Essentials of Terrorism

5th Edition

This book is dedicated to Sarah and Jonathan.

A man's fortunes are the fruit of his character. A man's friends are his magnetisms.

—Ralph Waldo Emerson, Essay on Fate (1860)

Sara Miller McCune founded SAGE Publishing in 1965 to support the dissemination of usable knowledge and educate a global community. SAGE publishes more than 1000 journals and over 800 new books each year, spanning a wide range of subject areas. Our growing selection of library products includes archives, data, case studies and video. SAGE remains majority owned by our founder and after her lifetime will become owned by a charitable trust that secures the company's continued independence.

Los Angeles | London | New Delhi | Singapore | Washington DC | Melbourne

Essentials of Terrorism

Concepts and Controversies

5th Edition

Gus Martin
California State University, Dominguez Hills

Los Angeles | London | New Delhi
Singapore | Washington DC | Melbourne

FOR INFORMATION:

SAGE Publications, Inc.
2455 Teller Road
Thousand Oaks, California 91320
E-mail: order@sagepub.com

SAGE Publications Ltd.
1 Oliver's Yard
55 City Road
London, EC1Y 1SP
United Kingdom

SAGE Publications India Pvt. Ltd.
B 1/I 1 Mohan Cooperative Industrial Area
Mathura Road, New Delhi 110 044
India

SAGE Publications Asia-Pacific Pte. Ltd.
3 Church Street
#10-04 Samsung Hub
Singapore 049483

Printed in the United States of America

Library of Congress Cataloging-in-Publication Data

Names: Martin, Gus, author.

Title: Essentials of terrorism : concepts and controversies / Gus Martin, California State University, Dominguez Hills, USA.

Description: Fifth edition. | Thousand Oaks, California : SAGE, [2019] | Includes references and index.

Identifiers: LCCN 2018022014 | ISBN 9781544342931 (pbk. : alk. paper)

Subjects: LCSH: Terrorism.

Classification: LCC HV6431 .M366 2019 | DDC 363.325–dc23 LC record available at https://lccn.loc.gov/2018022014

This book is printed on acid-free paper.

Acquisitions Editor: Jessica Miller
Editorial Assistant: Rebecca Lee
Content Development Editor: Adeline Wilson
Production Editor: Tracy Buyan
Copy Editor: Sarah Duffy
Typesetter: Hurix Digital
Proofreader: Susan Schon
Indexer: Will Ragsdale
Cover Designer: Candice Harman
Marketing Manager: Victoria Velasquez

SUSTAINABLE FORESTRY INITIATIVE
Certified Chain of Custody
Promoting Sustainable Forestry
www.sfiprogram.org
SFI-01268
SFI label applies to text stock

18 19 20 21 22 10 9 8 7 6 5 4 3 2 1

BRIEF CONTENTS

DETAILED CONTENTS

ABOUT THE AUTHOR

C. Augustus "Gus" Martin is a Professor of Criminal Justice Administration at California State University, Dominguez Hills, where he regularly teaches a course on the subject of terrorism and extremism. He has also served as Associate Vice President for Human Resources Management, Acting Associate Dean of the College of Business Administration and Public Policy, Associate Vice President for Faculty Affairs, and Chair of the Department of Public Administration and Public Policy. He began his academic career as a member of the faculty of the Graduate School of Public and International Affairs, University of Pittsburgh, where he was an Administration of Justice professor. His current research and professional interests are terrorism and extremism, homeland security, the administration of justice, and juvenile justice.

Dr. Martin is the author of several books on the subjects of terrorism and homeland security, including *Terrorism: An International Perspective* (with Fynnwin Prager, SAGE, 2019); *Understanding Terrorism: Challenges, Perspectives, and Issues* (SAGE, 2018); *Understanding Homeland Security* (SAGE, 2017); *The SAGE Encyclopedia of Terrorism*, second edition (SAGE, 2011); *Terrorism and Homeland Security* (SAGE, 2011); and *The New Era of Terrorism: Selected Readings* (SAGE, 2004). He is also the author of *Juvenile Justice: Process and Systems* (SAGE, 2005).

Prior to joining academia, Dr. Martin served as Managing Attorney for the Fair Housing Partnership of Greater Pittsburgh, where he was also director of a program created under a federal consent decree to desegregate public and assisted housing. He was also Special Counsel to the Attorney General of the U.S. Virgin Islands on the island of St. Thomas. As Special Counsel, he occupied a personal and confidential position in the central office of the Department of Justice, sat as hearing officer for disciplinary hearings and departmental grievances, served as chair of the Drug Policy Committee, served as liaison to the intergovernmental Law Enforcement Coordinating Committee as well as to the Narcotics Strike Force, and provided daily legal and policy advice to the attorney general. Prior to serving as Special Counsel, he was a "floor" Legislative Assistant to Congressman Charles B. Rangel of New York. As Legislative Assistant, he researched, evaluated, and drafted legislation in areas of foreign policy, foreign aid, human rights, housing, education, social services, and poverty; he also drafted House floor statements, *Congressional Record* inserts, press releases, and news articles, and he composed speeches, briefing materials, and legislative correspondence.

PREFACE

Welcome to the fifth edition of *Essentials of Terrorism: Concepts and Controversies.* This edition has been revised in several respects to enhance the educational quality of the study of terrorism. In the same spirit as the previous editions of *Essentials of Terrorism: Concepts and Controversies,* the fifth edition is designed as a foundational textbook to enhance the educational quality of the study of terrorism. It is a concise textbook for students and professionals who wish to explore the phenomenon of modern terrorist violence and who wish to use additional resources adapted for their specific instructional needs. Readers will acquire a solid foundation for understanding the nature of terrorism in a manner best suited for their classroom or professional program.

This book is also designed to be a resource for university students and professionals who require fundamental expertise in understanding terrorist violence. The content of the fifth edition of *Essentials of Terrorism: Concepts and Controversies* is directed to academic and professional courses whose subject areas have been selected for their specific educational program, including the study of terrorism, homeland security, international security, criminal justice administration, political conflict, armed conflict, and social environments. It can be incorporated into a variety of classes and seminars covering security studies, the administration of justice, the sociology of terrorism, conflict resolution, political theory, and other instruction in the social sciences. The intended level of instruction is undergraduate and master's students, as well as professionals with a need to understand terrorism.

No prerequisites are specifically recommended, but grounding in one of the following disciplines would be helpful: political science, government, administration of justice, sociology, history, or philosophy.

As will become readily apparent to instructors and students, the fifth edition of *Essentials of Terrorism: Concepts and Controversies* is an ideal anchor textbook for investigating the many aspects of terrorism, political violence, and homeland security. That it is easily adapted to these subjects means that instructors will be able to design a variety of instructional packages around it. In this way, the fifth edition is a versatile resource.

COURSE OVERVIEW AND PEDAGOGY

The fifth edition of *Essentials of Terrorism: Concepts and Controversies* introduces readers to terrorism in the contemporary era, focusing on the post–World War II period as its primary emphasis. It is a review of nations, movements, and individuals who have engaged in what many people would define as terrorist violence. It is also a review of the many kinds of terrorism that have existed in the post–World War II era. A serious exploration is made of the underlying causes of terrorism—for example, extremist ideologies, religious intolerance, and traumatic episodes in the lives of nations and people.

The pedagogical approach of the fifth edition is designed to stimulate critical thinking in readers. Students, professionals, and instructors will find that each chapter follows a sequence of instruction that builds on previous chapters and thus incrementally enhances the reader's knowledge of each topic. Chapters incorporate the following features:

- *Chapter Learning Objectives.* Using Bloom's taxonomy, chapter objectives are summarized at the beginning of each discussion.

- *Chapter Introduction.* Each chapter begins with an overview of the subject under investigation. The introduction provides perspective for the incorporation of each chapter's topic into the broader themes of the textbook.

- *Chapter Perspectives.* Chapters incorporate focused presentations of perspectives that explore people, events, organizations, and movements that are relevant to the subject matter of each chapter.

- *Chapter Summary.* A concluding discussion recapitulates the main themes of each chapter and introduces the subject matter of the following chapter.

- *Discussion Boxes.* These boxes present provocative information and pose challenging questions to stimulate critical thinking and further debate.

- *Key Terms and Concepts.* Important terms and ideas introduced in each chapter are listed for review and discussion. These are further explored and defined in the book's Glossary.

- *Terrorism on the Web.* Readers may log on to the Web-based study site at **https:// edge.sagepub.com/martiness5e** for additional Web sources and study resources.

- *Web Exercises.* Web exercises at the end of chapters have been designed for students, professionals, and instructors to explore and discuss information found on the Internet.

- *Recommended Readings.* Suggested readings listed at the end of each chapter provide either further information on or avenues of research into each topic.

CHAPTER GUIDE

This volume is organized into three thematic units, each consisting of several chapters. Appendix and a Glossary are included after the substantive chapters.

Part I: Understanding Terrorism: A Conceptual Review

The first section of the book is a comprehensive discussion of definitions of terrorism and the root causes of violent political extremism. Readers develop comprehensive, contextual, and critical skills for defining terrorism and for understanding the many causes of terrorist behavior. The discussion includes the informational war waged between adversaries and the role of the mass media. Readers investigate how the applications of the concepts of propaganda by deed and armed propaganda have been historically common to extremist violence.

Chapter 1. Defining Terrorism

This chapter investigates the reasons underlying why certain groups, movements, and individuals are labeled as terrorists or freedom fighters. It compares and contrasts radical and reactionary ideological tendencies as well as defines and investigates the characteristics of extremism. Terrorism is discussed at length by sampling official definitions, reviewing the American context, and summarizing several types of terrorism. Readers are introduced to several perspectives of terrorism that pose problems for definitional issues.

Chapter 2. Historical Perspectives and Ideological Origins

This chapter explores the historical and ideological origins of modern terrorism. Historical perspectives and the era of the New Terrorism are discussed in the context of conceptual themes used throughout the book. Ideological foundations for modern terrorist violence are also discussed at some length. The causes of left-wing and right-wing terrorism are identified, as are the qualities of ideological violence. Because both ideological poles were inextricably entwined during the 20th century and adherents continue to be active in the 21st century, it is important for readers to grasp the importance of the ideologies of class struggle, national liberation, order, and race. This chapter also discusses regional examples of ideological terrorism.

Chapter 3. Causes of Terrorist Violence

Readers become familiar with central factors in the personal and group histories of individuals and groups who become associated with terrorism. The motives of extremists and several explanations of terrorism are explored, including acts of political will, sociological explanations, and psychological explanations. An important discussion probes the degree to which a fresh generation of new terrorists is being forged in reaction to how the West and its allies have conducted the post–September 11, 2001, war on terrorism.

Chapter 4. Terrorist Violence and the Role of the Media

This chapter investigates and evaluates the centrality of the media and mass communications in the modern era of political violence. It first discusses the nature of mass communications and reporting in the context of terrorist environments. It also investigates the war of manipulation for favorable media coverage. In particular, readers assess the manipulation of information technologies and the media by modern terrorists. A discussion is also presented on the efficacy of regulating the media.

Part II: Terrorist Environments

Part II educates readers about the many manifestations of terrorism by helping them develop skills to critically assess and understand historical and modern examples of political violence. In particular, state- and dissident-initiated terrorism are discussed, compared, and contrasted. An examination is conducted of the availability of high-yield weaponry in the arsenals of dissident terrorists. Readers are also guided through how to distinguish between religious and international terrorism. Domestic terrorism in the United States is also explored.

Chapter 5. Terrorism by the State

This chapter investigates state-initiated repression and terror. A detailed discussion explores terrorism as foreign policy and terrorism as domestic policy. Important examples of state terrorism include the Khmer Rouge in Cambodia and the link between Janjaweed fighters and the government in Sudan.

Chapter 6. Terrorism by Dissidents

This chapter critically evaluates terrorism emanating from dissident movements. Several typologies and the morality of the New Terrorism are investigated. Finally, a detailed discussion explores antistate dissident terrorism and communal terrorism. Important examples include the modern use of child soldiers by extremists and Chechen terrorism against Russia.

Chapter 7. Religious Terrorism

This chapter evaluates the historical and modern origins and quality of religious terrorism. The goal is to engender critical discussion on the subject and to develop a contextual perspective for it. Because religious terrorism has become so prominent, it is important for readers to investigate different manifestations and to understand the contexts of regional case studies.

Chapter 8. International Terrorism

This chapter discusses recent and historical examples of international terrorism, defines what is meant by international terrorism, and explores the reasons for terrorist spillovers. Both the phenomenon of international terrorist networks and the concept of stateless revolutionaries are discussed. In this regard, readers evaluate newly emerging threats from groups and networks that have adapted the Al Qaeda example as a model.

Chapter 9. Domestic Terrorism in the United States

This chapter presents an overview of terrorism in post–World War II America. It probes the background to political violence and presents a detailed discussion of leftist and rightist terrorism in the United States. The chapter also evaluates prospects for violence emanating from modern extremists on the left and right and from religious extremism.

Part III: The Terrorist Battleground

Part III discusses the nuts and bolts of the terrorist trade, including counterterrorism and related responses to terrorist environments. Readers investigate how the applications of the concept of homeland security are applied in the United States and other countries. The future of terrorism is also explored.

Chapter 10. Counterterrorism and the War on Terrorism

This chapter explores counterterrorist options and security measures. Several categories of responses are assessed: the use of force, repressive operations other than war, conciliatory operations other than war, and legalistic responses. Contemporary controversies, such as the status and treatment of captured suspects, are explored.

Chapter 11. Homeland Security

This chapter provides readers with a fundamental introduction to homeland security in the United States. It prepares a contextual overview of the purpose of homeland security, defines the concept, and explains the mission of the homeland security bureaucracy.

Chapter 12. Future Trends and Projections

Readers are challenged to critically assess trends and other factors that can be used to project the near future of terrorism. In particular, this chapter presents theoretical models for evaluating terrorist environments and applying these models to project and evaluate emerging trends. Fresh discussions and data are offered for assessing the near future of ideological terrorism, religious terrorism, international terrorism, gender-selective political violence, and criminal dissident terrorism. A theoretical model is offered for assessing the decline and ending of terrorist campaigns.

NEW TO THIS EDITION

Updated information and other revisions are found throughout this volume. Detailed overviews of terrorist objectives, tactics, targets, and weapons are included in Chapters 1 and 6. Updated theoretical and historical information has been incorporated in Chapters 2, 6, and 7. Updated information and data are included in each chapter in Part II. The discussion of homeland security in Chapter 11 has been updated, as has the discussion of future trends in Chapter 12.

DIGITAL RESOURCES

edge.sagepub.com/martiness5e

This new *Essentials* edition comes with a variety of ancillaries to supplement instructor course preparation and student learning.

SAGE edge offers a robust online environment you can access anytime, anywhere, and features an impressive array of free tools and resources to keep you on the cutting edge of your learning experience.

SAGE edge for Students provides a personalized approach to help students accomplish their coursework goals in an easy-to-use learning environment.

- **Mobile-friendly eFlashcards** strengthen understanding of key terms and concepts.

- **Mobile-friendly practice quizzes** allow for independent assessment by students of their mastery of course material.

- **Exclusive access to various full-text SAGE journal articles** support and expand on the concepts presented in the chapters to help develop critical thinking skills.

- **Original videos** feature interviews with the author and provide contemporary examples that relate back to the chapter content.

- **Carefully selected web-based video resources** feature relevant interviews, lectures, personal stories, inquiries, and other content for use in independent or classroom-based explorations of key topics.

- **Multimedia content** includes videos that appeal to students with different learning styles.

SAGE edge for Instructors supports teaching by making it easy to integrate quality content and create a rich learning environment for students.

- **Original videos** feature interviews with the author to provide students with contemporary examples that relate back to the chapter content.

- **A Microsoft® Word test bank** is available containing multiple-choice, true/false, short-answer, and essay questions for each chapter. The test bank provides a diverse range of prewritten options, as well as the opportunity for editing any question and/or inserting personalized questions to assess students' progress and understanding.

- **Sample course syllabi for semester courses provide suggested models for use when creating the syllabi.**

- **Editable, chapter-specific Microsoft® PowerPoint® slides offer complete flexibility in easily creating a multimedia presentation for courses and highlight essential content and features.**

- **Exclusive access to various full-text SAGE journal articles** that support and expand on the concepts presented in the chapters. Combine cutting-edge academic journal scholarship with the topics in the course for a robust classroom experience that encourages students to think critically.

- **Multimedia content** includes videos that appeal to diverse learners.

ACKNOWLEDGMENTS

I am indebted for the support and encouragement of many people in bringing this venture to completion, with special appreciation for the professional and expert attention given to this project by the editorial group at SAGE. Without their patience and constructive criticism, this project would not have achieved the level of comprehensiveness and completeness that was my objective from the beginning.

Thanks are extended to colleagues who shared their expert advice and suggestions for crafting this volume. Deep appreciation is also due to the panel of peer reviewers assembled by the able editors and staff of SAGE during several rounds of review. The insightful, constructive comments and critical analyses of the following reviewers were truly invaluable:

John W. King, *Baldwin Wallace University*

Robert S. McDonnell, *University of North Carolina at Pembroke*

Marcos L. Misis, *Northern Kentucky University*

Joseph R. Rudolph Jr., *Towson University*

Jeff Schwartz, *Rowan University*

Finally, I thank my family for their constant support, encouragement, and humor during the course of this project.

PART ONE

UNDERSTANDING TERRORISM

A Conceptual Review

U.S. Department of Defense

▶ Asymmetrical warfare. The remains of a vehicular bomb inside the heavily fortified Green Zone of Baghdad. A suicide bomber attacked the U.S.-occupied area during the post-2003 insurgency phase of the war in Iraq.

CHAPTER ONE

DEFINING TERRORISM

Learning Objectives

This chapter will enable readers to do the following:

1. Explain the importance of identifying the common characteristics of extremism and understanding the world view of extremist adherents.

2. Demonstrate knowledge of the common features of formal definitions of terrorism.

3. Discuss whether violence should be classified as terrorism by recognizing the contextual perspectives of perpetrators and participants in terrorist environments.

4. Apply the Political Violence Matrix as a conceptual tool to interpret the quality of violence.

Terrorism, however defined, has always challenged the stability of societies and the peace of mind of everyday people. In the modern era, the impact of terrorism—that is, its ability to terrorize—is not limited to the locales or regions where the terrorists strike. In the age of television, the Internet, satellite communications, and global news coverage, graphic images of terrorist incidents are broadcast instantaneously into the homes of hundreds of millions of people. Terrorist groups understand the power of these images and manipulate them to their advantage as much as they can. Terrorist states also fully appreciate the power of instantaneous information and thus try to control the spin on reports of their behavior. In many respects, the 21st century is an era of globalized terrorism.

Some acts of political violence are clearly acts of terrorism. Most people would agree that politically motivated bombings of marketplaces, massacres of enemy civilians, and routine government use of torture are terrorist acts. However, as we begin our study of terrorism, it is important to appreciate that we will encounter many definitional gray areas. Depending on which side of the ideological, racial, religious, or national fence one sits on, political violence can be interpreted either as unmitigated terrorist barbarity or as freedom fighting for national liberation. These areas will be explored in the chapters that follow.

This chapter investigates definitional issues in the study of terrorism. Readers will probe the nuances of these issues and learn that the truism "one person's terrorist is another person's freedom fighter" is a significant factor in the definitional debate. It must be remembered that this debate occurs within a practical and real-life framework—in other words, a nontheoretical reality that some political, religious, or ethno-nationalist beliefs and behaviors are so reprehensible that they cannot be considered to be mere differences in opinion. Some violent incidents are *mala in se* acts of terrorist violence. For example, the New Terrorism of today is characterized by the threat of weapons of mass destruction, indiscriminate targeting, and efforts to inflict intentionally high casualty rates—as occurred in attacks on September 11, 2001, in the United States; March 11, 2004, in Spain; July 7, 2005, in Great Britain; November 26–29, 2008, in India; January and November 2015 in France; March 22, 2016, in Belgium; and repeated attacks in Nigeria, Syria, Iraq, and Pakistan. The use of indiscriminate targeting and tactics against civilians is indefensible, no matter what cause is championed by those who use them. The New Terrorism is discussed in detail in Chapter 2.

The discussion in this chapter will review the following:

- Understanding Political Extremism
- Formal and Informal Definitions
- Objectives and Goals of Terrorism
- Terrorists or Freedom Fighters?
- The Political Violence Matrix

UNDERSTANDING POLITICAL EXTREMISM

An important step toward defining terrorism is to develop an understanding of the causes of terrorism. To identify them, one must first understand the important role of extremism as a primary feature of all terrorist behavior.

Behind each incident of terrorist violence is some deeply held belief system that has motivated the perpetrator. Such systems are, at their core, extremist systems characterized by intolerance. One must keep in mind, however, that although terrorism is a violent expression of these beliefs, it is by no means the only possible manifestation of extremism. On a scale of activist behavior, extremists can engage in such benign expressions as sponsoring debates or publishing newspapers. They might also engage in vandalism and other disruptions of the normal routines of their enemies. Though intrusive and often illegal, these are examples of political expression that cannot be construed as terrorist acts. Our focus in this and subsequent chapters will be on violent extremist behavior that many people would define as acts of terrorism. First, we must briefly investigate the general characteristics of the extremist foundations of terrorism.

ABU BAKR AL-BAGHDADI
(ABU DU'A)
(IBRAHIM 'AWWAD
IBRAHIM 'ALI AL-BADRI)
Up to $25 Million Reward

STOP AL-BAGHDADI

UP TO $25 MILLION REWARD

Abu Bakr al-Baghdadi, also known as Abu Du'a, also known as Ibrahim 'Awwad Ibrahim 'Ali al-Badri, is the senior leader of the terrorist organization Islamic State of Iraq and the Levant (ISIL). Under al-Baghdadi, ISIL has been responsible for the deaths of thousands of civilians.

The U.S. Government is offering a reward of up to $25 million for information about al-Baghdadi. Absolute confidentiality is assured and relocation may be available. If you have information, please contact the nearest U.S. embassy or consulate or no2daesh@rewards4justice.co.

REWARDS FOR JUSTICE

Washington, D.C.
20533-0303 USA
no2daesh@rewards4justice.co
www.rewardsforjustice.net
☐ @Rewards4Justice
1-800-USREWARDS

U.S. Department of State, Rewards for Justice Program

▶ Abu Bakr Al-Baghdadi, founder and leader of ISIS. Wanted poster from the U.S. Department of State Rewards for Justice website.

Defining Extremism

Extremism is a quality that is "radical in opinion, especially in political matters; ultra; advanced."[1] It is characterized by intolerance toward opposing interests and divergent opinions and is the primary catalyst and motivation for terrorist behavior. Extremists who cross the line to become **terrorists** always develop noble arguments to rationalize and justify their acts of violence toward nations, people, religions, or other interests.

Extremism is a radical expression of political values. Both the content of one's beliefs and the style in which one expresses them are fundamental to extremism. Laird Wilcox summed up this quality as follows:

> Extremism is more an issue of style than of content. . . . Most people can hold radical or unorthodox views and still entertain them in a more or less reasonable, rational, and nondogmatic manner. On the other hand, I have met people whose views are fairly close to the political mainstream but were presented in a shrill, uncompromising, bullying, and distinctly authoritarian manner.[2]

Extremism is a precursor to terrorism—it is an overarching belief system terrorists use to justify their violent behavior. It is characterized by what a person's beliefs are as well as how a person expresses those beliefs. Thus, no matter how offensive or reprehensible one's thoughts or words are, they are not by themselves acts of terrorism. Only those who violently act out their extremist beliefs are terrorists.

The World of the Extremist

Extremists have very different—and at times fantastic—world views compared with non-extremists. They set themselves apart as protectors of a truth or as the true heirs of a legacy. They frequently believe that secret and quasi-mystical forces are arrayed against them and that these forces are the cause of worldwide calamities. One conspiracy theory widely believed among Islamist extremists in the aftermath of September 11, 2001, for example, was that Israeli agents were behind the attacks, that 4,000 Jews received telephone calls to evacuate the World Trade Center in New York, and that no Jews were among the victims of the attack.

As in the past, religion is often an underlying impetus for extremist activity. When extremists adopt a religious belief system, their world view becomes one of a struggle between supernatural forces of good and evil. They view themselves as living a righteous life that fits with their interpretation of God's will. Those who do not conform to the belief system are opposed to the one true faith. Those who live according to it are chosen, and those who do not are not chosen. These interpretations of behavior include elements of the underlying social or political environment. For example, as one student at a Pakistani religious school explained, "Osama [bin Laden] wants to keep Islam pure from the pollution of the infidels. . . . He believes Islam is the way for all the world. He wants to bring Islam to all the world."[3]

Extremists have a very clear sense of mission, purpose, and righteousness. They create a world view that sets them apart from society. Extremist beliefs and terrorist behaviors are thus logical to those who accept the belief system but illogical to those who reject it. For example, as discussed in Chapter Perspective 1.1, racial supremacy has historically promoted the extremist belief that some races are inherently superior to other races. Chapter Perspective 1.1 illustrates the rigid intolerance of a faction of the Ku Klux Klan in the United States, which justified its racism with references to its ideology of ethno-nationalist and religious authority.

Common Characteristics of Violent Extremists

Scholars and other experts have identified common characteristics exhibited by violent extremists. These characteristics are expressed in different ways, depending on a movement's particular belief system. The following commonalities are summaries of traits that experts have identified but are by no means an exhaustive inventory.[4]

Intolerance. Intolerance is the hallmark of extremist belief systems and terrorist behavior. The cause is considered to be absolutely just and good, and those who disagree with it (or some aspect of it) are cast as the opposition. Terrorists affix their opponents with certain negative or derisive labels to set them apart. These characterizations are often highly personalized so that individuals are identified who symbolize the opposing belief system or cause. Thus, during the Cold War, the American president was referred to by the pro-U.S. camp as the "leader of the free world" and by Latin American Marxists as the embodiment of "Yankee imperialism."[5]

Moral absolutes. Extremists adopt moral absolutes so that the distinction between good and evil is clear, as are the lines between the extremists and their opponents. The extremists' belief or cause is a morally correct vision of the world and is used to establish moral superiority over others. Violent extremists thus become morally and ethically pure elites who lead the oppressed masses to freedom. For example, religious terrorists generally believe that their one true faith is superior to all others and that any behavior committed in defense of the faith is fully justifiable.

Broad conclusions. Extremist conclusions are made to simplify the goals of the cause and the nature of the opponents. These generalizations are not debatable and permit no exceptions. Evidence for them is rooted in a belief system rather than based on objective data. For

CHAPTER PERSPECTIVE 1.1

We the Klan Believe

The United Klans of America (UKA) was a particularly violent and dogmatic faction of the Ku Klux Klan. The UKA arose in opposition to the civil rights movement in the United States during the 1950s to 1970s, and the organization actively tried to defeat the movement through the use of terrorist violence and other intimidation. For example, members of the UKA were linked to the 1963 bombing of the 16th Street Baptist Church in Birmingham, Alabama, which caused the deaths of four young African American girls. Members of the UKA were also linked to the 1965 murder in Alabama of Viola Liuzzo, a White civil rights worker from Michigan. The UKA ultimately failed to halt the civil rights movement through violence and intimidation, and members of the faction were eventually prosecuted for these acts of violence.

The following excerpts are from a pamphlet distributed by the United Klans of America during the 1970s.

We believe in the eternal separation of the church and state:

> Roman Catholicism teaches the union of church and state with the church controlling the state. . . .
>
> Every Roman Catholic holds allegiance to the Pope of Rome, and Catholicism teaches that this allegiance is superior to his allegiance to his country. . . .

We believe in white supremacy:

> The Klan believes that America is a white man's country, and should be governed by white men. Yet the Klan is not anti-Negro, it is the Negro's friend. The Klan is eternally opposed to the mixing of the white and colored races. Our creed: Let the white man remain white, the black man black, the yellow man yellow, the brown man brown, and the red man red. God drew the color line. . . .
>
> The Klan believes in England for Englishmen, France for Frenchman, Italy for Italians, and America for Americans. . . . The Klan is not anti-Catholic, anti-Jew, anti-Negro, anti-foreign, the Klan is pro-Protestant and pro-American. . . .
>
> We the Klan will never allow out [sic] blood bought liberties to be crucified on a Roman cross: and we will not yield to the integration of white and Negro races in our schools or any where else. . . .

The foregoing passage typifies racial supremacist belief systems that claim to be motivated by religious principles. The history, ideology, and activity of the Ku Klux Klan are discussed further in Chapter 9.

Source: Excerpts from "The Principle of the United Klans of America" (Tuscaloosa, AL: Office of the Imperial Wizard, 1974), in *Extremism in America: A Reader*, ed. Lyman Tower Sargent (New York, NY: New York University Press, 1995), 139.

example, ethno-nationalists frequently categorize all members of their opponent group as having certain broadly negative traits.

New language and conspiratorial beliefs. Language and conspiracies are created to demonize the enemy and set the terrorists apart from those not part of their belief system. Extremists thus become an elite with a hidden agenda and targets of that agenda. For example, some American far right conspiracy proponents express their anti-Semitic beliefs by using coded references to international bankers or a Zionist Occupied Government (ZOG). Neo-Nazi rightists degrade members of non-European races by referring to them as Mud People.

FORMAL AND INFORMAL DEFINITIONS

There is some consensus among experts—but no unanimity—on what kind of violence constitutes an act of terrorism. Governments, individual agencies within governments, and private agencies have each developed, adopted, and designed their own definitions, and academic experts have proposed and analyzed dozens of definitional constructs. This lack of unanimity, which exists throughout the public and private sectors, is an accepted reality in the study of political violence.

Terrorism would not, from a layperson's point of view, seem to be a difficult concept to define. Most people likely hold an instinctive understanding that terrorism is

- politically motivated violence,

- usually directed against **soft targets** (i.e., civilian and administrative government targets),

- intended to affect (terrorize) a target audience.

This instinctive understanding would also hold that terrorism is criminal, unfair, or an otherwise illegitimate use of force. Laypersons might presume that this is an easily understood concept, but defining terrorism is not that simple. Experts have for some time grappled with designing (and agreeing on) clear definitions of terrorism; the issue is, in fact, at the center of an ongoing debate. The result is a remarkable variety of approaches and definitions. Walter Laqueur noted that "more than a hundred definitions have been offered," including several of his own.[6] Even within the U.S. government, different agencies apply several definitions.

▶ Anwar al-Awlaki, American-born cleric who became a recruiter and propagandist for Al Qaeda in Yemen. He was assassinated during an American drone strike in Yemen in September 2011.

A significant amount of intellectual energy has been devoted to identifying formal elements of terrorism, as illustrated by Alex Schmid and Albert Jongman's surveys, which identified more than 100 definitions.[7]

Establishing formal definitions can, of course, be complicated by the perspectives of the participants in a terrorist incident, who instinctively differentiate freedom fighters from terrorists, regardless of formal definitions. Another complication is that most definitions focus on political violence perpetrated by dissident groups, even though many governments have practiced terrorism as both domestic and foreign policy.

Guerrilla warfare. One important observation must be kept in mind and understood at the outset: Terrorism is not synonymous with guerrilla warfare. The term **guerrilla** (little war) was developed during the early 19th century when Napoleon's army fought a long, brutal, and ultimately unsuccessful war in Spain. Unlike the Napoleonic campaigns elsewhere in Europe, which involved conventional armies fighting set-piece battles in accordance with rules of engagement, the war in Spain was a classic unconventional conflict. The Spanish people, as opposed to the Spanish army, rose in rebellion and resisted the invading French army. They liberated large areas of the Spanish countryside. After years of costly fighting—in which atrocities were common on both sides—the French were driven out. Thus, in contrast to *terrorists*, the term *guerrilla fighters* refers to

a numerically larger group of armed individuals, who operate as a military unit, attack enemy military forces, and seize and hold territory (even if only ephemerally during the daylight hours), while also exercising some form of sovereignty or control over a defined geographical area and its population.[8]

Dozens, if not scores, of examples of guerrilla warfare exist in the modern era. They exhibit the classic strategy of hit-and-run warfare. Many examples also exist of successful guerrilla campaigns against numerically and technologically superior adversaries.

A Sampling of Formal Definitions

The effort to formally define terrorism is critical because government antiterrorist policy calculations must be based on criteria that determine whether a violent incident is an act of terrorism. Governments and policy makers must piece together the elements of terrorist behavior and demarcate the factors that distinguish terrorism from other forms of conflict.

In Europe, countries that endured terrorist campaigns have written official definitions of terrorism. The British have defined terrorism as "the use or threat, for the purpose of advancing a political, religious, or ideological cause, of action which involves serious violence against any person or property."[9] In Germany, terrorism has been described as an "enduringly conducted struggle for political goals, which are intended to be achieved by means of assaults on the life and property of other persons, especially by means of severe crimes."[10] The European Interior Ministers note that "terrorism is . . . the use, or the threatened use, by a cohesive group of persons of violence (short of warfare) to effect political aims."[11]

Scholars have also tried their hand at defining terrorism. For example, Ted Gurr has described it as "the use of unexpected violence to intimidate or coerce people in the pursuit of political or social objectives."[12] J. P. Gibbs described it as "illegal violence or threatened violence against human or nonhuman objects," so long as that violence meets additional criteria such as secretive features and the use of unconventional warfare.[13] Bruce Hoffman wrote,

> We come to appreciate that terrorism is ineluctably political in aims and motives; violent—or, equally important, threatens violence; designed to have far-reaching psychological repercussions beyond the immediate victim or target; conducted by an organization with an identifiable chain of command or conspiratorial structure (whose members wear no uniform or identifying insignia); and perpetrated by a subnational group or non-state entity.
>
> We may therefore now attempt to define terrorism as the deliberate creation and exploitation of fear through violence or the threat of violence in the pursuit of change.[14]

To further illustrate the range of definitions, Whittaker notes the following descriptions by terrorism experts:[15]

- contributes the illegitimate use of force to achieve a political objective when innocent people are targeted (Walter Laqueur)

- a strategy of violence designed to promote desired outcomes by instilling fear in the public at large (Walter Reich)

- the use or threatened use of force designed to bring about political change (Brian Jenkins)

From this discussion, we can identify the common features of most formal definitions:

• the use of illegal force	• political motives
• subnational actors	• attacks against soft civilian and passive military targets
• unconventional methods	• acts aimed at purposefully affecting an audience

The emphasis, then, is on terrorists adopting specific types of motives, methods, and targets. One fact readily apparent from these formal definitions is that they focus on terrorist groups rather than terrorist states. As will be made abundantly clear in Chapter 5, state terrorism has been responsible for many more deaths and much more suffering than terrorism originating in small bands of terrorists.

Defining Terrorism in the United States

The United States has not adopted a single definition of terrorism as a matter of government policy, instead relying on definitions developed from time to time by government agencies. These definitions reflect the United States' traditional law enforcement approach to distinguishing terrorism from more common criminal behavior. The following definitions are a sample of the official approach.

The U.S. Department of Defense defines terrorism as "the unlawful use of, or threatened use of, force or violence against individuals or property to coerce and intimidate governments or societies, often to achieve political, religious, or ideological objectives."[16] The U.S. Code defines terrorism as illegal violence that attempts to "intimidate or coerce a civilian population; . . . influence the policy of a government by intimidation or coercion; or . . . affect the conduct of a government by assassination or kidnapping."[17] The **Federal Bureau of Investigation (FBI)** has defined terrorism as "the unlawful use of force or violence against persons or property to intimidate or coerce a Government, the civilian population, or any segment thereof, in furtherance of political or social objectives."[18] For the U.S. State Department, terrorism is "premeditated, politically motivated violence perpetrated against noncombatant targets by subnational groups or clandestine agents, usually intended to influence an audience."[19]

Using these definitions, the following common elements can be used to construct a composite American definitional model:

> Terrorism is a premeditated and unlawful act in which groups or agents of some principal engage in a threatened or actual use of force or violence against human or property targets. These groups or agents engage in this behavior intending the purposeful intimidation of governments or people to affect policy or behavior with an underlying political objective.

These elements indicate a fairly narrow and legalistic approach. When they are assigned to individual suspects, the suspects may be labeled and detained as terrorists. Readers, in evaluating the practical policy implications of this approach, should bear in mind that labeling and detaining suspects as terrorists is not without controversy. Some post–September 11 counterterrorist practices have prompted strong debate. For example, when enemy soldiers are taken prisoner, they are traditionally afforded legal protections as prisoners of war. This is well recognized under international law. In the war on terrorism, many suspected terrorists have been designated as enemy combatants and not afforded the same legal status as prisoners of war. Such practices have been hotly debated among proponents and opponents. Chapter Perspective 1.2 discusses the ongoing problem.

Nonterrorist Mass Violence in the United States

The United States periodically experiences incidents of nonterrorist mass homicides perpetrated by individuals who typically enter a facility and begin to randomly shoot victims, often using high-powered firearms such as assault rifles and high-caliber handguns. Perpetrators of mass firearm killings rarely justify their actions by citing political motivations, such as ideology, race, or religion, and thus do not fit the modern profile of terrorist operatives or political

CHAPTER PERSPECTIVE 1.2

The Problem of Labeling the Enemy in the New Era of Terrorism

When formulating counterterrorist policies, policy makers are challenged by two problems: first, the problem of defining terrorism, and second, the problem of labeling individual suspects. Although defining terrorism can be an exercise in semantics—and is often shaped by subjective political or cultural biases—there are certain fundamental elements that constitute objective definitions. In comparison, using official designations (labels) to confer special status on captured suspects has become a controversial process.

During the post–September 11, 2001, war on terrorism, it became clear to experts and the public that official designations and labels of individual suspected terrorists is a central legal, political, and security issue. Of essential importance is the question of a suspect's official *status* when he or she is taken prisoner.

Depending on one's designated status, certain recognized legal or political protections may or may not be observed by interrogators or others involved in processing specific cases.

According to the protocols of the third Geneva Convention, prisoners who are designated as *prisoners of war* and who are brought to trial must be afforded the same legal rights in the same courts as would soldiers from the country holding them prisoner. Thus, prisoners of war held by the United States would be brought to trial in standard military courts under the Uniform Code of Military Justice and would have the same rights and protections (such as the right to appeal) as all soldiers.

Suspected terrorists have not been designated as prisoners of war. Official and unofficial designations such as *enemy combatants, unlawful combatants,* and *battlefield detainees* have been used by U.S. authorities to differentiate them from prisoners of war. The rationale is that suspected terrorists are not soldiers fighting for a sovereign nation and are therefore ineligible for prisoner-of-war status. When hundreds of prisoners were detained at facilities such as the American base in Guantánamo Bay, Cuba, the United States argued that persons designated as enemy combatants were not subject to the protocols of the Geneva Conventions. Thus, such persons could be held indefinitely, detained in secret, transferred at will, and sent to allied countries for more coercive interrogations. Under enemy combatant status, conditions of confinement in Guantánamo Bay included open-air cells with wooden roofs and chain link walls. In theory, each case was to be reviewed by special military tribunals, and innocent prisoners would be reclassified as *nonenemy combatants* and released.

Civil liberties and human rights groups disagreed with the special status conferred on prisoners by the labeling system. They argued that basic legal and humanitarian protections should be granted to prisoners regardless of their designation. In June 2008, the U.S. Supreme Court held that foreign detainees held for years at Guantánamo Bay had the right to appeal to U.S. federal judges to challenge their indefinite imprisonment without charges. At the time of the decision, about 200 foreign detainees had lawsuits pending before federal court in Washington, D.C.

In one interesting development, the U.S. Department of Defense conferred *protected persons* status on members of the Iranian Mujahideen-e Khalq Organization (MKO), who were under guard in Iraq by the American military. The MKO is a Marxist movement opposed to the postrevolution regime in Iran. The group was regularly featured on the U.S. Department of State's list of terrorist organizations, and it was responsible for killing Americans and others in terrorist attacks.

lone-wolf actors. Rather, those who commit crimes of mass homicide are driven by the same antisocial motivations typically cited by other criminals. The distinctive difference is that they act out their antisocial rationales by engaging in mass firearm killings.

Nonterrorist mass shootings are not common among the world's prosperous democracies. The frequency of these incidents and the overall rate of firearm-related homicides are much higher in the United States than in similar high-income nations.

Types of Terrorism

The basic elements of terrorist environments are uncomplicated, and experts and commentators generally agree on the forms of terrorism found in modern political environments. For example, the following environments have been described by academic experts:

- Barkan and Snowden describe vigilante, insurgent, transnational, and state terrorism.[20]

- Hoffman discusses ethno-nationalist/separatist, international, religious, and state-sponsored terrorism.[21]

- While undertaking the task of defining the New Terrorism, Laqueur contextualizes far rightist, religious, state, exotic, and criminal terrorism.[22]

- Other experts evaluate **narco-terrorism**, toxic terrorism, and netwar.[23]

We will explore all of these environments in later chapters within the following contexts:

State terrorism. Terrorism from above committed by governments against perceived enemies. State terrorism can be directed externally against adversaries in the international domain or internally against domestic enemies.

Dissident terrorism. Terrorism from below committed by nonstate movements and groups against governments, ethno-nationalist groups, religious groups, and other perceived enemies.

Religious terrorism. Terrorism motivated by an absolute belief that an otherworldly power has sanctioned—and commanded—the application of terrorist violence for the greater glory of the faith. Religious terrorism is usually conducted in defense of what believers consider the one true faith.

International terrorism. **International terrorism** spills over onto the world's stage. Targets are selected because of their value as symbols of international interests, either within the home country or across state boundaries.

OBJECTIVES AND GOALS OF TERRORISM

Objectives and goals are parts of the process toward a final outcome. An objective is an incremental step in the overall process that leads to an ultimate goal. A goal is the final result of the process, the terminal point of a series of objectives. Thus, an objective in a revolutionary campaign could be the overthrow of an enemy government or social order; the goal could be to establish a new society. During a revolutionary campaign, many objectives have to be achieved to reach the final goal.

Typical Objectives

Politically violent groups and movements show certain similarities in their objectives. The following discussion identifies a few such commonalities. These are by no means either common to all violent extremists at all phases of their campaigns or exhaustive analyses. However, it is instructive to review a few central objectives:

- Changing the existing order
- Psychological disruption

- Social disruption
- Creating a revolutionary environment

Changing the Existing Order

At some level, all terrorists seek to change an existing order, even if it is simply a short-term objective to disrupt the normal routines of society by inflicting maximum casualties. When evaluating what it means to change an existing order, one must take into consideration the different profiles of terrorist movements, their motives, and the idiosyncrasies of individual terrorists. Here are a few examples:

- Ethno-nationalist terrorists seek to win recognition of their human rights, or a degree of national autonomy, from the present order.

- Nihilists wish to destroy systems and institutions without regard for what will replace the existing order.

- Religious terrorists act on behalf of a supernatural mandate to bring about a divinely inspired new order.

- Lone wolves have a vague and sometimes delusional assumption that their actions will further a greater cause against a corrupt or evil social order.

Psychological Disruption

An obvious objective is to inflict maximum psychological damage by applying dramatic violence against symbolic targets. "From the terrorists' perspective, the major force of terrorism comes not from its physical impact but from its psychological impact."[24] When terrorist violence is applied discerningly, the weak can influence the powerful, and the powerful can intimidate the weak. Cultural symbols, political institutions, and public leaders are examples of iconic (nearly sacred) targets that can affect large populations when attacked.

Social Disruption

Social disruption is an objective of propaganda by the deed. The ability of terrorists and extremists to disrupt the normal routines of society demonstrates both the weakness of the government and the strength of the movement; it provides terrorists with the potential for highly effective propaganda. When governments fail to protect the normal routines of society, discontent may spread throughout society, thus making the population susceptible to manipulation by a self-styled vanguard movement. For example, bombing attacks on public transportation systems certainly cause social disruption. A group might be attacked specifically to deter its members from traveling through a region or territory. Tourists, for example, have been targeted repeatedly in Egypt, including the July 2005 bombing incident in the resort city of Sharm el Sheikh on the Sinai Peninsula, which killed approximately 90 people.

Creating a Revolutionary Environment

Dissident extremists understand that they cannot hope to win in their struggle against the state without raising the revolutionary consciousness of the people. For many terrorists, propaganda by the deed is considered the most direct way to create a broad-based revolutionary environment so that "the destruction of one troop transport truck is more effective propaganda for the local population than a thousand speeches."[25] Revolutionary theorists have suggested that terrorism can force the state to overreact, the people to understand the true repressive nature of the state, thus fomenting mass rebellion—led, of course, by the revolutionary vanguard.

Playing to the Audience: Objectives, Victims, and Constituencies

Terrorists adapt their methods and selection of targets to the characteristics of their championed group and the idiosyncrasies of their environment. Targets are selected for specific symbolic reasons, with the objectives of victimizing specific groups or interests and sending symbolic messages to the terrorists' constituency. In a sense, the targeted groups or interests serve as conduits to communicate the extremist movement's message.

If skillfully applied, propaganda by the deed can be manipulated to affect specific audiences. These audiences can include the following segments of society:

Politically apathetic people. The objective of terrorist violence directed toward this group is to force an end to their indifference and, ideally, to motivate them to petition the government for fundamental changes.

The government and its allied elites. Terrorists seek to seriously intimidate or distract a nation's ruling bodies to force them to deal favorably with the underlying grievances of the dissident movement.

Potential supporters. An important objective of propaganda by the deed is to create a revolutionary consciousness in a large segment of society. This is more easily achieved within the pool of those who are sympathetic to the extremists' objectives but do not yet approve of their methods.

Confirmed supporters. Terrorists seek to assure their members and confirmed supporters that the movement continues to be strong and active. They communicate this through acts of symbolic violence.

Table 1.1 Constituencies and Enemies: Selecting Tactics and Targets

Terrorists select their methods within the context of their social and political environments. They appeal to specific constituencies and justify their choice of methods by championing the political cause of their constituencies. Their targeted interests (i.e., enemy interests) can be defined narrowly or broadly, so civilian populations can be included as legitimized targets.

Group or Movement	Activity Profile			
	Constituency	Objectives	Methods	Targeted Interest
Al-Aqsa Martyrs Brigade	Palestinians	Palestinian state	Suicide bombings; small-arms attacks	Israeli civilians; Israeli military
Iraqi and Syrian Islamist insurgents	Iraqi people	Collapse of Syrian and Iraqi regimes; establishment of Islamist state	Terrorist attacks; guerrilla warfare	Regime institutions; non-Sunnis
Al Qaeda and affiliates	Devout Muslims	Worldwide Islamic revolution	Well-planned bombings; indigenous insurrections	The West; secular Islamic governments
Provisional IRA	Irish Catholics	Union with the Irish Republic	Small-arms attacks; bombings	British; Ulster Protestants
Bosnian Serb militias	Bosnian Serbs	Serb state	Ethnic cleansing; communal terrorism	Bosnian Muslims; Bosnian Croats
Tamil Tigers	Sri Lankan Tamils	Tamil state	Terrorist attacks; guerrilla warfare	Sri Lankan government; Sinhalese

Depending on whom they claim to champion, extremist movements adapt their tactics to their environment as a way to communicate with (and attract) their defined constituency. With a few exceptions, terrorists and extremists usually direct their appeals to specific constituencies. These appeals are peculiar to the environment and idiosyncrasies of the movement, although leftists and ethno-nationalists have sometimes championed the same groups out of a sense of revolutionary solidarity. Table 1.1 illustrates the relationship between several extremist groups and their constituencies, objectives, methods, and targeted interests.

TERRORISTS OR FREEDOM FIGHTERS?

It should now be clear that defining terrorism can be an exercise in semantics and context, driven by one's perspective and world view. Absent definitional guidelines, these perspectives would be merely personal opinion and the subject of academic debate.

Perspective is a central consideration in defining terrorism. Those who oppose an extremist group's violent behavior—and who might be its targets—would naturally consider them terrorists. On the other hand, those who are being championed by the group—and on whose behalf the terrorist war is being fought—often see them as liberation fighters, even when they do not necessarily agree with the methods of the group. "The problem is that there exists no precise or widely accepted definition of terrorism."[26] We will consider several perspectives that illustrate this problem.

Perspective 1: Four Quotations

The term *terrorism* has acquired a decidedly pejorative meaning in the modern era so that few if any states or groups who espouse political violence ever refer to themselves as terrorists. Nevertheless, these same states and groups can be unabashedly extremist in their beliefs or violent in their behavior. They often invoke—and manipulate—images of a malevolent threat or unjust conditions to justify their actions. The question is whether these justifications are morally satisfactory (and thereby validate extremist violence) or whether terrorism is inherently wrong.

Evaluating the following aphorisms critically will help address difficult moral questions:

- "One person's terrorist is another person's freedom fighter."
- "One man willing to throw away his life is enough to terrorize a thousand."
- "Extremism in defense of liberty is no vice."
- "It became necessary to destroy the town to save it."[27]

"One person's terrorist is another person's freedom fighter"

Who made this statement is not known; it most likely originated in one form or another in the remote historical past. The concept it embodies is, very simply, perspective. It is a concept that will be applied throughout our examination of terrorist groups, movements, and individuals.

As will become abundantly clear, terrorists never consider themselves the bad guys in their struggle for what they would define as freedom. They might admit that they have been forced by a powerful and ruthless opponent to adopt terrorist methods, but they see themselves as freedom fighters—or, in the case of radical Islamists, obedient servants of God. Benefactors of terrorists always live with clean hands because they present their clients as plucky freedom fighters. Likewise, nations that use the technology of war to attack known civilian targets justify their sacrifice as incidental to the greater good of the cause.

"One man willing to throw away his life is enough to terrorize a thousand"

This concept originated with Chinese military philosopher **Wu Ch'i**, who wrote,

> Now suppose there is a desperate bandit lurking in the fields and one thousand men set out in pursuit of him. The reason all look for him as they would a wolf is that each one fears that he will arise and harm him. This is the reason one man willing to throw away his life is enough to terrorize a thousand.[28]

These sentences are the likely source for the better-known aphorism **"kill one man, terrorize a thousand."** Its authorship is undetermined but has been attributed to the leader of the Chinese Revolution, **Mao Zedong**, and to the Chinese military philosopher **Sun Tzu**. Wu Ch'i and Sun Tzu are often discussed in conjunction with each other, but Sun Tzu may be a mythical figure. Sun Tzu's book *The Art of War* has become a classic study of warfare. Regardless of who originated these phrases, their simplicity explains the value of a motivated individual who is willing to sacrifice himself or herself when committing an act of violence. They suggest that the selfless application of lethal force—in combination with correct timing, surgical precision, and an unambiguous purpose—is an invaluable weapon of war. It is also an obvious tactic for small, motivated groups that are vastly outnumbered and outgunned by a more powerful adversary.

"Extremism in defense of liberty is no vice"

Senator Barry M. Goldwater of Arizona made this statement during his bid for the presidency in 1964. His campaign theme was staunchly conservative and anti-Communist. However, because of the nation's rivalry with the Soviet Union at the time, every major candidate was overtly anti-Communist. Goldwater simply tried to outdo incumbent President Lyndon Johnson, his main rival, on the issue.[29]

This aphorism represents an uncompromising belief in the absolute righteousness of a cause. It defines a clear belief in good versus evil and a belief that the end justifies the means. If one simply substitutes *any cause* for the word *liberty*, one can fully understand how the expression lends itself to legitimizing uncompromising devotion to the cause. Terrorists use this reasoning to justify their belief that they are defending their championed interest (be it ideological, racial, religious, or national) against all perceived enemies—who are, of course, evil. Hence, the practice of ethnic cleansing was begun by Serb militias during the 1991–1995 war in Bosnia to forcibly remove Muslims and Croats from villages and towns. This was done in the name of Bosnian Serb security and historical claims to land occupied by others.[30] Bosnian and Croat paramilitaries later practiced ethnic cleansing to create their own ethnically pure enclaves.

"It became necessary to destroy the town to save it"

This quotation has been attributed to a statement by an American officer during the war in Vietnam. When asked why a village thought to be occupied by the enemy had been destroyed, he allegedly replied that American soldiers had destroyed the village to save it.[31] The symbolic logic behind this statement is seductive: If the worst thing that can happen to a village is for it to be occupied by an enemy, then destroying it is a good thing. The village has been denied to the enemy, and it has been saved from the horrors of enemy occupation. The symbolism of the village can be replaced by any number of symbolic values.

Terrorists use this kind of reasoning to justify hardships that they impose not only on a perceived enemy but also on their own championed group. For example, in Chapter 6, readers will be introduced to nihilist dissident terrorists, who are content to wage "revolution for revolution's sake." They have no concrete plan for what kind of society will be built on the rubble of the old one—their goal is simply to destroy an inherently evil system. To them, anything is better than the existing order. A historical example of this reasoning on an enormous scale is found in the great war between two totalitarian and terrorist states—Germany and the Soviet Union—from July 1941 to May 1945. Both sides used scorched-earth tactics as a matter of policy when their armies retreated, destroying towns, crops, roadways, bridges, factories, and other infrastructure as a way to deny resources to the enemy.

Perspective 2: Participants in a Terrorist Environment

Typically, the participants in a terrorist environment include the following actors, each of whom may advance different interpretations of an incident:[32]

The terrorist. Terrorists are the perpetrators of a politically violent incident. For them, the violent incident is a justifiable act of war against an oppressive opponent. "Insofar as terrorists seek to attract attention, they target the enemy public or uncommitted bystanders."[33] In their minds, this is a legitimate tactic, because in their view they are always freedom fighters, never terrorists. Propaganda by the deed, if properly carried out, carries powerful symbolic messages to the target audience and to large segments of an onlooker audience. Terrorists also attempt to cast themselves as freedom fighters, soldiers, and martyrs. If successful, their image will be of a vanguard movement representing the just aspirations of an oppressed people. When this occurs, political and moral pressure can be brought against their adversaries, possibly forcing them to grant concessions to the movement.

The supporter. Supporters of terrorists are patrons, in essence persons who provide a supportive environment or apparatus. Supporters will generally refer to the terrorist participants as freedom fighters. Even if supporters disagree with the use or with the application of force in an incident, they will often rationalize it as the unfortunate consequence of a just war. Supporters and patrons of terrorists often help with spinning the terrorists' cause and manipulating how incidents are reported. Supporters with sophisticated information departments—such as Northern Ireland's **Sinn Féin** or Lebanon's **Hezbollah**—can successfully use the media to deliver their message to a wide audience. Supporters will always defend the underlying grievances of the extremists and will often allude to these as the reason for the group's decision to use terrorist methods. The key for activist supporters is to convey the impression that the terrorists' methods are understandable under the circumstances.

The victim. Victims of political violence, and of warfare, will rarely sympathize with the perpetrators, regardless of the underlying motive. From their perspective, the perpetrators are little better than terrorists. From the terrorists' point of view, high-profile attacks that victimize an audience are useful as wake-up calls for the victims to understand the underlying grievances of the movement. Terrorists believe that although victims rarely sympathize with those who cause their suffering, propaganda arising from the deed can help educate them. Because they are the innocent **collateral damage** of a conflict, victims—with help from media commentators—will often question why they have become caught up in a terrorist environment. This process can theoretically cause public opinion shifts.

The target. Targets are usually symbolic. They represent some feature of the enemy and can be either property targets or human targets. Like the victims, human targets will rarely sympathize with the perpetrators. With the appropriate spin, terrorists can garner sympathy, or at least a measure of understanding, if the media convey their reasons for selecting the target. Assessing targeted interests is not unlike assessing the impact on victims, and media commentators assist with both. The difference is that the investigatory process is conducted with the understanding that targeted interests have been specifically labeled as an enemy interest. In many circumstances, targeted audiences can have a significant impact on public opinion and government policy.

The onlooker. Onlookers are the broad audience to the terrorist incident. They can be affected directly at the scene or indirectly by mass media. They may sympathize with the perpetrators, revile them, or remain neutral. Depending on the onlooker's world view, he or she might actually applaud an incident or an environment. Television is particularly effective for broadening the scope of who is an onlooker. This was evident during the live broadcasts of the attacks on the World Trade Center on September 11, 2001. The Internet also has become a primary medium for broadening the audience of terrorist acts, such as beheadings of hostages, bombings, and other incidents.

The analyst. The analyst is an interpreter of the terrorist incident. Analysts are important participants because they create perspectives, interpret incidents, and label other participants. Analysts can include political leaders, media experts, and academic experts. Very often, the analyst will simply define, for the other participants, who is—or is not—a terrorist. The media play a strong role as interpreters of the terrorist incident. They also play a role in how non-media analysts will have their views broadcast to a larger audience. Political leaders, experts, and scholars all rely on the media to promulgate their expert opinions.

The same event can be interpreted a number of ways, causing participants to adopt biased spins on that event. The following factors illustrate this problem:

- *Political associations* of participants can create a sense of identification with either the target group or the defended group. This identification can be either favorable or unfavorable, depending on the political association.

- *Emotional responses* of participants after a terrorist incident can range from horror to joy. This response can shape a participant's opinion of the incident or the extremist's cause.

- *Labeling* of participants can create either a positive or negative impression of an incident or cause. Labeling can range from positive symbolism on behalf of the terrorists to dehumanization of enemy participants (including civilians).

- *Symbolism* plays an important role in the terrorist's selection of targets. The targets can be inanimate objects that symbolize a government's power or human victims who symbolize an enemy people. Other participants sometimes make value judgments about the incident based on the symbolism of the target, thus asking whether the selected target was legitimate or illegitimate.

Perspective 3: Terrorism or Freedom Fighting?

Members of politically violent organizations tend to adopt the language of liberation, national identity, religious fervor, and even democracy. For example, ethno-nationalist or religious organizations such as the **Palestine Liberation Organization (PLO)** in Israel, the **Liberation Tigers of Tamil Eelam (LTTE)** in Sri Lanka, and the **Provisional Irish Republican Army (Provos)** in the United Kingdom have all declared that they were armies fighting on behalf of an oppressed people and were viewed by their supporters as freedom fighters. Conversely, many Israelis, Sinhalese, and British would label members of these groups as terrorists.

Governments have also adopted authoritarian measures to counter domestic threats from perceived subversives. Similarly, they rationalize their behavior as a proportional response to an immediate threat. Numerous cases of such rationalization exist, such as when the Chilean and Argentine armed forces seized power during the 1970s and engaged in widespread violent repression of dissidents. In Argentina, an estimated 30,000 people disappeared during the so-called **Dirty War** waged by its military government from 1976 to 1983.

Thus, from the perspective of many violent groups and governments, extremist beliefs and terrorist methods are logical and necessary, as well as rational and justifiable. They become mainstreamed within the context of their world view and political environment, which, in the minds of the extremists, offer no alternative to using violence to achieve freedom or maintain order. Conversely, those who oppose the practitioners of political violence reject their justifications of terrorist methods and disavow the opinion that these methods are morally proportional to the perceived political environment.

THE POLITICAL VIOLENCE MATRIX

To properly conceptualize modern terrorism, one must understand the qualities and scales of violence that define terrorist violence. The Political Violence Matrix is a tool that aids in this conceptualization.

Experts have identified and analyzed many terrorist environments. As readers will learn in the chapters that follow, these environments include state, dissident, religious, ideological, international, and criminal terrorism. One distinguishing feature in each model is the relationship between the *quality of force* used by the terrorists and the *characteristics of the intended target* of the attack. Figure 1.1 depicts how the relationship between quality of force and target characterisics often defines the type of conflict between terrorist and victim.

Figure 1.1 The Political Violence Matrix

The purpose of the Political Violence Matrix is to create a framework for classifying and conceptualizing political violence. This classification framework is predicated on two factors: **force** and **intended target**.

When force (whether conventional or unconventional) is used against *combatant* targets, it occurs in a warfare environment. When force is used against *noncombatant* or *passive military* targets, it often characterizes a terrorist environment. Violent environments can be broadly summarized as follows:

- **Total war**. Force is indiscriminately applied to destroy the military targets of an enemy combatant to absolutely destroy them.

- **Total war/unrestricted terrorism**. Indiscriminate force is applied against noncombatant targets without restraint, either by a government or by dissidents.

- **Limited war**. Discriminating force is used against a combatant target, either to defeat the enemy or to achieve a more limited political goal.

- **State repression/restricted terrorism**. Discriminating force is directed against noncombatant targets either as a matter of domestic policy or as the selective use of terrorism by dissidents.

This figure summarizes factors to be considered when evaluating the application of different scales of force against certain types of targets.

Indiscriminate force, combatant target	Total War (WWII Eastern Front)	Limited war (Korean War)	*Discriminate force, combatant target*
Indiscriminate force, noncombatant target	Total War (WWII bombing of cities)	State repression (Argentine "Dirty War")	*Discriminate force, noncombatant target*
	Unrestricted terrorism (Rwandan genocide)	Restricted terrorism (Italian Red Brigade)	

Source: Adapted from Peter C. Sederberg, *Terrorist Myths: Illusion, Rhetoric, and Reality.* Englewood Cliffs, NJ: Prentice Hall, 1989, p. 34.

Combatants, Noncombatants, and the Use of Force

Definitional and ethical issues are not always clearly drawn when one uses terms such as *combatant target*, *noncombatant target*, *discriminate force*, or *indiscriminate force*. Nevertheless, the association of these concepts and how they are applied to each other are instructive references for determining whether a violent incident may be defined as terrorism.

▶ Hijacked United Airlines Flight 175 from Boston crashes into the south tower of the World Trade Center and explodes at 9:03 a.m. on September 11, 2001, in New York City.

Spencer Platt/Getty Images News/Getty Images

Combatant and Noncombatant Targets

The term *combatants* certainly refers to conventional or unconventional adversaries who engage in armed conflict as members of regular military or irregular guerrilla fighting units. The term *noncombatants* obviously includes civilians who have no connection to military or other security forces. There are, however, circumstances in which these definitional lines become blurred. For example, in times of social unrest, civilians can become combatants. This has occurred repeatedly in societies where communal violence (e.g., civil war) breaks out between members of ethno-nationalist, ideological, or religious groups. Similarly, noncombatants can include off-duty members of the military in nonwarfare environments.[34] They become targets because of their symbolic status.

Indiscriminate and Discriminate Force

Indiscriminate force is the application of force against a target without attempting to limit the level of force or the degree of destruction of the target. *Discriminate force* is a more surgical use of limited force. Indiscriminate force is considered to be acceptable when used against combatants in a warfare environment. However, it is regularly condemned when used in *any* nonwarfare environment regardless of the characteristics of the victim.[35] There are, however, many circumstances when adversaries define "warfare environment" differently. When weaker adversaries resort to unconventional methods (including terrorism), they justify these methods by defining them as being necessary during a self-defined state of war. Discriminate force is considered to be a moral use of force when it is applied against specific targets with the intention to limit so-called collateral damage, or unintended destruction and casualties.

"Third World"),[a] who often entered into armed conflict. These conflicts could be ideological or communal in nature. Conflicts were often "proxy wars," wherein the Soviets or Americans sponsored rival insurgent groups (such as in Angola), or "**wars of national liberation**," which were nationalistic in nature (such as in Vietnam).

The following examples were several important "fronts" in the Cold War between the United States and the Soviet Union.

The Cuban Revolution

The U.S. influence in Cuba had been very strong since the United States granted the country independence in 1902 after defeating the Spanish in the Spanish-American War of 1898. The United States supported a succession of corrupt and repressive governments, the last of which was that of Fulgencio Batista. Batista's government was overthrown in 1959 by a guerrilla army led by **Fidel Castro** and **Ernesto "Che" Guevara**, an Argentine trained as a physician. Castro's insurgency had begun rather unremarkably, with significant defeats at the Moncada barracks in 1953 and a landing on the southeast coast of Cuba from Mexico in 1956 (when only 15 rebels survived to seek refuge in the Sierra Maestra mountains).

It was Batista's brutal reprisals against urban civilians that eventually drove many Cubans to support Castro's movement. When Batista's army was defeated and demoralized in a rural offensive against the rebels, Castro, his brother Raul, Guevara, and Camilo Cienfuegos launched a multifront campaign that ended in victory when their units converged on the capital of Havana in January 1959. The revolution had not been a Communist revolution, and the new Cuban government was not initially a Communist government. But by early 1960, Cuba began to receive strong economic and military support from the Soviet Union. Castro and his followers soon declared the revolution to be a Communist one, and the Soviet–American Cold War opened a new and volatile front. American attempts to subvert Castro's regime included the Bay of Pigs invasion in April 1961 and several assassination attempts against Castro.[b] The Soviets and Americans came close to war during the Cuban Missile Crisis in October 1962.

Cubans in Africa

In the postwar era, dozens of anticolonial and communal insurgencies occurred in Africa. During the 1970s, Africa became a central focus of the rivalry between Soviet- and Western-supported groups and governments. Thousands of Cuban soldiers were sent to several African countries on a mission that Fidel Castro justified as their "internationalist duty." For example, in the 1970s, Cuba sent 20,000 soldiers to Angola, 17,000 to Ethiopia, 500 to Mozambique, 250 to Guinea-Bissau, 250 to Equatorial Guinea, and 125 to Libya.[c]

Angola

Portugal was the colonial ruler of this southern African country for more than 500 years. Beginning in 1961, guerrillas began conducting raids in northern Angola, committing brutal atrocities that few can argue were not acts of terrorism. Three guerrilla movements eventually drove the Portuguese from Angola and declared independence in November 1975. These were the Front for the Liberation of Angola (FNLA), the National Union for the Total Independence of Angola (UNITA), and the Movement for the Liberation of Angola (MPLA).

In the civil war that broke out after the Portuguese withdrawal, the United States and China supported the FNLA, the Soviets and Cubans supported the MPLA, and the United States and South Africa supported UNITA. The MPLA became the de facto government of Angola. Cuban soldiers were sent to support the MPLA government, the United States and South Africa sent aid to UNITA, and South African and British mercenaries fought with UNITA. The FNLA never achieved much success in the field. Direct foreign support was withdrawn as the Cold War and South African apartheid ended, although the conflict continued through the 1990s. The MPLA finally forced UNITA to end its insurgency when UNITA leader Jonas Savimbi was killed in February 2002.

Nicaragua

U.S. influence and intervention in Nicaragua were common during most of the 20th century. Its governments had been supported by the United States, and its National Guard (the "Guardia") had been trained by the United States. These pro-American Nicaraguan governments had a long history of corruption and violent repression. Cuban-oriented Marxist guerrillas, the Sandinista National Liberation Front, overthrew the government of **Anastasio Somoza Debayle** in 1979 with Cuban and Soviet assistance.

During much of the next decade, the United States armed, trained, and supported anti-Sandinista guerrillas known as the Contras ("counterrevolutionaries"). This support included clandestine military shipments managed by the U.S. Central Intelligence Agency, the mining of Managua Harbor, and an illegal arms shipment program managed by Marine Lieutenant Colonel Oliver North.

Notes

a. At the time, the "First World" was defined as the developed Western democracies, the "Second World" was the Soviet bloc, and the "Third World" was the developing world, composed of newly emerging postcolonial nations.

b. At least one plot allegedly proposed using an exploding cigar.

c. See R. W. Cross, ed. *20th Century*. London: Purnell, 1979, p. 2365, and "The OAU and the New Scramble for Africa," pp. 2372–3.

Discussion Questions

1. Che Guevara is revered by many on the left as a "principled" revolutionary. He believed that a revolutionary spark was needed to create revolution throughout Latin America. Guevara was killed in Bolivia trying to prove his theory. Was Che Guevara an internationalist freedom fighter?

2. The United States used sabotage to destabilize Cuba's economy and government and plotted to assassinate Fidel Castro. Did the United States engage in state-sponsored terrorism? Compare this to Soviet support of its allies. Is there a difference?

3. The Soviet Union sponsored the Cuban troop presence in Africa during the 1970s. The wars in Angola, Ethiopia/Somalia, and Mozambique were particularly bloody. Did the Soviet Union engage in state-sponsored terrorism? Compare this to U.S. support of its allies. Is there a difference?

4. During the Soviet–United States rivalry in Angola, Jonas Savimbi commanded the pro-Western UNITA army. He was labeled as a freedom fighter by his U.S. patrons. Savimbi never overthrew the MPLA government. Promising efforts to share power after an election in 1992 ended in the resumption of the war when Savimbi refused to acknowledge his electoral defeat, and a 1994 cease-fire collapsed. From the U.S. perspective, has Jonas Savimbi's status as a freedom fighter changed? If so, when and how?

5. The Sandinistas overthrew a violent and corrupt government. The Contras were presented by the Reagan administration as an army of freedom fighters battling a totalitarian Communist government. Contra atrocities against civilians were documented. Were the Contras freedom fighters? How do their documented atrocities affect your opinion?

CHAPTER SUMMARY

This chapter presented readers with the nature of terrorism and probed the definitional debates about the elements of these behaviors. Several fundamental concepts were identified that continue to influence the motives and behaviors of those who support or engage in political violence.

It is important to understand the elements that help define terrorism. Common characteristics of the extremist beliefs that underlie terrorist behavior include intolerance, moral absolutes, broad conclusions, and a new language that supports a particular belief system. Literally scores of definitions of terrorism have been offered by laypersons, academics, and policy professionals to describe the elements of terrorist violence.

Many of these definitions are value laden and can depend on one's perspective as an actor in a terrorist environment. The role of perspective is significant in the definitional debate. Terrorists always declare that they are fighters who represent the interests of an oppressed group. They consider themselves freedom fighters and justify their violence as a proportional response to the object of their oppression. Their supporters will often mainstream the motives of those who violently champion their cause. In addition, the underlying principles of longstanding ideologies and philosophies continue to provide justifications for the support and use of political violence.

In the United States, official definitions have been adopted as a matter of policy. No single definition has been applied across all government agencies, but there is some commonality among their approaches. Commonalities include premeditation, unlawfulness, groups or agents, force or violence, human or property targets, intimidation, and a political objective.

KEY TERMS AND CONCEPTS

The following topics were discussed in this chapter and can be found in the Glossary:

Castro, Fidel   19
Collateral damage   15
Dirty War   16
Extremism   3
"Extremism in defense of liberty is no vice."   14
Federal Bureau of Investigation (FBI)   8
Freedom fighter   13
Guerrilla   6
Guevara, Ernesto "Che"   19
Hezbollah   15
International terrorism   10

"It became necessary to destroy the town to save it."   14
"Kill one man, terrorize a thousand."   14
Liberation Tigers of Tamil Eelam (LTTE)   16
Mao Zedong   14
Narco-terrorism   10
"One man willing to throw away his life is enough to terrorize a thousand."   14
"One person's terrorist is another person's freedom fighter."   13

Palestine Liberation Organization (PLO)   16
Provisional Irish Republican Army (Provos)   16
Sinn Féin   15
Soft targets   6
Somoza Debayle, Anastasio   20
Sun Tzu   14
Terrorism   6
Terrorist   3
Third World   19
Wars of national liberation   19
Wu Ch'i   14

WEB EXERCISE

Using this chapter's recommended websites listed on the student study site at edge.sagepub.com/martiness5e, conduct an online investigation of the fundamental characteristics of extremism.

1. What commonalities can you find in the statements of these groups?

2. Is there anything that strikes you as being particularly extremist? Why or why not?

For an online search of different approaches to defining extremism and terrorism, readers should enter the following keywords in their Web browser's search engine:

"Definitions of terrorism"

"Extremism"

RECOMMENDED READINGS

The following publications provide discussions for defining terrorism and terrorism's underlying extremist motivations.

Carr, M. (2007). *The infernal machine: A history of terrorism.* New York, NY: New Press.

Gerstenfeld, P. B. (2013). *Hate crimes: Causes, controls, and controversies.* Thousand Oaks, CA: Sage.

Hamm, M. S. (Ed.). (1994). *Hate crime: International perspectives on causes and control.* Highland Heights: Northern Kentucky University, Academy of Criminal Justice Sciences.

Howard, L. (Ed.). (1992). *Terrorism: Roots, impact, responses.* New York, NY: Praeger.

Kassimeris, G. (Ed.). (2007). *Playing politics with terrorism: A user's guide.* New York, NY: Hurst/Columbia University Press.

Laqueur, W. (1999). *The new terrorism: Fanaticism and the arms of mass destruction.* New York, NY: Oxford University Press.

Lawrence, F. M. (1999). *Punishing hate: Bias crimes under American law.* Cambridge, MA: Harvard University Press.

Sederberg, P. C. (1989). *Terrorist myths: Illusion, rhetoric, and reality.* Englewood Cliffs, NJ: Prentice Hall.

CHAPTER TWO

HISTORICAL PERSPECTIVES AND IDEOLOGICAL ORIGINS

Terrorism has been a dark feature of human behavior since history was first recorded. Great leaders have been assassinated, groups and individuals have committed acts of incredible violence, and entire cities and nations have been put to the sword—all in the name of defending a greater good.

The modern era of terrorism is primarily, though not exclusively, a conflict between adversaries waging, on one side, a self-described war on terrorism and, on the other, a self-described holy war in defense of their religion. It is an active confrontation, evidenced by the fact that the incidence of significant terrorist attacks often spikes to serious levels. Although such trends are disturbing, it is critical for one to keep these facts in perspective because the modern terrorist environment is in no manner a unique circumstance in human history.

It will become clear in the following pages that the history of terrorist behavior extends into antiquity and that themes and concepts recur. State terrorism, dissident terrorism, and other types of political violence are common to all periods of civilization. It will also become clear to readers that certain *justifications*—rooted in basic beliefs—have been used to rationalize terrorist violence throughout history. The following themes are introduced here:

- Historical Perspectives on Terrorism
- Ideological Origins of Terrorism
- September 11, 2001, and the New Terrorism

Learning Objectives

This chapter will enable readers to do the following:

1. Demonstrate knowledge of the historical context of modern terrorist violence.

2. Understand the classical ideological continuum.

3. Classify some ideologies and activism as left-wing phenomena.

4. Explain the attributes and behavior of left-wing terrorism.

5. Classify some activism and extremism as right-wing phenomena.

6. Explain the attributes and behavior of right-wing terrorism.

HISTORICAL PERSPECTIVES ON TERRORISM

It is perhaps natural for each generation to view history narrowly, from within its own political context. Contemporary commentators and laypersons tend to interpret modern events as though they have no historical precedent. However, terrorism is by no means a modern phenomenon and has in fact a long history. Nor does terrorism arise from a political vacuum.

Antiquity

In the ancient world, cases and stories of state repression and political violence were common. Several ancient writers championed **tyrannicide** (the killing of tyrants) as necessary for the greater good of the citizenry and to delight the gods. Some assassins were honored by the public. For example, after Aristogeiton and Harmodius were executed for assassinating the Greek tyrant Hipparchus, statues were erected to honor them.[1] Conquerors often set harsh examples by exterminating entire populations or forcing the conquered into exile. An example of this practice is the Babylonian Exile, which followed the conquest of the kingdom of Judea. Babylon's victory resulted in the forced removal of the Judean population to Babylon in 598 and 587 BCE. Those in authority also repressed the expression of ideas from individuals they deemed dangerous, sometimes violently. In ancient Greece, Athenian authorities sentenced the great philosopher Socrates to death in 399 BCE for allegedly corrupting the city-state's youth and meddling in religious affairs. He drank hemlock and died among his students and followers.

The Roman Age

During the time of the Roman Empire, the political world was rife with many violent demonstrations of power, which were arguably examples of what we would now term state terrorism. These include the brutal suppression of Spartacus's followers after the Servile War of 73–71 BCE, after which the Romans crucified surviving rebels along the Appian Way. **Crucifixion** was a common form of public execution: The condemned were affixed to a cross or other wooden frame, either tied or nailed through the wrist or hand, and later died by suffocation as their bodies sagged.

Warfare was waged in an equally hard manner, such as the final conquest of the North African city-state of Carthage in 146 BCE. The city was reportedly allowed to burn for 10 days, the rubble was cursed, and salt was symbolically plowed into the soil to signify that Carthage would forever remain desolate. During another successful campaign in 106 CE, the Dacian nation (modern Romania) was eliminated, its population was enslaved, and many Dacians perished in gladiatorial games. In other conquered territories, conquest was often accompanied by similar demonstrations of terror, always with the intent to demonstrate that Roman rule would be wielded without mercy against those who did not submit to the authority of the empire.

Regicide (the killing of kings) was also fairly common during the Roman period. Perhaps the best known was the assassination of Julius Caesar in 44 BCE by rivals in the Senate. Other Roman emperors also met violent fates: Caligula and Galba were killed by the Praetorian Guard in 41 and 68 CE, respectively; Domitian was stabbed to death in 96 CE; a paid gladiator murdered Commodus in 193 CE; and Caracalla, Elagabalus, and other emperors either were assassinated or died suspiciously.[2]

The Ancient and Medieval Middle East

Cases exist of movements in the ancient and medieval Middle East that used what modern analysts would consider to be terrorist tactics. For example, in the *History of the Jewish War*—a seven-volume account of the first Jewish rebellion against Roman occupation (66–73 CE)—the historian Flavius Josephus describes how one faction of the rebels, the **Sicarii** (who took their name from their preferred weapon, the *sica*, a short curved dagger), attacked both Romans and members of the Jewish establishment.[3] They were masters of guerrilla warfare and the destruction of symbolic property and belonged to a group known as the **Zealots** (from the Greek *zelos*, meaning ardor or strong spirit), who opposed the Roman occupation of Palestine. The modern term *zealot*, used to describe uncompromising devotion to radical change, is derived from the name of this group. Assassination was a commonly used tactic. Some Sicarii Zealots were present at the siege of Masada, a hilltop fortress that held out against the Romans for 3 years before the defenders committed suicide in 74 CE rather than surrender.

The Dark Ages

During the period from the Assassins (13th century) to the French Revolution (18th century), behavior that would later be considered terrorism was commonly practiced in medieval warfare. In fact, a great deal of medieval conflict involved openly brutal warfare. However, the modern terrorist profile of politically motivated dissidence attempting to change an existing order, or state repression to preserve state hegemony, was uncommon. Nation states in the modern sense did not exist in medieval Europe, and recurrent warfare was motivated by religious intolerance and political discord between feudal kings and lords. The post-Assassin Middle East also witnessed periodic invasions, discord between leaders, and religious warfare but not modern-style terrorism. It was not until the rise of the modern nation state in the mid-17th century that the range of intensity of conflict devolved from open warfare to include behavior that the modern era would define as insurgency, guerrilla warfare, and terrorism.

The French Revolution: Prelude to Modern Terrorism

During the French Revolution, British statesman and philosopher **Edmund Burke** coined the word *terrorism* in its modern context. He used the word to describe the *régime de la terreur*, commonly known in English as the **Reign of Terror** (June 1793 to July 1794).[4] The Reign of Terror, led by the radical Jacobin-dominated government, is a good example of state terrorism carried out to further the goals of a revolutionary ideology.[5] During the Terror, thousands of opponents to the Jacobin dictatorship—and others merely perceived as enemies of the new revolutionary Republic—were arrested and put on trial before the **Revolutionary Tribunal**. Those found to be enemies of the Republic were beheaded by a new instrument of execution—the guillotine. With the capability to execute victims one after the other in assembly-line fashion, it was regarded by Jacobins and other revolutionaries of the time as an enlightened and civilized tool of revolutionary justice.[6]

The ferocity of the Reign of Terror is reflected in the number of victims. Between 17,000 and 40,000 persons were executed, and perhaps 200,000 political prisoners died in prisons from disease and starvation.[7] Two incidents illustrate the communal nature of this violence. In Lyon, 700 people were massacred by cannon fire in the town square. In Nantes, thousands were drowned in the Loire River when the boats they were detained in were sunk.[8]

The Revolutionary Tribunal, a symbol of revolutionary justice and state terrorism, has its modern counterparts in 20th-century social upheavals. Recent examples include the **struggle meetings** of revolutionary China (public criticism sessions, involving public humiliation and confession) and revolutionary Iran's Islamic Revolution Committees, also known as **komitehs** (ad hoc tribunals that enforced Islamic laws).[9]

Nineteenth-Century Europe: Two Examples From the Left

Modern left-wing terrorism is not a product of the 20th century. Its ideological ancestry dates to the 19th century, when anarchist and communist philosophers began to advocate the destruction of capitalist and imperial society—what **Karl Marx** referred to as the "spectre . . . haunting Europe."[10] Some revolutionaries readily encouraged the use of terrorism in the new cause. One theorist, **Karl Heinzen** in Germany, anticipated the late-20th-century fear that terrorists might obtain weapons of mass destruction when he supported the acquisition of new weapons technologies to destroy the enemies of the people. According to Heinzen, these weapons should include poison gas and new high-yield explosives.[11]

During the 19th century, several terrorist movements championed the rights of the lower classes. These movements were prototypes for 20th-century groups and grew out of social and political environments unique to their countries. To illustrate this point, two examples are drawn from early industrial England and from semifeudal Russia.

The **Luddites** were English workers in the early 1800s who objected to the social and economic transformations of the Industrial Revolution. Their principal objection was that industrialization threatened their jobs, and thus they targeted the machinery of the new textile factories. They attacked, for example, stocking looms that mass-produced stockings at the expense of skilled stocking weavers who made them by hand.

A mythical figure, Ned Ludd, was the supposed founder of the Luddite movement. The movement was active from 1811 to 1816 and was responsible for sabotaging and destroying wool and cotton mills and weaving machinery. The British government eventually suppressed the movement by passing anti-Luddite laws, including establishing the crime of "machine breaking," which was punishable by death. After 17 Luddites were executed in 1813, the movement gradually died out. Although historians debate whether Luddites clearly fit the profile of terrorists, modern antitechnology activists and terrorists, such as the **Unabomber, Theodore "Ted" Kaczynski**, in the United States, are sometimes referred to as neo-Luddites.

People's Will (Narodnaya Volya) in Russia was a direct outgrowth of student dissatisfaction with the czarist regime in the late 19th century. Many young Russian university students, some of whom had studied abroad, became imbued with the ideals of anarchism and Marxism. Many became radical reformists who championed the rights of the people, particularly the peasant class. A populist revolutionary society, Land and Liberty (Zemlya Volya), was founded in 1876 with the goal of fomenting a mass peasant uprising by settling radical students among them to raise their class consciousness. After a series of arrests and mass public trials, Land and Liberty split into two factions in 1879. One faction, Black Repartition, kept to the goal of

CHAPTER PERSPECTIVE 2.1

The Gunpowder Plot of Guy Fawkes

The reign of James I, King of England from 1603 to 1625, took place in the aftermath of a religious upheaval. During the previous century, King Henry VIII (1509–1547) wrested from Parliament the authority to proclaim himself the head of religious affairs in England. King Henry had requested permission from Pope Clement VII to annul his marriage to Catherine of Aragon when she failed to give birth to a male heir to the throne. His intention was to then marry Anne Boleyn. When the Pope refused his request, Henry proclaimed the Church of England and separated the new church from papal authority. The English crown confiscated Catholic Church property and shut down Catholic monasteries. English Catholics who failed to swear allegiance to the crown as supreme head of the church were repressed by Henry and later by Queen Elizabeth I (1558–1603).

When James I was proclaimed king, Guy Fawkes and other conspirators plotted to assassinate him. They meticulously smuggled gunpowder into the Palace of Westminster, intending to blow it up along with King James and any other officials in attendance on the opening day of Parliament. Unfortunately for Fawkes, one of his fellow plotters attempted to send a note to warn his brother-in-law to stay away from Westminster on the appointed day. The note was intercepted, and Fawkes was captured on November 5, 1605, while guarding the store of gunpowder.

Guy Fawkes suffered the English penalty for treason. He was dragged through the streets, hanged until nearly dead, his bowels were drawn from him, and he was cut into quarters—an infamous process known as hanging, drawing, and quartering. Fawkes had known that this would be his fate, so when the noose was placed around his neck he took a running leap, hoping to break his neck. Unfortunately, the rope broke, and the executioner proceeded with the full ordeal.

a peasant revolution. The other, People's Will, fashioned itself into a conspiratorial terrorist organization.

People's Will members believed that they understood the underlying problems of Russia better than the uneducated masses of people did and concluded that they were therefore better able to force government change. This was, in fact, one of the first examples of a revolutionary vanguard strategy, in which People's Will believed that they could both demoralize the czarist government and expose its weaknesses to the peasantry. Group members quickly embarked on a terrorist campaign against carefully selected targets. Incidents of terror committed by People's Will members—and other revolutionaries who emulated them—included shootings, knifings, and bombings targeting government officials. In one successful attack, Czar Alexander II was assassinated by a terrorist bomb on March 1, 1881. The immediate outcome of the terrorist campaign was the installation of a repressive police state in Russia that, although not as efficient as later police states would be in the Soviet Union or Nazi Germany, succeeded in harassing and imprisoning most members of People's Will.

The Modern Era

David C. Rapoport designed a theory holding that modern terrorism has progressed through three waves that lasted for roughly 40 years each and that we now live in a fourth wave. His four waves are as follows:

- the anarchist wave: 1880s to the end of World War I

- the anticolonial wave: end of World War I until the late 1960s

- the New Left wave: late 1960s to the near present

- the religious wave: about 1980 until the present

It is useful in developing a critical understanding of modern extremist behavior to understand that the modern threat of the New Terrorism adds a unique dimension to the terrorist environment of the 21st century. This is because "the new terrorism is different in character, aiming not at clearly defined political demands but at the destruction of society and the elimination of large sections of the population."[12]

The new breed of terrorists "would feel no compunction over killing hundreds of thousands if they had the means to do so."[13] In addition, the modern environment is characterized by a horizontal organizational arrangement wherein independent cells operate autonomously without reporting to a hierarchical (vertical) command structure. The attacks in September 2001 in the United States, March 2004 in Spain, and July 2005 in Great Britain and Egypt are examples of this new environment. Many of these new terrorists are motivated by religious or nationalist precepts that do not fit easily into the classical ideological continuum discussed in the next section.

IDEOLOGICAL ORIGINS OF TERRORISM

Ideologies are systems of belief derived from theories that explain human social and political conditions. Literally scores of belief systems have led to acts of terrorist violence. Because there are so many belief systems, it is difficult to classify them with precision. Nevertheless, a classical ideological continuum rooted in the politics of the French Revolution has endured to the present time.[14] This is instructive for our discussion of politically motivated violence because the concepts embodied in the continuum have continued and will continue to be relevant.

The Classical Ideological Continuum: The Case of the French Revolution

At the beginning of the French Revolution in 1789, a parliament-like assembly was convened to represent the interests of the French social classes. Although its name changed during the revolution—from National Constituent Assembly, to Legislative Assembly, to National Convention—the basic ideological divisions were symbolically demonstrated by where representatives sat during assembly sessions. On the left side of the assembly sat those who favored radical change, some advocating a complete reordering of French society and culture. On the right side of the assembly sat those who favored either the old order or slow and deliberate change. In the center of the assembly sat those who either favored moderate change or simply could not make up their minds to commit to either the left or right. These symbolic designations—**left, center, and right**—have become part of our modern political culture. Table 2.1 summarizes the progression of these designations from their origin during the French Revolution.

It is readily apparent from the French Revolution that the quality of the classical continuum depended very much on the political environment of each society. For example, in American culture, mainstream values include free enterprise, freedom of speech, and limited government.[15] Depending on where one falls on the continuum, the interpretation can be very different. Thus, the continuum summarizes the conventional political environment of the modern era. Many nationalist or religious terrorists, however, do not fit easily into the classical continuum. For example, "to argue that the Algerian terrorists, the Palestinian groups, or the Tamil Tigers are 'left' or 'right' means affixing a label that simply does not fit. . . . The Third World groups . . . have subscribed to different ideological tenets at different periods."[16] Nevertheless, the continuum is still useful for categorizing terrorist behaviors and extremist beliefs. Table 2.2 compares the championed groups, methodologies, and desired outcomes of typical political environments.

An Ideological Analysis: From the Extreme Left to the Extreme Right

Fringe left ideology is usually an extreme interpretation of Marxist ideology, using theories of class warfare or ethno-nationalist liberation to justify political violence. At the leftist fringe, violence is seen as a perfectly legitimate option because the group considers itself at war with an oppressive system, class, or government. The key justification is the notion of the group as a righteous champion of the poor and downtrodden.

Table 2.1   The Classical Ideological Continuum: The Case of the French Revolution

After the dissolution of the monarchy, the victorious revolutionaries began a complete restructuring of French society. Perhaps the most important priority was to create a new elective constituent assembly to represent the interests of the people. The configuration of this new assembly changed repeatedly as the revolution progressed from one ideological phase to the next.

Legislative Body	Political and Ideological Orientation		
	Left	**Center**	**Right**
National Constituent Assembly 1789–1791	Patriots (republicans)	Moderates (constitutional monarchists)	Blacks (reactionaries)
Legislative Assembly 1791–1792	Mountain (republicans)	Plain (near-republicans)	Constitutionalists (constitutional monarchists)
National Convention 1792	Mountain (radicals)	Marsh (uncommitted bourgeois)	Girondins (bourgeois republicans)

Table 2.2 The Classical Ideological Continuum: Modern Political Environments

Activism on the left, right, and center can be distinguished by a number of characteristics. A comparison of these attributes is instructive. The representation here compares their championed groups, methodologies, and desired outcomes.

	Left Fringe	Far Left	Liberalism	Moderate Center	Conservatism	Far Right	Fringe Right
Championed groups	Class/ nationality	Class/ nationality	Demographic groups	General society	General society	Race, ethnicity, nationality, religion	Race, ethnicity, nationality, religion
Methodology/ process	Liberation movement	Political agitation	Partisan democratic processes	Consensus	Partisan democratic processes	Political agitation	"Order" movement
Desired outcome	Radical change	Radical change	Incremental reform	Status quo slow change	Traditional values	Reactionary change	Reactionary change

This type of ideological movement frequently concerns itself only with destroying an existing order in the name of the championed class or national group, not with building the new society in the aftermath of the revolution. For example, **Gudrun Ensslin**, a leader of the terrorist Red Army Faction in West Germany, stated, "As for the state of the future, the time after victory, that is not our concern. . . . We build the revolution, not the socialist model."[17]

Far left ideology frequently applies Marxist theory to promote class or ethno-nationalist rights. It is best characterized as a radical worldview because political declarations often direct public attention against perceived forces of exploitation or repression. Far left groups do not necessarily engage in political violence and often fully participate in democratic processes. In Western Europe, for example, Communist parties and their affiliated Communist labor unions have historically been overt in agitating for reform through democratic processes.[18] It is important to note that this environment of relatively peaceful coexistence occurs only in societies where dissent is tolerated. In countries with weaker democratic traditions, far left dissent has erupted in violence and been met by extreme repression. Latin America has many examples of this kind of environment.

Far right ideology is characterized by strong adherence to social order and traditional values. A chauvinistic racial or ethnic dimension is often present, as is an undercurrent of religion or mysticism (the latter is especially prevalent in the United States). As with the far left, far right groups do not necessarily engage in political violence and have fully participated in democratic processes. Organized political expression is often overt. For example, right-wing political parties in many European countries are a common feature of national politics. Their success has been mixed, and their influence varies in different countries. In Spain, Greece, and Great Britain, they have little popular support.[19] However, those in Austria, Belgium, France, and Italy have enjoyed significant popular support in the recent past.

Not all far right political movements are the same, and a comparison of the American and European contexts is instructive. In Europe, some rightist parties are nostalgic and neofascist, such as the German People's Union. Others are more populist, such as the National Front in France.[20] In the United States, the far right is characterized by activism among local grassroots organizations such as the Tea Party movement and has no viable political party. Some American groups have a religious orientation, others are racial, others embody a politically paranoid survivalist lifestyle, and some incorporate all three tendencies.

Fringe right ideology is usually rooted in an uncompromising belief in ethno-nationalist or religious superiority, and terrorist violence is justified as a protection of the purity and superiority of the group. Terrorists on the fringe right picture themselves as champions of an ideal order that has been usurped, or attacked, by inferior interests or unwanted religious values. Violence is an acceptable option against those who are not members of the group because they are considered obstacles to the group's natural assumption of power. For example, in Europe rightist violence is often directed against non-European migrants from the Middle East and Africa.[21] Like their counterparts on the fringe left, right-wing terrorists often have only a vague notion of the characteristics of the new order after the revolution. They are concerned only with asserting their value system and, if necessary, destroying the existing order. Significantly, rightist terrorists have been more likely than their leftist counterparts to engage in indiscriminate bombings and other attacks that produce higher numbers of victims.

Table 2.3 applies this discussion to the American context.

Table 2.3   The Classical Ideological Continuum: The Case of the United States

The United States is a good case in point for the application of the classical ideological continuum. Its political environment has produced organizations that represent the ideologies included in the continuum. The representation here compares organizations that have economic, group rights, faith, and legal agendas.

Left Fringe	Far Left	Liberalism	Moderate Center	Conservatism	Far Right	Fringe Right
Economic/class agenda						
May 19 Communist Organization	Communist Party, USA	American Federation of State, County and Municipal Employees	American Federation of Labor and Congress of Industrial Organizations	Teamsters Union	Lyndon Larouche groups	Posse Comitatus
Activist/group rights agenda						
Fuerzas Armadas de Liberación Nacional Puertorrequeña	Black Panther Party for Self Defense	National Council of La Raza	National Bar Association	Heritage Foundation	Euro-American Unity and Rights Organization	Aryan Republican Army
Religious/faith agenda						
Liberation theology	Catholic Worker movement	American Friends Service Committee	National Conference of Christians and Jews	Southern Baptist Convention	Moral Majority	Army of God
Legal/constitutional agenda						
Individual lawyers	National Lawyers Guild	American Civil Liberties Union	American Bar Association	Thomas More Law Center	American Center for Law and Justice	Freemen

Ideology in Practice: From Anarchism to Fascism

Anarchism

Anarchism is a leftist philosophy that was an ideological by-product of the social upheavals of mid-19th-century Europe, a time when civil unrest and class conflict swept the continent and culminated in the revolutions of 1848. Anarchists were among the first antiestablishment radicals who championed what they considered the downtrodden peasant and working classes. They abhorred central government control and private property. Frenchman **Pierre-Joseph Proudhon**, who published a number of articles and books on the virtues of anarchism, coined an enduring slogan among anarchists: **"Property is theft!"**

The radical undercurrent of anarchist thought began with that proposition. **Mikhail Bakunin** and his philosophical associates, **Sergei Nechayev** and **Petr Kropotkin**, all Russians, were the founders of modern anarchism. They supported destruction of the state, radical decentralization of power, atheism, and individualism. They also opposed capitalism and Karl Marx's revolutionary doctrine of building a socialist state.

▶ Architects of Communism. Russian revolutionary leader Vladimir Ilyich Lenin (left) with Leon Trotsky, head of the Red Army and future ideological rival of Joseph Stalin.

Early anarchists never offered a concrete plan for replacing centralized state authority because they had no clearly defined vision of postrevolutionary society. They considered the destruction of the state their contribution to the future.

They advocated achieving propaganda victories by violently pursuing the revolution, which became known as **propaganda by the deed**. Terrorism was advocated as the principal way to destroy state authority. Interestingly, anarchists argued that terrorists should organize themselves into small groups, or cells, a tactic that modern terrorists have adopted. Anarchists actively practiced propaganda by the deed, as evidenced by the many acts of violence against prominently symbolic targets. In Russia, People's Will conducted a terrorist campaign from 1878 to 1881, and other anarchist terrorist cells operated in Western Europe. Around the turn of the 20th century, anarchists assassinated Russian czar Alexander II, Austro-Hungarian empress Elizabeth, Italian king Umberto I, and French president Marie François Sadi Carnot. An alleged anarchist, Leon Czolgosz, assassinated U.S. president William McKinley.

Marxism

Radical socialism, like anarchism, is a leftist ideology that began in the turmoil of mid-19th-century Europe and the uprisings of 1848. Socialists championed the emerging industrial working class and argued that the wealth produced by these workers should be more equitably distributed rather than concentrated in the hands of the wealthy elite.

Karl Marx is regarded as the founder of modern socialism. He and his associate **Friedrich Engels**, both Germans, argued that their approach to socialism was grounded in the scientific discovery that human progress and social evolution is the result of a series of historical conflicts and revolutions. Each era was based on the working group's unequal relationship to the **means of production** (e.g., slaves, feudal farmers, industrial workers) vis-à-vis the ruling group's enjoyment of the fruits of the working group's labor. In each era, a ruling thesis group maintained the status quo and a laboring antithesis group challenged it (through agitation and revolution), resulting in a socioeconomic synthesis that created new relationships with the means of production. Thus, human society evolved into the next era. According to Marx, the most advanced era of social evolution would be the synthesis Communist era, which he argued would be built after the antithesis industrial working class overthrew the thesis capitalist system. Marx theorized that the working class would establish the **dictatorship of the proletariat** in the Communist society and build a just and egalitarian social order.

Figure 2.1 illustrates the class pyramid during the Industrial Age, which Marx considered to be the final age of human society prior to the dictatorship of the proletariat.

Marx and Engels collaborated on the *Manifesto of the Communist Party*, a short work completed in 1847 and published in 1848. It became one of the most widely read documents of the 20th century. In it, Marx and Engels explained the revolutionary environment of the industrial era and how this era was an immediate precursor to the Communist era.

Marxist socialism was pragmatic, revolutionary, and action oriented, and many revolutionary leaders and movements throughout the 20th century adopted it. Terrorism, both state and dissident, was used during the revolutions and the consolidations of power after victory. It is interesting to note that none of these Marxist revolutions was led by the industrial working class; all occurred in preindustrial developing nations, often within the context of anticolonial warfare waged by peasants and farmers. Chapter Perspective 2.2 summarizes the Marxist-influenced political philosophies of the New Left, which arose in Western countries during the 1960s.

Fascism

Fascism was a rightist ideological counterpoint to Marxism and anarchism that peaked before World War II. Like Marxism and anarchism, fascism's popular appeal grew out of social turmoil in Europe, this time as a reaction to the 1917 Bolshevik (Communist) Revolution in Russia, the subsequent Bolshevik-inspired political agitation elsewhere in Europe, and the widespread unrest during the Great Depression of the 1930s. It was rooted in a brand of extreme nationalism that championed the alleged superiority of a particular national heritage or ethno-racial group. Fascism was anti-Communist, antimonarchist, antidemocratic, and anti-intellectual (though there were some fascist writers). It demanded extreme obedience to law, order, and the state. Fascism also required cultural **conservatism**—often looking backward in history to link the ancient past to the modern state. Fascists created their own conceptualizations of traditional values such as military duty, the Christian church, and motherhood. Strong antidemocratic leadership was centralized in the state, usually under the guidance of a single charismatic leader

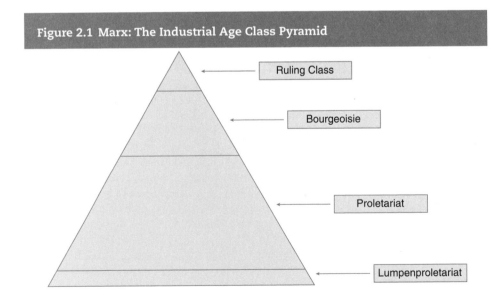

Figure 2.1 Marx: The Industrial Age Class Pyramid

CHAPTER PERSPECTIVE 2.2

Required Reading on the "New Left"

In the postwar West, many leftist terrorists were inspired not by orthodox Marxism but by examples of revolutionaries in the developing world such as Mao Zedong, Ho Chi Minh, Fidel Castro, and Che Guevara. Realizing as a practical matter that building guerrilla units in the countryside was impossible—and that the working class was not sufficiently prepared for revolution—many young radicals became nihilistic dissident revolutionaries. They concluded that revolution was a goal in itself, and "revolution for the hell of it"[a] became a slogan and a practice for many left-wing radicals in the West. For them, there was little vision of what kind of society would be built on the rubble of the old. In fact,

> The central question about the rationality of some terrorist organizations, such as the West German groups of the 1970s or the Weather Underground in the United States, is whether or not they had a sufficient grasp of reality . . . to calculate the likely consequences of the courses of action they chose.[b]

Nevertheless, from the perspective of radical activists and intellectuals, nihilist dissident behavior was rational and logical.

Several books inspired radical leftists in the West. These books provided a rational justification for revolutionary agitation against democratic institutions in relatively prosperous societies. They came to define the New Left of the 1960s and 1970s, which rejected the rigid ideological orthodoxy of the "Old Left" Marxists. They created a new interpretation of revolutionary conditions. On the short list of required reading among radical activists were three books:[c]

- Frantz Fanon's *The Wretched of the Earth*
- Herbert Marcuse's *One-Dimensional Man*
- Carlos Marighella's *Mini-Manual of the Urban Guerrilla*

The Wretched of the Earth

In *The Wretched of the Earth,* Fanon analyzed the role of indigenous people living in countries controlled by imperial governments that exploited local resources and imposed a foreign culture and values. He concluded that revolutionary violence was perfectly justifiable under these conditions. In fact, it was required because, in addition to liberating one's country, one had to liberate oneself as an individual; only "liberating violence" could do this. Young radicals in the West agreed with this analysis, and some concluded that liberating violence in a prosperous society was justified. They also rationalized their violent political behavior by establishing a sense of revolutionary solidarity with "the wretched of the earth."

One-Dimensional Man

Marcuse was a German philosopher who, along with Jean-Paul Sartre, was prominent among existentialist writers. He argued in *One-Dimensional Man* that capitalist society—no matter how prosperous or democratic—created "manacles" of privilege that kept the public docile and content. He explained that the people's oppression should be measured by how much they had been co-opted by the accouterments of capitalist comfort. Using this analysis, middle-class college students who considered themselves to be Marxists could justify revolutionary activism, even though they were far removed from the working class. Thus, they were rejecting their "manacles" of privilege and fighting in common cause with other revolutionaries worldwide.

Mini-Manual of the Urban Guerrilla

As discussed in Chapter 5, Carlos Marighella's book was extremely influential on leftist revolutionary strategy in Latin America, Western Europe, and the United States. It was a blueprint for revolution in urban societies, and Marighella's guidelines for using urban terrorism to create revolutionary conditions were widely followed. However, as noted previously, the assumption that the exploited group would join the revolution at the right time rarely happened in practice.

These works of dissident philosophy shaped the ideological justifications for the tactics of many revolutionary movements. For example, the motivation behind West Germany's Red Army Faction has been described as having three central elements. These elements reflect the revolutionary literature and theory of the time:[d]

- the concept of the "armed struggle" and the model of Third World liberation movements

(Continued)

(Continued)

- the Nazi "connection" and "formal democracy" in the Federal Republic
- the rejection of consumer society[e]

Notes

a. The title of a book by the American New Left radical Abbie Hoffman. See Hoffman, Abbie. *Revolution for the Hell of It*. New York: Dell, 1968.

b. Reich, Walter. *Origins of Terrorism: Psychologies, Theologies, States of Mind*. Washington, DC: Woodrow Wilson Center, 1990, p. 9.

c. Fanon, Frantz. *The Wretched of the Earth*. New York: Grove, 1963; Marcuse, Herbert. *One-Dimensional Man*. Boston: Beacon, 1964; Marighella, Carlos. *Mini-Manual of the Urban Guerrilla*. Chapel Hill, NC: Documentary, 1985.

d. Marighella, *Mini-Manual*.

e. Pridham, Geoffrey. "Terrorism and the State in West Germany During the 1970s: A Threat to Stability or a Case of Political Over-Reaction?" In *Terrorism: A Challenge to the State*, edited by Juliet Lodge. Oxford, UK: Martin Robinson, 1981. Quoted in Whittaker, David J., ed. *The Terrorism Reader*. New York: Routledge, 2001, pp. 189–91.

▶ Architects of fascism. German *Führer* Adolf Hitler (front left) stands beside Italian *Duce* Benito Mussolini. Behind them are ranking members of the Nazi and Fascist regimes.

Istituto Nazionale Luce/Alinari Archives/Getty Images

who symbolically embodied the virtues of the state, the people, and the underlying fascist ideology.

Italian dictator **Benito Mussolini** was the first to consolidate power and create a fascist state. Beginning with his March on Rome in 1922, he gradually eliminated all opposition and democratic institutions. He was a mentor to **Adolf Hitler**, who led the fascist National Socialist German Worker's (Nazi) Party to power in Germany in 1933. Both the Italian and German fascist regimes sent troops to fight on the side of right-wing Spanish rebels led by **Francisco Franco** during the Spanish Civil War.[22]

Although the first fascist movement largely collapsed in 1945, right-wing groups and political parties have continued to promote neofascist ideals. Some terrorist groups in Europe and the United States have been overtly fascist and racist. Dictatorships have also arisen since World War II that adopted many features of prewar fascism. For example, Latin American regimes arose in Chile, Argentina, Uruguay, and El Salvador—to name a few—that fit the fascist pattern.

The Just War Doctrine

The **just war doctrine** is an ideal and a moralistic philosophy rather than an ideology. The concept has been used by ideological and religious extremists to justify acts of extreme violence. Throughout history, nations and individuals have gone to war with the belief that their cause was just and their opponents' cause unjust. Similarly, attempts have been made for millennia to write fair and just laws of war and rules of engagement. For example, in the late 19th and early 20th centuries, the **Hague Convention** produced at least 21 international agreements on the rules of war.[23]

The just war debate asks who can morally be defined as an enemy and what kinds of targets it is morally acceptable to attack. In this regard,

> there are two separate components to the concept of just war (which philosophers call the just war tradition): the rationale for initiating the war (war's ends) and the method of warfare (war's means). Criteria for whether a war is just are divided into jus ad bellum (justice of war) and jus in bello (justice in war) criteria.[24]

Thus, **jus in bello** is correct behavior while waging war, and **jus ad bellum** is having the correct conditions for waging war in the first place. These concepts have been debated by philosophers and theologians for centuries. The early Christian philosopher **Saint Augustine** concluded in the fifth century that war is justified to punish injuries inflicted by a nation that has refused to correct wrongs committed by its citizens. The Christian religious tradition, especially the Roman Catholic Church, has devoted a great deal of intellectual effort to clarifying Augustine's concept. Saint Augustine was, of course, referring to warfare between nations and cities, and Church doctrine long held that an attack against state authority was an offense against God.[25] Likewise, the Hague Convention dealt only with rules of conflict between nations and afforded no legal rights to spies or antistate rebels. Neither system referred to rules of engagement for nonstate or antistate conflicts.

▶ Antifascist protesters rally against a Unite the Right demonstration in Charlottesville, Virginia, in August 2017.

In the modern era, both dissidents and states have adapted the just war tradition to their political environments. Antistate conflict and reprisals by states are commonplace. Dissidents always consider their cause just and their methods proportional to the force the agents of their oppressors use. Antiterrorist reprisals launched by states are also justified as appropriate and proportional applications of force—in this case as a means to root out bands of terrorists.

Rules of war and the just war tradition are the result of many motivations. Some rules and justifications are self-serving, others are pragmatic, and others are grounded in ethno-nationalist or religious traditions. Hence, the just war concept can be easily adapted to justify ethnic, racial, national, and religious extremism in the modern era.

Table 2.4 summarizes the ideals and ideologies discussed here.

Table 2.4   A Comparison of Ideologies

Social conflict in the 20th century was deeply rooted in the application of ideals and ideologies to practice. The adoption of these social and philosophical systems frequently inspired individuals and motivated movements to engage in armed conflict with perceived enemies. This table matches proponents, outcomes, and case studies of four ideals and ideologies.

| | Ideological Orientation | | | |
	Anarchism	Marxism	Fascism	Just War
Proponents	Proudhon/Bakunin	Marx/Engels	Mussolini/Hitler	Saint Augustine
Desired social outcome	Stateless society	Dictatorship of the proletariat	New order	Legitimized conflict
Applications	Narodnaya Volya	Russian Revolution	WWII-era Italy and Germany	State and dissident violence

SEPTEMBER 11, 2001, AND THE NEW TERRORISM

The death of **Al Qaeda** leader Osama bin Laden in May 2011 occurred on the eve of the 10th anniversary of the September 11, 2001, terrorist attacks on U.S. soil. The attacks were seen by many as a turning point in the history of political violence. In the aftermath of these attacks, journalists, scholars, and national leaders repeatedly described the emergence of a new international terrorist environment. It was argued that within this new environment, terrorists were now quite capable of using—and very willing to use—weapons of mass destruction to inflict unprecedented casualties and destruction on enemy targets. These attacks seemed to confirm warnings from experts during the 1990s that a New Terrorism,[26] using "asymmetrical" methods, would characterize the terrorist environment in the new millennium.

September 11, 2001

One of the worst incidents of modern international terrorism occurred in the United States on the morning of September 11, 2001. It was carried out by 19 Al Qaeda terrorists who were on a suicidal "martyrdom mission." They committed the attack to strike at symbols of American (and Western) interests in response to what they perceived to be a continuing process of domination and exploitation of Muslim countries. They were religious terrorists fighting in the name of a holy cause against perceived evil emanating from the West. Their sentiments were born in the religious, political, and ethno-nationalist ferment that has characterized the politics of the Middle East for much of the modern era.

Nearly 3,000 people were killed in the attack. The sequence of events occurred as follows:

7:59 a.m. American Airlines Flight 11, carrying 92 people, leaves Boston's Logan International Airport for Los Angeles.

8:14 a.m. United Airlines Flight 175, carrying 65 people, leaves Boston for Los Angeles.

8:20 a.m. American Airlines Flight 77, carrying 64 people, takes off from Washington's Dulles Airport for Los Angeles.

8:42 a.m. United Airlines Flight 93, carrying 44 people, leaves Newark (New Jersey) International Airport for San Francisco.

8:46 a.m. American Flight 11 crashes into the north tower of the World Trade Center.

9:03 a.m. United Flight 175 crashes into the south tower of the World Trade Center.

9:37 a.m. American Flight 77 crashes into the Pentagon. Trading on Wall Street is called off.

9:59 a.m. Two World Trade Center—the south tower—collapses.

10:03 a.m. United Flight 93 crashes 80 miles southeast of Pittsburgh, Pennsylvania.

10:28 a.m. One World Trade Center—the north tower—collapses.[27]

The United States had previously been the target of international terrorism at home and abroad but had never suffered a strike on this scale on its territory. The most analogous historical event was the Japanese attack on the naval base at Pearl Harbor, Hawaii, on December 7, 1941. The last time so many people had died from an act of war on American soil was during the Civil War in the mid-19th century.

After the Al Qaeda assault and the subsequent anthrax crisis, American culture shifted away from openness to security. The symbolism of the attack, combined with its sheer scale, drove the United States to war and dramatically changed the American security environment. Counterterrorism in the United States shifted from a predominantly law enforcement mode to a security mode. Measures included unprecedented airport and seaport security, border searches, visa scrutiny, and more intensive immigration procedures. Hundreds of people were administratively detained and questioned during a sweep of persons fitting the profile of the 19 attackers. These detentions set off a debate about the constitutionality of the methods and the fear of many that civil liberties were in jeopardy. In October 2001, the USA PATRIOT Act was passed, granting significant authority to federal law enforcement agencies to engage in surveillance and other investigative work. On November 25, 2002, 17 federal agencies (later increased to 22) were consolidated to form a new Department of Homeland Security.

CHAPTER PERSPECTIVE 2.3

Waging War in the Era of the New Terrorism

A war on terrorism was declared in the aftermath of the September 11, 2001, attacks. This is a new kind of conflict against a new form of enemy. From the outset, policy makers understood that the war would be fought unconventionally, primarily against shadowy terrorist cells and elusive leaders. It is not a war against a nation, but rather against ideas and behavior.

The mobilization of resources in this war necessitated the coordination of law enforcement, intelligence, and military assets in many nations across the globe. Covert operations by special military and intelligence units became the norm rather than the exception. Suspected terrorist cells were identified and dismantled by law enforcement agencies in many countries, and covert operatives worked secretly in other countries. Although many suspects were detained at the U.S. military base in Guantanamo Bay, Cuba, other secret detention facilities were also established. These detentions stimulated a vigorous debate among political, judicial, and human rights experts.[a]

However, the war has not been fought solely in the shadows. In contrast to the deployment of small law enforcement and covert military or intelligence assets, the U.S.-led invasions of Afghanistan and Iraq involved the commitment of large conventional military forces. In Afghanistan, reasons given for the invasion included the need to eliminate state-sponsored safe havens for Al Qaeda and other international *mujahideen* (holy warriors). In Iraq, reasons given for the invasion included the need to eliminate alleged stockpiles of weapons of mass destruction and alleged links between the regime of Saddam Hussein and terrorist networks.[b] The U.S.-led operation in Iraq was symbolically named Operation Iraqi Freedom.

One significant challenge for waging war against extremist behavior—in this case, against terrorism—is that victory is not an easily definable condition. For example, on May 1, 2003, U.S. president George W. Bush landed on the aircraft carrier *Abraham Lincoln* to deliver a speech in which he officially declared that the military phase of the Iraq invasion had ended and that the overthrow of the Hussein government was "one victory in a war on terror that began on September 11th, 2001, and still goes on."[c] Unfortunately, the declaration was premature. A widespread insurgency took root in Iraq, with the resistance employing both classic hit-and-run guerrilla tactics and terrorism. Common cause was found between remnants of the Hussein regime and non-Iraqi Islamist fighters. Thousands of Iraqis and occupation troops became casualties during the insurgency. In particular, the insurgents targeted foreign soldiers, government institutions, and so-called collaborators such as soldiers, police officers, election workers, and interpreters. Sectarian violence also spread, with Sunni and Shi'a religious extremists killing many civilians. Domestic security in Iraq further devolved, after the withdrawal of coalition forces, with the rise of extremist movements such as the Islamic State of Iraq and the Levant (ISIS).

Is the war on terrorism being won? How can victory reasonably be measured? Assuming that the New Terrorism will continue for a time, perhaps the best measure for progress in the war is to assess the degree to which terrorist behavior is being successfully managed—in much the same way that progress against crime is assessed. As the global community continues to be challenged by violent extremists during the new era of terrorism, the definition of victory is likely to continue to be refined and redefined by nations and leaders.

Notes

a. See, e.g., Spencer Ackerman, "Island Mentality: Why the Bush Administration Defends Guantanamo." *The New Republic*, August 2, 2005.

b. In 2006, the Senate Intelligence Committee issued a 356-page report saying that it had discovered no evidence linking Al-Qaeda to the regime of Saddam Hussein. See Greg Miller, "Senate: Hussein Wasn't Allied With Al Qaeda." *Los Angeles Times*, September 9, 2006.

c. David E. Sanger, "In Speech, Bush Focuses on Conflicts Beyond Iraq." *New York Times*, May 1, 2003.

The symbolism of a damaging attack on homeland targets was momentous because it showed that the American superpower was vulnerable to small groups of determined revolutionaries. The Twin Towers had dominated the New York City skyline since 1972. They were a symbol of global trade and prosperity and the pride of the largest city in the United States. The Pentagon, of course, is a unique building that symbolizes American military power, and its location across the river from the nation's capital showed the vulnerability of the seat of government to attack.

On May 30, 2002, a 30-foot-long steel beam, the final piece of debris from the September 11 attack, was ceremoniously removed from the "Ground Zero" site in New York City.

The New Terrorist Morality

The morality of terrorism in the latter decades of the 20th century differed from 19th-century and early 20th-century anarchist terrorism and other violent movements. The new generation did not share the same moralistic scruples of the previous generation. Terrorism in late 19th- and early 20th-century Russia, for example, was "surgical" in the sense that it targeted specific individuals to assassinate, specific banks to rob, and specific hostages to kidnap. In fact, not only did the **Social Revolutionary Party** in Russia (founded in 1900) engage in an extensive terrorist campaign in the early 20th century, but its tactics actually became somewhat popular because its victims were often government officials who were hated by the Russian people.

In contrast, during the post–World War II era, the definitions of who an enemy was, what a legitimate target could be, and which weapons to use became much broader. This redefining of what constitutes a legitimate target, as well as the appropriate means to attack that target, led to a new kind of political violence. Late 20th-century dissident terrorism was "new" in the sense that it was "indiscriminate in its effects, killing and maiming members of the general public . . . , arbitrary and unpredictable . . . , refus[ing] to recognize any of the rules or conventions of war . . . [and] not distinguish[ing] between combatants and non-combatants."[38] Operationally, the new terrorist morality can be spontaneous and quite gruesome. For example, in March 2004, four American private contractors were killed in an ambush in the Iraqi city of Fallujah. Their corpses were burned, dragged through the streets, and then displayed from a bridge. In Iraq and Syria, the Islamic State of Iraq and the Levant (ISIS) recorded and promulgated graphic executions, including the beheadings of several Western civilian prisoners in 2014, and the public burning of a captured Jordanian pilot in 2015. These events were recorded and posted on social networking media and the Internet.

When terrorists combine this new morality with the ever-increasing lethality of modern weapons, the potential for high casualty rates and terror on an unprecedented scale is very real. For example, this combination was put into practice during the long-term terrorist suicide campaigns in Israel with the Palestinians' two *intifadas* in 1987–1993 and 2000–2005. The combination of a new morality and lethality were especially put into practice by Al Qaeda-inspired attacks in September 2001 in the United States, March 2004 in Madrid, and July 2005 in London. It was also put into practice by ISIS-inspired attacks in November 2015 in Paris and March 2016 in Brussels. Should terrorists obtain high-yield weapons—such as chemical, biological, nuclear, or radiological weapons—the new morality would provide an ethical foundation for their use.

The New Terrorism

It is clear from human history that terrorism is deeply woven into the fabric of social and political conflict. This quality has not changed, and in the modern world, states and targeted populations are challenged by the New Terrorism, which is characterized by the following:

- loose, cell-based networks with minimal lines of command and control
- desired acquisition of high-intensity weapons and weapons of mass destruction
- politically vague, religious, or mystical motivations

- asymmetrical methods that maximize casualties
- skillful use of the Internet and **manipulation of the media**

The New Terrorism should be contrasted with traditional terrorism, which is typically characterized by the following:

- clearly identifiable organizations or movements
- use of conventional weapons, usually small arms and explosives
- explicit grievances championing specific classes or ethno-nationalist groups
- relatively "surgical" selection of targets

New information technologies and the Internet create unprecedented opportunities for terrorist groups, and violent extremists have become adept at bringing their wars into the homes of literally hundreds of millions of people. Those who specialize in suicide bombings, car bombs, or mass-casualty attacks correctly calculate that carefully selected targets will attract the attention of a global audience. Thus, cycles of violence not only disrupt normal routines, but they also produce long periods of global awareness. Such cycles can be devastating. For example, during the winter and spring of 2005, Iraqi suicide bombings increased markedly in intensity and frequency, from 69 in April 2005 (a record rate at that time) to 90 in May.[28] Likewise, the renewal of sectarian violence in 2014, exacerbated by intensive combat with ISIS, was a reinvigoration of the sectarian bloodletting that occurred during the U.S.-led occupation of Iraq in the early 2000s. These attacks resulted in many casualties, including hundreds of deaths, and greatly outpaced the previous cycle of car bombings by more than two to one.

Table 2.5 Ten Countries With the Most Terrorist Attacks

	Total Attacks		Total Deaths*		Deaths per Attack*		Total Injured*		Injured per Attack*		Total Kidnapped/ Hostages	
	2016	2015	2016	2015	2016	2015	2016	2015	2016	2015	2016	2015
Iraq	2,965	2,417	9,764	6,973	3.44	3.01	13,314	11,900	4.74	5.25	8,586	4,008
Afghanistan	1,340	1,716	4,561	5,312	3.58	3.24	5,054	6,250	4.03	3.99	1,673	1,134
India	927	798	337	289	0.38	0.38	636	500	0.73	0.66	317	866
Pakistan	734	1,010	955	1,087	1.34	1.11	1,729	1,338	2.43	1.37	450	279
Philippines	482	490	272	260	0.58	0.54	418	430	0.90	0.90	216	127
Nigeria	466	588	1,832	4,940	4.35	9.13	919	2,786	2.66	7.70	265	858
Syria	363	387	2,088	2,767	6.42	7.91	2,656	2,830	9.16	9.63	1,406	1,476
Turkey	363	309	657	337	1.81	1.11	2,282	828	6.37	2.78	18	141
Yemen	363	460	628	1,517	1.89	3.90	793	2,599	2.44	6.97	173	456
Somalia	359	241	740	659	2.18	3.05	943	463	2.91	2.28	373	161
Worldwide	11,072	12,121	25,621	29,424	2.44	2.56	33,814	37,419	3.32	3.40	15,543	12,264

Source: U.S. Department of State, Bureau of Counterterrorism and Countering Violent Extremism, *Country Reports on Terrorism 2016* (Washington, DC: U.S. Department of State, 2017).

*Includes perpetrators.

All of these threats offer new challenges for policy makers about how to respond to the behavior of terrorist states, groups, and individuals. The war on terrorism, launched in the aftermath of the attacks of September 11, 2001, seemed to herald a new resolve to end terrorism. This has proved to be a difficult task. The war has been fought on many levels, as exemplified by the invasions of Afghanistan and Iraq, the disruption of terrorist cells on several continents, and counterterrorist campaigns against movements such as the self-proclaimed Islamic State. There have been serious terrorist strikes such as those in Madrid, Spain; Bali, Indonesia; London, England; and Sharm el Sheikh, Egypt. In addition, differences arose within the post–September 11 alliance, creating significant strains. It is clear that the war will be a long-term prospect, likely with many unanticipated events. Table 2.5 reports the scale of violence in 2015 and 2016 for 10 countries with active terrorist environments.

DISCUSSION BOX

TOTAL WAR

This chapter's Discussion Box is intended to stimulate critical debate about the legitimacy of using extreme force against civilian populations.

Total war is "warfare that uses all possible means of attack, military, scientific, and psychological, against both enemy troops and civilians."[a] It was the prevailing military doctrine applied by combatant nations during World War II and was prosecuted by marshalling a total mobilization of industrial and human resources.

Allied and Axis military planners specifically targeted civilian populations. In the cases of German and Japanese strategists, the war was fought as much against indigenous populations as against opposing armies. The massacres and genocide directed against civilian populations at Auschwitz, Dachau, Warsaw, Lidice, and Nanking—and countless other atrocities—are a dark legacy of the 20th century.

The estimated number of civilians killed during the war is staggering:[b]

Belgium	90,000
Britain	70,000
China	20,000,000
Czechoslovakia	319,000
France	391,000
Germany	2,000,000
Greece	391,000
Japan	953,000
Poland	6,000,000
Soviet Union	7,700,000
Yugoslavia	1,400,000

An important doctrine of the air war on all sides was widespread bombing of civilian populations in urban areas (so-called saturation bombing) so that the cities of Rotterdam, Coventry, London, Berlin, Dresden, and Tokyo were deliberately attacked. It is estimated that the American atomic bombs dropped on Hiroshima and Nagasaki in Japan killed 70,000 and 35,000 people, respectively.[c]

Notes

a. *Webster's New Twentieth Century Dictionary of the English Language*, Unabridged, 2d ed. New York: Publishers Guild, 1966.

b. Mercer, Derrik, ed. *Chronicle of the Second World War.* Essex, UK: Longman Group, 1990, p. 668.

c. Jablonski, Edward. *Flying Fortress.* New York: Doubleday, 1965, p. 285.

CHAPTER SUMMARY

This chapter introduced readers to some of the historical and modern attributes of terrorism, with a central theme that terrorism is deeply rooted in the human experience. The impact of extremist ideas on human behavior should not be underestimated because certain historical examples of political violence in some ways parallel modern terrorism.

The relationship between extremist ideas and terrorist events was discussed as a nexus, whereby terrorism is the violent manifestation of extremist beliefs. Ideologies are the belief systems at the root of political violence.

Whether terrorist acts are **mala in se** or **mala prohibita** is often relative. Depending on one's perspective, gray areas may challenge us to be objective about the true nature of political violence. Most, if not all, nations promote an ideological doctrine to legitimize the power of the state and to convince the people that their systems of belief are worthy of loyalty, sacrifice, and (when necessary) violent defense. Conversely, when a group of people perceives that an alternative ideology or condition should be promoted, revolutionary violence may occur against the defenders of the established rival order. In neither case would those who commit acts of political violence consider themselves unjustified in their actions or label themselves as terrorists.

KEY TERMS AND CONCEPTS

The following topics were discussed in this chapter and can be found in the Glossary:

WEB EXERCISE

Using this chapter's recommended websites listed on the student study site at **edge.sagepub.com/martiness5e**, conduct an online investigation of organizations that monitor extremist sentiment and terrorist behavior. Compare and contrast these organizations.

1. What are the primary agendas of these organizations?

2. How would you describe the differences between research, government, and social activist organizations?

3. In your opinion, are any of these organizations more comprehensive than other organizations? Less comprehensive?

For an online search of research and monitoring organizations, readers should enter the following keywords in their Web browser's search engine:

- "Terrorism research"

- "Human rights organizations"

RECOMMENDED READINGS

The following publications provide introductions to terrorism and ideological perspectives.

Anti-Defamation League. (1995). *The skinhead international: A worldwide survey of neo-Nazi skinheads.* New York, NY: Anti-Defamation League.

Bar-On, T. (2007). *Where have all the Fascists gone?* Aldershot, UK: Ashgate.

Bergen, P. I. (2011). *A very long war: The history of the war on terror and the battles with Al Qaeda since 9/11.* New York, NY: Free Press.

Coll, S. (2008). *The bin Ladens: An Arabian family in the American century.* New York, NY: Penguin.

Cronin, I. (Ed.). (2002). *Confronting fear: A history of terrorism.* New York, NY: Thunder's Mouth Press.

Fanon, F. (1963). *The wretched of the earth.* New York, NY: Grove.

Farber, D. (Ed.). (2007). *What they think of us: International perceptions of the United States since 9/11.* Princeton, NJ: Princeton University Press.

Gage, B. (2009). *The day Wall Street exploded: A story of America in its first age of terror.* Oxford, UK: Oxford University Press.

Griset, P. L., & Mahan, S. (2007). *Terrorism in perspective* (2nd ed.). Thousand Oaks, CA: Sage.

Haberfeld, M. R., & von Hassel, A. (Eds.). (2009). *A new understanding of terrorism: Case studies, trajectories, and lessons learned.* New York, NY: Springer.

Heinze, E. A., & Steele, B. J. (Eds.). (2009). *Ethics, authority, and war: Non-state actors and the just war tradition.* New York, NY: Palgrave Macmillan.

Hersh, S. M. (2004). *Chain of command: The road from 9/11 to Abu Ghraib.* New York, NY: HarperCollins.

Heymann, P. B., & Kayyem, J. N. (2005). *Protecting liberty in an age of terror.* Cambridge, MA: MIT Press.

Hobsbawm, E. J. (2008). *On empire: America, war, and global supremacy.* New York, NY: Pantheon.

Hoffman, B. (2006). *Inside terrorism.* New York, NY: Columbia University Press.

Kaczynski, T. (2010). *Technological slavery: The collected writings of Theodore J. Kaczynski, a.k.a. "The Unabomber."* Port Townsend, WA: Feral House.

Kaplan, J., & Bjørgo, T. (Eds.). (1998). *Nation and race: The developing Euro-American racist subculture*. Boston, MA: Northeastern University Press.

Kelly, R. J., & Meghan, J. (Eds.). (1998). *Hate crime: The global politics of polarization*. Carbondale: Southern Illinois University Press.

Laqueur, W. (Ed.). (2004). *Voices of terror: Manifestos, writings, and manuals of Al-Qaeda, Hamas and other terrorists from around the world and throughout the ages*. New York, NY: Reed Press.

Lee, M. A. (1999). *The beast reawakens: Fascism's resurgence from Hitler's spymasters to today's neo-Nazi groups and right-wing extremists*. New York, NY: Routledge.

Lipstadt, D. E. (1994). *Denying the Holocaust: The growing assault on truth and memory*. New York, NY: Plume.

Marcuse, H. (1964). *One-dimensional man*. Boston, MA: Beacon.

Marighella, C. (1985). *Mini-manual of the urban guerrilla*. Chapel Hill, NC: Documentary.

Marshall, P. (2010). *Demanding the impossible: A history of anarchism*. Oakland, CA: PM Press.

National Commission on Terrorist Attacks Upon the United States. (2004). *The 9/11 Commission report*. New York, NY: Norton.

Reed, C., & Ryall, D. (Eds.). (2007). *The price of peace: Just war in the twenty-first century*. Cambridge, UK: Cambridge University Press.

Scheuer, M. (2004). *Imperial hubris: Why the West is losing the war on terror*. Dulles, VA: Brassey's.

Scheuer, M. (2011). *Osama bin Laden*. New York, NY: Oxford University Press.

Tanner, S. (2009). *Afghanistan: A military history from Alexander the Great to the war against the Taliban* (Updated ed.). New York, NY: Da Capo.

CHAPTER THREE

CAUSES OF TERRORIST VIOLENCE

Learning Objectives

This chapter will enable readers to do the following:

1. Demonstrate the ability to interpret revolutionary ideologies and cultural factors to assess whether the use of political violence is a strategic choice.

2. Apply sociological theories of intergroup conflict and collective violence to posit explanations for political violence.

3. Apply criminological theories of criminality to posit explanations for political violence.

4. Apply psychological theories of group- and individual-level dynamics to posit explanations for political violence.

5. Interpret justifications for political violence, as reported by extremists, within the context of moral reasoning.

This chapter investigates the causes of terrorism. Many explanations have been given for terrorism, and scholars and other experts have devoted a great deal of effort to explaining terrorist behavior. This has not been a simple task. Explanatory models consider many factors, including political history, government policy, contemporary politics, cultural tensions, ideological trends, economic trends, individual idiosyncrasies, and other variables.

In the following discussion, readers will encounter factors that explain why individuals and groups choose to engage in terrorist violence. Readers will also explore and critically assess the sources of ideological belief systems and activism and the reasons why such activism sometimes results in terrorist violence. For example, is the terrorist option somehow forced on people who have no other alternative? Is terrorism simply one choice from a menu of options? Is politically motivated violence perhaps a pathological manifestation of personal or group dysfunction?

It is useful in the beginning of our discussion to identify broad causes of terrorism at the individual and group levels.

At the *individual level*, some experts have distinguished rational, psychological, and cultural origins:

> Rational terrorists think through their goals and options, making a cost-benefit analysis. . . . Psychological motivation for resorting to terrorism derives from the terrorist's personal dissatisfaction with his/her life and accomplishments. . . . A major cultural determinant of terrorism is the perception of "outsiders" and anticipation of their threat to ethnic group survival.[1]

At the *group level*, terrorism can grow out of an environment of political activism, when a group's goal is to redirect a government's or society's attention toward the grievances of an activist social movement. It can also grow out of dramatic events in the experience of a people or a nation. Although these two sources—social movements and dramatic events—are generalized concepts, it is instructive to briefly review their importance.

Social Movements. Social movements are campaigns that try either to promote change or to preserve something that is perceived as threatened. Movements involve mass action on behalf of a cause, not simply the actions of individuals promoting their personal political beliefs. Examples include the Irish Catholic civil rights movement of the 1960s in Northern Ireland and the African American civil rights movement in the American South during the same decade. Proponents of this type of movement seek the moral high ground as a way to rally sympathy and support for their cause and to bring pressure on those at odds with the cause. In both cases, radicalized sentiment grew out of frustration with the slow pace of change and the violent reaction of some opponents.

Dramatic Events. Also called traumatic events, these occur when an individual, a nation, or an ethno-nationalist group suffers from an event that has a traumatizing and lasting effect. At the personal level, children of victims of political violence may grow up to oppose perceived oppressors with violence. This is likely to occur in regions of extended conflict, such as the war between Tamils and Sinhalese in Sri Lanka, the Troubles in Northern Ireland, or the Palestinian **intifada**.

Regardless of the specific precipitating cause of a particular terrorist's behavior, the fact that so many individuals, groups, and nations resort to terrorist violence suggests that common motives and explanations can be found. The discussion in this chapter will review the following:

- Political Violence as the Fruit of Injustice
- Political Violence as Strategic Choice
- Moral Justifications for Political Violence

POLITICAL VIOLENCE AS THE FRUIT OF INJUSTICE

Sociological Explanations of Terrorism: Intergroup Conflict and Collective Violence

The sociological approach argues that terrorism is a group-based phenomenon, selected by weaker groups as the only available strategy. From the perspective of an opponent group, "terrorism and other forms of collective violence are often described as 'senseless,' and their participants are often depicted as irrational."[2] However, this is not an entirely complete analysis, because

> if "rational" means goal directed . . . then most collective violence is indeed rational . . . . Their violence is indeed directed at achieving certain, social change-oriented goals, regardless of whether we agree with those goals or with the violent means used to attain them. If "rational" further means sound, wise, and logical, then available evidence indicates that collective violence is rational . . . because it sometimes can help achieve their social goals.[3]

In essence, the disadvantaged group asserts its rights by selecting a methodology—in this case, terrorism—that from the group's perspective is its only viable option. The selection process is based on the insurgent group's perceptions and its analysis of those perceptions.

Theoretical Foundations for Sociological Explanations

Two sociological concepts, structural theory and relative deprivation theory, provide useful explanatory analysis for this process.[4]

Structural theory has been used in many policy and academic disciplines to identify social conditions (structures) that affect group access to services, equal rights, civil protections, freedom, or other quality-of-life measures. Examples of social structures include government policies, administrative bureaucracies, spatial (geographic) location of the group, the role of security forces, and access to social institutions. Applying this theory to the context of terrorism,

> structural theories of revolution emphasize that weaknesses in state structures encourage the potential for revolution. . . . According to this view, a government beset by problems such as economic and military crises is vulnerable to challenges by insurgent forces. . . . Other governments run into trouble when their . . . policies alienate and even anger elites within the society.[5]

The state is the key actor in structural theories of revolution. Its status is the precipitating factor for popular revolutions. Popular discontent, the alienation of elites, and a pervasive crisis are the central ingredients for bringing a society to the brink of revolution.[6]

Relative deprivation theory is a theory cited by sociologists and political scientists, principally arguing that "feelings of deprivation and frustration underlie individual decisions to engage in collective action."[7] As explained by Ted Robert Gurr in his seminal book *Why Men Rebel*, the gap between expected and achieved well-being breeds resentment and discontent.[8] In this type of environment, deprived and disenfranchised populations will weigh the utility of force. Thus, "when people feel deprived relative to some other group or find that their hopes and expectations for improved conditions have been frustrated, their discontent and thus likelihood of engaging in protest increases."[9]

In essence, their motive for engaging in political violence is their observation that they are *relatively* deprived, vis-à-vis other groups, in an unfair social order. According to this theory, when a group's rising expectations are met by sustained repression or second-class status, the group's reaction may include political violence. For example, research has posited that the gap between expected and achieved well-being among educated Palestinians and Israelis is higher among Palestinians and that this may to some degree explain social unrest emanating from the Palestinian population.[10]

Relative deprivation should be contrasted with **absolute deprivation**, when a group has been deprived of the basic necessities for survival by a government or social order. In this environment, a group is denied adequate shelter, food, healthcare, and other basic necessities. These conditions can also lead to political violence, the rationale being that absolutely deprived populations have little to lose by engaging in collective violence.

One observation must be made about relative deprivation theory: Although it was, and is, a popular theory among many experts, three shortcomings have been argued:

- Psychological research suggests that aggression happens infrequently when the conditions for relative deprivation are met.

- The theory is more likely to explain individual behavior than group behavior.

- Empirical studies have not found an association between relative deprivation and political violence.[11]

▶ Bloody Sunday (January 30, 1972): A British soldier runs down an Irish Catholic demonstrator during protests and rioting in the city of Londonderry in Northern Ireland. The confrontations resulted in elite paratroopers firing on Catholic civilians. The incident was a seminal event that rallied many Catholics to support the Provisional Irish Republican Army.

This debate persists. Nevertheless, many sociologists and political scientists continue to reference relative deprivation as an explanatory theory when investigating the characteristics and motivations of social movements.

Sociological Explanations in an International Context

Examples of movements that are motivated against a government or social order include ethno-nationalist movements among Irish Catholics in Northern Ireland and Palestinians in Israel. Sociological explanations for these movements are summarized below.

Irish Catholic nationalism in Northern Ireland dates to the 16th century, when English King James I granted Scottish Protestant settlers land in Ireland, thus beginning a long process of relegating Irish Catholics to second-class status in their own country. Protestant (Scotch-Irish) and English domination was secured in 1690 at the Battle of the Boyne. Catholic independence was finally won in 1919 and 1920, but the island was formally divided between the independent Irish Republic in the south and the British-administered six-county region of Northern Ireland. Since that time, some Irish republicans in the north, especially the Provisional Irish Republican Army, engaged in armed resistance against Protestant and British political domination. They seek union with the southern republic.

Palestinian nationalism dates to the formal creation of the state of Israel on May 14, 1948. The next day, the Arab League—Lebanon, Egypt, Jordan, and Syria—declared war on Israel. Israel was victorious, and in the subsequent consolidation of power, hundreds of thousands of Palestinians either left Israel or were expelled. Since that time, Palestinian nationalists, especially the Palestine Liberation Organization and HAMAS, have fought a guerrilla and terrorist war against Israel to establish a Palestinian state.

Table 3.1 summarizes the constituencies and enemies of groups promoting these causes.

Table 3.1	Nationalism and Sociological Explanations of Terrorism: Examining Four Cases of Constituencies and Adversaries

Nationalism is an expression of ethno-nationalist identity. Nationalist activism can range in scale from the promotion of cultural heritage to armed insurrection. Its goals can range from a desire for equal political rights to complete national separation.

Some ethnonational groups have engaged in nationalist activism to preserve their cultural heritage and have opposed what they consider to be national and cultural repression. Within these ethnonational groups, violent extremists have engaged in terrorism.

This table summarizes the constituencies and adversaries of four nationalist movements that have used terrorism to obtain autonomy from social orders they perceive to have repressed their national and cultural aspirations.

| Group | Activity Profile | |
	Constituency	Adversary
Irish Republican Army factions	Northern Irish Catholics	British and Ulster Protestants
ETA factions	Spanish Basques	Spaniards
Secular and religious Palestinian groups	Palestinians	Israelis
FLQ	French-speaking residents of Quebec (Québécois)	English-speaking Canadians

Psychological Explanations of Terrorism: Rationality and Terrorist Violence

Psychological approaches to explaining terrorism broadly examine the effects of internal psychological dynamics on individual and group behavior. This kind of analysis incorporates many of the concepts discussed later in this chapter, such as moral convictions and simplified definitions of good and evil.

At the outset, it is useful to examine the presumption held by a number of people—experts, policy makers, and laypersons—that terrorism is a manifestation of insanity or mental illness or that terrorism is the signature of a lunatic fringe. This presumption suggests that terrorism is a priori (fundamentally) irrational behavior and that only deranged individuals or deranged collections of people would select terrorist violence as a strategy. Most experts agree that this blanket presumption is incorrect. Although individuals and groups do act out of certain idiosyncratic psychological processes, their behavior is neither insane nor necessarily irrational.

Individual-Level Psychological Explanations

Some experts argue that the decision to engage in political violence is frequently an outcome of significant events in individual lives that give rise to antisocial feelings. They actively seek improvement in their environment or desire redress and revenge from the perceived cause of their condition.

Research has *not* found a pattern of psychopathology among terrorists. In comparing nonviolent and violent activists, studies reported "preliminary impressions . . . that the family backgrounds of terrorists do not differ strikingly from the backgrounds of their politically active counterparts."[12] There is evidence of some psychosocial commonalities among violent activists. For example, research on 250 West German terrorists reported "a high incidence of fragmented families," "severe conflict, especially with the parents," conviction in juvenile court, and "a pattern of failure both educationally and vocationally."[13]

Group-Level Psychological Explanations

In a number of social and political contexts, political violence is a familiar social phenomenon for some people. When it is combined with "the pronounced need to belong to a group,"[14] individuals can in the end "define their social status by group acceptance." Thus, at the group level,

> another result of psychological motivation is the intensity of group dynamics among terrorists. They tend to demand unanimity and be intolerant of dissent . . . [and] pressure to escalate the frequency and intensity of operations is ever present. . . . Compromise is rejected, and terrorist groups lean toward maximalist positions.[15]

An important outcome of these dynamics is the development of a self-perpetuating cycle of rationalizations of political violence. This occurs because

> the psychodynamics also make the announced group goal nearly impossible to achieve. A group that achieves its stated purpose is no longer needed; thus, success threatens the psychological well-being of its members.[16]

Generalized Psychological Explanations

Psychological explanations are fairly broad approaches. Both individual and group theories attempt to generalize reasons for the decision to initiate political violence and the processes that perpetuate such violence. These explanations may be summarized as follows:

- Terrorism is simply a choice among violent and less violent alternatives. It is a rational selection of one methodology.

- Terrorism is a technique for maintaining group cohesion and focus. Group solidarity overcomes individualism.

- Terrorism is a necessary process to build the esteem of an oppressed people. Through terrorism, power is established over others, and the weak become strong. Attention itself becomes self-gratifying.

- Terrorists consider themselves an elite vanguard. They are not content to debate the issues because they have found a truth that needs no explanation. Action is superior to debate.

- Terrorism provides a means to justify political violence. The targets are depersonalized, and symbolic labels are attached to them. Thus, symbolic buildings become legitimate targets even when occupied by people, and individual victims become symbols of an oppressive system.

In essence, then, psychological explanations of terrorist behavior use theories of individual motivations and group dynamics to explain why people decide to adopt strategies of political violence and why groups continue campaigns of violence. Pressures to conform to the group, combined with pressures to commit acts of violence, form a powerful psychological drive to carry on in the name of the cause even when victory is logically impossible. These pressures become so prevalent that victory becomes secondary to the unity of the group.[17] Having said this, it is inadvisable to generalize about psychological causes of terrorism because "most terrorists do not demonstrate serious psychopathology" and "there is no single personality type."[18]

Case: The Stockholm Syndrome. In August 1973, three women and one man were taken hostage by two bank robbers in Stockholm, Sweden. The botched robbery led to a hostage crisis that lasted for six days. During the crisis, the robbers threatened to kill the four hostages if the authorities tried to rescue them. At the same time, the hostages received treatment from the robbers that they began to think of as kindness and consideration. For example, one hostage was told that he would not be killed but rather shot in the leg if the police intervened and that he should play dead. Another hostage, who suffered from claustrophobia, was let out of the bank vault on a rope leash.

During the six-day episode, all of the hostages began to sympathize with the robbers and gradually came to identify with them. They eventually denounced the authorities' attempts to free them. After the situation was resolved, the hostages remained loyal to their former captors for months. They refused to testify against them and raised money for their legal defense. One of the female former hostages actually became engaged to one of the robbers. This was, to say the least, surprising behavior. The question is whether this was an isolated phenomenon or whether it is possible for it to occur in other hostage crises.

Experts are divided about whether the **Stockholm syndrome** is a prevalent condition. Those who contend that it can occur and has occurred in other situations argue that the syndrome sets in when a prisoner suffers a psychological shift from captive to sympathizer. In theory, the prisoner will try to keep his or her captor happy in order to stay alive whenever he or she is unable to escape, isolated, or threatened with death. This becomes an obsessive identification with what the captor likes and dislikes, and the prisoner eventually begins to sympathize with the captor. The psychological shift theoretically requires three or four days to set in.

Criminological Explanations of Terrorism: The Path to Political Criminality

Criminological explanations generally hold that terrorism is a product of the same socialization processes that cause individuals to engage in criminal behavior. Such processes explain why individuals become terrorists or criminals and why groups of people establish terrorist or criminal organizations. The criminological approach argues that terrorism and crime are explainable within the framework of established theoretical perspectives used to explain criminal deviance.

Differential Association Theory. Edwin Sutherland described the theory of differential association in his 1939 book, *Principles of Criminology.* Differential association is a process of social learning in which criminals and law-abiding people learn their behavior from associations with others. People imitate or otherwise internalize the quality of these associations. Criminality (and by implication, political extremism) are learned behaviors that are acquired from interacting with others who participate in criminal politically activist lifestyles so that the difference between offenders and nonoffenders lies in individual choices. In other words, offenders and nonoffenders strive for similar goals, but they choose different avenues to achieve those goals. These choices are based on the lessons they take from exposure to certain kinds of life experiences. In particular, those who grow up in criminal or politically polarized milieus will adopt values that can result in crime or political extremism.

Although differential association theory has been criticized for relying on variables that are difficult to operationalize, it remains a potent and influential approach to explaining crime. Its appeal is perhaps grounded in its proposition that all persons possess the same learning processes, which are developed through communicating and interacting with groups of people. The difference between criminals and noncriminals is that they base their choices on different lessons learned from their different experiences. Norms and values are similarly learned, but some people internalize deviant norms and values.

Anomie and Strain Theories. The great sociologist Émile Durkheim's concept of anomie[19] was applied to criminology during the 1930s by Robert Merton and others, who studied the tension between socially acceptable goals and the means one is permitted by society to use for achieving those goals.[20] Merton's application of anomie theory focused on the *availability* of goals and means. He posited that the greater society encourages its members to use acceptable means to achieve acceptable goals. For example, in the United States "acceptable means" include hard work, prudent savings, and higher education. Acceptable goals include comfort, leisure time, social status, and wealth. However, not all members of society have an equal availability of resources to achieve society's recognized goals, thus creating *strain* for these less-empowered members. Strain is manifested as a desire to achieve these goals, and one's inability to acquire the legitimate means to attain them. In theory, those who do not have access to acceptable means may resort to illegitimate and illicit avenues to achieve their goals. In other words, those without resources and access may become criminals to achieve comfort, leisure, status, and wealth.

The implications of Merton's and his fellow researchers' findings are clear: Lack of opportunity and inequality are central causal factors for crime, and by implication political extremism. However, anomie and strain theory have been criticized for placing too much emphasis on deviance emanating from the poorer classes and for failing to adequately explain why so many youths and adults who suffer from strain do not turn to crime or political extremism.

Routine Activity Theory. This theory, first posited by Cohen and Felson,[21] holds that political extremism and criminal behavior require the convergence of three societal elements. The adaptation of this theory to the convergence of extremism and crime is summarized as follows:

- A steady supply of motivated offenders. At a fundamental level of analysis, this element holds that the political motivations of terrorists and the profit-based motivations of criminals require observable benefits for individuals. Examples of such benefits may include increased status, greed satisfaction, vengeance, or sheer adventure. Within this framework, the political violence option is an attractive motivation because it provides individuals with an outlet to express their indignation with a sense of glory.

- The ready availability of attractive victims and targets of opportunity. This element holds that terrorists and criminals profit from the presence of victims who will provide them with certain benefits. For terrorists, appropriate victims will return maximum symbolic and political effect when they strike. For criminals, appropriate victims and customers will return maximum profit-making opportunities.

- The presence, or lack thereof, of social guardians. Examples of guardians include the police, surveillance systems, and social networks. Thus, a critical societal element for the calculus of terrorists and criminals is whether the social or political environment possesses weak guardianship and is therefore ripe for exploitation. In this regard, relatively weak antiterrorist or anticrime barriers will create a sociopolitical vacuum in which dedicated terrorists or criminals may perceive an opportunity for exploitation.

Radical Criminology. During the 1960s and 1970s, a good deal of theory and research on criminality reflected the political and social discord of the period. Critical theorists challenged previous conventions of criminal causation, arguing that delinquency and criminality were caused by society's inequitable ideological, political, and socioeconomic makeup.[22] Proponents of the emergent radical approach argued that because power and wealth have been unequally distributed, those who have been politically and economically shut out understandably resort to criminal antagonism against the prevailing order. According to radical criminologists, these classes will continue to engage in behavior labeled as criminal until society remedies the plight of the powerless and disenfranchised.

Critical theories similar to radical criminology frequently use Marxist theory to critique the role of capitalist economics in creating socioeconomic inequities.[23] Marxist perspectives on criminology argue that the ruling capitalist classes exploit the labor of the lower classes and co-opt them by convincing them that capitalism is actually beneficial for them.[24] Marxist-oriented radical criminologists hold that ruling elites have used their own interpretations of justice to maintain their status. Hence, the criminal justice system is inherently exploitative and unfair toward criminals who originate from the lower classes. The fact that social minorities and the poor are overrepresented in prisons is explained as a manifestation of the inherent unfairness at the core of the existing capitalist establishment.

Critical theories and Marxist ideological tendencies have been used to explain the role of gender in radical movements. Women have historically been prominently represented in many extremist movements and organizations. Chapter Perspective 3.1 investigates the subject of gender and terrorism by discussing women as terrorists.

CHAPTER PERSPECTIVE 3.1

Women as Terrorists

From October 23 to 26, 2003, Chechen terrorists seized 700 hostages in a Moscow theater. The episode ended with the deaths of scores of hostages and all of the terrorists. Russian authorities reported that many of the hostage takers were women who had suicide explosive vests strapped to their bodies. The presence of female suicide bombers was not uncommon in the Chechen resistance movement. As a result, the Russian media dubbed the women among Chechen terrorists "Black Widows" because they were allegedly relatives of Chechen men who died in the ongoing war in Chechnya.

How common is terrorism by women? What motivates women to become terrorists? In which environments are female terrorists typically found?[a]

Women have been active in a variety of roles in many violent political movements.[b] Historically, some women held positions of leadership during terrorist campaigns and were well integrated into the command systems and policy decision-making processes in extremist groups. In the modern era, women were central figures in Sri Lanka's Tamil Tigers, Germany's Red Army Faction, Italy's Red Brigade,[c] Spain's Basque ETA, and the Japanese Red Army. During the Palestinian *intifada* against Israel, a number of Palestinian suicide bombers were young women. More commonly, women serve as combatants rather than leaders, or women are recruited to participate as support functionaries, such as finding safe houses and engaging in surveillance.

Regardless of the quality of participation, it is clear that such involvement belies the common presumption that terrorism is an exclusively male preserve. In fact, some of the most committed revolutionaries around the world are women.

The following examples are instructive:

- Prior to the 1917 Bolshevik revolution, Russian women were leading members of violent extremist groups such as People's Will (Narodnaya Volya) and the Social Revolutionary Party.

- Female anarchists such as Emma Goldman in the United States demonstrated that women could be leading revolutionary theorists.

- Leila Khaled became a well-respected and prominent member of the Palestinian nationalist movement after her participation in two airline hijacking incidents.

- During the unrest leading up to the Iranian Revolution in the late 1970s, women participated in numerous antigovernment attacks.

- Gudrun Ensslin, Ulrike Meinhof, and other women were leaders and comrades-in-arms in Germany's Red Army Faction during the 1970s.

- During the 1970s and 1980s, other Western European terrorist groups such as France's Direct Action, Italy's Red Brigade, and Belgium's Communist Combat Cells fully integrated women into their ranks.

- Women were leaders in the nihilistic Japanese Red Army during the 1970s and 1980s, and the movement was founded by a woman named Shigenobu Fusako.

- During the latter quarter of the 20th century, many Provisional Irish Republican Army (IRA) "soldiers" were women, reflecting the fact that the IRA was a nationalist and mildly socialist movement.

- Women became renowned leaders among Sri Lanka's Tamil Tigers group during the 1990s and thereafter when many male leaders were killed or captured, and female terrorists known as Freedom Birds engaged in many attacks, including numerous suicide bombings.

- Among Chechen rebels, since 2002, young women have been recruited, manipulated, or coerced into becoming suicide fighters, known among Russians as Black Widows.

- Since around 2002, the Al-Aqsa Martyr Brigades unit of the Palestine Liberation Organization has actively recruited and deployed women as suicide bombers.[d]

- Female combatants have been found in the ranks of many insurgent groups, such as

Colombia's FARC and ELN, India's Naxalites, the Communist Party of Nepal, Peru's Shining Path (Sendero Luminoso), and Mexico's Zapatistas.

- In Iraq, the number of female suicide bombers increased markedly from eight in all of 2007 to more than 20 in the first half of 2008. This was because Iraqi insurgents learned that women were much less likely to be searched or otherwise scrutinized by security forces and could therefore more easily penetrate many levels of security.

- In March 2011 the recruitment of women took an interesting turn when Al Qaeda published a magazine for women, titled *al Shamikha* ("The Majestic Woman"). Examples of content include articles on beauty advice and suicide bombing.

- Beginning in 2014, Nigeria's Boko Haram often deployed young women and girls, some as young as eight years old, as suicide bombers. By 2016, an estimated one in five Boko Haram suicide bombers were children, mostly girls.[e]

Active participation of women is arguably more common among left-wing and nationalist terrorist movements than in right-wing and religious movements. Rightist and religious movements yield some cases of women as terrorists but very few examples of female leaders. One reason for these characteristics is that, on one hand, many leftists adopt ideologies of gender equality and many nationalists readily enlist female fighters for the greater good of the group.[f] On the other hand, right-wing and religious movements often adopt ideologies that relegate women to secondary roles within the group. Among religious movements, ideologies of male dominance and female subordination have been common, so women rarely participate in attacks, let alone in command systems and policy decision-making processes. Having said this, the incidence of female suicide bombings increased markedly in some conflicts (especially in Iraq and Israel) because extremists realized that women were less likely to be scrutinized by security forces.

In a particularly disturbing trend, young girls have been recruited as fighters by paramilitary groups, such as the Lord's Resistance Army in Uganda and the Revolutionary United Front (RUF) in Sierra Leone. Some of these "Small Girls Units" were made to participate in the brutalization of local populations.[g] Boko Haram in Nigeria used girls extensively as suicide bombers.

Notes

a. For a good discussion of these and other issues, see Rhiannon Talbot, "Myths in the Representation of Women Terrorists," *Eire-Ireland* 35 (2001): 165–86.

b. For a discussion of the roles of women in terrorist movements, see Rhiannon Talbot, "The Unexpected Face of Terrorism," *This Is the Northeast,* January 31, 2002.

c. For a good discussion of Italian women in violent organizations, see Alison Jamieson, "Mafiosi and Terrorists: Italian Women in Violent Organizations," *SAIS Review* (Summer/Fall 2000): 51–64.

d. For interviews with female Al-Aqsa Martyr Brigades volunteers, see Michael Tierney, "Young, Gifted and Ready to Kill," *The Herald* (Glasgow, UK), August 3, 2002.

e. United Nations Children's Fund. "Beyond Chibok: Over 1.3 Million Children Uprooted by Boko Haram Violence." New York: UNICEF Regional Office for West and Central Africa, April 2016.

f. Mia Bloom, "Female Suicide Bombers: A Global Trend," *Daedalus* (Winter 2007): 94–102.

g. Susan McKay, "Girls as 'Weapons of Terror' in Northern Uganda and Sierra Leonean Rebel Fighting Forces," *Studies in Conflict & Terrorism* (April 2005): 385–97.

POLITICAL VIOLENCE AS STRATEGIC CHOICE

Making Revolution: Acts of Political Will

An **act of political will** is an effort to force change. It is a choice, a rational decision from the revolutionary's perspective, to adopt specific tactics and methodologies to defeat an adversary. These methodologies are instruments of rational strategic choice, in which terrorism is adopted as an optimal strategy. All that is required for final victory is the political and strategic will to achieve the final goal. Selecting terrorism is a process based on the experiences of each insurgent group and thus the outcome of an evolutionary political progression.

As a result, terrorism is simply a tool, an option, selected by members of the political fringe to achieve a goal. Terrorism is a deliberate strategy, and success is ensured as long as the group's political and strategic will remains strong.

The evolution of Marxist revolutionary strategy illustrates the essence of political will. Karl Marx argued that history and human social evolution are inexorable forces that will inevitably end in the triumph of the revolutionary working class. He believed that the prediction of the eventual collapse of capitalism was based on scientific law. **Vladimir Ilyich Lenin**, however, understood that capitalism's demise would not come about without a push from an organized and disciplined vanguard organization such as the Communist Party. This organization would lead the working class to victory. In other words, the political will of the people can make history if they are properly indoctrinated and led. An important conceptual example will help readers better understand the theory of revolutionary change through acts of political will. It is a strategy known as **people's war**. The context in which it was first developed and applied was the Chinese Revolution.

Mao Zedong led the Communist Red Army to victory during the Chinese Revolution by waging a protracted war—first against Chiang Kai-shek's Nationalists (Kuomintang), then in alliance with the Nationalists against the invading Japanese, and finally driving Chiang's forces from mainland China in 1949. The Red Army prevailed largely because of Mao's military-political doctrine, which emphasized waging an insurgent people's war. His strategy was simple: Indoctrinate the army; win over the people; and hit, run, and fight forever.

People's war was a strategy born of necessity, originating when the Red Army was nearly annihilated by the Nationalists before and during the famous Long March campaign of 1934 and 1935. During the Long March, the Red Army fought a series of rearguard actions against pursuing Nationalist forces, eventually finding refuge in the northern Shensi province after a reputed 6,000-mile march. After the march, while the Red Army rested and was refitted in Shensi, Mao developed his military doctrine. People's war required protracted warfare (war drawn out over time), fought by an army imbued with an iron ideological will to wear down the enemy.[25]

According to Mao, the Red Army should fight a guerrilla war with roving bands that would occasionally unite. The strategy was to fight by consolidating the countryside and then gradually moving into the towns and cities. Red Army units would avoid conventional battle with the Nationalists, giving ground before superior numbers. Space would be traded for time, and battle would be engaged only when the Red Army was tactically superior at a given moment. Thus, an emphasis was placed on avoidance and retreat. In people's war, assassination was perfectly acceptable, and targets included soldiers, government administrators, and civilian collaborators. Government-sponsored programs and events—no matter how beneficial they might be to the people—were to be violently disrupted to show the government's weakness. A successful people's war required the cooperation and participation of the civilian population, so Mao ordered his soldiers to win their loyalty by treating the people appropriately.

Mao's contribution to modern warfare—and to the concept of political will—was that he deliberately linked his military strategy to his political strategy; they were one and the same. Terrorism was a perfectly acceptable option. The combination of ideology, political indoctrination, guerrilla tactics, protracted warfare, and popular support made people's war a very potent strategy and an effective synthesis of political will.

Perception and Cultural Disconnect:
Adversaries in the War on Terrorism

One final consideration is necessary to fully appreciate the modern causes of terrorism. This theory is rooted in the political environment that gave rise to the new era of terrorism.

The concept of "one person's terrorist is another person's freedom fighter" is pertinent to how the behavior of the West, and particularly the behavior of the United States, is perceived around the world. When the September 11 attacks occurred, many Americans and other Westerners saw them as an attack on Western-style civilization. Reasons given for the subsequent U.S.-led war on terrorism included the argument that war is necessary to defend civilization from a new barbarism. From the official American and allied point of view, the war is simply a counteraction against the enemies of democracy and freedom. However, many Muslims have a wholly different perspective.

Interestingly, many young Muslims are keen to adopt some degree of Western culture yet remain loyal to the Muslim community. One student commented,

> Most of us here like it both ways, we like American fashion, American music, American movies, but in the end, we are Muslims. . . . The Holy Prophet said that all Muslims are like one body, and if one part of the body gets injured, then all parts feel that pain. If one Muslim is injured by non-Muslims in Afghanistan, it is the duty of all Muslims of the world to help him.[26]

The argument, then, is that the cause of anti-American and anti-Western sentiment is the behavior of those nations—that is, their actions rather than their values or their culture. In the opening paragraph of his controversial book *Imperial Hubris*, former ranking CIA official Michael Scheuer presented the central precept of this argument:

> In America's confrontation with Osama bin Laden, Al Qaeda, their allies, and the Islamic world, there lies a startlingly clear example of how loving something intensely can stimulate an equally intense and purposeful hatred of things by which it is threatened. This hatred shapes and informs Muslim reactions to U.S. policies and their execution, and it is impossible to understand the threat America faces until the intensity and pervasiveness of this hatred is recognized.[27]

Can Muslim perceptions and Western behaviors be reconciled? What are the prospects for mitigating this source of terrorism in the modern era? Several events portend a continued disconnect, at least for the immediate future:

- the American-led occupation of Iraq and the protracted insurgency that arose

- an open-ended presence of Western troops in or near Muslim countries

- broadcast images of civilian casualties and other collateral damage during military operations

- broadcast images and rumors of the mistreatment of prisoners in American-run detention facilities

- cycles of chronic violence between Israelis and Palestinians and the perception that the United States and the West unfairly favor Israel

In this regard, a July 2007 report by the CIA's National Intelligence Council concluded that the terrorist threat to the U.S. homeland remained high and that Al Qaeda remained a potent adversary in the war on terrorism.[28] The 2007 National Intelligence Council's estimate essentially reiterated the 2004 estimate, which had warned that the war in Iraq created a new training ground for professional terrorists, much as the 1979–1989 Soviet war in Afghanistan created an environment that led to the rise of Al Qaeda and other international *mujahideen* (Islamic holy warriors).[29] It also projected that veterans of the Iraq war would disperse after the end of the conflict, thus constituting a new generation of international mujahideen who would supplant the first Afghanistan-trained generation. This was a plausible scenario because many foreigners volunteered to fight in Iraq out of a sense of pan-Islamic solidarity.[30] This trend continued when thousands of foreign fighters joined the self-proclaimed Islamic State's military campaign in Syria and Iraq.

MORAL JUSTIFICATIONS FOR POLITICAL VIOLENCE

Although not all extremists become terrorists, some do cross the line. For them, terrorism is a morally acceptable strategy, a specifically selected method to further a just cause. To facilitate critical understanding of the morality of terrorists, the following four motives are reviewed:

1. Moral convictions of terrorists

2. Simplified definitions of good and evil

3. Seeking utopia

4. Codes of self-sacrifice

Moral Convictions of Terrorists

Moral conviction refers to terrorists' unambiguous certainty of the righteousness of their cause. The goals and objectives of their movement are considered principled beyond reproach and their methods absolutely justifiable. This conviction can arise in several environments, including the following two settings:

In the first, a group of people can conclude that they have been morally wronged and that a powerful, immoral, and evil enemy is arrayed against them. This enemy is considered adept at betrayal, exploitation, violence, and repression. These conclusions can have some legitimacy, especially when a history of exploitation has been documented. This historical evidence is identified and interpreted as being the source of the group's modern problems. For example, many leftist insurgents in Latin America characterized the United States as an imperialist enemy because of its long history of military intervention, economic penetration, and support for repressive regimes in the region.[31]

In later generations, native populations who shared this kind of history and who interpreted it as being part of an ongoing pattern in contemporary times developed strong resentment against their perceived oppressor—in this case, the United States and the governments it supported. To them, there was no need to question the morality of their cause; it was quite clear.

A second setting in which moral conviction may arise is when a group or a people concludes that it is inherently and morally superior. This can be derived from ideological convictions, ethno-nationalist values, or religious beliefs. From this perspective, the cause is virtually holy; in the case of religious beliefs, it *is* holy. A sense of moral purity becomes the foundation for the simplification of good and evil. In this setting, extremists decide that no compromise is possible and that terrorism is a legitimate option.

For example, a major crisis began in the Yugoslavian territory of **Kosovo** in 1998 when heavy fighting broke out between Serb security forces, the **Kosovo Liberation Army (KLA)**, and the Serb and Albanian communities. The conflict ended when the North Atlantic Treaty Organization (NATO) and Russian troops occupied Kosovo and the Serb security units were withdrawn. The strong Serb bond with Kosovo had originated in 1389 when the Serb hero Prince Lazar was defeated by the Ottoman Turks in Kosovo. Kosovo had been the center of the medieval Serb empire, and this defeat ended the Serb nation. Over the next 500 years, as the Turks ruled the province, Albanian Muslims migrated into Kosovo and gradually displaced Serb Christians. Nevertheless, Serbs have always had strong ethno-nationalist ties to Kosovo, considering it a kind of spiritual homeland. It is at the center of their national identity. Thus, despite the fact that 90% of Kosovo's population was Albanian in 1998, Serbs considered their claim to the territory paramount to anyone else's. From their perspective, the morality of their position was clear.

Chapter Perspective 3.2 illustrates the application of selective and moral terrorism. It is an excerpt from a document captured during the war in Vietnam from the **Viet Cong** by American soldiers of the First Cavalry Division. It is a directive explaining procedures for suppressing counterrevolutionary elements,[32] remarkable for its instructions on how to correctly conduct the campaign.

CHAPTER PERSPECTIVE 3.2

A Viet Cong Directive Ordering Selective Terrorism

The Viet Cong were southern Vietnamese communists who fought alongside the North Vietnamese Army against American forces and the Republic of South Vietnam. The communist forces considered this war to be one phase in an ongoing effort to unify the North and South into a single nation.

During the American phase of their long war, Vietnamese communists in South Vietnam routinely used terrorism to eliminate enemies. Assassinations and kidnappings were common, and targets regularly included civilians. Thousands fell victims to this policy.

The following excerpt is from a passage concerning the suppression of counterrevolutionaries in areas under American or South Vietnamese control. It is interesting because it orders Viet Cong operatives to be very selective in choosing their targets.[a]

DIRECTIVE

Concerning a number of problems that require thorough understanding in Z's task of repressing counterrevolutionary elements . . .

2. In areas temporarily under enemy control:

(1) We are to exterminate dangerous and cruel elements such as security agents, policemen, and other cruel elements in espionage organizations, professional secret agents in organizations to counter the Revolution, henchmen with many blood debts . . . in village administrative machines, in the puppet system, in enemy military and paramilitary organizations, and in [South Vietnamese political parties].

(2) We are to establish files immediately and prepare the ground for later suppression of dangerous henchmen whom we need not eliminate yet or whose elimination is not yet politically advantageous. . . .

While applying the above-mentioned regulations, we must observe the following:

—Distinguish . . . the elimination of tyrants and local administrative personnel while fighting from the continuous task of repressing counterrevolutionaries in the liberated areas.

—Distinguish the ringleaders, the commissioned officers, from the henchmen.

—Distinguish exploiting elements from the basic elements and distinguish persons determined to oppose the Revolution from those who are forced to do so or those who are brought over and have no political understanding.

—Distinguish between persons with much political and religious influence and those who have no influence or very little influence.

—Distinguish between historical problems and present-day problems.

—Distinguish major crimes with many bad effects from minor crimes or innocence.

—Distinguish determined and stubborn antirevolutionary attitudes from attitudes of submission to the Revolution and true repentance, and willingness to redeem by contribution to the Revolution.

—Distinguish counterrevolutionary elements from backward and dissatisfied persons among the masses.

Note

a. Quoted in Jay Mallin, *Terror and Urban Guerrillas: A Study of Tactics and Documents* (Coral Gables, FL: University of Miami Press, 1971), 33, 39–40.

Source: People's Liberation Armed Forces (The Viet Cong) (1960).

Simplified Definitions of Good and Evil

Revolutionaries universally conclude that their cause is honorable, their methods are justifiable, and their opponents are representations of implacable evil. They arrive at this conclusion in innumerable ways, often—as in the case of Marxists—after devoting considerable intellectual energy to political analysis. Nevertheless, their final analysis is uncomplicated: Our cause is just, and the enemy's is unjust. Once this line has been clearly drawn between good and evil, the methods used in the course of the struggle are justified by the ennobled goals and objectives of the cause.

A good example of the application in practice of simplified delineations of good and evil is found in the influential *Mini-Manual of the Urban Guerrilla*, written by Brazilian revolutionary **Carlos Marighella**.[33] In this document, Marighella clearly argues that terrorism is necessary against a ruthless enemy. The *Mini-Manual* was read, and its strategy implemented, by leftist revolutionaries throughout Latin America and Europe. Marighella advocated terrorism as a correct response to the oppression of the Brazilian dictatorship. He wrote,

> The accusation of assault or terrorism no longer has the pejorative meaning it used to have.... Today to be an assailant or a terrorist is a quality that ennobles any honorable man because it is an act worthy of a revolutionary engaged in armed struggle against the shameful military dictatorship and its monstrosities.[34]

One fact is clear: There is a moment of decision among those who choose to rise in rebellion against a perceived oppressor. This moment of decision is a turning point in the lives of individuals, people, and nations.

Seeking Utopia

The book *Utopia*, written by the English writer Sir Thomas More in the 16th century, was a fictional work that described an imaginary island with a society having an ideal political and social system. Countless philosophers, including political and religious writers, have since created their own visions of the perfect society.[35] Terrorists likewise envision some form of **utopia**, although for many this can simply mean the destruction of the existing order. For such **nihilist dissidents**, any system is preferable to the existing one, and its destruction alone is a justifiable goal. The question is what kind of utopia terrorists seek. This depends on their belief system. For example, religious terrorists seek to create a God-inspired society on earth that reflects the commandments, morality, and values of their religious faith. Political terrorists define their ideal society according to their ideological perspective. Regardless of which belief system terrorists adopt, they uniformly accept the proposition that the promised good (a utopia) outweighs their present actions, no matter how violent those actions are. The revolution will bring utopia after a period of trial and tribulation so that **the end justifies the means**. This type of reasoning is particularly common among religious, ethno-nationalist, and ideological terrorists.

U.S. Department of Defense

▶ Photographs that shocked the world. An American soldier pulls an Iraqi detainee with a leash in Abu Ghraib prison in Baghdad in late 2003. Such images served to rally opposition to the U.S.-led occupation.

Codes of Self-Sacrifice

Terrorists invariably have faith in the justness of their cause and live their lives accordingly. Many consequently adopt **codes of self-sacrifice** that are at the root of their everyday lives. They believe that these codes are superior codes of living and that those who follow the code are superior to those who do not. The code accepts a basic truth and applies it to everyday life. This truth usually has a religious, ethno-nationalist, or ideological foundation. Any actions taken within the accepted parameters of these codes—even terrorist actions—are justified because the code cleanses the true believer.

A good example of ideological codes of self-sacrifice is found on the fringe left among the first anarchists. Many anarchists did not simply believe in revolution; they lived the revolution. They crafted a lifestyle that was consumed by the cause. Among some, an affinity for death became part of the revolutionary lifestyle. The Russian anarchist Sergei Nechayev wrote in *Revolutionary Catechism* , "The revolutionary is a man committed. He has neither personal interests nor sentiments, attachments, property, nor even a name. Everything in him is subordinated to a single exclusive interest, a single thought, a single passion: the revolution."[36]

Codes of self-sacrifice explain much terrorist behavior. Those who participate in movements and organizations adopt belief systems that justify their behavior and absolve them of responsibility for normally unacceptable behavior. Such systems cleanse participants and offer them a sense of participating in a higher or superior morality.

Chapter Perspective 3.3 discusses the motives and behavior of two Palestinian nationalists, Leila Khaled and Abu Nidal.

CHAPTER PERSPECTIVE 3.3

Profiles of Violent Extremists: Leila Khaled and Abu Nidal

▶ Palestinian terrorist or freedom fighter? Leila Khaled in a photograph dating from the 1970s.

The processes that cause people to become political extremists and terrorists are very idiosyncratic. Individuals adopt extremist beliefs and engage in terrorist behaviors for many of the reasons discussed in this chapter.

A comparison of two revolutionaries championing the Palestinian cause is very useful for critically assessing why nationalists engage in terrorist violence. These are cases that illustrate the origins of the motives and ideologies of politically violent individuals.

Leila Khaled: Freedom Fighter or Terrorist?

During the early 1970s, Leila Khaled was famous both because of her exploits as a Palestinian revolutionary and because she was for a time the best-known airline hijacker in the world.

Khaled was born in Haifa in Palestine. After the Israeli war of independence, she and her family became refugees in a camp in the city of Tyre, Lebanon, when she was a young child. Khaled has said that she was politicized from a very young age and became a committed revolutionary by the time she was 15. Politically, she was influenced by leftist theory. One of her revolutionary heroes was Ernesto "Che" Guevara, whom she considered to be a "true" revolutionary, unlike other Western radicals.

In August 1969, at the age of 23, Leila Khaled hijacked a TWA flight on behalf of the Popular Front for the Liberation of Palestine (PFLP). The purpose of the hijacking was to direct the world's attention to the plight of the Palestinians. It was a successful operation, and she reportedly forced the pilots to fly over her ancestral home of Haifa before turning toward Damascus. In Damascus, the passengers were released into the custody of the Syrians and the plane was blown up. Afterward, a then-famous photograph was taken of her.

In preparation for her next operation (and because the photograph had become a political icon), Khaled underwent plastic surgery in Germany to alter her appearance. She participated in a much larger operation on September 6 and 9, 1970, when the PFLP attempted to hijack five airliners. One of the hijackings failed; one airliner was flown to a runway in Cairo, where it was

(Continued)

(Continued)

destroyed; and the remaining three airliners were flown to Dawson's Field in Jordan, where they were blown up by the PFLP on September 12. Khaled had been overpowered and captured during one of the failed attempts on September 6—an El Al (the Israeli airline) flight from Amsterdam. She was released on September 28 as part of a brokered deal exchanging Palestinian prisoners for the hostages.

Leila Khaled published her autobiography in 1973, titled *My People Shall Live: The Autobiography of a Revolutionary*.[a] She eventually settled in Amman, Jordan, and became a member of the Palestinian National Council, the Palestinian parliament. She has never moderated her political beliefs, has always considered herself to be a freedom fighter, and takes pride in being one of the first to use extreme tactics to bring the Palestinians' cause to the world's attention. Khaled considers the progression of Palestinian revolutionary violence—such as the *intifada* ("shaking off") uprisings—to be a legitimate means to regain Palestine.

Abu Nidal: Ruthless Revolutionary

Sabri al-Banna, a Palestinian, adopted the nom de guerre of "Abu Nidal," which has become synonymous with his Abu Nidal Organization (ANO). He was a radical member of the umbrella Palestine Liberation Organization (PLO) from an early point in its history. Yasir Arafat's nationalist Al Fatah organization was the dominant group within the PLO. Unlike the Fatah mainstream, Abu Nidal was a strong advocate of a dissident ideology that was pan-Arabism, meaning he believed that national borders in the Arab world were not sacrosanct. Abu Nidal long argued that Al Fatah membership should be open to all Arabs, not just Palestinians. In support of the Palestinian cause, he argued that Palestine must be established as an Arab state. Its borders must stretch from the Jordan River in the east to the Mediterranean Sea. According to pan-Arabism, however, this is only one cause among many in the Arab world.

After the 1973 Yom Kippur war, when invading Arab armies were soundly defeated by Israel, many in the mainstream Al Fatah group argued that a political solution with Israel should be an option. In 1974, Abu Nidal split from Al Fatah and began his "rejectionist" movement to carry on a pan-Arabist armed struggle. He and his followers immediately began engaging in high-profile international terrorist attacks, believing that the war should not be limited to the Middle East. At different periods in his struggle, he successfully solicited sanctuary from Iraq, Libya, and Syria—all of which have practiced pan-Arabist ideologies.

The ANO became one of the most prolific and bloody terrorist organizations in modern history. It carried out attacks in approximately 20 countries and was responsible for killing or injuring about 900 people. The ANO's targets included fellow Arabs, such as the PLO, Arab governments, and moderate Palestinians. Its non-Arab targets included the interests of France, Israel, the United Kingdom, and the United States. Many of these attacks were spectacular, such as an attempted assassination of the Israeli ambassador to Great Britain in June 1982, simultaneous attacks on the Vienna and Rome airports in December 1985, the hijacking of a Pan Am airliner in September 1986, and several assassinations of top PLO officials in several countries. It has been alleged that Abu Nidal collaborated in the 1972 massacre of 11 Israeli athletes by the Black September group at the Munich Olympics.

Abu Nidal remained a dedicated pan-Arabist revolutionary and never renounced his worldwide acts of political violence. His group has several hundred members, a militia in Lebanon, and international resources. The ANO operated under numerous names, including the Al Fatah Revolutionary Council, Arab Revolutionary Council, Arab Revolutionary Brigades, Black September, Black June, and Revolutionary Organization of Socialist Muslims. The group seemingly ended its attacks against Western interests in the late 1980s. The only major attacks attributed to the ANO in the 1990s were the 1991 assassinations of PLO deputy chief Abu Iyad and PLO security chief Abu Hul in Tunis, and the 1994 assassination of the senior Jordanian diplomat Naeb Maaytah in Beirut.

The whereabouts of Abu Nidal were usually speculative, but he relocated to Iraq in December 1998. In August 2002, he was found dead in Iraq of multiple gunshot wounds. The official Iraqi account of Abu Nidal's death was that he committed suicide. Other unofficial accounts suggested that he was shot when Iraqi security agents came to arrest him, dying either of self-inflicted wounds or during a shootout.

Note

a. Leila Khaled, *My People Shall Live: The Autobiography of a Revolutionary* (London, UK: Hodder & Stoughton, 1973).

DISCUSSION BOX

BLOODY SUNDAY AND BLACK SEPTEMBER

This chapter's Discussion Box is intended to stimulate critical debate about seminal incidents in the history of national groups.

Bloody Sunday

In the late 1960s, Irish Catholic activists calling themselves the Northern Ireland Civil Rights Association attempted to emulate the African American civil rights movement as a strategy to agitate for equality in Northern Ireland. They thought that the same force of moral conviction would sway British policy to improve the plight of the Catholics. Their demands were similar to those of the American civil rights movement: equal opportunity, better employment, access to housing, and access to education. This ended when mostly peaceful demonstrations gradually became more violent, leading to rioting in the summer of 1969, an environment of generalized unrest, and the deployment of British troops. After 1969, the demonstrations continued, but rioting, fire bombings, and gun battles gradually became a regular feature of strife in Northern Ireland.

On January 30, 1972, elite British paratroopers fired on demonstrators in Londonderry. Thirteen demonstrators were killed. After this incident, many Catholics became radicalized and actively worked to drive out the British. The Irish Republican Army received recruits and widespread support from the Catholic community. In July 1972, the Provos launched a massive bombing spree in central Belfast.

Black September

When Leila Khaled and her comrades attempted to hijack five airliners on September 6 and 9, 1970, their plan was to fly all of the planes to an abandoned British Royal Air Force (RAF) airfield in Jordan, hold hostages, broker the release of Palestinian prisoners, release the hostages, blow up the planes, and thereby force the world to focus on the plight of the Palestinian people. On September 12, 255 hostages were released from the three planes that landed at Dawson's Field (the RAF base), and 56 were kept to bargain for the release of seven Palestinian prisoners, including Leila Khaled. The group then blew up the airliners.

Unfortunately for the hijackers, their actions greatly alarmed King Hussein of Jordan. Martial law was declared on September 16, and the incident led to civil war between Palestinian forces and the Jordanian army. Although the Jordanians' operation was precipitated by the destruction of the airliners on Jordanian soil, tensions had been building between the army and Palestinian forces for some time. King Hussein and the Jordanian leadership interpreted this operation as confirmation that radical Palestinian groups had become too powerful and were a threat to Jordanian sovereignty.

On September 19, Hussein asked for diplomatic intervention from Great Britain and the United States when a Syrian column entered Jordan in support of the Palestinians. On September 27, a truce ended the fighting. The outcome of the fighting was a relocation of much of the Palestinian leadership and fighters to their Lebanese bases. The entire incident became known among Palestinians as Black September and was not forgotten by radicals in the Palestinian nationalist movement. One of the most notorious terrorist groups took the name Black September, and the name was also used by Abu Nidal.

Discussion Questions

1. What role do you think these incidents had in precipitating the IRA's and PLO's cycles of violence?

2. Were the IRA's and PLO's tactics and targets justifiable responses to these incidents?

3. What, in your opinion, would have been the outcome in Northern Ireland if the British government had responded peacefully to the Irish Catholics' emulation of the American civil rights movement?

4. What, in your opinion, would have been the outcome if the Jordanian government had not responded militarily to the Palestinian presence in Jordan?

5. How should the world community have responded to Bloody Sunday and Black September?

CHAPTER SUMMARY

This chapter introduced readers to the theoretical causes of terrorism and presented examples that represent some of the models developed by scholars and other researchers. Individual profiles, group dynamics, political environments, and social processes are at the center of the puzzle of explaining why people and groups adopt fringe beliefs and engage in terrorist behavior. Social movements and dramatic (or traumatic) events have been identified as two sources of terrorism, with the caveat that they are generalized explanations.

Not all extremists become terrorists, but certainly all terrorists are motivated by extremist beliefs. Motives behind terrorist behavior include a range of factors. One is morality, an unambiguous conviction of the righteousness of one's cause. Terrorists believe that the principles of their movement are unquestionably sound. A second is simplified notions of good and evil, with no shades of gray, when terrorists presume that their cause and methods are completely justifiable because their opponents represent inveterate evil. A third is utopian ideals, whereby an idealized end justifies violence. Such ends are often vague concepts, such as Karl Marx's dictatorship of the proletariat . The fourth factor is critical to understanding terrorist behavior. It is codes of self-sacrifice, when an ingrained belief system forms the basis for a terrorist's lifestyle and conduct. Collectively, these factors form a useful theoretical foundation for explaining terrorist motives.

Explanations of terrorism also include a range of factors. The theory of acts of political will is a rational model in which extremists choose to engage in terrorism as an optimal strategy to force change. Sociological explanations of terrorism look at intergroup dynamics, particularly conflict that results in collective violence. Perception is an important factor in the decision.

Psychological explanations broadly explain individual motivations and group dynamics. Psychological theories also help explain the cohesion of terrorist organizations and why they perpetuate violent behavior even when victory is logically impossible.

One final point should be considered when evaluating the causes of terrorism. When experts build models and develop explanatory theories for politically motivated violence, their conclusions sometimes "reflect the political and social currents of the times in which the scholars writing the theories live."[37] It is plausible that

> to a large degree, the development of theories . . . reflects changing political and intellectual climates. When intellectuals have opposed the collective behavior of their times . . . they have tended to depict the behavior negatively. . . . When scholars have instead supported the collective behavior of their eras . . . they have painted a more positive portrait of both the behavior and the individuals participating in it.[38]

This is not to say that analysts are not trying to be objective or that they are purposefully disingenuous in their analyses. But it is only logical to presume that new explanatory theories will be affected by factors such as new terrorist environments and new ideologies that encourage political violence. The progression of explanations by the social and behavioral sciences in the future will naturally reflect the sociopolitical environments of the times in which they are developed. The examples of Bloody Sunday and Black September presented in this chapter's Discussion Box illustrate several explanatory theories.

KEY TERMS AND CONCEPTS

The following topics were discussed in this chapter and can be found in the Glossary:

Absolute deprivation 46	Black September 62	End justifies the means, The 58
Abu Nidal Organization (ANO) 60	Black Widows 52	Freedom Birds 52
Act of political will 53	Bloody Sunday 62	Intifada 45
Al Fatah 60	Codes of self-sacrifice 58	Khaled, Leila 59

WEB EXERCISE

Using this chapter's recommended websites listed on the student study site at **edge.sagepub.com/martiness5e**, conduct an online investigation of the causes of extremist agitation and terrorist violence.

1. What issues do these groups consider to have unquestioned merit? What reasons do they give for this quality?

2. What scenarios do you think might cause these groups to engage in direct confrontation or violence?

3. Act as devil's advocate and defend one of these causes that you disagree with.

For an online search of factors that are commonly cited as causes for terrorist violence, readers should enter the following keywords in their Web browser's search engine:

"Intifada (or intifadeh)"

"Just war"

RECOMMENDED READINGS

The following publications provide discussions about the causes of extremism and terrorist behavior.

Bloom, M. (2011). *Bombshell: Women and terrorism.* Philadelphia: University of Pennsylvania Press.

Chenoweth, E., & Moore, P. (2018). *The politics of terror.* New York, NY: Oxford University Press.

Crotty, W. (Ed.). (2005). *Democratic development and political terrorism: The global perspective.* Boston, MA: Northeastern University Press.

Djilas, M. (1973). *Memoir of a revolutionary.* New York, NY: Harcourt Brace Jovanovich.

Eager, P. W. (2008). *From freedom fighters to terrorists: Women and political violence.* Burlington, VT: Ashgate.

Forest, J. J. F. (Ed.). (2006). *The making of a terrorist: Recruitment, training, and root causes.* Westport, CT: Praeger Security International.

Franks, J. (2006). *Rethinking the roots of terrorism.* New York, NY: Palgrave Macmillan.

Freilich, J. D., LaFree, G., & Winterdyk, J. (Eds.). (2015). *Criminology theory and terrorism: New applications and approaches.* New York, NY: Routledge.

Gurr, T. R. (1970). *Why men rebel.* Princeton, NJ: Princeton University Press.

Huntington, S. P. (1996). *The clash of civilizations and the remaking of world order.* New York, NY: Touchstone.

Khaled, L. (1973). *My people shall live: The autobiography of a revolutionary.* London, UK: Hodder & Stoughton.

Martinez, T., & Guinther, J. (1988). *Brotherhood of murder.* New York, NY: Simon & Schuster.

McKelvey, T. (Ed.). (2007). *One of the guys: Women as aggressors and torturers*. Emeryville, CA: Seal Press.

Nassar, J. R. (2009). *Globalization and terrorism: The migration of dreams and nightmares* (2nd ed.). Lanham, MD: Rowman & Littlefield.

Ocalan, A. (2007). *Prison writings: The roots of civilization*. London, UK: Pluto.

Pedahzur, A., & Perliger, A. (2009). *Jewish terrorism in Israel*. New York, NY: Columbia University Press.

Perry, B. (2001). *In the name of hate: Understanding hate crimes*. New York, NY: Routledge.

Reich, W. (Ed.). (1998). *Origins of terrorism: Psychologies, ideologies, states of mind*. Washington, DC: Woodrow Wilson Center.

Shultz, R. H., & Dew, A. J. (2006). *Insurgents, terrorists, and militias: The warriors of contemporary combat*. New York, NY: Columbia University Press.

Simon, J. D. (2013). *Lone wolf terrorism: Understanding the growing threat*. New York, NY: Prometheus Books.

Sjoberg, L., & Gentry, C. E. (2007). *Mothers, monsters, whores: Women's violence in global politics*. London, UK: Zed Books.

Skaine, R. (2006). *Female suicide bombers*. Jefferson, NC: McFarland.

Staub, E. (2011). *Overcoming evil: Genocide, violent conflict, and terrorism*. New York, NY: Oxford University Press.

CHAPTER FOUR

TERRORIST VIOLENCE AND THE ROLE OF THE MEDIA

This chapter explores the role of the media in a terrorist environment—the frequent interplay between media reporting and the use of violence by extremist movements. If terrorism is a strategy characterized by symbolic attacks on symbolic targets, it is also a strategy characterized by intentional manipulation of the news media: "Terrorist attacks are often carefully choreographed to attract the attention of the electronic media and the international press."[1] The truism that **information is power** is clearly understood by all parties—the media and governments as well as terrorists, their audiences, and their adversaries.

Terrorists understand that instantaneous media exposure for their grievances requires simply a dramatic incident to attract the world's press. Terrorists seeking publicity are likely to garner a large audience if they dramatically carry out targeted hijackings, bombings, hostage takings, assassinations, or other acts of violence. The press also has its own incentives to report major terrorist incidents. From the media's point of view—and aside from its fundamental theoretical responsibility to objectively report the news—drama guarantees increased attention from viewers and is therefore often at the forefront of reported news.

The discussion in this chapter will review the following:

- Understanding the Role of the Media

- A New Battleground: The War for the Information High Ground

UNDERSTANDING THE ROLE OF THE MEDIA

In societies that champion freedom of the press, tension exists between the media's professional duty to objectively report the news and the terrorists' desire to promote their cause, and between the necessity to keep the public informed and deliberate attempts to disseminate propaganda through the media. Organizations, movements, and governments use propaganda to spread their interpretations of the truth or to invent a new truth. Propaganda can incorporate truths, half-truths, and lies. Underlying all extremist propaganda is a particular political agenda.

Learning Objectives

This chapter will enable readers to do the following:

1. Explain the perspectives of the media and governments.

2. Understand the role of the media.

3. Describe the conflict for manipulating the "spin" of media reporting.

4. Discuss issues arising from the debate concerning media regulation.

John Downing/Express/Hulton Archive/Getty Images

▶ The nature of the job. A British war correspondent travels with southern Sudanese rebels. The rebels, who practice Christianity or traditional religions, fought a long and brutal war against the northern Islamic government.

The media sometime tread a fine line between providing news and disseminating the terrorists' message when they report the details of terrorist incidents, broadcast interviews with terrorists and their extremist supporters, or investigate the merits of the terrorists' grievances. In theory, the media will be mindful of the fine line and carefully weigh what news to report and how to report it. In practice, some media outlets are blatantly sympathetic to one side of a conflict and completely unsympathetic to the other. In authoritarian states, this occurs as a matter of routine because the government heavily regulates the media. In democracies, the **free press** enjoys the liberty to apply whatever **media spin** is deemed desirable in their reporting practices. Some media purposely use provocative language and photographs to attract an audience.

The following discussion will review several factors one should consider in understanding the role of the media:

- Mass Communications and the Terrorists' Message

- Mass Communications and the "New Media"

- Reporting Terrorism

Mass Communications and the Terrorists' Message

The technological capability to convey considerable amounts of information to a large number of people, **mass communications** include printed material, audio broadcasts, video broadcasts, and expanding technologies such as the Internet and social media. Today's revolutionaries consider mass communications an invaluable tool for achieving the goals of their cause. In fact, the theories of armed propaganda are partly technology driven. Furthermore, the mass media are used as a recruiting tool by violent extremists and in this regard have become a **force multiplier** for revolutionary movements.

For terrorists, efficiency and timeliness are critical components to mass communication. Efficiency is necessary so that delivery of the message will be orderly (as opposed to garbled or chaotic) and the message itself will be intelligible and easily understood. Timeliness is also necessary because the message must be received while it is still fresh and relevant. It makes little sense to send a message before an issue has had an opportunity to ripen; it likewise makes little sense to send a message after an issue has become moot. Thus, if one's message is efficiently delivered and timely, it will have a stronger impact on the target audience.

Since the advent of printing presses using industrial-age technologies in the 19th century, terrorists and extremist movements have used virtually every available mass communications technology. The following technologies are commonly used by political extremists today:

- print media

- radio

- television

- the Internet and social media

Print Media

Dissident movements relied on the printed word throughout the 20th century. Sympathetic publishers and clandestine printing presses were instrumental in promulgating propaganda on behalf of dissident causes. Governments readily understood the power of the press to sway public sentiment as well as their own power to crack down on aboveground newspapers. There are also many examples of the deployment of security forces to locate and shut down clandestine presses. In an interesting example of how political blackmail can be used to promulgate an extremist message, the *New York Times* and *Washington Post* published the political manifesto of Ted Kaczynski, the so-called Unabomber, on September 19, 1995. Earlier in 1995, Kaczynski stated that he would cease his bombing campaign if major newspapers published his manifesto. If they did not do so, he promised to continue his campaign. On the recommendation of the U.S. Department of Justice, which hoped Kaczynski's writing style would be recognized, the *Times* and *Post* published his document, titled *Industrial Society and Its Future*.

Radio

Radio broadcasts were used by many dissident movements before the advent of television. Many 20th-century movements continued to broadcast over the radio in societies where large numbers of people were unable to receive uncensored television broadcasts and where shortwave radio was widely used. In 1969, for example, the Brazilian groups National Liberation Action and MR-8 kidnapped the American ambassador to Brazil, successfully demanding—in the terms for his release—that their manifesto be broadcast over the radio. Historically, clandestine radio broadcasts have been instrumental in publicizing the cause to selected audiences, including potential supporters; shortwave radio was particularly effective in reaching a broad audience. As with dissident printing presses, governments have used security forces to root out clandestine radio stations.

Television

Television became a medium of choice for terrorists in the era of cable and digital feeds because it provides immediate visibility and increases the size of the audience. It also allows for dramatic images, many of which are relatively uncensored in sympathetic markets. Especially significant, of course, is that televised news breaks very quickly—often within minutes of an incident—and is broadcast worldwide. Satellite feeds can be linked from almost anywhere in the world. Television has thus become quite useful for promulgating the terrorists' message both visually and with dramatic on-the-scene audio. All they need to do is manipulate the media into broadcasting a sympathetic spin for their grievances.

If successful, terrorists can bring images of their war into the homes of hundreds of millions of people worldwide nearly instantaneously—possibly with content that might sway large audiences to their cause or serve as a recruiting tool for potential fighters.

The Internet and Social Media

Computer and social communication technologies are used extensively by many terrorist groups and extremist movements. It is not uncommon for websites to be visually attractive, user-friendly, and interactive. Music, photographs, videos, and written propaganda are easily posted on webpages or disseminated via social media.

Tweeting, texting, and other social media platforms are used to record incidents (often graphically) and tout claimed successes. The fundamental attraction of social media is that they afford the capability to send messages and images live, as they occur. This is an advantage for media outlets or individuals who wish to be the first to break a story. Activists quickly adapted to this capability, first and most notably during the Arab Spring in 2011, when protesters tweeted and texted videos and other information during antigovernment demonstrations. Extremists also took advantage of social media by recording and disseminating real-time images of fighting, executions, beheadings, and casualties.

Many Internet postings portray the sense of a peaceful and rich culture of a downtrodden group. Graphic, gory, or otherwise moving images are skillfully posted, sometimes as photo essays that "loop" for continuous replay. Bloggers have posted links to hundreds of websites where viewers may obtain jihadist videos.[2] E-mail addresses, mailing addresses, membership applications, and other means to contact the movement are also common, so a "virtual world" of like-minded extremists thrives on the Internet.[3] One apt example of the anonymity and scope of the Internet is the activities of a purported member of the Iraqi resistance who called himself Abu Maysara al-Iraqi. Al-Iraqi regularly posted alleged updates and communiqués about the Iraqi resistance on sympathetic Islamic websites. It proved very difficult to verify his authenticity or even whether he (or they) was based in Iraq, given how accomplished he was in one online account or another.[4] As a counterpoint to such online materials, organizations independently monitor extremist websites for their origin and content.

Mass Communications and the "New Media"

The traditional and new resources just discussed are not the only media outlets. In the United States, there is a growing market in, and consumer demand for, the so-called **New Media**. New Media use existing technologies and alternative broadcasting formats to analyze and disseminate information. These alternative formats include talk-show models, tabloid (sensational) styles, celebrity status for hosts, blatant entertainment spins, and strong and opinionated political or social commentary.[5] Common types of New Media include "political talk radio . . . television talk . . . electronic town meetings . . . television news magazines . . . MTV . . . and print and television tabloids."[6] These media are innovative in their formats and sensational in their delivery. They do not hesitate to make admittedly provocative and completely biased statements. An important quality of the New Media is that they are very innovative and frequently experiment with untried formats and issues. Some extremist groups have appeared in the New Media, but terrorists have not been particularly active in attempting to manipulate it as a resource.[7]

Reporting Terrorism

The propensity of those in print and broadcast media has been to give priority to terrorist incidents in their news reports. This is understandable, given the influence terrorism can have on policy making and either domestic or international political environments. However, the media have not been consistent about which incidents they report or how they report them. They frequently cover some acts of political violence extensively but provide little if any information about others.[8] For example, during invasions of Afghanistan and Iraq after September 11, 2001, American cable news outlets focused on the military campaign, lacing their broadcasts with on-the-scene reporting from embedded journalists advancing with the troops. In contrast, Qatar's **Al Jazeera** cable news outlet regularly broadcasted images of injured civilians or destruction from the fighting, lacing its broadcasts with on-the-scene reporting from journalists on the streets and inside hospitals. Similarly, media reports are inconsistent in labeling perpetrators of political violence, and media interest in the sheer violent nature of terrorism can be disproportionate to exploration of the underlying causes of this violence.

Because of such disparities, organizations such as the Middle East Media Research Institute were established to bridge the language gap between Western and Middle Eastern media outlets.

Market Competition

The news media are owned and controlled by large corporations largely motivated by market share and profit. This affects their style, content, and reporting practices. Objective reporting is often outweighed by other factors, such as trying to acquire a larger share of the viewing market. The scoop and the news exclusive are prized objectives. Coverage can thus be quite selective, often allowing public opinion and government pronouncements to set the agenda for how the news will be spun. In such a political and market environment, the media will often forgo criticism of counterterrorist policies. Coverage can also be quite subjective, with the biases of executives, editors, and commentators reported to the public as if they were the most salient features of an issue.

Deciding Which Incidents to Report

The process for deciding which events to report (**news triage**) is often driven by evaluating what kind of news is likely to attract an audience. If it is decided that dramatic incidents will bring in sizable shares of viewers, the media will not hesitate to prioritize such incidents for the day's editions or broadcasts. The media can be highly selective about which terrorist incidents to report. The ultimate decision tends to weigh in favor of what most affects readers or the viewing public.

The personal stories of participants in a terrorist environment are particularly appealing to the media. Strong emotions such as outrage, grief, and hatred play well to many audiences. Certain kinds of terrorist incidents are particularly susceptible to the human interest spin. The key task for the media is to find personal stories that resonate well with their readers or viewers. Stories that do not resonate are likely to be left out of the mix.

Deciding How to Report Incidents

Deciding how to report terrorist incidents is, from the readers' or viewers' perspective, seemingly a subjective exercise. Media reports have never been consistent in their descriptions of the perpetrators of terrorist incidents, nor have they been consistent in characterizing examples of extremist violence as terrorism per se. **Labeling** vacillates from the pejorative to the somewhat positive, from *terrorist* to *commando*, for example. This point is further demonstrated by the following sequence of reporting that occurred in 1973:

> One *New York Times* leading article . . . [described] it as "bloody" and "mindless" and [used] the words "terrorists" and "terrorism" interchangeably with "guerrillas" and "extremists." . . . The *Christian Science Monitor* reports of the Rome Pan Am attack . . . avoided "terrorist" and "terrorism" in favor of "guerrillas" and "extremists"; an Associated Press story in the next day's *Los Angeles Times* also stuck with "guerrillas," while the two *Washington Post* articles on the same incident opted for the terms "commandos" and "guerrillas."[9]

These labels reflect a tendency to use indirect or vague language to describe what might otherwise be appalling behavior.[10] Euphemisms that apply words outside of their normal meaning to mask or soften the language of violence are also common among governments, policy makers, and others. This practice is deliberately media oriented so that the press and general public will more easily accept an incident or policy.

Terrorist-Initiated Labeling

Terrorist groups also use labeling and **euphemistic language**, most often in two circumstances: first, when they label enemy interests as potential targets and, second, when they label themselves. This language is promulgated in communiqués to supporters and journalists.

Labeling enemies and targets. Using symbolism to dehumanize potential targets is a universal trait among violent extremists, regardless of ideology. For example, leftists might recast Western business travelers as imperialists. Armenian nationalists might symbolically hold Turkish diplomats to account for the Armenian genocide of the early 20th century.

Table 4.1 Public Relations: The Organizational Titles of Violent Extremists

Terrorists seek to project an image that casts them in the role of liberators and soldiers. They are often conscious of their public image and can become quite media savvy.

This table illustrates how organizational titles reflect terrorists' self-designations as military organizations, the purpose of their movements, and their championed groups.

Organizational Title	Self-Designation	Purpose	Championed Group
Popular Front for the Liberation of Palestine (Israel/Palestine)	A united front; a forward position in a war	Liberation of a people	Palestine and Palestinians
Islamic State in Iraq and the Levant (Iraq/Syria)	A prototypical nation	Liberation movement creating a caliphate	Faithful Muslims in the region
Irish Republican Army (Northern Ireland)	An army; members are soldiers	Republican unification	Northern Irish Catholics
New People's Army (Philippines)	An army; members are soldiers	The continuation of a people's liberation movement	The people
Party of God/Hezbollah (Lebanon)	Movement representing God's will	Carry out God's will on earth	The faithful
Liberation Tigers of Tamil Eelam (Sri Lanka)	Warriors possessing the fierceness of tigers	Liberation	Tamils
Quebec Liberation Front (Canada)	A united front; a forward position in a war	Liberation of a people	Quebec and people of Quebec

Anti-Semitic and religious terrorists might label a Jewish community center as a Zionist interest. Al Qaeda and its sympathizers denounce Western culture and values as contrary to Islam and the values of the faithful; they also denounce secular Arab governments as apostasies. This labeling process creates important qualifiers for acts of extreme violence, allowing terrorists to justify their behavior even though their victims are often noncombatants.

Self-labeling. Choosing an organization or movement name is a significant decision. Those who engage in political violence consider themselves an elite—a vanguard—waging war against an implacable foe. They consciously use labels and euphemisms to project their self-image. Members of the cause become self-described martyrs, soldiers, or freedom fighters. An image of freedom, sacrifice, or heroism is a given. This pattern is universal among groups on the extremist fringe and is likely to continue. Table 4.1 surveys a few examples of self-labeling and euphemistic language.

A NEW BATTLEGROUND: THE WAR FOR THE INFORMATION HIGH GROUND

Mass communications technologies can become weapons of war in both conventional and asymmetrical conflicts. Adversaries in a terrorist environment frequently try to shape the character of the environment by manipulating the media. For terrorists, the media serve several useful purposes: first, dissemination of information about the cause; second, the delivery of messages to supporters and adversaries; and, third, as a "front" in the war to shape official governmental policies or influence the hearts and minds of the audience. For governments, the media can be a powerful tool in suppressing terrorist propaganda and manipulating the opinions of large segments of society. This is why every regime will be aggressive in delivering selective information to the media or, as in authoritarian regimes, officially suppress some stories.

Practical Considerations: Using the Media

Terrorists and their supporters use time-honored techniques to attract media attention. In the tradition of mainstream media-savvy organizations (and aside from acts of dramatic violence), terrorists have invited the media to press conferences, issued press releases, granted interviews, released audio and video productions, and produced attractive photographic essays. There is a tendency for the media to sensationalize information so that broadcasts of terrorist audio and video recordings, news conferences, or written statements often take on an entertainment quality.

Terrorists' Manipulation of the News "Scoop"

News outlets compete in trying to preempt the newsworthiness of their competitors' stories—known colloquially as a **news scoop**, that is, being the first to report breaking news. "This is a situation that, however unwittingly, is tailor-made for terrorist manipulation and contrivance."[11] Terrorists and other radicals have in fact successfully manipulated this propensity for scooping and sensationalizing news on a number of occasions. Several examples follow:

- **Ilich Ramirez Sanchez**, also known as **Carlos the Jackal**, did not make his escape during the December 1975 OPEC hostage crisis until the television cameras arrived. Only then did he dramatically and publicly make his getaway from Vienna to Algeria with 35 hostages in tow.[12]

- During the November 1979 to January 1981 seizure of the American embassy in Iran, Iranian crowds played to the cameras several times. Crowds would come alive when the cameras were on them, while parts of the crowd not under scrutiny were rather quiescent.[13]

- In May 1986, ABC News broadcast a short interview with Abu Abbas, the leader of the Palestine Liberation Front (PLF). The PLF was notorious at the time because a PLF terrorist unit had carried out the October 1985 hijacking of the *Achille Lauro* cruise ship, in which American passengers were terrorized and one was murdered. During the interview, Abbas threatened to carry out acts of terrorism in the United States and referred to President Ronald Reagan as Enemy Number One.

Points of Criticism

Because of these and other examples of overt (often successful) manipulation, critics have identified a number of problems in news reporting:

1. Critics argue that journalists sometime cross the line between reporting the news and disseminating terrorist propaganda.

2. Critics argue that the media's behavior sometimes shifts from objectivity to sensational opinion during particularly intense incidents.

3. Critics argue that the ability of the mass media to reach large audiences, when combined with the first two factors, can lead to realignments in the political environment.

Thus, in the aftermath of the September 11 attacks, political and media critics hotly debated whether the media should continue to broadcast feeds from Al Jazeera news service. Al Jazeera is one of the rare independent news services in the Middle East, and it broadcast extensive footage of injured Afghani and Iraqi civilians, whom the United States classifies as the unfortunate collateral damage of war. Al Jazeera also aired film clips of Al Qaeda leaders Osama bin Laden and Ayman al-Zawahiri that Al Qaeda had delivered to the station. The fear in the United States was that uninterpreted broadcasts of these images could spread enemy propaganda or send messages to sleeper cells. For this reason, American news services were asked to limit their use of Al Jazeera coverage.

Counterpointing the Criticism

As a counterpoint to these criticisms, and in defense of journalistic reporting of terrorist incidents, some proponents of the free press argue that full exposure of terrorism and the terrorists' grievances should be encouraged. This way, the public can become fully informed about the nature of terrorism in general and about the motives of specific terrorists. Thus, "defenders of media coverage feel that it enhances public understanding of terrorism and reinforces public hostility toward terrorists."[14]

Chapter Perspective 4.1 discusses the case of WikiLeaks and the unauthorized reporting of private and classified information.

CHAPTER PERSPECTIVE 4.1

WikiLeaks

WikiLeaks is an independent organization founded by Australian Julian Assange and others in 2007. It maintains an international online presence through its domain, wikileaks.org, operating in accordance with self-described central principles, which include

> the defence of freedom of speech and media publishing, the improvement of our common historical record and the support of the rights of all people to create new history. We derive these principles from the Universal Declaration of Human Rights. In particular, Article 19 inspires the work of our journalists and other volunteers. It states that everyone has the right to freedom of opinion and expression; this right includes freedom to hold opinions without interference and to seek, receive and impart information and ideas through any media and regardless of frontiers. We agree, and we seek to uphold this and the other Articles of the Declaration.[a]

WikiLeaks publishes documents and other information obtained from anonymous volunteers, including classified information not intended for release. In particular, WikiLeaks has obtained information from volunteers who may be subject to criminal prosecution or other sanctions if their anonymity is compromised. This occurred when United States Army Private First Class Chelsea Manning, who formerly went by the name Bradley, was arrested in May 2010 for allegedly delivering hundreds of thousands of classified documents to WikiLeaks.

The documents and information released by WikiLeaks have on occasion incited strong international debate about wartime policies. For example, in 2010 WikiLeaks released U.S. military reports under the titles "Afghan War Diary" and "Iraq War Logs." These releases together accounted for one of the most voluminous releases of classified information in modern U.S. history.

Other controversial releases of information included the 2012 release of U.S. Department of Defense documents concerning Guantanamo Bay detainees and several million e-mails from the private intelligence company Stratfor. In June 2015, WikiLeaks released classified reports and documents from the U.S. National Security Agency, which WikiLeaks titled "Espionnage Élysée." It reported NSA surveillance of French government officials.

Note

a. WikiLeaks website. http://www.wikileaks.org/About.html.

Information Is Power: The Media as a Weapon

For terrorists and other extremists, information can be wielded as a weapon of war, making **media as a weapon** an important concept. Because symbolism is at the center of most terrorist incidents, the media are explicitly identified by terrorists as potential supplements to their arsenal. When terrorists successfully—and violently—manipulate important symbols, relatively weak movements can influence governments and societies. Even when a terrorist unit fails to complete its mission, intensive media exposure can lead to a propaganda victory. For example, during the 1972 Munich Olympics attack by Black September terrorists, "an estimated 900 million persons in at least a hundred different countries saw the crisis unfold on their television screens."[15] As one Palestine Liberation Organization (PLO) leader later observed, "World opinion was forced to take note of the Palestinian drama, and the Palestinian people imposed their presence on an international gathering that had sought to exclude them."[16]

▶ TWA Flight 847. A terrorist waves a gun to cut short a press interview with TWA pilot John Testrake during the hijacked airliner's odyssey around the Mediterranean. The terrorists skillfully manipulated the international press.

Case: Hezbollah and the Hijacking of TWA Flight 847

Lebanon's Hezbollah has demonstrated its skill at conducting extraordinary strikes, some of which ultimately affected the foreign policies of France, Israel, and the United States. It regularly markets itself to the media by disseminating grievances as press releases, filming and photographing moving images of its struggle, compiling human interest background stories on Hezbollah fighters and Shi'a victims, and packaging its attacks as valiant assaults against Western and Israeli invaders and their proxies. This has been done overtly and publicly, and incidents are manipulated to generate maximum publicity and media exposure. For example, the January 1987 kidnapping in Beirut, Lebanon, of Terry Waite, the archbishop of Canterbury's envoy, was broadcast globally. He was released in November 1991.

On June 14, 1985, three Lebanese Shi'a terrorists hijacked **TWA Flight 847** as it flew from Athens, Greece, to Rome, Italy. It was diverted to Beirut, Lebanon, and then to Algiers, Algeria. It was then flown back to Beirut, made a second flight to Algiers, and then flew back to Beirut a second time. During the odyssey, the terrorists released women, children, and those who were not American, until 39 American men remained on board the aircraft. At the final stop in Beirut, the hostages were offloaded and dispersed throughout the city.

As the hijacking unfolded, the media devoted an extraordinary amount of airtime to the incident. The U.S. television networks ABC, CBS, and NBC broadcast almost 500 news reports, or 28.8 per day, and devoted two thirds of their evening news programs to the crisis.[17] "During the 16 days of the hijacking, CBS devoted 68% of its nightly news broadcasts to the event while the corresponding figures at ABC and NBC were 62% and 63%, respectively."[18]

The hijackers were masterful as puppeteers of the world's media. They granted carefully orchestrated interviews, held press conferences, and selected the information they permitted the news outlets to broadcast. It was reported later that they had offered to arrange tours of the airliner for the networks for a $1,000 fee and an interview with the hostages for $12,500.[19] After the hostages were dispersed in Beirut, **Nabih Berri**, the leader of Lebanon's Syrian-backed Shi'a **Amal** movement (an ally and occasional rival of the Shi'a Hezbollah movement), was interviewed by news networks as part of the negotiations to trade the hostages for concessions. In the end, the terrorists' media-oriented tactics were effective. They broadcast their grievances and demands to the world community and achieved their objectives. "[The] media exposure of the hostages generated enough pressure for the American president to make concessions."[20]

The hostages were released on June 30, 1985.

The Contagion Effect

The **contagion effect** refers to the theoretical influence of media exposure on the future behavior of other like-minded extremists.[21] This concept can also be applied "to a rather wide range of violent behavior [other than terrorism], including racial disturbances."[22] In theory, when terrorists successfully garner wide exposure or a measure of sympathy from the media and their audience, other terrorists may be motivated to replicate the tactic or strategy. This may be especially true if concessions have been forced from the targeted interest. Assuming that contagion theory has merit (the debate on this point continues), the question becomes the extent to which the contagion effect influences behavior.

Assessments of the contagion effect have produced some consensus that the media do have an effect on terrorist cycles. For example, empirical studies have indicated a correlation between media coverage and time lags between terrorist incidents.[23] These studies have not definitively proved that contagion is a behavioral fact but do suggest that the theory may have some validity.

The era of the New Terrorism arguably presents an unprecedented dynamic for contagion theory because transnational cell-based movements are a new model for—and may suggest new assessments of—the theory. Transnational organizations such as Al Qaeda engage in a learning process from the lessons of attacks by their operatives around the world. The advent of communication technologies such as faxes, cellular telephones, e-mail, text messaging, and the Internet—especially in combination with focused manipulation of the media—means that the terrorists' international learning curve can be quick and efficient. Hence, in theory, the contagion effect may be enhanced within New Terrorism movements on a global scale.

▶ Disseminating information. A Rewards for Justice program poster disseminated by the U.S. Department of State's Diplomatic Security Service. It depicts the aftermath of the 1993 bombing of the World Trade Center in New York City.

Problems on the New Battleground: The Risk of Backlash

Unfortunately for terrorists, this widespread exposure does not always work to their advantage. Governments are also experts at spinning the nature of violence to the media. When the violence is truly horrific, and when the victims, targets, or onlooker audiences recoil in popular disgust, the terrorists significantly diminish their influence over their adversary. They can, in effect, actually strengthen the adversary's resolve.

Public opinion among victims, targets, and onlooker audiences is critical to the success of **media-oriented terrorism**. However, one should bear in mind that terrorists often play to their supporter audiences so that success is always a relative term in the battle for the media.

Freedom of the Press and Regulating the Media

Freedom of the press is an ideal standard—and arguably an ideology—in many democracies. The phrase embodies a conceptual construct that suggests that the press should enjoy the liberty to independently report information to the public, even when the information might be unpopular. News editors and journalists, when criticized for their reports, frequently cite the people's right to know as a justification. The counterpoint to freedom of the press is regulation of the press. This issue arises when the media publish unpleasant facts (often in lurid prose) about subjects that the public or the government would rather not consider. Regulation is also a genuine option when matters of national security are at stake.

The international media operate under many rules inherent to and defined by their cultural environments. Some media have few if any codes of professional self-regulation, whereas others have adopted rather strict self-standards.[24] The Netherlands Broadcasting Corporation has traditionally had no formal code of operations, for example, whereas its British counterpart operates under a detailed set of rules.[25] Consensus indicates that ethical standards should be observed when reporting terrorist incidents.

Gatekeeping. In societies that champion freedom of the press, one model professional environment is **journalistic self-regulation**, sometimes referred to as **media gatekeeping**. If conducted under established standards of professional conduct, self-regulation obviates the need for official regulation and censorship. In theory, moral arguments brought to bear on the press from political leaders and the public will pressure them to adhere to model standards of fairness, accuracy, and objectivity.

This is, of course, an ideal free press environment; in reality, critics argue that journalistic self-regulation is a fluid and inconsistent process. Chapter Perspective 4.2 illustrates this criticism by contrasting different standards of gatekeeping by the American media when reporting news about several U.S. presidents.

CHAPTER PERSPECTIVE 4.2

Self-Regulation and the American Media

Gatekeeping is a process of self-regulation by the press, using professional standards of restraint and industry guidelines about fair and objective journalism. The American media have traditionally practiced self-regulation with relatively little hindrance from government regulators, except in time of war (particularly during World War II).

Reporters working in the White House press pool, or otherwise reporting on the U.S. presidency, have developed gatekeeping standards that until recently ensured that the personal lives of presidents would not become front-page news. This hands-off approach to reporting details of presidential personal qualities has not been consistent.

For example, the reporting of Franklin Delano Roosevelt's administration was highly self-censored. FDR was the United States' only president with a limiting disability. His legs were paralyzed, and he used a wheelchair from the age of 39. Roosevelt wore thick braces on his legs to prop him up when he delivered speeches. And yet, no photographs of him in his wheelchair were published by the media, most likely because American culture at the time was biased against people with disabilities. During his last years in office, he has

been described as a dying man. Nevertheless, his declining health was never reported extensively to the public. The press also never reported persistent rumors about FDR's alleged long-term extramarital affair.

Likewise, the reporting of John F. Kennedy's administration was self-censored. JFK symbolized the youth and idealism of a new generation. However, he suffered from poor health during much of his adult life. For example, he had Addison's disease, severe allergies, and spinal problems, and he contracted malaria during the World War II in the South Pacific. The media were captivated by JFK, portraying him as a man of great vigor and youth. As was the case with FDR, the press never reported rumors of JFK's alleged extramarital affairs.

In contrast, the reporting of Bill Clinton's personal life was lurid and long term. Extramarital rumors were reported, interviews were broadcast of his accusers, and the Monica Lewinsky episode was front-page news around the world. For Clinton, the media's self-regulatory gatekeeping practices were virtually nonexistent—particularly in comparison with the reporting of the personal lives of previous presidents such as Roosevelt and Kennedy.

Regulation of the free press. Many governments occasionally regulate or otherwise influence their press community while advocating freedom of reporting. Governments selectively release information, or release none, during terrorist incidents. The rationale is that proper investigation, by definition, requires limitations. This occurs as a matter of routine during wartime or other national crises.

A number of democracies have state-run and semiprivate radio and television stations—for example, Great Britain, France, Germany, and other European democracies. These networks are expected to promote accepted standards of professional conduct and to practice self-regulation for the sake of good taste and national security. In some democracies, the law permits the government to suppress the reporting of news.

The State-Regulated Press

State-regulated media exist in environments in which the state routinely intervenes, even in societies that otherwise have a measure of democratic freedoms. For example, the **state-regulated presses** of most countries in the Middle East led many people in those countries to believe that the September 11 attacks either were not the work of Al Qaeda or were the work of Zionists. Some disseminated far-fetched rumors. As noted earlier, some Middle Eastern mainstream commentators reported and supported a popular conspiracy theory that anonymous telephone calls warned thousands of Jewish workers in the World Trade Center to leave the buildings before the attack and that therefore no Jews were among the casualties.

Scales of intervention range from permitting independent but regulated newspapers to creating government-controlled propaganda enterprises. In **authoritarian** and **totalitarian regimes**, terrorists have no chance to rely on the media to sensationalize their deeds. In these societies, the media serve to promote the government's interests and often to disseminate government propaganda. There are no gripping stories that might sway an audience. The general public is never privy to sympathetic human interest stories or to an extremist manifesto's call to arms. When terrorist incidents occur, they are either underreported by the government or manipulated to the absolute advantage of the regime.

In very restrictive societies, the media are used as outlets for propaganda on behalf of the existing regime. For example, the late Iraqi dictator Saddam Hussein created an extensive **cult of personality** not unlike that of dictators Joseph Stalin in the Soviet Union and Kim Il Sung, son Kim Jong Il, and grandson Kim Jong Un in North Korea. Cults of personality are used by dictatorial regimes to promote the leader or ruling party as the source of absolute wisdom, truth, and benevolence. Likenesses of the leader are widely distributed, usually in a variety of symbolic poses. Saddam Hussein, for example, was regularly depicted as a visionary, a warrior, the good father, a common citizen, a devout Muslim, and the medieval leader Saladin. Hussein, Stalin, and the Kim family promoted themselves, their regimes, and their policies by completely controlling the dissemination of information.

DISCUSSION BOX

FREEDOM OF REPORTING AND SECURITY ISSUES

This chapter's Discussion Box is intended to stimulate critical debate about seminal incidents in the history of national groups.

During times of crisis, governments restrict media access to information about matters that affect security policy. The logic is quite understandable: Governments believe that the war effort (or counterterrorism policy) requires limitations to be imposed to prevent information from helping the enemy and to prevent the enemy from spreading its propaganda. For example, the British **Official Secrets Act** was designed to manage the flow of information both *from* adversaries and *to* adversaries.

The challenge for democracies is to strike a balance between governmental control over information—for the sake of national security—and unbridled propaganda. The following examples illustrate how the United States and Great Britain managed the flow of information during international crises:

- During the Vietnam War, journalists had a great deal of latitude in the field to visit troops in the field and observe operations. Vietnam was the first "television war," so violent and disturbing images were broadcast into American homes on a daily basis. These reports were one reason why American public opinion turned against the war effort.

- During the 1982 Falklands War, news about operations was highly controlled and censored

by the British government. Press briefings were strictly controlled by the government, under the rationale that useful information could otherwise be received by the Argentines and jeopardize the war effort.

- During the 1990–1991 Persian Gulf War, news was likewise highly controlled. Unlike during the Vietnam War, the media received their information during official military press briefings. They were not permitted to travel into the field except under highly restrictive conditions.

- During the Afghan phase of the war on terrorism in late 2001, news was highly restricted. Official press briefings were the norm, and requests were made for cooperation in not broadcasting enemy propaganda.

- During the 2003 conventional phase of the invasion of Iraq, reporters were embedded with military units and reported events as they unfolded. Official press briefings were the norm.

Discussion Questions

1. Should the United States adopt information-control regulations similar to Britain's Official Secrets Act?

2. What are the policy implications of permitting journalists to have the same degree of access to information as occurred during the Vietnam War?

3. What are the policy implications of permitting journalists to have the same degree of access to information as occurred during the Gulf War?

4. Under what circumstances should the state increase restrictions on the media? How would you justify these restrictions?

5. Do you think that the media in democracies are more prone to manipulation by terrorists? Is this a myth?

CHAPTER SUMMARY

This chapter investigated the role of the media in terrorist environments. Particular attention was given to terrorists' efforts to publicize the cause, their manipulation of mass communications, and the potential impact of the New Media. Issues related to reporting terrorism include questions about which incidents to report and how to report them. The concepts of information as power and media-oriented terrorism were defined and explored as critical considerations in understanding the role of the media.

Evaluation of the new battleground for information requires that readers first explore the issue from the perspectives of participants in terrorist environments.

Practical considerations for terrorists' treatment of the media include their manipulation of the media's desire to scoop their competitors. The contagion effect and the example of the hijacking of TWA Flight 847 demonstrate how media exposure can become an effective weapon in a terrorist arsenal.

Regulation of the media is a challenge for every government. For authoritarian and totalitarian regimes, this challenge is easily resolved by simply prohibiting certain kinds of reporting practices. It is a more complex issue in most democratic systems, though most have adapted by adopting laws and practices that restrict media access to operational information.

KEY TERMS AND CONCEPTS

The following topics were discussed in this chapter and can be found in the Glossary:

Achille Lauro 71	Force multiplier 66	Media-oriented terrorism 74
Al Jazeera 68	Free press 66	New Media 68
Amal 73	Information is power 65	News scoop 71
Authoritarian regimes 76	Journalistic self-regulation 75	News triage 69
Berri, Nabih 73	Labeling 69	Official Secrets Act 77
Carlos the Jackal 71	Mass communications 66	Sanchez, Ilich Ramirez 71
Contagion effect 74	Media as a weapon 73	State-regulated press 76
Cult of personality 76	Media gatekeeping 75	Totalitarian regimes 76
Euphemistic language 69	Media spin 66	TWA Flight 847 73

WEB EXERCISE

Using this chapter's recommended websites listed on the student study site at **edge.sagepub.com/martiness5e**, conduct an online investigation of the reporting of terrorism by the media.

1. Compare and contrast the reporting of political violence by the referenced media services. What patterns of reporting can you identify?

2. To what extent are the media services biased in their reporting? How so?

3. To what extent are the media services objective in their reporting? How so?

For an online search of media reporting of terrorism, readers should enter the following keywords in their Web browser's search engine:

- "Media and terrorism"

- "Propaganda and terrorism"

RECOMMENDED READINGS

The following publications provide discussions for evaluating the role of the media in the reporting of terrorism, national conflict, and political dissent.

Davies, N. (2009). *Flat earth news: An award-winning reporter exposes falsehood, distortion, and propaganda in the global media*. London, UK: Vintage Books.

Davis, R., & Owen, D. (1998). *New media and American politics*. New York, NY: Oxford University Press.

Edwards, D., & Cromwell, D. (2009). *Newspeak in the 21st century*. London, UK: Pluto Press.

Gitlin, T. (1980). *The whole world is watching: Mass media in the making and unmaking of the New Left*. Los Angeles: University of California Press.

Herbst, P. (2003). *Talking terrorism: A dictionary of the loaded language of political violence*. Westport, CT: Greenwood.

Kavoori, A. P., & Fraley, T. (Eds.). (2006). *Media, terrorism, and theory: A reader*. Lanham, MD: Rowman & Littlefield.

Knightley, P. (2004). *The first casualty: The war correspondent as hero and myth maker from the Crimea to Iraq*. Baltimore, MD: Johns Hopkins University Press.

Nacos, B. L. (2007). *Mass-mediated terrorism: The central role of the media in terrorism and counterterrorism*. Lanham, MD: Rowman & Littlefield.

Nacos, B. L., Bloch-Elkon, Y., & Shapiro, R. Y. (2011). *Selling fear: Counterterrorism, the media, and public opinion*. Chicago, IL: University of Chicago Press.

Paletz, D. L., & Schmid, A. P. (Eds.). (1992). *Terrorism and the media*. Newbury Park, CA: Sage.

Pludowski, T. (2007). *How the world's news media reacted to 9/11: Essays from around the globe*. Spokane, WA: Marquette Books.

Seib, P. (Ed.). (2007). *New media and the new Middle East*. New York, NY: Palgrave Macmillan.

Tuman, J. S. (2010). *Communicating terror: The rhetorical dimensions of terrorism* (2nd ed.). London, UK: Sage.

Weimann, G., & Winn, C. (1994). *The theater of terror: Mass media and international terrorism*. New York, NY: Longman.

TERRORIST ENVIRONMENTS

▸ The Pentagon on the morning of September 11, 2001.

U.S. Army

CHAPTER FIVE

TERRORISM BY THE STATE

Learning Objectives

This chapter will enable readers to do the following:

1. Understand and explain the state terrorism paradigm.

2. Interpret some incidents of state-initiated international violence as state terrorism.

3. Interpret some incidents of state-initiated domestic violence as state terrorism.

4. Discuss scales of violence perpetrated by states.

This chapter explores the characteristics of terrorism from above—state terrorism—committed by governments and quasi-governmental agencies and personnel against perceived enemies. State terrorism can be directed externally against foreign adversaries or internally against domestic enemies. Readers will explore the various types of state terrorism and acquire an appreciation for the qualities that characterize each state terrorist environment. A state terrorist paradigm will be discussed and cases will be examined to understand what is meant by terrorism as foreign policy and terrorism as domestic policy.

Political violence by the state is the most organized and potentially the most far-reaching application of terrorist violence. Because of the many resources available to the state, its ability to commit acts of violence far exceeds that perpetrated by dissident terrorists in scale and duration. Only communal dissident terrorism (group-against-group violence) potentially approximates the scale and duration of state-sponsored terror.[1] Terrorism by states is characterized by official government support for policies of violence, repression, and intimidation. Such violence and coercion are directed against perceived enemies that the state has determined threaten its interests or security. Although the perpetrators of state terrorist campaigns are frequently government personnel acting in obedience to directives originating from government officials, those who carry out the violence are also quite often unofficial agents the government uses and encourages.

For example, some governments have adopted a strategy of using violent state-sponsored paramilitaries as an instrument of official state repression. The rationale behind supporting these paramilitaries is that they can be deployed to violently enforce state authority and at the same time permit the state to deny responsibility for their behavior. Such deniability can be useful for propaganda purposes because the government can officially argue that its paramilitaries represent a spontaneous grassroots reaction against their opponents.

The discussion in this chapter will review the following:

- Perspectives on Terrorism by Governments
- Domestic Terrorism by the State
- Terrorism as Foreign Policy

Experts and scholars have designed a number of models to describe state terrorism. These constructs have been developed to identify distinctive patterns of state-sponsored terrorist behavior. Experts agree that several models can be differentiated. For example, one model[2] describes state-level participants in a security environment as including the following:

- *sponsors* of terrorism, meaning those states that actively promote terrorism and have been formally designated as rogue states or state sponsors under U.S. law[3]

- *enablers* of terrorism, or those states that operate in an environment in which "being part of the problem means not just failing to cooperate fully in countering terrorism but also doing some things that help enable it to occur"[4]

- *cooperators* in counterterrorism efforts, including unique security environments in which "cooperation on counter terrorism is often feasible despite significant disagreements on other subjects"[5]

State terrorism incorporates many types and degrees of violence. The intensity of this violence may range in scale from single acts of coercion to extended campaigns of terrorist violence. Another model describes the scale of violence as including the following:

- In **warfare**, the conventional military forces of a state are marshaled against an enemy. The enemy is either a conventional or guerrilla combatant and may be an internal or external adversary. This is a highly organized and complicated application.

- In **genocide**, the state applies its resources toward the elimination of a scapegoat group. The basic characteristic of state-sponsored genocidal violence is that it does not differentiate between enemy combatants and enemy civilians; all members of the scapegoat group are considered enemies. Like warfare, this is often a highly organized and complicated application.

- **Assassinations** are selective applications of homicidal state violence, in which a person or a specified group is designated for elimination. This is a lower scale application.

- **Torture** is used by some states as an instrument of intimidation, interrogation, and humiliation.[6] Like assassinations, it is a selective application of state violence directed against a single person or a specified group of people. Although it is often a lower scale application of state violence, many regimes make widespread use of torture during states of emergency.[7]

Understanding State-Sponsored Terrorism:

State Patronage and Assistance

Links between regimes and terrorism can range from very clear lines of sponsorship to very murky and indefinable associations. Governments inclined to use terrorism as an instrument of statecraft are often able to control the parameters of their involvement so that they can sometimes manage how precisely a movement or an incident can be traced back to personnel.

Thus, state sponsorship of terrorism is not always a straightforward process. In fact, it is usually a covert, secret policy that allows states to claim deniability when accused of sponsoring terrorism. Because of these veiled parameters, a distinction must be made between **state patronage** and **state assistance**. These two subtly distinct concepts are summarized in Table 5.1.

Table 5.1 State Sponsorship of Terrorism

State participation in terrorist and extremist behavior can involve either direct or indirect sponsorship and can be conducted in the international or domestic policy domains. State *patronage* refers to relatively direct linkages between a regime and political violence. State *assistance* refers to relatively indirect linkages.

This table distinguishes state patronage and assistance in the international and domestic policy domains.

Domain	Type of Sponsorship	
	Patronage	Assistance
International	International violence conducted on government orders	International violence with government encouragement and support
	Case: 2008 assassination of Hezbollah commander Imad Mughniyeh by car bomb in Damascus, Syria, neither confirmed nor denied by Israel	Case: Covert Pakistani assistance for Afghan Taliban through its Interservices Intelligence agency
Domestic	Domestic repression by government personnel	Domestic repression by progovernment extremists
	Case: Syrian government's violent suppression campaign against the 2011 Arab Spring movement	Case: Violence by state-supported progovernment proxy gangs in Iran during the 2011–2012 Green Revolution protests

State Sponsorship: The Patronage Model

State patronage for terrorism refers to active participation in and encouragement of terrorist behavior. Its basic characteristic is that the state, through its agencies and personnel, actively takes part in repression, violence, and terrorism. Thus, state patrons adopt policies that *initiate* terrorism and other subversive activities—including directly arming, training, and providing sanctuary for terrorists.

State Patronage in Foreign Policy

In the foreign policy domain, state patronage for terrorism occurs when a government champions a politically violent movement or group—a proxy—that is operating beyond its borders. Under this model, the state patron directly assists the proxy in its cause and continues its support even when the movement or group has become known to commit acts of terrorism or other atrocities. When these revelations occur, patrons typically reply to this information with rationalizations. The patron will do one of four things:

- accept the terrorism as a necessary tactic

- deny that what occurred should be labeled as terrorism

- deny that an incident occurred in the first place

- issue a blanket and moralistic condemnation of all such violence as unfortunate

The 1981 to 1988 U.S.-directed guerrilla war against the leftist Sandinista regime in Nicaragua incorporated elements of the state patronage model.[8] Although it was not a terrorist war per se, the U.S. proxy did commit human rights violations. It is therefore a good case study of state patronage for a proxy that was quite capable of engaging in terrorist behavior. The most important component was U.S. support for anti-Sandinista Nicaraguan counterrevolutionaries, known as the **Contras**.

From December 1981 until July 1983, the Contras were sustained by U.S. arms and funding. Without this patronage, they would not have been able to operate against the **Sandinistas**. Unfortunately for the United States, evidence surfaced that implicated the Contras in numerous human rights violations. These allegations were officially dismissed or explained away.

State Patronage in Domestic Policy

In the domestic policy domain, state patronage of terrorism occurs when a regime engages in direct violent repression against a domestic enemy. Patronage is characterized by the use of state security personnel in an overt policy of political violence. State patrons typically rationalize policies of repression by arguing that they are necessary to

- suppress a clear and present domestic threat to national security,

- maintain law and order during times of national crisis,

- protect fundamental cultural values that are threatened by subversives,

- restore stability to governmental institutions that have been shaken, usurped, or damaged by a domestic enemy.

The Syrian government's 1982 suppression of a rebellion by the **Muslim Brotherhood** is an apt case study. The Muslim Brotherhood is a transnational Sunni Islamic fundamentalist movement very active in several North African and Middle Eastern countries. Beginning in the early 1980s, it initiated a widespread terrorist campaign against the Syrian government. In 1981, the Syrian army and other security units moved in to crush the Muslim Brotherhood in the cities of Aleppo and Hama, killing at least 200 people. Syrian president Hafez al-Assad increased security restrictions and made membership in the organization a capital offense. In 1982, another Muslim Brotherhood revolt broke out in Hama. The Syrian regime sent in troops and tanks, backed by artillery, to put down the revolt; they killed approximately 25,000 civilians and destroyed large sections of the city. After the suppression of the Hama revolt, the Muslim Brotherhood and other religious fundamentalist groups posed little threat to the Syrian regime, which is a secular government dominated by a faction of the nationalistic Ba'ath Party. Nevertheless, when the Ba'athist regime was again challenged by mass protests during the 2011 Arab Spring uprisings, it again deployed the army and other security forces to violently attack centers of protest nationwide and again assaulted Hama.[9] A civil war ensued, with antigovernment forces initially comprising a loose coalition of disparate militias, collectively known as the Free Syrian Army. A potent well-armed Islamist movement eventually rose to challenge both the Free Syrian Army and the Ba'athist government.

State Sponsorship: The Assistance Model

State assistance for terrorism refers to tacit participation in and encouragement of terrorist behavior. Its basic characteristic is that the state, through sympathetic proxies and agents, implicitly takes part in repression, violence, and terrorism. In contrast to state patrons of terrorism, state assisters are less explicit in their sponsorship, and links to state policies and personnel are more ambiguous. State assistance includes policies that help sympathetic extremist proxies engage in terrorist violence, whereby the state indirectly arms, trains, and provides sanctuary for terrorists.

State Assistance in Foreign Policy

In the foreign policy domain, state assistance for terrorism occurs when a government champions a politically violent proxy operating beyond its borders. Under this model, the assistance is indirect, and the state may or may not continue its support if the movement or group becomes known for committing acts of terrorism or other atrocities. When the proxy's terrorism becomes known, state assisters typically weigh political costs and benefits when crafting a reply to the allegations. The ambiguity that the assister has built into its links with the proxy is intended to provide deniability when accused of complicity.

The Contra insurgency against the Sandinistas was introduced as a case study of the state patronage model—with the caveat that it was not per se a terrorist war. The later phases of the war are also a good example of the state assistance model.

Several incidents undermined congressional support for the Reagan administration's policy in Nicaragua. In December 1982, Congress passed the **Boland Amendment**, which forbade the expenditure of U.S. funds to overthrow the Sandinista government. In late 1984, a second Boland Amendment forbade all U.S. assistance to the Contras. These legislative measures were the catalyst for a highly covert effort to continue supplying the Contras. The most effective effort to circumvent the congressional ban was the resupply network set up by Marine Lieutenant Colonel Oliver North, an official of the National Security Council. North successfully set up a resupply program that shipped large amounts of arms to the Contras. This program was intended to wait out congressional opposition to arming the Contras and was successful, because in June 1986 Congress approved $100 million in aid for the Contras. Congressional support for this disbursement was severely shaken when a covert American cargo plane was shot down inside Nicaragua, an American mercenary was captured, and the press published reports about North's operations. This combination of factors—known as the **Iran-Contra scandal**—ended congressional support for the Contra program.

State Assistance in Domestic Policy

In the domestic policy domain, state assistance for terrorism occurs when a regime engages in indirect violent repression against an enemy. Under this model, the assistance is characterized by the use of sympathetic proxies. This can occur in an environment where the proxy violence coincides with that of state security personnel. Thus, the overall terrorist environment may include both state patronage (direct repression) and state assistance (indirect repression). State assisters typically rationalize policies of indirect repression by adopting official positions that

- blame an adversary group for the breakdown of order and call on the people to assist the government in restoring order,

- argue that the proxy violence is evidence of popular patriotic sentiment to suppress a threat to national security,

- call on all parties to cease hostilities but focus blame for the violence on an adversary group,

- assure everyone that the government is doing everything in its power to restore law and order but that the regime is unable to immediately end the violence.

The **Great Proletarian Cultural Revolution** in China, which lasted from 1965 to 1969,[10] is a good example of state assistance for an ideologically extremist movement. Launched by national leader Mao Zedong and the Chinese Communist Party Central Committee, it was a mass movement that mobilized the young postrevolution generation. Its goal was to eliminate what it called revisionist tendencies in society and create a newly indoctrinated revolutionary generation. The period was marked by widespread upheaval and disorder. Maoists mobilized millions of young supporters in the **Red Guards**, who waged an ideological struggle to

CHAPTER PERSPECTIVE 5.1

The State-Sponsored Janjaweed Militia Campaign in Darfur, Sudan

Darfur is a region in western Sudan with a population that is almost entirely Muslim. Although inhabitants are classified as either African or Arab, these distinctions are largely cultural. In practical terms, those classified as Arabs are mostly culturally "Arabized" Africans, and the government of Sudan is dominated by Arabized Sudanese.

In early 2003, two Darfur rebel movements, the Sudanese Liberation Army (SLA) and the Justice and Equality Movement (JEM), attacked government troops stationed in Darfur. Because the government had few soldiers in the region, and because it did not trust those who were there, it organized an alliance of Arab militias known as the Janjaweed. The term *Janjaweed* is roughly translated as "men on horses" because the Arabized population are herdsmen and often travel on camels with horses tied behind them. African residents in Darfur tend to be farmers.

From its inception, the war was brutal. With government arms and air support, the Janjaweed embarked on a policy of de facto ethnic cleansing and methodically burned African villages, killed many inhabitants, and drove others off the land.[a] About 2 million Africans were forced from the land, many taking refuge in neighboring Chad. Although both the Janjaweed and their adversaries were Muslims, Janjaweed fighters burned mosques. More than 50,000 people died.

As has occurred in many communal conflicts elsewhere, African women and girls were systematically sexually assaulted by Janjaweed fighters. One purpose of the assaults was to debase the culture of African Muslims by "defiling" their women. Another, more genocidal, purpose was to impregnate the women and thereby create "light" babies, which under local tradition would take on the ethnicity of their fathers.[b]

Governments and human rights agencies declared the Janjaweed campaign of systematic rape to be a conscious policy of using sexual assault as a weapon of war.[c]

Notes

a. For a discussion of genocide in Darfur, see Mike De and John McCain, "It's Happening Again," *Washington Post*, June 23, 2004.

b. Emily Wax, "'We Want to Make a Light Baby,'" *Washington Post*, June 30, 2004.

c. See Amnesty International, *Darfur: Rape as a Weapon of War: Sexual Violence and Its Consequences* (London, UK: Amnesty International, July 19, 2004).

---

eliminate what were known as the Four Olds: Old Ideas, Old Culture, Old Customs, and Old Habits.[11] The Red Guards were the principal purveyors of the Cultural Revolution and were strongly encouraged to attack the Four Olds publicly and with great vigor. This led to widespread turmoil. For approximately 18 months, beginning in early 1967, the Red Guards seized control of key government bureaucracies. Because they had no experience in government operations, the government ceased to operate effectively. It was not until violent infighting within the Red Guards began that Mao ordered an end to the Cultural Revolution and deployed the People's Liberation Army to restore order.

Chapter Perspective 5.1 discusses the case of the Janjaweed militia campaign in Darfur, Sudan, as an example of a government proxy operating domestically.

DOMESTIC TERRORISM BY THE STATE

State terrorism as domestic policy refers to a state's politically motivated application of force inside its own borders. Military, law enforcement, and other security institutions are used to suppress perceived threats and can be supplemented by unofficial paramilitaries and death squads. The purpose of domestically focused terrorism is to demonstrate the supreme power of the government and to intimidate or eliminate the opposition. In environments where the central government perceives its authority to be seriously threatened, this force can be extreme.

South Africa during the final years of **apartheid**, the system of racial separation, is a good example. When confronted by a combination of antiapartheid reformist agitation, mass unrest, and terrorist attacks, the South African government began a covert campaign to root out antiapartheid leaders and supporters. This included government support for the Zulu-based **Inkatha Freedom Party** in its violence against the multiethnic and multiracial **African National Congress (ANC)**. The South African government also assigned security officers to command death squads called **Askaris**, who assassinated ANC members both inside South Africa and in neighboring countries.

Legitimizing State Authority

Every type of regime seeks to legitimize its authority and maintain its conception of social order. How this is done often depends on the political environment at a particular point in a nation's history and occurs with varying degrees of restraint. Stable democracies with strong constitutional traditions are usually characterized by measured restraint. Regimes with weak constitutional traditions or those in a period of national crisis often show little or no restraint. Examples of state domestic authority can be summarized as follows:

- *Democracy* is a system of elected government in which authority is theoretically delegated by the people to elected leaders. Under this model, a strong constitution grants authority for elected leaders to govern the people and manage the affairs of government. The power of the state is clearly delimited.

- *Authoritarianism* is a system of government in which authority and power come from the state rather than being delegated by the people to elected leaders. Law, order, and state authority are emphasized. Authoritarian regimes can have elected leaders, but these leaders have authoritarian power and often rule for indefinite periods. Constitutions do not have enough authority to prohibit abuses by the state.

- *Totalitarianism* is a system under which all national authority originates from the government, which enforces its own vision of an ordered society.

- *Crazy states*[12] are those whose behavior is not rational; in such states, the people live at the whim of the regime or a dominant group. Some **crazy states** are failed states that have little or no central authority and are ravaged by warlords or militias. Other crazy states have capricious, impulsive, and violent regimes in power that act out with impunity.

Table 5.2 illustrates these models of domestic state authority by summarizing sources of state authority and giving examples of these environments.

▶ North Korean soldiers, carrying a large portrait of late North Korean leader Kim Il Sung, marching during a grand military parade to celebrate the 75th anniversary of the founding of the Korean People's Army.

KCNA/AFP/Getty Images

State Domestic Authority

The following discussion is a domestic state terrorist model adapted from one designed by Peter C. Sederberg.[13] It defines and differentiates broad categories of domestic state terrorism that are useful in critically analyzing the motives and behaviors of terrorist regimes. They signify the varied qualities of state-sponsored terrorism directed against perceived domestic enemies:

- Unofficial Repression: Vigilante Domestic State Terrorism

- Repression as Policy: Official Domestic State Terrorism

- Mass Repression: Genocidal Domestic State Terrorism

Table 5.2 State Domestic Authority

Several models can be constructed that illustrate the manner in which state authority is imposed and the degree of coercion that is used to enforce governmental authority. Sources of state authority differ depending on which model of authority characterizes each regime.

Models of State Authority	Sources of State Authority		Examples of Authority Models
	Legitimization of Authority	Center of Authority	
Democracy	Secondary role of security institutions; strong constitution and rule of law	Government with constrained authority	Japan United States Western Europe
Authoritarianism	Central role of official security institutions; strong constitution possible	Government with minimally constrained authority	Belarus Egypt Myanmar (Burma)
Totalitarianism	Central role of official security institutions	Government with unconstrained authority	China North Korea Taliban Afghanistan
Crazy states	Central roles of official and unofficial security institutions	Government with unconstrained authority, unconstrained paramilitaries, or both	Liberia (1990s) Somalia Uganda under Idi Amin

Unofficial Repression: Vigilante Domestic State Terrorism

Vigilante terrorism is political violence perpetrated by nongovernmental groups and individuals. These groups can receive unofficial support from agents of the state.

Why do regimes encourage vigilante violence? What are the benefits of such support? From the perspective of the state, what are the values being safeguarded by the vigilantes? Vigilante violence committed on behalf of a regime is motivated by the perceived need to defend a demographic group or cultural establishment. The overall goal of **vigilante state terrorism** is to violently preserve the preferred order. In a classic terrorist rationalization process, the end of an orderly society justifies the means of extreme violence.

The vigilante terrorists, sometimes alongside members of the state security establishment, unofficially wage a violent suppression campaign against an adversarial group or movement. Such a campaign occurs when civilians and members of the state's security forces perceive that the state is threatened. This can occur in warlike environments or when an alternative social movement or ideology challenges the established order. Civilians and members of the security establishment who participate in vigilante violence adhere to a code of duty and behavior and thus believe that their actions are absolutely justifiable. Nongovernmental vigilantes often organize themselves into paramilitaries and operate as death squads. Death squads have committed many documented massacres and atrocities, including assassinations, disappearances, and random terrorist attacks.

Repression as Policy: Official Domestic State Terrorism

State-sponsored repression and political violence were practiced regularly during the 20th century. Many regimes deliberately adopted domestic terrorism as a matter of official policy, and directives ordering government operatives to engage in violent domestic repression frequently originated with ranking government officials.

Why do regimes resort to official policies of domestic violence? What are the benefits of such programs? From the perspective of the state, who are the people who deserve this kind of violent repression? The goals of **official domestic state terrorism** are to preserve an existing order and to maintain state authority through demonstrations of state power. Regimes that officially selected violent repression as a policy choice rationalized their behavior as a legitimate method of protecting the state from an internal threat. Two manifestations of official state terrorism in the domestic domain must be distinguished: overt and covert.

Overt official state terrorism refers to the visible application of state-sponsored political violence. A policy of unconcealed and explicit repression against a domestic enemy is common in totalitarian societies, such as Stalinist Russia, Nazi Germany, Khmer Rouge Cambodia, and Taliban Afghanistan.

Covert official state terrorism refers to the secretive application of state-sponsored political violence. A policy of concealed and implicit repression against a domestic enemy, it is common in countries with extensive secret police services, such as Syria during the regimes of Presidents Hafez al-Assad and his son Bashar, Saddam Hussein's Iraq, General Augusto Pinochet's Chile, and Argentina during the Dirty War.

Official state terrorism is not always directed against subversive elements. It is sometimes conducted to cleanse society of an undesirable social group. These groups are perceived as purveyors of a decadent lifestyle or immoral values or as otherwise unproductive drains on society. Chapter Perspective 5.2 discusses how extremist regimes have solved this problem by engaging in so-called **social cleansing** and **ethnic cleansing**.

CHAPTER PERSPECTIVE 5.2

Cleansing Society

Among the euphemisms used by propagandists to characterize state-initiated domestic terrorism, perhaps the most commonly applied term is that of "cleansing" society. Conceptually, an image is constructed that depicts an undesirable group as little more than a virus or bacterium that has poisoned society. The removal of this group is considered to be a necessary remedy for the survival of the existing social order.

This imagery has been invoked repeatedly by extremist regimes. An example from Fascist Italy illustrates this point:

"Terror? Never," Mussolini insisted, demurely dismissing such intimidation as "simply . . . social hygiene, taking those individuals out of circulation like a doctor would take out a bacillus."[a]

For society to solve its problems, the bacterium represented by the group must be removed. Acceptance of this characterization makes domestic terrorism palatable to many extremist regimes. The following "cleansing" programs include examples of recent uses of this imagery.

Social Cleansing

Social cleansing refers to the elimination of undesirable social elements. These undesirable elements are considered to be blights on society and can include street children, prostitutes, drug addicts, criminals, homeless people, transvestites, and homosexuals. In Colombia, undesirable social elements are commonly referred to as *disposables*.

Social cleansing has occurred in a number of countries. The term was probably coined in Latin America, where social cleansing took on the attributes of vigilante state domestic terrorism in Brazil, Guatemala, Colombia, and elsewhere. Participants in cleansing campaigns have included members of the police and death squads. In societies where social cleansing has occurred, the "disposables" have been killed, beaten, and violently intimidated.

Ethnic Cleansing

The term *ethnic cleansing* was coined during the war in Bosnia in the former Yugoslavia. It refers to the expulsion of an ethno-nationalist group from a geographic region as a means to create an ethnically "pure" society. During the war in Bosnia, Serb soldiers and paramilitaries initiated a cycle of ethnic cleansing. They officially and systematically expelled, killed, raped, and otherwise intimidated Bosnian Muslims to create Serb-only districts. The most intensive campaigns of Serb-initiated ethnic cleansing in Bosnia occurred in 1992 and 1993. As the war progressed, Croats and Bosnians also engaged in ethnic cleansing, so that there were periods during the war in which all three groups "cleansed" areas populated by members of the other groups.

Since the war in Bosnia, the term has become widely used to describe present and past campaigns to systematically and violently remove ethno-nationalist groups from geographic regions.

Note

a. Bruce Hoffman, *Inside Terrorism* (New York, NY: Columbia University Press, 1998), p. 24, quoting Walter Laqueur, *The Age of Terrorism* (Boston, MA: Little, Brown, 1987), p. 66.

Mass Repression: Genocidal Domestic State Terrorism

The word *genocide* was first used by **Raphael Lemkin** in 1943 and first appeared in print in his influential book *Axis Rule in Occupied Europe*, published in 1944.[14] It is derived from the Greek word *genos*, meaning race or tribe, and the Latin-derived suffix *cide*, meaning killing. Genocide is first and generally defined as the elimination of a group as a matter of state policy or communal dissident violence by one group against another. The second refers to campaigns of substate, group-against-group terrorism.

Whether perpetrated at the state or communal level, genocide is considered an unacceptable social policy and an immoral application of force. It has been deemed a crime under international law since 1946, when the General Assembly of the United Nations adopted Resolution 96(I). In 1948, the General Assembly adopted the Convention on the Prevention and Punishment of the Crime of Genocide. Under Article 2 of the convention, genocide is formally defined as follows:

> Any of the following acts committed with intent to destroy, in whole or in part, a national, ethnic, racial, or religious group, such as:
>
> a. Killing members of the group;
>
> b. Causing serious bodily or mental harm to members of the group;
>
> c. Deliberately inflicting on the group conditions of life calculated to bring about its physical destruction in whole or in part;
>
> d. Imposing measures intended to prevent births within the group;
>
> e. Forcibly transferring children of the group to another group.[15]

Why do regimes resort to genocidal policies against their populace? What are the benefits to a regime of eliminating a particular group? From the perspective of the state, why do some groups deserve to be eliminated? One practical reason for terrorist regimes is that scapegoating a defined enemy is a useful strategy to rally the nation behind the ruling government. The goal is to enhance the authority and legitimacy of the regime by targeting internal enemies for genocidal violence.

States have available to them, and frequently marshal, enormous resources to use against an undesired group. Such resources can include the military, security services, civilian paramilitaries, legal systems, private industry, social institutions, and propaganda resources. When the

▶ A mother and child lie dead after a "cleansing" sweep by paramilitaries in Bosnia.

decision is made to eliminate or culturally destroy a group, state resources can be brought to bear with devastating efficiency. Chapter Perspective 5.3 discusses a case in point, Iraq's genocidal **Anfal campaign** against its Kurdish population in 1988.

Genocidal domestic state terrorism occurs, then, when the resources of a nation are mobilized to eliminate a targeted group. The group can be a cultural minority—such as a racial, religious, or ethnic population—or a designated segment of society—such as believers in a banned ideology or a socioeconomically unacceptable group. When ideological or socioeconomic groups are singled out, the resulting environment is one in which members of the same ethnic or religious group commit genocide against fellow members, a practice known as **auto-genocide** (self-genocide). This occurred during the reign of the Khmer Rouge in Cambodia, which Chapter Perspective 5.4 explores.

CHAPTER PERSPECTIVE 5.3

The Anfal Campaign: Genocidal State Terrorism in Iraq

During the regime of Saddam Hussein, political power in Iraq was highly centralized in the Ba'ath Party, which Hussein led. The Ba'ath Party, one faction of which governs Syria under the leadership of Bashar al-Assad, is secular, Arab, and nationalist. In Iraq, Ba'athist functionaries were personally loyal to Hussein and commanded key government institutions, the military, and the security services. Hussein and the Ba'ath Party legitimized state authority through force of arms. Dissent was severely repressed, and rebellion was dealt with mercilessly. Iraqi armed forces were unleashed to quell rebellions among the so-called Marsh Arabs in the country's southeastern region and among its Kurdish population in the north.

Iraq's Anfal campaign was an instance of genocidal state terrorism waged against the Iraqi Kurdish minority from February to September 1988.

Had history been kinder to the Kurds, they might have established their own sovereign nation of Kurdistan. Unfortunately, Kurdistan is a geographic region politically divided between Iraq, Iran, Turkey, and Syria. The Iraqi Kurds have historically sought political self-governance in their region. Some Iraqi Kurds seeking complete independence resorted to armed insurrection. Iraqi policy during its suppression campaigns against Kurdish rebellions was brutal and included the use of poison gas.

In 1987, Saddam Hussein's cousin Ali Hassan al-Majid was assigned the task of securing Iraqi governmental authority in Kurdistan. His carefully planned campaign was code-named al-Anfal, or the spoils, named for passages in the Quran that describe the Prophet Muhammed's revelations after his first great victory and advise the prophet to severely punish unbelievers when necessary. When the Anfal campaign was launched, it had eight phases, during which civilians were uprooted, many killed en masse. Males in particular were singled out for death. During the campaign, Iraq dropped chemical weapons, including mustard gas and nerve agents, on Kurdish villages.[a] One attack was described as follows:

> The planes dropped bombs. They did not produce a big noise. A yellowish cloud was created and there was a smell of rotten parsley or onions. There were no wounds. People would breathe the smoke, then fall down and blood would come from their mouths.[b]

Between 50,000 and 100,000 Kurds may have died.[c] After the campaign, that particular round of the Kurdish rebellion was quelled, and approximately 2.5 million Iraqi Kurds were forced into exile. It is a good case study of how regimes in which state power is centralized in a ruling body may use terrorism and other violent repression to maintain domestic authority.

As a postscript, Ali Hassan al-Majid, nicknamed Chemical Ali and the Butcher of Kurdistan for his actions in the Anfal campaign, was captured by U.S. troops in August 2003 and condemned to death by an Iraqi court in June 2007.

Notes

a. Walter Laqueur, *The Age of Terrorism* (Boston, MA: Little, Brown, 1987), 66, quoted in Bruce Hoffman, *Inside Terrorism* (New York, NY: Columbia University Press, 1998), 24.

b. Cited in Jessica Stern, *The Ultimate Terrorists* (Cambridge, MA: Harvard University Press, 1999), 107.

c. See Human Rights Watch, *Iraq's Crime of Genocide: The Anfal Campaign Against the Kurds* (New York: Human Rights Watch, 1994).

CHAPTER PERSPECTIVE 5.4

The Khmer Rouge: Genocidal State Terrorism in Cambodia

Colonial Cambodia was governed as part of French Indochina, which also included what are now the countries of Laos and Vietnam. In 1944, Vietnamese nationalists led by Ho Chi Minh rebelled against the French colonial regime, which had essentially collaborated with Japanese occupiers during World War II. Cambodian intellectuals and activists joined with the Vietnamese during their resistance against the French. One Cambodian activist was Pol Pot, who joined the underground Indochinese Communist Party in about 1946.

When the French withdrew after their defeat in 1954 at Dien Bien Phu in Vietnam,[a] Cambodia became a republican monarchy ruled by Prince Norodom Sihanouk.

Many of the Cambodians who participated in anti-French agitation during World War II were nationalist communists. Some of them gathered abroad after the war and established strong ideological bonds. Pol Pot lived and studied for four years in France, where he was an unremarkable student but met with other Indochinese activists and became a dedicated Marxist revolutionary. When he returned to Cambodia in 1953, he became a member of the People's Revolutionary Party of Kampuchea, which was Communist. In 1960, the Cambodian Communist Party was founded. Pol Pot became its leader in 1963 and soon fled with his followers into the jungle after Prince Sihanouk suppressed Communist Party activities.

It was in the jungle in the mid-1960s that the guerrilla movement known as the Khmer Rouge (Red Khmers, given that most Cambodians are ethnic Khmers), led by Pol Pot, took up arms. The Khmer Rouge was an extreme left-wing movement that sought to completely redesign and restructure society. In 1967, it staged an armed rebellion that was put down by Sihanouk's forces. In 1970, a civil war broke out after a right-wing coup—led

▶ The Killing Fields. Skulls are displayed of victims of Cambodia's genocidal Khmer Rouge regime. The Khmer Rouge waged a campaign of domestic terrorism that claimed the lives of at least one million Cambodians.

by Cambodian Prime Minister Lon Nol and Prince Sirik Matak—toppled the Sihanouk government. Prince Sihanouk eventually joined Pol Pot and the Khmer Rouge to fight against the new regime. Khmer Rouge forces swelled with new recruits when U.S. forces bombed and invaded Cambodia in 1970.[b] Despite massive U.S. assistance, the Lon Nol government suffered one defeat after another at the hands of the Khmer Rouge.

In January 1975, the Khmer Rouge seized the capital of Phnom Penh (now swollen by 2 million refugees), renamed the country Democratic Kampuchea, set the calendar to Year Zero and began a four-year reign of state domestic terror. Their first act was to depopulate Phnom Penh through mass evacuations of the inhabitants to the countryside. There, they toiled in the fields to build the Khmer Rouge's vision of an ideal communist society. The era of the Killing Fields had begun, when hundreds of thousands of Cambodians (possibly as many as 2 million) died in the countryside from executions, starvation, and arduous forced labor.

(Continued)

(Continued)

Notes

a. France lost 15,000 soldiers at Dien Bien Phu. For a good history of the battle, see Bernard Fall, *Hell in a Very Small Place: The Siege of Dien Bien Phu* (Philadelphia, PA: Lippincott, 1963).

b. See William Shawcross, *Sideshow: Kissinger, Nixon, and the Destruction of Cambodia* (New York, NY: Simon & Schuster, 1979).

Unlike vigilante and official state terrorism, the scale of violence during campaigns of state-sponsored genocidal terrorism can be virtually unlimited. In some cases, no check whatsoever is placed on what violence can be used against an adversary group, and the targeted group may suffer casualties in the many thousands or millions.

It is important to understand that the elimination of a group does not necessarily entail their physical extermination. The state's goal might also be to destroy a culture. This can be accomplished through forced population removals or prohibitions against practicing religious, linguistic, or other measures of cultural identification.

Most cases of state genocide are not examples of a precipitous policy under which the security services or paramilitaries are suddenly unleashed against a targeted group. More commonly, the methodology and purpose behind genocidal policies require a coordinated series of events, perhaps in phases over months or years. During these phases, cultural or other measures of identification can be suppressed in a number of ways—perhaps with the ultimate goal of physical extermination.

Table 5.3 identifies several examples of state-sponsored genocidal campaigns directed against domestic groups.

Table 5.3 State-Initiated Genocide

Genocidal state terrorism is directed against populations within countries that the state declares to be undesirable. When this occurs, governments and extremist regimes have designed policies of elimination that can include cultural destruction, mass resettlement, violent intimidation, or complete extermination. Historically, state-initiated genocide is not an uncommon policy selection.

As summarized in this table, state-initiated genocide has occurred in every region of the world.

Country	Activity Profile		
	Incident	Target Group	Outcome
Rwanda	Rwandan president Habyarimana assassinated	Tutsis and Hutu moderates	Genocidal violence; approximately 500,000 people killed by Rwandan army and Hutu militants
Cambodia	Victory on the battlefield by the Khmer Rouge; imposition of a new regime	City dwellers, educated people, upper class, Buddhists, fellow Khmer Rouge	The Killing Fields; up to 2 million deaths
Bosnia	The breakup of Yugoslavia and Serb resistance to the declarations of independence by Slovenia, Croatia, and Bosnia	Muslims living in territory claimed by Serbs	Ethnic cleansing assisted by Serbia, population removals, massacres, systematic rape, and cultural destruction
Germany	Racially motivated genocide by the Nazi regime	German Jews	The Holocaust; deaths of most of Germany's Jewish population
United States	Conquering the frontier and 19th-century frontier wars	Native Americans	Annihilation of some tribes; resettlement of others on reservations

Table 5.4 Vigilante Terrorism: The Case of the Paramilitaries

Paramilitaries are armed nongovernmental groups or gangs. Progovernment paramilitaries generally consider themselves to be the defenders of an established order that is under attack from a dangerously subversive counterorder. Some paramilitaries are well armed and receive direct official support from government personnel. Others are semi-independent vigilante groups.

Reactionary right-wing paramilitaries in Latin America have been implicated in numerous atrocities, including massacres and assassinations. This table summarizes several of these groups.

Paramilitary Group	Benefactor	Target
United Self-Defense Groups (AUC)	Colombian security services, Colombian landholders	Marxist FARC rebels and suspected supporters
Civil Patrols (CAP)	Guatemalan security services, Guatemalan landholders	Marxist rebels and suspected supporters
Chiapas paramilitaries	Possibly Mexican security force members; Mexican landholders	Zapatistas and suspected supporters
Argentine Anti-Communist Alliance (Triple-A)	Argentine security services	Leftists

Table 5.4 identifies several paramilitaries that have operated in Latin America with the support of government security services.

TERRORISM AS FOREIGN POLICY

During the 20th century, military forces were used by states to pursue policies of aggression, conquest, and cultural or ethnic extermination. In the latter half of the century, especially in the latter quarter, many governments used terrorism as an instrument of foreign policy. As a policy option, state-sponsored terrorism is a logical option because states cannot always deploy conventional armed forces to achieve strategic objectives. As a practical matter for many governments, it is often not logistically, politically, or militarily feasible to confront an adversary directly. For example, few states can hope to be victorious in a conventional military confrontation with the United States—as Saddam Hussein's well-entrenched Iraqi army learned both in Kuwait during the Gulf War of 1990–1991 and in the U.S.-led invasion of March and April 2003. Terrorism thus becomes a relatively acceptable alternative for states pursuing an aggressive foreign policy against a superior adversary.

Governments use terrorism and other confrontational propaganda because, from their point of view, it is an efficient way to achieve strategic objectives. As a practical matter for aggressive regimes, state terrorism in the international domain is advantageous in several respects:

State terrorism is inexpensive. The costs of patronage and assistance for terrorist movements are relatively low. Even poor nations can strike and injure a prosperous adversary in a single spectacular incident.

State terrorism has limited consequences. State assisters that are clever can distance themselves from culpability for a terrorist incident. They can cover their involvement, disclaim responsibility, and thus escape possible reprisals or other penalties.

State terrorism can be successful. Weaker states can raise the stakes beyond what a stronger adversary is willing to bear. Aggressor states that wish to remain anonymous can likewise successfully destabilize an adversary in a proxy movement. They can do so with one or more spectacular incidents or by assisting in a campaign of terror.

To simplify matters for our discussion, we will discuss the following four policy frameworks. They signify the varied qualities of state-sponsored terrorism in the international domain:

1. Moral support: politically sympathetic sponsorship	3. Selective participation: episode-specific sponsorship
2. Technical support: logistically supportive sponsorship	4. Active participation: joint operations supportive sponsorship

Table 5.5 summarizes these policy frameworks by placing them within the context of state patronage and state assistance for terrorism.

Table 5.5 State-Sponsored Terrorism: The Foreign Policy Domain

State participation in terrorism in the international domain can involve several types of backing for championed causes and groups. This backing can range in quality from relatively passive political sympathy to aggressive joint operations.

This table distinguishes state patronage and assistance in four policy frameworks. Each framework—a type of state backing—is summarized within the state sponsorship model that distinguishes between patronage and assistance.

Policy Framework (Type of State Backing)	Type of Sponsorship	
	Patronage	Assistance
Politically sympathetic (moral support)	Overt political support and encouragement for a championed group's motives or tactics	Implicit political support and encouragement for a championed group's motives or tactics
	Case: Official Arab governments' political support for the objectives of the PLO and HAMAS	Case: Iran's ideological connection with Lebanon's Hezbollah and other armed Shi'a movements
Logistically supportive (technical support)	Direct state support, such as sanctuary, for a championed cause to the group	The provision of state assistance to a group, such as providing matériel (military hardware)
	Case: Jordanian facilitation of PLO fedayeen bases inside Jordan for raids on Israel prior to the Black September incidents in 1970	Case: Syria's provision of sanctuary, resupply, and other facilities for extremist movements prior to the 2011 Arab Spring uprisings
Episode-specific (selective participation)	Direct involvement by government personnel for a specific incident or campaign	The provision of state assistance to a group or movement for a specific goal
	Case: Yugoslavia's and Serbia's deployment of Army units to Bosnia and Kosovo during the 1991–2001 Yugoslav civil war	Case: Iran's attempted delivery of 50 tons of munitions to the PLO in January 2002
Joint operations (active participation)	Operations carried out by government personnel jointly with its proxy	Indirect state support for a proxy using allied personnel
	Case: The American–South Vietnamese Phoenix Program during the U.S. war in Vietnam	Case: Soviet deployment of Cuban troops to Ethiopia and Angola during the 1970s and 1980s

Moral Support: Politically Sympathetic Sponsorship

Politically sympathetic sponsorship occurs when a government openly embraces the main beliefs and principles of a cause. This embrace can range in scope from political agreement with a movement's motives, though not its tactics, to complete support for both. Such support may be delivered either overtly or covertly. Although politically sympathetic governments act as ideological role models for their championed groups, such support is often a way for a state to pursue its national agenda.

Iran's support for several violent movements in the Middle East is an example of an unambiguous policy of mentorship for groups known to have engaged in acts of terrorism. Iran consistently provided politically sympathetic and logistically supportive sponsorship for several movements, including Lebanon's Hezbollah, **Palestine Islamic Jihad (PIJ)**, and HAMAS. All of these organizations adopted religious revolutionary ideologies—including strong anti-Israel goals—which created a sense of revolutionary common cause among religious hard-liners in Iran.

Technical Support: Logistically Supportive Sponsorship

Logistically supportive sponsorship occurs when a government provides aid and comfort to a championed cause. This can include directly or indirectly facilitating training, arms resupply, safe houses, or other sanctuary for the movement. These options are relatively passive types of support that allow state sponsors of terrorism to promote an aggressive foreign policy agenda but deny their involvement in terrorist incidents.

An excellent case study is the foreign policy Syria adopted during the rule of Hafez al-Assad. During that time, from February 1971 to June 2000, Syria fought two wars against Israel, strongly backed the Palestinian cause, occupied the Beka'a Valley in Lebanon, and supported the Lebanese militias Amal and Hezbollah. Assad's regime could certainly be aggressive in the international domain, but despite this activism, Syria was rarely linked directly to terrorist incidents. "There is no evidence that either Syria or Syrian government officials have been directly involved in the planning or execution of international terrorist attacks since 1986."[16]

Selective Participation: Episode-Specific Sponsorship

Episode-specific sponsorship refers to government support for a single incident or series of incidents. For this type of operation, the government will provide as much patronage or assistance as is needed. Sometimes members of the proxy will carry out the incident, and at other times agents of the state sponsor will.

One example of episode-specific support was the bombing of **Pan Am Flight 103**, which exploded over Lockerbie, Scotland, on December 21, 1988. Two hundred seventy people were killed, all 259 passengers and crew and 11 persons on the ground. In November 1991, the United States and Great Britain named two Libyan nationals as the masterminds of the bombing. The men—**Abdel Basset al-Megrahi** and **Lamen Khalifa Fhima**—were alleged to be agents of Libya's **Jamahiriya Security Organization (JSO)**. This was a significant allegation because the JSO was repeatedly implicated in numerous acts of terrorism, including killing political rivals abroad, laying mines in the Red Sea, attacking Western interests in Europe, and providing logistical support and training facilities for terrorists from around the world. Libyan leader **Muammar el-Qaddafi** denied any involvement of the Libyan government or its citizens. Both men were prosecuted in Scotland for the bombing; Megrahi was convicted and sentenced to life imprisonment, and Fhima was acquitted. In August 2009, a Scottish judge released Megrahi and returned him to Libya, citing humanitarian reasons because Megrahi was reportedly terminally ill with prostate cancer. He died in May 2012 in Tripoli, Libya.

Active Participation: Joint Operations Supportive Sponsorship

Joint operations supportive sponsorship occurs when government personnel carry out campaigns in cooperation with a championed proxy. Close collaboration is typical, with the sponsor providing primary operational support for the campaign. Joint operations are often undertaken during a large-scale and ongoing conflict.

An example is the **Phoenix Program**, a campaign conducted during the Vietnam War to disrupt and eliminate the administrative effectiveness of the Viet Cong, the Communist guerrilla movement recruited from among southern Vietnamese. It was a three-year program that focused on the infrastructure of the Viet Cong. Both American and allied South Vietnamese squads were to wage the campaign by pooling intelligence information and making lists of persons to be targeted. The targets were intended to be hard-core Communist agents and administrators, and they were supposed to be arrested rather than assassinated.

In practice, although the Communists were significantly disrupted, many innocent Vietnamese were swept up in the campaign. Also, "despite the fact that the law provided only for the arrest and detention of the suspects, one-third of the 'neutralized agents' were reported dead."[17] Corruption was rampant among South Vietnamese officials.

Thus, terrorism and sponsorship for subversive movements are methods of statecraft that many types of governments have adopted, from stable democracies to aggressive and revolutionary regimes. It is certainly true that democracies are less likely to engage in this behavior than aggressively authoritarian states. However, democracies have been known to resort to terrorist methods when operating in certain security or political environments.

Chapter Perspective 5.5 discusses the officially defined threat inherent in the authoritarian government of Saddam Hussein that precipitated the U.S.-led invasion of Iraq in 2003.

CHAPTER PERSPECTIVE 5.5

Calculation or Miscalculation? The Threat From Weapons of Mass Destruction and the Iraq Case

One of the most disturbing scenarios involving state-sponsored terrorism is the delivery of weapons of mass destruction (WMDs) to motivated terrorists by an aggressive authoritarian regime. This scenario was the underlying rationale given for the March 2003 invasion of Iraq by the United States and several allies.

In January 2002, U.S. president George W. Bush identified Iraq, Iran, and North Korea as the "axis of evil" and promised that the United States "will not permit the world's most dangerous regimes to threaten us with the world's most destructive weapons." In June 2002, President Bush announced during a speech at the U.S. Military Academy at West Point that the United States would engage in preemptive warfare if necessary.

Citing Iraq's known possession of weapons of mass destruction in the recent past and its alleged ties to international terrorist networks, President Bush informed the United Nations in September 2002 that the United States would unilaterally move against Iraq if the UN did not certify that Iraq no longer possessed WMDs. Congress authorized an attack on Iraq in October 2002. UN weapons inspectors returned to Iraq in November 2002. After a three-month military buildup, Iraq was attacked on March 20, 2003, and Baghdad fell to U.S. troops on April 9, 2003.

The Bush administration had repeatedly argued that Iraq still possessed a significant arsenal of WMDs at the time of the invasion, that Hussein's regime had close ties to terrorist groups, and that a preemptive war was necessary to prevent the delivery of these weapons to Al Qaeda or another network. Although many experts discounted links between Hussein's regime and religious terrorists, it was widely expected that WMDs would be found. Iraq was known to have used chemical weapons against Iranian troops during the Iran–Iraq War of 1980 to 1988 and against Iraqi Kurds during the Anfal campaign of 1987 (discussed in Chapter Perspective 5.3).

In actuality, UN inspectors identified no WMDs prior to the 2003 invasion, nor were WMDs found by U.S. officials during the occupation of Iraq. Also, little evidence was uncovered to substantiate allegations of strong ties between Hussein's Iraq and Al Qaeda or similar networks. The search for WMDs ended in December 2004, and an inspection report submitted to Congress by U.S. weapons hunter Charles A. Duelfer essentially "contradicted nearly every prewar assertion about Iraq made by Bush administration officials."[a]

Policy makers and experts bear two fundamental questions for critical analysis and debate:

- Did the reasons given for the invasion reflect a plausible threat scenario?

- Was the invasion a well-crafted policy option centered on credible political, military, and intelligence calculations?

Note

a. Dafna Linzer, "Search for Banned Arms in Iraq Ended Last Month," *Washington Post*, January 12, 2005.

DISCUSSION BOX

AUTHORITARIANISM AND DEMOCRACY

This chapter's Discussion Box is intended to stimulate critical debate about the application of authoritarian methods by democratic governments and the justifications used by these governments for such methods.

Democracies are constrained by strong constitutions from summarily violating the rights of their citizens. Most democracies have due process requirements in place when security services wish to engage in surveillance, search premises, seize evidence, or detain suspects. However, when confronted by serious security challenges, democracies have resorted to authoritarian security measures. Germany, Italy, France, the United Kingdom, and the United States have all adopted aggressive policies to suppress perceived threats to national security.

For example, in the United States, periodic anti-Communist "**Red Scares**" occurred when national leaders reacted to the perceived threat of Communist subversion. Government officials reacted by adopting authoritarian measures to end the perceived threats. The first Red Scare occurred after the founding of the Communist Party–USA in 1919, and a series of letter bombs were intercepted. President Woodrow Wilson allowed Attorney General **A. Mitchell Palmer** to conduct a series of raids—the so-called **Palmer Raids**—against Communist and other leftist radical groups. Offices of these groups were shut down, leaders were arrested and put on trial, and hundreds were deported.

A second Red Scare occurred in the 1930s. This Scare resulted in the creation of the **House Un-American Activities Committee** and the passage of the Smith Act in 1940, which made advocacy of the violent overthrow of the government a federal crime. In the late 1940s, Communists were prosecuted, and high-profile investigations were made of people such as Alger Hiss.

A third Red Scare occurred in the 1950s when **Senator Joseph McCarthy** of Wisconsin held a series of hearings to expose Communist infiltration in government, industry, and Hollywood. Hundreds of careers were ruined, and many people were "**blacklisted**," meaning that they were barred from obtaining employment.

In Northern Ireland, the British government has periodically passed legislation to combat terrorism by the IRA. These laws granted British forces authoritarian powers in Northern Ireland. One such law was the 1973 Northern Ireland Emergency Provisions Act, which provided the military with sweeping powers to temporarily arrest and detain people and to search homes in Northern Ireland without warrants. Under the Act, the army detained hundreds of people and searched more than 250,000 homes. This sweep was actually fairly successful in that thousands of weapons were found and seized.

1. Are authoritarian methods morally compatible with democratic principles and institutions?

2. Under what circumstances are authoritarian policies justifiable and necessary, even in democracies with strong constitutional traditions?

3. The postwar Red Scare investigations in the United States have been labeled by many as "witch hunts." Were these investigations nevertheless justifiable, considering the external threat from the Soviet Union?

4. The British security services detained hundreds of innocent people and searched the homes of many thousands of non-IRA members. Considering the threat from the IRA, were these inconveniences nevertheless justifiable?

5. Assume for a moment that some security environments justify the use of authoritarian measures by democracies. What kind of "watchdog" checks and balances are needed to ensure that democracies do not move toward permanent authoritarianism?

CHAPTER SUMMARY

This chapter introduced readers to the terror from above that characterizes state-sponsored terrorism and outlined the nature of state terrorism. The purpose of this discussion was to identify and define several state terrorist environments, to differentiate state terrorism in the foreign and domestic policy domains, and to provide cases in point for these concepts.

The state terrorism paradigm identified several approaches experts use to define and describe state terrorism. Included in this discussion was a comparison of the underlying characteristics of the state patronage and state assistance models of terrorism. The patronage model is characterized by situations in which regimes act as active sponsors of, and direct participants in, terrorism. Under the assistance model, regimes tacitly participate in violent extremist behavior and indirectly sponsor terrorism.

In the domestic policy domain, several models of state domestic authority and legitimacy were identified and summarized, and their sources of authority and centers of power contrasted. The models were democracy, authoritarianism, totalitarianism, and crazy states. Because the methodologies of state domestic terrorism differ from case to case, several models provided a useful approach to understanding the characteristics of particular terrorist environments. These models were vigilante, overt official, covert official, and genocidal state domestic terrorism.

The discussion of state terrorism as foreign policy applied a model that categorized terrorism in the foreign domain as politically sympathetic, logistically supportive, episode specific, or joint operations. Each category described different aspects in the scale of support and directness of involvement by state sponsors. Several examples clarified the behavioral distinctions across categories.

KEY TERMS AND CONCEPTS

The following topics were discussed in this chapter and can be found in the Glossary:

African National Congress (ANC) 88

al-Megrahi, Abdel Basset 97

Anfal campaign 92

Apartheid 88

Askaris 88

Assassination 83

Auto-genocide 92

Axis of evil 98

Ba'ath Party 92

Blacklisted 99

Boland Amendment 86

WEB EXERCISE

Using this chapter's recommended websites listed on the student study site at **edge.sagepub.com/martiness5e**, conduct an online investigation of state terrorism.

1. Are there certain governmental or institutional profiles that distinguish repressive regimes from nonrepressive regimes?

2. Read the mission statements of the monitoring organizations. Do they reflect objective and professionally credible approaches for monitoring the behavior of states?

3. In your opinion, how effective are these organizations?

For an online search of state terrorism, readers should enter the following keywords in their Web browser's search engine:

"State terrorism"

"Terrorist states"

RECOMMENDED READINGS

The following publications provide discussions on state-sponsored terrorism.

Bullock, A. (1958). *Hitler: A study in tyranny*. New York, NY: Harper.

Byman, D. (2005). *Deadly connections: States that sponsor terrorism*. New York, NY: Cambridge University Press.

Dror, Y. (1980). *Crazy states: A counterconventional strategic problem*. New York, NY: Kraus, Milwood.

Goren, R., & Becker, J. (Eds.). (1984). *The Soviet Union and terrorism*. London, UK: Allen & Unwin.

Mann, M. (2005). *The dark side of democracy: Explaining ethnic cleansing*. New York, NY: Cambridge University Press.

McSherry, J. P. (2005). *Predatory states: Operation Condor and covert war in Latin America*. Lanham, MD: Rowman & Littlefield.

O'Sullivan, M. L. (2003). *Shrewd sanctions: Statecraft and state sponsors of terrorism.* Washington, DC: Brookings Institution.

Stohl, M., & Lopez, G. (Eds.). (1984). *The state as terrorist: The dynamics of governmental violence and repression.* Westport, CT: Greenwood.

Tucker, R. C. (1990). *Stalin in power: The revolution from above, 1928–1941.* New York, NY: Norton.

Wright, T. C. (2007). *State terrorism in Latin America: Chile, Argentina, and international human rights.* Lanham, MD: Rowman & Littlefield.

Want a better grade?

Get the tools you need to sharpen your study skills. Access practice quizzes, eFlashcards, video, and multimedia at **edge.sagepub.com/martiness5e**.

CHAPTER SIX

TERRORISM BY DISSIDENTS

This chapter discusses the characteristics of terrorism from below—**dissident terrorism**—committed by nonstate movements, groups, and so-called lone-wolf extremists against governments, ethno-nationalist groups, religious groups, and other perceived enemies. Dissident terrorism is a distinct terrorist typology (among other typologies) that encompasses subnational political violence, and it is therefore important for readers to engage in a focused examination of the nuances of dissident political violence. Readers will probe the different types of dissident terrorism and develop an understanding of the qualities that differentiate each dissident terrorist environment.

It is important to understand that political violence by nonstate actors has long been viewed as a necessary evil by those sympathetic to their cause. Revolutionaries, terrorists, and assassins have historically justified their deeds as indispensable tactics to defend a higher cause. The methods can range in intensity from large-scale wars of national liberation—such as the many anticolonial wars of the 20th century—to individual assassins who strike down enemies of their cause. In the United States, for example, when Confederate sympathizer **John Wilkes Booth** assassinated President Abraham Lincoln during a play at Ford's Theater in Washington, D.C., he leaped from Lincoln's balcony to the stage after shouting "Sic semper tyrannis!" ("Thus always to tyrants!").

The U.S. Department of State publishes an annual report that identifies and describes an official list of foreign terrorist organizations. Table 6.1 reproduces a typical list of these organizations.

Why do people take up arms against governments and social systems? What weapons are available to the weak when they decide to confront the strong? Do the ends of antistate dissident rebels justify their chosen means? State repression and exploitation are frequently cited as grievances to explain why nonstate actors resort to political violence. Such grievances are often ignored by state officials, who refuse to act until they are forced to do so.

An example illustrating this grievance-related concept is the rebellion in Mexico waged by rebels calling themselves the **Zapatista National Liberation Front** (Ejército Zapatista de Liberacion Nacional). The Zapatistas were leftists who championed the cause of Indians native to Mexico's Chiapas state, where starvation and disease were endemic

Learning Objectives

This chapter will enable readers to do the following:

1. Understand and explain the dissident terrorism paradigm.

2. Interpret some incidents of dissident-initiated political violence as antistate terrorism.

3. Interpret some incidents of dissident-initiated political violence as communal terrorism.

4. Discuss central operational attributes of the New Terrorism.

Table 6.1 Foreign Terrorist Organizations, 2016

Foreign Terrorist Organization (FTO) designations are an important element of our counterterrorism efforts. Designations of foreign terrorist groups expose and isolate these organizations, deny them access to the U.S. financial system, and create significant criminal and immigration consequences for their members and supporters. Moreover, designations can assist or complement the law enforcement actions of other U.S. agencies and other governments.

In 2016, the Department of State designated the following terrorist groups as FTOs: ISIS-Khorasan, ISIL-Libya, and al-Qa'ida in the Indian Subcontinent. The Department of State also amended the FTO designations of al-Nusrah Front on November 10 to include the alias Jabhat Fath al-Sham and of Lashkar e-Tayyiba on December 28 to include the alias Al-Muhammadia Students.

Legal Criteria for Designation under Section 219 of the INA as amended:

1. It must be a *foreign organization*.
2. The organization must *engage in terrorist activity*, as defined in section 212 (a)(3)(B) of the INA (8 U.S.C. § 1182(a)(3) (B)), or *terrorism*, as defined in section 140(d)(2) of the Foreign Relations Authorization Act, Fiscal Years 1988 and 1989 (22 U.S.C. § 2656f(d)(2)), *or retain the capability and intent to engage in terrorist activity or terrorism*.
3. The organization's terrorist activity or terrorism must threaten the security of U.S. nationals or the national security (national defense, foreign relations, or the economic interests) of the United States.

U.S. Government Designated Foreign Terrorist Organizations

Abdallah Azzam Brigades (AAB)
Abu Nidal Organization (ANO)
Abu Sayyaf Group (ASG)
Al-Aqsa Martyrs Brigade (AAMB)
Ansar al-Dine (AAD)
Ansar al-Islam (AAI)
Ansar al-Shari'a in Benghazi (AAS-B)
Ansar al-Shari'a in Darnah (AAS-D)
Ansar al-Shari'a in Tunisia (AAS-T)
Army of Islam (AOI)
Asbat al-Ansar (AAA)
Aum Shinrikyo (AUM)
Basque Fatherland and Liberty (ETA)
Boko Haram (BH)
Communist Party of Philippines/New People's Army (CPP/NPA)
Continuity Irish Republican Army (CIRA)
Gama'a al-Islamiyya (IG)
HAMAS
Haqqani Network (HQN)
Harakat ul-Jihad-i-Islami (HUJI)
Harakat ul-Jihad-i-Islami/Bangladesh (HUJI-B)
Harakat ul-Mujahideen (HUM)
Hizballah
Indian Mujahedeen (IM)
Islamic Jihad Union (IJU)
Islamic Movement of Uzbekistan (IMU)
Islamic State of Iraq and Syria (ISIS)
Islamic State's Khorasan Province (ISIS-K)
ISIL-Libya
ISIL Sinai Province (ISIL-SP)
Jama'atu Ansarul Muslimina Fi Biladis-Sudan (Ansaru)

Jemaah Ansharut Tauhid (JAT)
Jemaah Islamiya (JI)
Jundallah Kahane Chai
Kata'ib Hizballah (KH)
Kurdistan Workers' Party (PKK)
Lashkar e-Tayyiba (LeT)
Lashkar i Jhangvi (LJ)
Liberation Tigers of Tamil Eelam (LTTE)
Mujahidin Shura Council in the Environs of Jerusalem (MSC)
Al-Mulathamun Battalion (AMB)
National Liberation Army (ELN)
Al-Nusrah Front (ANF)
Palestine Islamic Jihad (PIJ)
Palestine Liberation Front–Abu Abbas Faction (PLF)
Popular Front for the Liberation of Palestine (PFLP)
Popular Front for the Liberation of Palestine-General Command (PFLP-GC)
Al-Qa'ida (AQ)
Al-Qa'ida in the Arabian Peninsula (AQAP)
Al-Qa'ida in the Indian Subcontinent (AQIS)
Al-Qa'ida in the Islamic Maghreb (AQIM)
Real IRA (RIRA)
Revolutionary Armed Forces of Colombia (FARC)
Revolutionary People's Liberation Party/Front (DHKP/C)
Revolutionary Struggle (RS)
Al-Shabaab (AS)
Shining Path (SL)
Tehrik-e Taliban Pakistan (TTP)
Jaish-e-Mohammed (JeM)
Jaysh Rijal Al-Tariq Al-Naqshabandi (JRTN)

Source: U.S. Department of State, Bureau of Counterterrorism and Countering Violent Extremism, *Country Reports on Terrorism 2016* (Washington, DC: U.S. Department of State, 2017).

and the government had long supported large landowners in exploiting Indian peasants. In January 1994, the Zapatistas began attacking Mexican army troops and police stations in Chiapas. During this initial campaign, approximately 145 people were killed before the rebels retreated into the jungle to continue the conflict. A low-intensity guerrilla insurgency continued, with the government gradually agreeing to address the grievances of all of Mexico's 10 million Indians. By 2001, the Zapatistas had evolved into an aboveground political movement lobbying for the civil rights of Mexico's Indians and peasants. A key reason for the Zapatistas' success was their ability to adopt a Robin Hood image for their movement and thereby garner support from many Mexicans.

The discussion in this chapter will review the following:

▶ The IRA at work. A photograph of members of the Provisional Irish Republican Army as they conduct training exercises and a demonstration.

- Perspectives on Violent Dissent
- The Practice of Dissident Terrorism
- Terrorist Targets and Weapons
- Dissidents and the New Terrorism

PERSPECTIVES ON VIOLENT DISSENT

Policy experts and academics have designed a number of models that define dissident terrorism. For example, one model places dissident terrorism into a larger framework of "three generalized categories of political action":[1]

- revolutionary terrorism—the threat or use of political violence aimed at effecting complete revolutionary change
- subrevolutionary terrorism—the threat or use of political violence aimed at effecting various changes in a particular political system (but not aimed at abolishing it)
- establishment terrorism—the threat or use of political violence by an established political system against internal or external opposition[2]

Other models develop specific types of dissident terrorism, such as single-issue, separatist, and social revolutionary.[3] Likewise, insurgent terrorism has been defined as violence "directed by private groups against public authorities [that] aims at bringing about radical political change."[4]

To simplify our analysis, the discussion here presents a dissident terrorist model adapted from one by Peter Sederberg.[5] It defines and differentiates broad categories of dissident terrorism useful for critically analyzing terrorist motives and behaviors. Although each category— **revolutionary**, **nihilist**, and **nationalist dissident terrorism**—is specifically defined for our discussion, one should keep in mind that the same terms are applied by experts in many different contexts.

Revolutionary Dissident Terrorism: A Clear World Vision

The goals of revolutionary dissidents are to destroy an existing order through armed conflict and to build a relatively well-designed new society. This vision can be the result of nationalist aspirations, religious principles, ideological dogma, or some other rationale.

Keystone/Hulton Archive/Getty Images

▶ Ulrike Meinhof and Gudrun Ensslin, prominent members of West Germany's Red Army Faction, also known as the Baader-Meinhof Gang. Both committed suicide in prison.

Revolutionaries view the existing order as regressive, corrupt, and oppressive; their envisioned new order will be progressive, honest, and just. Revolutionary dissident terrorists are not necessarily trying to create a separate national identity; they are activists seeking to build a new society on the rubble of an existing one. Many Marxist revolutionaries, for example, have a general vision of a Communist Party–led egalitarian classless society with centralized economic planning. Many Islamic revolutionaries also have a grand vision—that of a spiritually pure culture justly based on the application of *shari'a*, or God's law. An example of the latter is the Hezbollah (Party of God) organization in Lebanon, which is actively agitating for its own vision of a spiritually pure Lebanon; to that end, Hezbollah has its own political movement, armed militia, and social services. Various factions of the Muslim Brotherhood also advocate a rather clear program.

As a practical matter, revolutionary dissidents are often outnumbered and outgunned by the established order. Their only hope for victory is to wage an unconventional war to destabilize the central authority. Terrorism thus becomes a pragmatic tactical option to disrupt government administration and symbolically demonstrates the weakness of the existing regime.

Good case studies for terrorism as a legitimate tactic are found in the Marxist revolutionary movements in Latin America from the 1950s to the 1980s. For example, during the Cuban Revolution, which began in 1956, rebels operating in rural areas waged classic hit-and-run guerrilla warfare against the Batista government's security forces. Fidel Castro and Ernesto "Che" Guevara led these rural units. In urban areas, however, the rebels commonly carried out terrorist attacks because the rural model was impractical in urban-focused conflict. Urban terrorist tactics successfully disrupted government administration and thereby undermined public confidence in Batista's ability to govern. Marxist revolutionaries throughout Latin America used this urban-focused model repeatedly, usually unsuccessfully, so that urban terrorism became a widespread phenomenon in many countries during this period. Carlos Marighella, the Brazilian revolutionary and author of the *Mini-Manual of the Urban Guerrilla*, detailed the logic of urban terrorism in the Latin American context.[6]

Nihilist Dissident Terrorism: Revolution for the Sake of Revolution

Nihilism was a 19th-century Russian philosophical movement of young dissenters who believed that only scientific truth could end ignorance. Religion, nationalism, and traditional values (especially family values) were, they believed, at the root of ignorance. Nihilists had no vision for a future society, asserting only that the existing society was intolerable. Nihilism was, at its core, a completely negative and critical philosophy. Modern nihilist dissidents exhibit a similar disdain for the existing social order but, despite a vague goal of justice, offer no clear alternative for the aftermath of its destruction. The goal of modern nihilists is to destroy the existing order through armed conflict with little forethought to the configuration of the new society; victory is defined simply as the destruction of the old society.

Nihilist dissidents have never been able to lead broad-based revolutionary uprisings among the people or to mount sustained guerrilla campaigns against conventional security forces. Thus, the only armed alternative among hard-core nihilists has been to resort to terrorism. Examples of modern nihilist dissident terrorists include the leftist Red Brigade in Italy and the Weather Underground Organization (WUO) in the United States, each of which had only a vaguely Marxist model for postrevolutionary society. Another example is the Palestinian terrorist Abu Nidal, who had no postrevolution vision. Arguably, Osama bin Laden's Al Qaeda network fits the model because although Al Qaeda has a generalized goal of defending Islam and fomenting a pan-Islamic revival, it offers no specific model for how the postrevolution world will be shaped, and its long-term goals are not clearly defined.

Nationalist Dissident Terrorism: The Aspirations of a People

Nationalist dissidents champion the national aspirations of groups of people distinguished by their cultural, religious, ethnic, or racial heritage. The championed people generally live in an environment in which their interests are subordinate to the interests of another group or a national regime. The goal of nationalist dissidents is to mobilize a particular demographic group against another group or government. They are motivated by the desire for some degree of national autonomy, such as democratic political integration, regional self-governance, or national independence.

Nationalist sentiment has been commonplace—particularly during the 19th and 20th centuries—and can arise in many social and political environments. For example, the championed group may be a minority living among a majority group, such as the Basques of northern Spain. It may also be a majority national group living in a region politically dominated by the government of another ethnic group, such as Tibetans and the Chinese. The group may be a minority with a separate cultural and linguistic identity, such as the French Canadians in Quebec. Some national groups have a distinct cultural, ethnic, and regional identity that exists within the borders of several countries, such as the Kurds, whose Kurdistan is divided across Iran, Iraq, Turkey, and Syria.

Many nationalist dissidents have used terrorism to achieve their goals. This has often been a practical option because their opponents have overwhelming military and political superiority and would quickly prove victorious during a guerrilla or conventional conflict. Examples include Palestinian dissident organizations and the Provisional Irish Republican Army (Provos). In other contexts, the armed opposition must operate in urban areas, which always favors the dominant group or regime because of the impossibility of maneuver, the concentration of security forces, and sometimes the lack of mainstream support from the championed group. Examples include Islamist-inspired terrorists in Western countries and the **Basque Fatherland and Liberty (Euskadi Ta Azkatasuna, or ETA)** organization in the Basque region of northern Spain. These are logical operational policies because for nationalists, "the basic strategy is to raise the costs to the enemy occupiers until they withdraw."[7]

Chapter Perspective 6.1 explores a troubling practice found among many revolutionary, nihilist, and nationalist paramilitaries and rebel groups. This is the phenomenon of recruiting and training so-called child soldiers.

CHAPTER PERSPECTIVE 6.1

Child Soldiers

One disturbing—and common—trend among paramilitaries and other armed groups has been the conscription of children as fighters. Child soldiers are a serious humanitarian issue, with "children as young as six . . . being used in combat by government and rebel forces in civil wars throughout the world."[a]

"Thousands of children are serving as soldiers in armed conflicts around the world. These boys and girls, some as young as 8-years-old, serve in government forces and armed opposition groups. They may participate in suicide missions, and act as spies, messengers, or lookouts. Paramilitaries and rebel movements have

(Continued)

(Continued)

assigned child soldiers to heavy combat on the front lines. Some children are drugged prior to entering into combat and have been known to commit atrocities under orders. Girls may be forced into sexual slavery. Many are abducted or recruited by force, while others join out of desperation, believing that armed groups offer their best chance for survival."[b] Here are some examples:

- In India, "Maoist 'Naxalite' rebels in Chhattisgarh use children as soldiers. The Maoists induct children as young as six into children's associations and use children as young as 12 in armed squads that receive weapons training and may participate in armed encounters with government security forces."[c]

- In Sierra Leone during the 1990s and early 2000s, the Revolutionary United Front abducted thousands of children and organized those under the age of 15 into Small Boy Units and Small Girl Units.

- In Democratic Republic of Congo, "children serve in the government armed forces as well as various rebel forces. At the height of DRC's war, the UN estimated that more than 30,000 boys and girls were fighting with various parties to the conflict."[d]

- In Central African Republic, "hundreds of children, some as young as 12, serve with various rebel groups."[e]

- In Colombia, "thousands of children—both boys and girls—serve[d] in Colombia's irregular armed groups. The majority serve[d] in the FARC guerrillas, with smaller numbers

in the UC-ELN guerrillas. Children [were] also recruited into successor groups to paramilitaries."[f]

- In Afghanistan "insurgent groups, including the Taliban and other armed groups, use children as fighters, including in suicide attacks. The UN also reports recruitment of children by the Afghan National Police."[g]

- In Nigeria, Boko Haram kidnapped hundreds of boys and girls to use as fighters, "wives" for their fighters, and suicide bombers. The use of children, especially girls, "has become one of the defining, and alarming features of the conflict."[h]

Notes

a. Amnesty International, *Killings by Government* (London, UK: Amnesty International, 1983), Quoted in Peter Iadicola and Anson Shupe, *Violence, Inequality, and Human Freedom* (Dix Hills, NY: General Hall, 1998), 255.

b. Human Rights Watch, "Child Soldiers" (2014), http://www.hrw.org/node/105699.

c. Human Rights Watch, "Child Soldiers Worldwide" (2014), http://www.hrw.org/node/105699.

d. Ibid.

e. Ibid.

f. Ibid.

g. Ibid.

h. United Nations Children's Fund, "Beyond Chibok: Over 1.3 Million Children Uprooted by Boko Haram Violence" (New York, NY: UNICEF Regional Office for West and Central Africa, April 2016).

Revolutionaries, Nihilists, and Nationalists: Freedom Fighters?

Table 6.2 gives examples of how terrorists perceive themselves. Regardless of their ideology, methodology, or goals, there is unanimity in positive self-perception: Terrorists perceive themselves as members of an enlightened fighting elite. The names terrorist organizations adopt reflect this self-perception, but, as indicated in Table 6.2, organizational names often have nothing to do with the reality of the group's composition.

Table 6.2 Self-Perception or Self-Deception? Dissident Terrorists as Freedom Fighters

Dissident terrorists adopt organizational names that characterize themselves as righteous defenders of a group or principle. These monikers are always positive representations that project the "higher purpose" of the group. The following categories and examples illustrate the self-perception of armed dissident groups.

Liberation Fighters	Military Units	Defensive Movements	Retribution Organizations	Distinctive Alliances
Basque Fatherland and Liberty	Alex Boncayo Brigade	Islamic Resistance Movement	Revolutionary Justice Organization	Aum Shinrikyo ("Supreme Truth")
Liberation Tigers of Tamil Eelam	Irish Republican Army	Revolutionary People's Struggle	International Justice Group	Middle Core Faction
Palestine Islamic Jihad	Japanese Red Army	National Council of Resistance	Palestinian Revenge Organization	Al Qaeda ("The Base")
Revolutionary People's Liberation Party	New People's Army	Jewish Defense League	Black September	Orange Volunteers

THE PRACTICE OF DISSIDENT TERRORISM

Concept: Asymmetrical Warfare

The concept of **asymmetrical warfare** refers to the use of unconventional, unexpected, and nearly unpredictable methods of political violence. Terrorists intentionally strike at unanticipated targets and apply unique and idiosyncratic tactics. This way, they can seize the initiative and redefine the international security environment and overcome the traditional protections and deterrent policies that societies and the international community use.

The Appeal of Asymmetrical Conflict

Dissident terrorists are quantitatively and qualitatively weaker than conventional security forces. In today's intensive security environment, they simply cannot prevail or last indefinitely in an urban-based guerrilla campaign. Because of this, state-level rivals must resort to unconventional and subversive methods to confront U.S., Western, and other governmental interests. At the same time, they must also deliver maximum propaganda and symbolic blows against the seemingly overwhelming power of enemy states or societies. New Terrorism is thus characterized by a new doctrine that allows for the use of weapons of mass destruction, indiscriminate attacks, maximum casualties, technology-based terrorism, and other exotic and extreme methods.

In adopting asymmetrical methods, inherently weaker extremists essentially wage total war by engulfing an entire enemy interest in their conflict. They are trying to break the enemy's will to resist by whatever means are at their disposal.

Netwar: A New Organizational Theory

The New Terrorism incorporates maximum flexibility into its organizational and communications design. Semiautonomous cells either are prepositioned around the globe as sleepers (such as the 2004 Madrid terrorists) or travel to locations where an attack is to occur (such as the September 11 hijackers in the United States). They communicate using new cyber and digital technologies. An important concept in the new terrorist environment is the notion of **netwar**, which refers to dispersed groups of extremists who organize themselves and communicate using modern networking technologies. In this way they are able to coordinate their efforts in an "internetted" fashion without direct command and control. The new internetted movements have made a strategic decision to establish virtual linkages via the Internet and other technologies.

Resources for Funding and Financing Dissident Terrorism

Terrorists and their supporters have amassed sizable amounts of money from a variety of sources, including transnational crime, personal fortunes, extortion, and private charities and foundations.

Large portions of these assets were in the recent past deposited in anonymous bank accounts, thus allowing funds to be electronically transferred between banking institutions and other accounts internationally in mere minutes. During the months following the September 11, 2001, attacks, government agencies from a number of countries made a concerted effort to identify and trace the terrorists' bank accounts. Law enforcement and security agencies also began to closely scrutinize the activities of private charities and foundations in an attempt to determine whether they were "front groups" secretly funneling money to supporters of terrorist organizations. Since September 11, 2001, government agencies such as the U.S. Treasury Department have covertly tracked global bank data to monitor transfers of money and other banking activities.

Terrorists adapted quickly to the new focus on financial counterterrorist measures. Implementing a process that apparently began during the global crackdown after September 11, 2001, terrorists and their supporters began to transfer their assets out of international financial institutions, where they were vulnerable to seizure. Operatives removed assets from financial institutions and began investing in valuable commodities such as gold, diamonds, and other precious metals and gems.[8] From the perspective of counterterrorist officials, this tactic can potentially cripple the global effort to electronically monitor, track, and disrupt terrorist finances. From the perspective of terrorists and their supporters, the chief encumbrance of this adaptation is the fact that they could become literally burdened with transporting heavy suitcases filled with precious commodities. However, this is an acceptable encumbrance because it is very difficult for counterterrorist agents to identify and interdict couriers or to locate and raid repositories.

Another adaptation used by terrorists is through an ancient practice known as *hawala*. Hawala is a transnational system of brokers who know and trust each other. Persons wishing to transfer money approach hawala brokers and, for a fee, ask the broker to transfer money to another person. Using the name and location of the recipient, the initial broker will contact a broker in the recipient's country. The recipient of the money contacts the local hawala broker, who delivers the money. To prevent fraud, the sending broker gives the recipient broker a code number (such as the string of numbers on a $20 bill). The recipient (who receives the code from the sender) must give the broker this code number in order to pick up his or her funds. No records are kept of the transaction, thus ensuring anonymity. This is a useful system because it relies on an honor system to succeed, and money is never physically moved.

Antistate Dissident Terrorism

A good deal of terrorism from below is by definition antistate. It is directed against existing governments and political institutions and attempts to destabilize the existing order as a precondition to a new society. As discussed earlier, antistate dissidents can have a clear vision of the new society (revolutionary dissidents), a vague vision of the new society (nihilist dissidents), national aspirations (nationalist dissidents), or a profit motive (criminal dissidents). Regardless of which model fits a particular movement, the common goal is to defeat the state and its institutions.

Intensities of Conflict: Antistate Terrorist Environments

With few exceptions, **antistate terrorism** is directed against specific governments or interests and occurs either within the borders of a particular country or where those interests are found in other countries. Thus, antistate terrorist environments are defined by the idiosyncrasies of each country, each dissident movement, and each terrorist organization. The histories of every nation give rise to specific antistate environments that are unique to their societies. The following examples from North America and Europe illustrate this point.

In the United States, leftist terrorism predominated during the late 1960s through the late 1970s, at the height of the anti–Vietnam War and people's rights movements. Acts of political violence—such as bank robberies, bombings, and property destruction—took place when some black, white, and Puerto Rican radicals engaged in armed protest. This changed in the 1980s, when the leftist remnants either gave up the fight or were arrested. Around this time, right-wing terrorism began to predominate when some racial supremacists, religious extremists, and antigovernment members of the Patriot movement adopted strategies of violence.[9]

In the United Kingdom, the terrorist environment was shaped by the sectarian conflict in Northern Ireland, which was characterized by both antistate and communal violence from 1969 until the peace settlement in 1999. The nationalist Provisional IRA[10] was responsible for most acts of antistate political violence directed against British administration in Northern Ireland. During the same period, Protestant Loyalist terrorism tended to meet the criteria for communal terrorism rather than antistate terrorism because Loyalist paramilitaries targeted pro-IRA Catholics rather than symbols of governmental authority. The IRA responded in kind so that more than 3,500 people had been killed on both sides by the 1999 cease-fire.[11]

In West Germany, from the late 1960s through the mid-1980s, the leftist **Red Army Faction (RAF)** engaged in a large number of bank robberies, bombings, assassinations, and other acts of antistate violence aimed at destabilizing the West German government. The RAF also targeted the North Atlantic Treaty Organization (NATO) presence in West Germany, primarily focusing on U.S. military personnel. After the fall of the Communist Eastern Bloc in 1989 and the reunification of Germany, RAF-style leftist terrorism waned. Around this time, rightist neo-Nazi violence increased—much of it directed against non-German *Gastarbeiters*, or guest workers. The perpetrators of this violence were often young **skinheads** and other neofascist youths. Many of these rightist attacks occurred in the former East Germany.

In Italy, the leftist Red Brigade was responsible for thousands of terrorist incidents from the early 1970s through the mid-1980s. Originating in the student-based activism of the late 1960s and early 1970s, Red Brigade members were young urban terrorists whose campaign is best described as a nihilist attempt to undermine capitalism and democracy in Italy. By the late 1980s, Italian police had eliminated Red Brigade cells and imprisoned their hard-core members. During this period, Italian neofascists also engaged in terrorist violence, eventually outlasting the leftist campaign, and remained active into the 1990s.

In Spain, antistate terrorism has generally been nationalistic or leftist. Without question, the most prominent was the nationalist and vaguely Marxist ETA. ETA was founded in 1959 to promote Basque independence. The Basques are a culturally and linguistically distinct people who live in northern Spain and southwestern France. Although ETA adopted terrorism as a tactic in response to the Franco government's violent repression of Basque nationalism, "of the more than 600 deaths attributable to ETA between 1968 and 1991, 93 per cent occurred after [General Francisco] Franco's death."[12] ETA was rife with factional divisions—at least six factions and subfactions were formed—but their terrorist campaign continued, despite the considerable political rights the Spanish government granted them and the loss of popular support among the Basque people. A right-wing terrorist group, Spanish National Action (Accion Nacional Espanila), was formed as a reaction to ETA terrorism.

Sometimes antistate dissident movements, because of their history and political environment, take on elements of both antistate and communal conflict. In Israel, for example, the Palestinian nationalist movement is made up of numerous organizations and movements that have mostly operated under the umbrella of the Palestine Liberation Organization (PLO), founded by **Yasir Arafat** and others in 1964. From its inception, the PLO has sought to establish an independent Palestinian state. Because it claims the same territory as the state of Israel, the PLO and its affiliates have attacked targets inside Israel and abroad. Until recently, Palestinian armed resistance was characterized by a series of dramatic hit-and-run raids, hijackings, bombings, rocket attacks, and other acts of violence. Israeli and Jewish civilians were often targeted.

Since September 28, 2000, Palestinian resistance has taken on the characteristics of a broad-based uprising—and communal terrorism. On that date, Israeli general Ariel Sharon visited the Temple Mount in Jerusalem. The Temple Mount is sacred to both Muslims and Jews. After Sharon's visit, which Palestinians perceived as a deliberate provocation, enraged Palestinians began a second round of massive resistance, or *intifada*. The new dissident environment included violent demonstrations, street fighting, and suicide bombings. This violence was characterized by attacks against civilian targets. Thus, the Palestinian nationalist movement arguably entered a phase distinguished by the acceptance of communal dissident terrorism as a strategy.

The Logic of Narco-Terrorism

The term *narco-terrorism* was first used in 1983 by Peruvian president Belaunde Terry when Peruvian drug traffickers waged war against antidrug security forces. Although its original meaning referred to a theorized semimonolithic Marxist (hence, Soviet) control of the trade, narco-terrorism continues to be an important concept in the post–Cold War world. The U.S. Drug Enforcement Administration differentiates between narco-terrorism and drug-related violence, pointing out that the latter occurs visibly and every day in major urban areas around the world, whereas narco-terrorism is less visible and not as pervasive.

The logic of narco-terrorism is uncomplicated: Because of the frequent difficulty in obtaining direct state sponsorship, some indigenous terrorist and revolutionary groups have turned to drug trafficking and arms trading to raise money for their movements. Among traditional criminal enterprises, drug traffickers have been especially prone to engage in criminal dissident terrorism because their product must be grown, refined, packaged, and transported from production regions within the borders of sovereign nations. Thus, among transnational criminals, drug traffickers in particular must necessarily establish a political environment that is conducive to their illegal enterprise.

Communal Terrorism

Dissident terrorism is not always directed against a government or national symbols. It is also often directed against entire population groups—people who are perceived to be ethnonationalist, racial, religious, or ideological enemies. Because the scope of defined enemies is so broad, it is not unusual for this type of terrorism to be characterized by extreme repression and violence on a massive scale. Often deeply rooted in long cultural memories of conflict, **communal terrorism** sometimes descends into genocidal behavior because "while the rival combatants often lack the weapons of destruction available to the major powers, they often disregard any recognized rules of warfare, killing and maiming civilians through indiscriminate car bombings, grenade attacks, and mass shootings."[13]

Communal terrorism is essentially group-against-group terrorism, in which subpopulations of society wage internecine (i.e., mutually destructive) violence. As with other types of violence, it occurs in varying degrees of intensity and in many contexts. The scale of violence frequently surprises the world, for these conflicts "often do not command the headlines that rivet world attention on international wars and guerrilla insurgencies, but they frequently prove more vicious and intractable."[14]

There are many sources of communal violence, and it is useful to review a few broad categories and illustrative cases. These categories—ethno-nationalist, religious, and ideological—are explored in the following discussion.

Ethno-nationalist Communal Terrorism

Ethno-nationalist communal terrorism involves conflict between populations that have distinct histories, customs, ethnic traits, religious traditions, or other cultural idiosyncrasies. Numerous adjectives have been used to describe this type of dissident terrorism, including "separatist, irredentist, . . . nationalist, tribal, racial, indigenous, or minority."[15] It occurs when one group asserts itself against another, many times, to defend its cultural identity. This rationale is not uncommon and has been used in Bosnia, the Caucasus, Sri Lanka, Indonesia, and elsewhere. In these conflicts, all sides believed themselves vulnerable and use this perception to rationalize their violence.

The scale of ethno-nationalist communal violence can vary considerably from region to region, depending on many factors—such as unresolved historical animosities, levels of regional development, and recurrent nationalist aspirations. It can be waged across national borders (as in the Congo-Rwanda-Burundi region of East Africa), inside national borders (as in Afghanistan), within ethnically polarized provinces (as in the Nagorno-Karabakh territory of Azerbaijan), at the tribal level (as in Liberia), and even at the subtribal clan level (as in Somalia).

Religious Communal Terrorism

Sectarian violence refers to conflict between religious groups and is sometimes one element of discord in a broader conflict between ethno-nationalist groups. Many of the world's ethnic populations define their cultural identity partly through their religious beliefs so that violence committed by and against them has both ethnic and religious qualities. This link is common in regions where ethnic groups with dissimilar religious beliefs have long histories of conflict, conquest, and resistance. In Sri Lanka, for example, the civil war between the Hindu Tamils and the Buddhist Sinhalese was exceptionally violent, with massacres and indiscriminate killings a common practice. The war ended with the defeat of the Tamil Tigers in 2009.

The following examples of **religious communal terrorism** further illustrate the ethno-nationalist quality of some religious conflicts:

Yugoslavia. Some intra-ethnic internecine conflict occurs because of combined nationalist aspirations and regional religious beliefs. The breakup of Yugoslavia led to internecine fighting, the worst of which occurred in Bosnia from 1992 to 1995. During fighting between Orthodox Christian Serbs, Muslim Bosnians, and Roman Catholic Croats, ethnic cleansing—the forcible removal of rival groups from claimed territory—was practiced by all sides. Significantly, all three religious groups are ethnic Slavs.

Israel. Religion is used in Israel by both Jewish and Muslim militants to justify communal violence. This has been encouraged by members of radical organizations such as the late Rabbi Meir Kahane's **Kach (Kahane Chai)** (meaning "thus") movement, which has advocated the expulsion of all Arabs from biblical Jewish territories. Settlers generally rationalize their attacks as reprisals for Palestinian attacks and sometimes cite Jewish religious traditions as a basis for their actions.

Intractable religious sentiment exists on both sides of the conflict in Israel and Palestine, then, with Islamic extremists waging a holy war to expel Jews and Jewish settler extremists seeking to reclaim biblical lands and expel Arabs.

Northern Ireland. Communal dissident terrorism between Catholic nationalists (Republicans) and Protestant unionists (Loyalists) became a regular occurrence in Northern Ireland

▶ A soldier of the Ugandan rebel group the Lord's Resistance Army poses with his machine gun. The LRA engaged in one of Africa's longest-running conflicts.

during the unrest that began in 1969. Targets included civilian leaders, opposition sympathizers, and random victims. One study notes that from 1969 to 1989, of the 2,774 recorded deaths, 1,905 were civilians; of the civilian deaths, an estimated 440. were Catholic or Protestant terrorists.[16] Another study notes that between 1969 and 1993, 3,284 people died. During this period, Loyalist paramilitaries killed 871 people, Republican paramilitaries killed 829, and British forces killed 203.[17]

Sudan. In Sudan, long-term animosity exists between the mostly Arabized[18] Muslim north and mostly black Christian and animist (traditional religions) south. Civil war has been a feature of Sudanese political life since its independence in 1956, generally between progovernment Muslim groups and antigovernment Christian and animist groups. The war has been fought by conventional troops, guerrilla forces, undisciplined militias, and vigilantes. In addition, the Sudanese government began arming and encouraging Arabized militants in the Darfur region to attack black Muslims. Tens of thousands died in this conflict, which approached genocide in scale.

Lebanon. In Lebanon, bloody religious communal fighting killed more than 125,000 people during the 16-year Lebanese civil war that began in 1975. Militias were formed along religious affiliations so that Maronite Christians, Sunni Muslims, Shi'a Muslims, and Druze all contended violently for political power. Palestinian fighters, Syrian troops, and Iranian revolutionaries were also part of this environment, which led to the breakdown of central government authority.

Ideological Communal Terrorism

Ideological communal terrorism in the post–World War II era reflected the global rivalry between the United States and the Soviet Union. The capitalist democratic West competed with the authoritarian Communist East for influence in the postcolonial developing world and in countries ravaged by invading armies during the war. A common pattern was for civil wars to break out after European colonial powers or Axis armies[19] were driven out of a country. These civil wars were fought by indigenous armed factions drawn from among the formerly occupied population. In China, Yugoslavia, Malaysia, and elsewhere, Communist insurgents vied with traditional monarchists, nationalists, and democrats for power. Civilian casualties were high in all of these conflicts.

Examples of ideological communal conflict have occurred in the following countries and regions:[20]

Greece. The five-year civil war in Greece from 1944 to 1949 was a complicated and brutal affair that in the end took at least 50,000 to 65,000 lives. It involved fighting among conventional troops, guerrilla groups, gendarmerie (armed police), and armed bands. The Greek Communist Party, which had led a resistance group during World War II, fought against the Greek government in several phases after liberation in 1944. The Greek Communist Party eventually lost, in the only attempted Communist takeover in post–World War II Europe to be defeated by force of arms.

Angola. Former anti-Portuguese allies in Angola fought a long conflict after independence in 1975. The ruling Movement for the Liberation of Angola (MPLA) is a Marxist-Leninist movement whose ideology promotes a multicultural and nationalistic (rather than ethnic or regional) agenda. Its principal adversary is the National Union for the Total Independence of Angola (UNITA), mostly made up of the Ovimbundu tribal group. Because the MPLA leadership identified with the international ideological left, the Soviet Union and Cuba supported the MPLA, while the United States and South Africa supported UNITA. This is a rare example of conflict between a multicultural ideological movement and a regional ethnic movement.

Indonesia. The Indonesian Communist Party (PKI) was implicated in an October 1965 abortive coup attempt. The army rounded up PKI members and sympathizers, and many Indonesians took to the streets to purge the Communist presence. During a wave of anti-Communist communal violence, much of it done by gangs supported by the government, roughly 500,000 Communists, suspected Communists, and political opponents of the government were killed.

Ideology was used repeatedly in the 20th century to bind together nations or distinctive groups. It has become, in many conflicts, a means to discipline and motivate members of a movement. When applied to rationalize behavior in communal conflicts, the effect can be devastatingly brutal. Antistate and communal terrorist environments are very dynamic over time, and never static. Table 6.3 reports the top five perpetrator groups with the most attacks worldwide in 2015 and 2016.

Defeat Is Unthinkable: The Terrorists' Faith in Victory

Why do small groups of individuals violently confront seemingly invincible enemies? Why do they engage powerful foes by force of arms when their envisioned goal is often illogical or unattainable? For antistate dissidents, their armed struggle is never in vain. They believe not only that their cause is likely to end in victory but that victory is in fact inevitable. To outside observers, terrorists are almost certainly fighting a losing battle yet persist in their war.

Although antistate dissident terrorists avoid direct confrontation out of a pragmatic acceptance of their comparative weakness, they nevertheless believe in the ultimate victory of their cause. They have a utopian vision that not only justifies their means but also guarantees their idealized ends. Violent confrontation in the present—often horrific in scope—is acceptable

Table 6.3 Five Perpetrator Groups With the Most Attacks Worldwide, 2015 and 2016								
	Total Attacks		Total Deaths*		Total Injured*		Total Kidnapped/ Hostages	
	2016	2015	2016	2015	2016	2015	2016	2015
Islamic State of Iraq and Syria (ISIS)**	1,133	969	9,114	6,178	7,671	6,608	8,379	4,805
Taliban	848	1,104	3,615	4,535	3,572	4,758	1,498	975
Maoists/Communist Party of India-Maoist (CPI-Maoist)	336	347	174	177	141	156	171	707
Al-Shabaab	332	226	740	836	921	561	375	559
Houthi Extremists	267	292	374	978	568	1,704	137	387

Source: U.S. Department of State, Bureau of Counterterrorism and Countering Violent Extremism, *Country Reports on Terrorism 2016, Annex of Statistical Information* (Washington, DC: U.S. Department of State, 2017).

* Includes perpetrators.

** Excludes attacks attributed to branches of ISIS or ISIS-inspired individuals.

because of the promised good at the end of the struggle. For example, religious antistate dissidents believe that God will ensure them final victory.

Nonreligious antistate dissidents also hold an enduring faith in final victory. Some have adopted a strategy similar to the urban terrorist (or urban guerrilla) model that Carlos Marighella developed. He maintained that rebels should organize themselves in small cells in major urban areas. He argued that terrorism, when correctly applied against the government, will create sympathy among the population, which in turn forces the government to become more repressive, thus creating an environment conducive to a mass uprising.[21] This model has failed repeatedly because the people tend not to rise up, and repressive states usually crush the opposition. Nonetheless, it exemplifies the faith antistate dissidents have in their victory scenarios—no matter how far-fetched those scenarios may be.

Chapter Perspective 6.2 summarizes the coalitional features of the Palestinian movement. Attention should be given to the PLO and its role as an umbrella for numerous ideological factions.

CHAPTER PERSPECTIVE 6.2

The Palestinian Movement[a]

Some antistate dissident environments are longstanding and have generated many contending factions. A good example of this phenomenon is the Palestinian movement. Palestinian activism against the state of Israel has as its ultimate goal the creation of an independent Palestinian state. The antistate strategies of most of these groups were replaced by a broad-based communal dissident environment (the *intifada*), combined with maintaining Palestinian governing authority in Gaza and the West Bank. The following organizations have been prominent in the Palestinian nationalist movement.

Palestine Liberation Organization (PLO)

Formed in 1964, the Palestine Liberation Organization is not a religious movement but rather a secular nationalist umbrella organization comprising numerous factions. Its central and largest group is Al Fatah, founded by PLO chairman Yasir Arafat in October 1959. The PLO is the main governing body for the Palestinian Authority in Gaza and the West Bank. Force 17 is an elite unit that was originally formed in the 1970s as a personal security unit for Yasir Arafat. It has since been implicated in paramilitary and terrorist attacks. The Al-Aqsa Martyr Brigades is a "martyrdom" society of fighters drawn from Al Fatah and other factions; it includes suicide bombers. Traditionally a secular nationalistic movement, the PLO has received significant challenges from HAMAS for the mantle of champion of the Palestinian people.

Islamic Resistance Movement (Harakat al-Muqawama Al-Islamiya, or HAMAS, meaning "zeal")

HAMAS (Islamic Resistance Movement) is an Islamic fundamentalist movement founded in 1987, with roots in the Palestinian branch of the Muslim Brotherhood. HAMAS is a comprehensive movement rather than simply a terrorist group, providing social services to Palestinians while at the same time committing repeated acts of violence against Israeli interests. Its armed groups operate as semiautonomous cells and are known as the Izzedine al-Qassam Brigade (named for a famous *jihadi* in the 1920s and 1930s). HAMAS has always been at the forefront of the communal dissident *intifada*. In February 2006, HAMAS assumed control of the Palestinian parliament, and in June 2007, the movement seized military control of Gaza from the PLO after fierce fighting. After several years of negotiations, in 2011, HAMAS and Al Fatah reached an accord in Cairo seeking gradual rapprochement and operational cooperation. However, fundamentalist splinter factions such as the Al Qaeda–inspired Jund Ansar Allah (Soldiers of the Companions of God) group formed to challenge HAMAS as being too moderate. A second round of reconciliation talks between HAMAS and Al Fatah resulted in an April 2014 accord. During this period, tensions escalated markedly between Israel and HAMAS, as HAMAS fired hundreds of rockets into Israeli territory, eventually resulting in an Israeli military suppression campaign in July 2014. Fighting ended in August 2014 after thousands of casualties. HAMAS has several thousand members, mostly in Gaza, and continues to engage in terrorist violence against Israel.

Palestine Islamic Jihad (PIJ)

The Palestine Islamic Jihad began not as a single organization but a loose affiliation of factions. It is an Islamic fundamentalist revolutionary movement that seeks to promote jihad, or holy war, to form a sectarian Palestinian state. The PIJ operates primarily from Gaza and is responsible for numerous bombings, rocket attacks, assassinations, and suicide operations. With approximately 1,000 followers, the group actively recruits and trains new members.

Abu Nidal Organization (ANO)

Led by Sabri al-Banna, the Abu Nidal Organization is named for al-Banna's nom de guerre. The ANO split from the PLO in 1974 and is an international terrorist organization, having launched attacks in 20 countries at the cost of 900 people killed or wounded. Most of these attacks occurred during the 1980s, and none have been directed against the West since that time. The ANO at one time boasted several hundred members and a militia in Lebanon, but in recent years its strength is unknown. It has operated under other names, including Fatah Revolutionary Council, Arab Revolutionary Council, and Black September. The ANO has operated from bases in Libya, Lebanon, and Sudan.

Popular Front for the Liberation of Palestine (PFLP)

The Popular Front for the Liberation of Palestine was founded in 1967 by George Habash. It is a Marxist-Leninist organization that advocates a multinational Arab revolution. The PFLP was most active during the 1960s and 1970s, and is responsible for dramatic, and lethal, international terrorist attacks. Its hijacking campaign in 1969 and 1970, its collaboration with Western European terrorists, and its mentorship of Carlos the Jackal arguably established the model for modern international terrorism. George Habash died in January 2008. The PFLP continued its terrorist attacks against Israel during the 2000s, engaging in suicide bombings, attacks against security forces, mortar and rocket attacks, and lethal assaults on Israeli civilians.

Popular Front for the Liberation of Palestine–General Command (PFLP-GC)

Ahmed Jibril formed the Popular Front for the Liberation of Palestine–General Command in 1968 when he split from the PFLP because he considered the PFLP to be too involved in politics and not sufficiently committed to the armed struggle against Israel. The group carried out dozens of attacks internationally during the 1970s and 1980s, but since that time its attacks have occurred with less frequency. The group allied itself with Lebanon's Hezbollah and is responsible for rocket and bombing operations against Israel. The PFLP-GC has several hundred members and receives support from Syria and Iran.

Palestine Liberation Front (PLF)

The Palestine Liberation Front split from the PFLP-GC in the mid-1970s and further split into pro-PLO, pro-Syrian, and pro-Libyan factions. The pro-PLO faction was led by Abu Abbas, who committed a number of attacks against Israel. The group was very active during the 1980s and 1990s, committing high-profile attacks such as the 1985 seajacking of the cruise ship *Achille Lauro*. The PLF remained dormant for years after the capture and death of Abu Abbas during Operation Iraqi Freedom, but the group has carried out a few attacks since 2008. It is unknown how many followers the PLF has; estimates range from about 50 to 500 members.

Democratic Front for the Liberation of Palestine (DFLP)

The Democratic Front for the Liberation of Palestine split from the PFLP in 1969 and further split into two factions in 1991. It is a Marxist-Leninist organization that believes in ultimate victory through mass revolution. The DFLP engaged in terrorist attacks against Israeli targets primarily during the 1970s and 1980s, although it has participated in operations since that time. The group was active during the second intifada during the early 2000s. With several hundred members, it has committed primarily small bombings and assaults against Israel, including border raids.

Note

a. Most of these data were found in *Country Reports on Terrorism, 2015* (Washington, DC: U.S. Department of State, 2016).

TERRORIST TARGETS AND WEAPONS

Terrorists select their targets with the expectation that any moral ambiguities of the deed will be outweighed by the target's propaganda value. Terrorists must calculate that they can manipulate the incident into a positive propaganda context. In many campaigns, the objective has been to disrupt society to the point where the routines of life cannot be managed and the government cannot maintain order. To accomplish this, some terrorist movements have incrementally adapted their methods to new targets.

The following sampling of typical targets indicates that terrorists and extremists must rely on a process of redefining who constitutes an enemy group, thereby turning them into a legitimate target.

The Symbolism of Targets

In light of our previous discussions about terrorist groups, environments, and incidents, one conclusion should now be readily apparent: Terrorists select their targets because of their symbolic and propaganda value. High-profile, sentimental, or otherwise significant targets are chosen with the expectation that the terrorists' constituency will be moved and that the victims' audience will in some way suffer. On occasion, terrorists attempt to demonstrate the weakness of an enemy and terrorize those who trust in that enemy. The following targets are often selected for their anticipated high return in propaganda value.

Embassies and Diplomatic Personnel

The symbolism of embassy attacks and operations against diplomats can be profound. Embassies represent the sovereignty and national interests of nations. Diplomatic personnel are universally recognized as official representatives of their home countries, and attacks on embassy buildings or embassy personnel are conceptually the same as direct attacks on the nations they represent. Assaults on embassies also guarantee a large audience.

International Symbols

Many nations deploy military representatives to other countries. They also encourage international investment by private corporations, which consequently set up offices and other facilities. These interests are understandable targets for terrorists because they can be manipulated to depict exploitation, imperialism, or other representations of repression. Thus, terrorists and extremists redefine military facilities, corporate offices, military personnel, and company employees as enemy interests and legitimate targets.

Symbolic Buildings and Sites

Buildings and sentimental sites often represent the prestige and power of a nation or the identity of a people and can evoke strong psychological and emotional reactions from people who revere them. Terrorists and extremists select these cultural symbols because they know that the target audience will be affected. Interestingly, the target audience can be affected even without violence—their perception of these sites as having been desecrated can involve nothing more than a show of strength at a site.

Symbolic People

Terrorists frequently assault individuals because of the symbolic value of their status—security personnel, political leaders, journalists, and business executives are typical targets. Kidnappings and physical violence are common. In hostage situations, videos and photographs are sometimes released for propaganda value.

Passenger Carriers

From the terrorists' perspective, passenger carriers are logical targets. If the carrier is big, such as an airliner, it provides a large number of potential victims or hostages who are confined inside a mobile prison. International passenger carriers readily lend themselves to immediate international media and political attention. Chapter Perspective 6.3 applies the foregoing discussion to several symbolic attacks against American interests.

Weapons Old and New

Twenty-first-century weaponry can be classified along a sliding scale of technological sophistication and threat potential. This scale includes a high, medium, and low range, summarized as follows:[22]

High range. The New Terrorism is defined in part by the threatened acquisition of **chemical agents**, **biological agents**, or **nuclear weapons**. This threat includes the development of **radiological agents** that spread highly toxic radioactive materials by detonating conventional explosives. The first case of widespread use of a biological agent by terrorists occurred when **anthrax** was deliberately sent through the mail in the United States in the aftermath of the September 11 attacks.

Medium range. Terrorists currently have extensive access to military-style weaponry. These include automatic weapons, rocket launchers, and military-grade explosives of many varieties. Sympathetic state sponsorship and the international arms black market facilitate procurement of a virtually unlimited array of conventional small arms and munitions. These arms have been the weapons of choice for terrorists in innumerable incidents.

Low range. Often forgotten in the discussions about the threat from medium- and high-range weaponry are the powerful homemade weapons that can be manufactured from commercial-grade components. For example, ammonium nitrate and fuel oil (ANFO) bombs can be easily manufactured from readily available materials. Iraqi insurgents became quite adept at deploying **improvised explosive devices (IEDs)**, commonly referred to as "**roadside bombs**," against U.S.-led occupation troops.

Firearms

Small arms and other handheld weapons have been, and continue to be, the most common types of weapon that terrorists use. These are light and heavy infantry weapons and include pistols, rifles, submachine guns, assault rifles, machine guns, **rocket-propelled grenades (RPGs)**, mortars, and precision-guided munitions. Typical firearms include the following:

Submachine guns. Originally developed for military use, **submachine guns** are now used primarily by police and paramilitary services. Although new models have been designed, such as the famous Israeli Uzi and the American Ingram, World War II–era models are still on the market and have been used by terrorists.

Assault rifles. Usually capable of both automatic (repeating) and semiautomatic (single-shot) fire, **assault rifles** are military-grade weapons that are used extensively by terrorists and other irregular forces. The **AK-47**, invented by **Mikhail Kalashnikov** for the Soviet army, is the most successful assault rifle in terms of production numbers and widespread adoption by standing armies, guerrillas, and terrorists. The American-made **M-16** has likewise been produced in large numbers and adopted by a range of conventional and irregular forces.

CHAPTER PERSPECTIVE 6.3

The Symbolism of Targets: Terrorist Attacks Against the United States

Many targets are selected because they symbolize the interests of a perceived enemy. This selection process requires that these interests be redefined by extremists as representations of the forces against whom they are waging war. This redefinition process, if properly communicated to the terrorists' target audience and constituency, can be used effectively as propaganda on behalf of the cause.

The following attacks were launched against American interests.

Embassies and Diplomatic Missions

- June 1987: A car bombing and mortar attack were launched against the U.S. embassy in Rome, most likely by the Japanese Red Army.

- February 1996: A rocket attack was launched on the American embassy compound in Greece.

- August 1998: The U.S. embassies were bombed in Dar es Salaam, Tanzania, and Nairobi, Kenya. More than 200 people were killed.

- September 2012: Islamist insurgents attacked a U.S. diplomatic compound and an annex in Benghazi, Libya. The U.S. ambassador and a foreign service officer were killed at the compound. Two Central Intelligence Agency (CIA) contractors were killed at the annex.

International Symbols

- April 1988: A USO club in Naples, Italy, was bombed, most likely by the Japanese Red Army. Five people were killed.

- November 1995: Seven people were killed when anti-Saudi dissidents bombed an American military training facility in Riyadh, Saudi Arabia.

- November 2015: Four people, including two American trainers, were shot and killed by a Jordanian police captain at a police training facility near Amman, Jordan.

Symbolic Buildings and Events

- January 1993: Two were killed and three injured when a Pakistani terrorist fired at employees outside the CIA headquarters in Langley, Virginia.

- February 1993: The World Trade Center in New York City was bombed, killing six and injuring more than 1,000.

- September 2001: Attacks in the United States against the World Trade Center and the Pentagon killed approximately 3,000 people.

- January 2011: A viable antipersonnel pipe bomb was found in Spokane, Washington, along the planned route of a memorial march commemorating the Reverend Dr. Martin Luther King Jr.

Symbolic People

- May 2001: The Filipino Islamic revolutionary movement Abu Sayyaf took three American citizens hostage. One of them was beheaded by members of the group in June 2001.

- January 2002: An American journalist working for the *Wall Street Journal* was kidnapped in Pakistan by Islamic extremists. His murder was later videotaped by the group.

- August and September 2014: ISIS broadcast the beheadings of two captive American journalists.

Passenger Carrier Attacks

- August 1982: A bomb exploded aboard Pan Am Flight 830 over Hawaii. The Palestinian group 15 May committed the attack. The plane was able to land.

- April 1986: A bomb exploded aboard TWA Flight 840. Four were killed and nine injured, including a mother and her infant daughter who fell to their deaths when they were sucked out of the plane. The plane landed safely.

- December 2001: An explosive device malfunctioned aboard American Airlines Flight 63 as it flew from Paris to Miami. Plastic explosives had been embedded in the shoe of passenger Richard Reid.

- December 2009: An explosive device malfunctioned aboard Northwest Airlines Flight 253 as it approached Detroit, Michigan. Plastic explosives had been embedded in the underwear of passenger Umar Farouk Abdulmutallab.

Rocket-propelled grenades. Light self-propelled munitions are common features of modern infantry units. The **RPG-7** has been used extensively by dissident forces throughout the world, particularly in Latin America, the Middle East, and Asia. Manufactured in large quantities by the Soviets, Chinese, and other Communist nations, it is an uncomplicated and powerful weapon that is useful against armor and fixed emplacements such as bunkers or buildings.

Precision-guided munitions. Less commonly found among terrorists but extremely effective when used, **precision-guided munitions (PGMs)** are weapons that can be guided to their targets by using infrared or other tracking technologies. The American-made **Stinger** is a shoulder-fired surface-to-air missile that uses an infrared targeting system. It was delivered to the Afghan mujahideen during their anti-Soviet jihad and used very effectively against Soviet helicopters and other aircraft. The Soviet-made **SA-7**, also known as the **Grail**, is also an infrared-targeted surface-to-air missile. Both the Stinger and the Grail pose a significant threat to commercial airliners and other aircraft.

Common Explosives

Terrorists regularly use explosives to attack symbolic targets. Along with firearms, explosives are staples of the terrorist arsenal. The vast majority of terrorist bombs are self-constructed improvised weapons rather than premanufactured military-grade bombs. The one significant exception to this rule is the heavy use of military-grade **mines**. These are buried in the soil or rigged to be detonated as booby traps. Some improvised bombs are constructed from commercially available explosives such as **dynamite** and **TNT**, whereas others are manufactured from military-grade compounds. Examples of compounds found in terrorist bombs include the following:

Plastic explosives. **Plastic explosives** are putty-like explosive compounds that can be easily molded. The central component of most plastic explosives is a compound known as **RDX**. Nations that manufacture plastic explosives often use chemical markers to tag each batch manufactured. The explosives can thus be traced back to their source.

Semtex is a potent plastic explosive of Czech origin. During the Cold War, Semtex appeared on the international market, and Libya obtained a large supply. It is popular among terrorists.

Invented in the United States, **Composite-4 (C-4)** is a high-grade and powerful plastic explosive. It is more expensive and more difficult to obtain than Semtex.

Ammonium nitrate and fuel oil (ANFO). These explosives are manufactured from common ammonium nitrate fertilizer that has been soaked in fuel oil. Using ammonium nitrate as a base for the bomb, additional compounds and explosives can be added to intensify the explosion. These devices require hundreds of pounds of ammonium nitrate, so are generally constructed as car or truck bombs.

Triggers

Regardless of the type of explosive that is used, some bomb makers construct sophisticated triggering devices and are able to shape explosive charges to control the direction of the blast. Examples of triggering devices include the following:

Timed twitches. Time bombs are constructed from acid-activated or electronically activated triggers. They are rigged to detonate after a period of time.

Fuses. A very old and low-technology method to detonate bombs is to light a fuse that detonates the explosive. It can be timed by varying the length of the fuse. Shoe bomber Richard Reid was overpowered after a flight attendant smelled burning matches as he tried to light a fuse in his shoe.

Pressure triggers. Using **pressure triggers**, weapons such as mines are detonated when physical pressure is applied to a trigger. Car bombers in Iraq apparently attached broom handles or other poles to the front of their vehicles as plungers and then rammed their target with the plunger. A variation on physical pressure triggers is trip-wire booby traps. More sophisticated pressure triggers react to atmospheric (barometric) pressure, such as changes in pressure when an airliner ascends or descends.

Electronic triggers. Remotely controlled bombs are commonly employed by terrorists. **Electronic triggers** are activated by a remote electronic or radio signal.

High-technology triggers. Some sophisticated devices may use triggers that are activated by motion, heat, or sunlight.

Types of Bombs

Gasoline bombs. The most easily manufactured (and common) explosive weapon dissidents use is nothing more than a gasoline-filled bottle with a flaming rag for its trigger. A **gasoline bomb** is thrown at targets after the rag is stuffed into the mouth of the bottle and ignited. Tar, Styrofoam, or other ingredients can be added to create a gelling effect for the bomb, which causes the combustible ingredient to stick to surfaces. These weapons are commonly called **Molotov cocktails**, named for **Vyacheslav Molotov**, the Soviet Union's foreign minister during World War II. The name was coined during the 1939–1940 Winter War by Finnish soldiers, who used the weapon effectively against Soviet troops.

Pipe bombs. These devices are easily constructed from common pipes and filled with explosives (usually gunpowder) and then capped on both ends. Nuts, bolts, screws, nails, and other shrapnel are usually taped or otherwise attached, to be released as projectiles on detonation. Terrorists have used many hundreds of **pipe bombs**.

Vehicular bombs. Ground vehicles that have been wired with explosives are a frequent weapon in the terrorist arsenal. **Vehicular bombs** can include car bombs and truck bombs; they are mobile, covert in the sense that they are not readily identifiable, capable of transporting large amounts of explosives, and rather easily constructed. They have been used on scores of occasions throughout the world.

Barometric bombs. These sophisticated devices use triggers that are activated by changes in atmospheric pressure. An altitude meter can be rigged to become a triggering device when a specific change in pressure is detected. Thus, an airliner can be blown up in midair as the cabin pressure changes.

Improvised rockets. Examples exist of the deployment of self-designed rockets by terrorist groups. These are basic designs that are fired without precision at intended targets, but some designs have been significantly upgraded in sophistication. The most famous and frequently used improvised rocket is the **Qassam**, deployed by HAMAS and Palestine Islamic Jihad against Israel.

Case: Weapons of Mass Destruction

Within the context of threats from high-range weapons, it is important to understand the basic differences between four types of weapons: biological agents, chemical agents, radiological agents, and nuclear weapons.

Biological agents. These weapons are organisms or other contagious substances that are manufactured in order to spread disease or cause death. Once biological components are obtained, the problem of converting them into weapons can be difficult. However, experts generally agree that the most likely biological agents terrorists might use would be the following:

- *Anthrax.* A disease that afflicts livestock and humans, anthrax can exist as spores or suspended in aerosols. Humans contract anthrax through cuts in the skin (cutaneous anthrax), through the respiratory system (inhalation anthrax), or by eating contaminated meat. Obtaining lethal quantities of anthrax is difficult but not impossible.

- *Smallpox.* Eradicated in nature, **smallpox** is a virus that is very difficult to obtain because samples exist solely in laboratories, apparently only in the United States and Russia. Its symptoms appear after about 12 days of incubation and include flu-like symptoms and a skin condition that eventually leads to pus-filled lesions. It is highly contagious and can be deadly if it progresses to a hemorrhagic (bleeding) stage known as the black pox.

- *Botulinum toxin (botulism).* Also known as **botulism**, **botulinum toxin** is a rather common form of food poisoning. It is a bacterium rather than a virus or fungus and can be deadly if inhaled or ingested even in small quantities.

- *Bubonic plague.* A bacterium that leads to the disease known as the Black Death in medieval Europe, **bubonic plague** is highly infectious, often fatal, and spread by bacteria-infected fleas that infect hosts when bitten.

Chemical agents. As weapons, these are manufactured chemicals or similar substances that can be spread as solids, liquids, or gases. These are toxic substances that harm or destroy organic material. Some chemical agents, such as pesticides, are commercially available. Others can be manufactured using available instruction guides. Because of many plausible threat scenarios, experts believe that chemical weapons in the possession of terrorists pose a more likely possibility than do biological, radiological, or nuclear weapons. Examples of possible weaponized chemical agents in the arsenals of terrorists could include the following:

- **Phosgene gas** causes the lungs to fill with water, choking the victim.

- **Chlorine gas** destroys the cells that line the respiratory tract.

- **Mustard gas** is actually a mist rather than a gas. It is a blistering agent that blisters skin, eyes, and the nose and can severely damage the lungs if inhaled.

- **Nerve gases**, such as **sarin**, tabun, and VX, block (or short-circuit) nerve messages in the body. A single drop of a nerve agent, whether inhaled or absorbed through the skin, can shut down the body's neurotransmitters.

Radiological agents. To become threatening to life or health, these radioactive substances must be absorbed into a person by being inhaled, swallowed, or otherwise absorbed through the skin. Non-weapons-grade radiological agents could theoretically be used to build a toxic **dirty bomb** that would use conventional explosives to release a cloud of radioactive contaminants. Absent large quantities of radioactive materials, this type of weapon would likely cause minimal casualties outside of the blast radius of the bomb, but its psychological effect could be quite disruptive.

Nuclear weapons. These high-explosive military weapons use high-grade plutonium and uranium. Explosions from nuclear bombs devastate the area within their blast zone, irradiate an area outside the blast zone, and are capable of sending dangerous radioactive debris into the atmosphere that falls to earth as toxic **fallout**. Nuclear devices are sophisticated and difficult to manufacture, even for highly motivated governments. Although it is conceivable that terrorists could do the same, the challenge is technically and logistically formidable. Most threat scenarios thus envision that terrorists have acquired tactical nuclear weapons such as artillery shells.

DISSIDENTS AND THE NEW TERRORISM

The dissident terrorist paradigm is a good model for analyzing the environments, motives, and behaviors of modern terrorism. Categorizing the goals and strategies of dissident terrorists as revolutionary, nihilistic, or nationalistic is a useful way to understand dissident violence. However, one must remember that terrorism is an evolutionary phenomenon and that terrorist environments are never static. Methodologies and organizational configurations continue to evolve.

Toward the end of the 20th century, two important developments came to characterize the terrorist environment, moving it into a new phase: a new morality (see full discussion in Chapter 2) and decentralization.

Case: Suicide Bombers and the New Dissident Terrorist Morality

"Human bombs" have become an accepted method of political violence in a number of conflicts. Although some examples of suicidal behavior by ideological extremists can be cited, most incidents have been committed by ethno-nationalist and religious terrorists. When considering the tactical and symbolic value of **suicide bombers**, it is instructive to recall the words of the Chinese military philosopher Wu Ch'i: "One man willing to throw away his life is enough to terrorize a thousand."

In some conflicts, suicide bombings have occurred only rarely. For example, the IRA, ETA, and European leftists and rightists did not use suicidal violence. In others, suicide attacks became common. The Tamil Tigers in Sri Lanka, Hezbollah (Islamic Jihad) in Lebanon, several Palestinian groups in Israel, and Al Qaeda are all examples. In other conflicts, suicide operations became a **signature method**, as with Chechen rebels and Iraqi insurgents. The following cases illustrate this behavior:

Religion-motivated suicide and the Lebanon model. Lebanon descended into anarchy for approximately 15 years during the 1970s and 1980s. The fighting was mostly religious, among contending paramilitaries drawn from the Shi'a, Sunni, Druze, and Christian communities.

The group that pioneered suicide bombing as an effective method of terrorist violence in the Middle East was Lebanon's Hezbollah. The group conducted a series of suicide bombings from 1983 through 1985 against Israeli, American, and French interests. The October 1983 attacks against the French and American peacekeeping troops in Beirut were particularly effective—the attackers killed 58 French paratroopers and 241 U.S. Marines, forcing the peacekeepers to withdraw. This tactic continued through the 1990s during Hezbollah's campaign against the Israeli occupation of Lebanon's southern border region. An important aspect of the Lebanese example is that each suicide bomber was later glorified as a martyr. This concept of martyrdom is an important motivation behind the recruitment of young suicide bombers.

Intifada-motivated suicide in Israel. Israel has experienced more suicide attacks than perhaps any other nation. Readers may recall that the Islamic Resistance Movement, better known as HAMAS, is a Palestinian Islamic fundamentalist movement founded in December 1987 when the first Palestinian intifada broke out. HAMAS's military wing is the Izzedine al-Qassam Brigade, which first appeared in January 1992.

HAMAS made a concerted effort from 1994 to 1996 to establish itself as the preeminent Palestinian liberation organization. It was during this period that it set the precedent—and honed the methodology—for suicide bombings. In 1995 and 1996, its campaign became more deadly as its bombs became increasingly sophisticated. This was the handiwork of an electrical engineer named **Yehiya Ayyash**, the master bomb maker better known as **The Engineer**.

HAMAS had launched the campaign in retaliation for the February 1994 Hebron massacre when Baruch Goldstein killed and wounded scores of Muslim worshippers at the Ibrahim Mosque on the holy site of the Cave of the Patriarchs (for a discussion of Goldstein's attack, see Chapter 7). HAMAS recruited human-bomb candidates into its Izzedine al-Qassam Brigade cells, with the specific mission to attack Israeli civilian targets—primarily at commuter transportation sites. The suicide bombers used shrapnel-laden vehicular bombs, satchel charges (bagged bombs), and garment-strapped bombs, attacks that inflicted significant damage on Israel in terms of the number of Israeli casualties. Four HAMAS bombers, for example, killed 59 Israelis in 1996.

Beginning in 2001, suicide bombers from sectarian HAMAS and the secular PLO-affiliated Al-Aqsa Martyr Brigades carried out dozens of attacks against civilian targets, killing scores of people. The targets, often buses, were selected to disrupt everyday life in Israel. This was not the first suicide bombing campaign in Israel, but it was by far the most sustained and lethal campaign. From 2001 to 2004, approximately 125 suicide bombings occurred, many carried out by young women.

Table 6.4 summarizes the scale of violence experienced during the suicide bombing campaign waged by the Palestinians during a short period of the intifada. It is important that the targets were almost exclusively civilians and that the death toll was acceptable from the terrorists' perspective—200 people killed at a cost of 13 human bombs.

Chapter Perspective 6.4 explores the new morality within the context of Chechen terrorism in Russia. The Chechen Republic lies in the Caucasus region of the Russian Federation. Also known as Chechnya, it has a long history of opposition to Russian rule that dates at least to the 18th century. In the modern era, the region has been at war since 1994.

Terrorist Cells and Lone Wolves: New Models for a New War

A newly predominant organizational profile—the **cell**—also emerged as the 20th century drew to a close. Terrorist organizations had traditionally been rather clearly structured, many with hierarchical command and organizational configurations. They commonly had aboveground political organizations and covert military wings.

During the heyday of group-initiated New Left and Middle Eastern terrorism from the 1960s to the 1980s, it was not unusual for dissident groups to issue formal communiqués. These would officially claim credit for terrorist incidents committed on behalf of championed causes. Formal press conferences were also held on occasion.

The vertical organizational models began to be superseded by less structured horizontal models during the 1990s. Such cell-based movements have indistinct command and organizational configurations. Modern terrorist networks are often composed of a hub that may guide the direction of a movement but has little direct command and control over operational units. These units are typically autonomous or semiautonomous cells that act on their own, often after lying dormant for long periods as sleepers in a foreign country. The benefit of this configuration is that if one cell is eliminated or its members are captured, they can do little damage to other independent cells. It also permits aboveground supporters to have deniability over the tactics and targets of the cells.

Table 6.4 The Intifada Suicide Bombers

The Palestinian intifada increased in scale and ferocity during 2001 and 2002. Fighting in Gaza and the West Bank became pitched battles between Palestinian guerrillas and the Israeli military. Street fighting broke out in Bethlehem, Nablus, Ramallah, and other ancient cities. At the same time, a deadly and unpredictable new weapon was applied extensively by the Palestinians—the human bomb.

Initially used by radical Islamic movements such as HAMAS and Palestine Islamic Jihad, suicide bombing became a regular weapon of secular Palestine Liberation Organization fighters. The Al-Aqsa Martyr Brigades was a secular "martyrdom" society linked to the mainstream Al Fatah organization of the PLO.

This table is a 10-month snapshot of the activity profiles of human bombing incidents.

"Martyr" Profile	Activity Profile		
	Date	Target	Fatalities
22-year-old man, Jordanian	June 1, 2001	Tel Aviv discothèque	20 killed
23-year-old man, HAMAS activist	August 9, 2001	Jerusalem pizzeria	15 killed, including 7 children
48-year-old man, first known Arab Israeli bomber	September 9, 2001	Train depot	3 killed
21-year-old man, engaged to be married	December 2, 2001	Haifa passenger bus	15 killed
28-year-old woman, first female suicide bomber	January 27, 2002	Jerusalem shopping district	1 killed
21-year-old woman, English student	February 27, 2002	Israeli roadblock	3 hurt
19-year-old man	March 2, 2002	Bar Mitzvah celebration	9 killed
20-year-old man	March 9, 2002	Café near Prime Minister Ariel Sharon's residence	11 killed
20-year-old man	March 20, 2002	Commuter bus	7 killed
23-year-old man, wanted fugitive	March 27, 2002	Passover celebration Seder	21 killed
18-year-old woman, engaged to be married	March 29, 2002	Jerusalem supermarket	2 killed
23-year-old man	March 30, 2002	Tel Aviv restaurant	32 hurt
22-year-old man	March 31, 2002	Haifa restaurant	15 killed

Source: Created from Ripley, Amanda, "Why Suicide Bombing Is Now All the Rage," *Time,* April 15, 2002.

A good example of how a cell can be as small as a single person—the **lone-wolf model**—is the case of Richard C. Reid, a British resident who converted to Islam. Reid was detected by an alert flight attendant and overpowered by passengers on December 22, 2001, when he attempted to ignite plastic explosives in his shoe on a Boeing 767 carrying 198 passengers and crew from Paris, France, to Miami, Florida. Reid was apparently linked to Al Qaeda and had been trained by the organization in Afghanistan. He was sentenced to life imprisonment after pleading guilty before a federal court in Boston, Massachusetts.

CHAPTER PERSPECTIVE 6.4

Chechen Terrorism in Russia

During the pending collapse of the Soviet Union, a group of Chechens perceived an opportunity for independence and in 1991 declared the new Chechen Republic of Ichkeria to be independent from Russia. Their rationale was that they were no different from the Central Asian, Eastern European, and Baltic states that had also declared their independence. The Russian Federation refused to recognize Chechnya's independence and in 1994 invaded with 40,000 troops. The Chechens resisted fiercely, inflicting severe casualties on Russian forces, and in 1996, Russia agreed to withdraw its troops after approximately 80,000 Russians and Chechens had died.

Tensions mounted again in 1999 as Russian troops prepared to reenter Chechnya. In September 1999, several blocks of apartments were destroyed by terrorist explosions in Dagestan and Moscow; hundreds were killed. The Russian army invaded Chechnya, thus beginning a protracted guerrilla war that also witnessed repeated Chechen terrorist attacks in Russia. Although guerrillas inside Chechnya were mostly suppressed, approximately 100,000 Russians and Chechens died during the second invasion.

Because Chechnya is a Muslim region, Russian authorities have tried to link their conflict with the global war on terrorism. At the same time, some Chechen fighters have become Islamists and sought support from the Muslim world. Russian president Vladimir Putin repeatedly voiced a strong and aggressive tone against Chechen terrorists, stating on one occasion that "Russia doesn't conduct negotiations with terrorists—it destroys them."[a]

During the Russian occupation, Chechen separatists waged an ongoing terrorist campaign on Russian soil. Their attacks have been dramatic and deadly. Examples of the quality of their attacks include the following incidents:

From October 23 through 26, 2002, approximately 50 Chechen terrorists seized about 750 hostages in a Moscow theater. During the 57-hour crisis, the Chechens wired the theater with explosives and threatened to destroy the entire building with everyone inside. Several of the female terrorists also wired themselves with explosives. Russian commandos eventually pumped an aerosol anesthetic, or "knockout gas" (possibly manufactured with opiates), into the theater, and 129 hostages died, most of them from the effects of the gas, which proved to be more lethal than expected in a confined area. All of the Chechens were killed by the commandos as they swept through the theater during the rescue operation.

On February 6, 2004, a bomb in a Moscow subway car killed 39 people and wounded more than 100.

On August 24, 2004, two Russian airliners crashed, virtually simultaneously. Investigators found the same explosive residue at both crash sites. Chechen suicide bombers were suspected, and a group calling itself the Islambouli Brigades of Al Qaeda claimed responsibility.

On August 31, 2004, a woman detonated a bomb near a Moscow subway station, killing herself and nine other people and wounding 100. The Islambouli Brigades of Al-Qaeda claimed responsibility.

On September 1, 2004, Chechens seized a school in Beslan, taking 1,200 hostages. On September 3, as explosives were detonated and special forces retook the school, more than 330 people were killed, about half of them schoolchildren. Russian authorities displayed the bodies of 26 Chechens.

The number and intensity of terrorist incidents declined in 2005 and 2006, largely because of negotiations and Russian success in eliminating prominent Chechen opposition leaders. In March, the president of a separatist Chechen government was killed by Russian troops, and in July 2006, famed rebel leader Shamil Basayev was killed by an explosion that many attributed to Russian security forces.

The conflict has by no means ended. "Incidents of violence rose from 795 in 2008 to 1,100 in 2009, and suicide bombings quadrupled in 2009, the majority of which occurred in Chechnya."[b] In 2010, 39 people were killed when two metro stations in Moscow were attacked by two female suicide bombers, for which Chechen leader Doku Umarov claimed responsibility. A Chechen suicide assault on the Domodedovo Airport in Moscow in 2011 killed 36 people. The National Consortium for the Study of Terrorism and Responses to Terrorism reported that in 2012, 150 terrorist attacks occurred in Russia from all sources.

Notes

a. Judith Ingram, "Rush Hour Blast Hits Moscow Metro," *Washington Post*, February 6, 2004.

b. Preeti Bhattacharji, "Chechen Terrorism (Russia, Chechnya, Separatist)." In *Backgrounder* (Washington, DC: Council on Foreign Relations, 2010).

DISCUSSION BOX

THE TAMIL TIGERS

This chapter's Discussion Box is intended to stimulate critical debate about the legitimacy of dissident movements using guerrilla and terrorist tactics.

The Democratic Socialist Republic of Sri Lanka is an island nation in the Indian Ocean off the southeast coast of India. Its population is about 74% Sinhalese and 18% Tamil; the rest of the population is a mixture of other ethnic groups.[a]

In April 1987, more than 100 commuters were killed when terrorists—most likely Liberation Tigers of Tamil Eelam (Tamil Tigers)—exploded a bomb in a bus station in the capital city of Colombo. This type of attack was typical in the Tigers' long war of independence against the Sri Lankan government. The organization was founded in 1976 and champions the Tamil people of Sri Lanka against the majority Buddhist Sinhalese.

The goal of the movement was to carve out an independent state from Sri Lanka, geographically in the north and east of the island. To accomplish this, the Tamil Tigers used conventional, guerrilla, and terrorist tactics to attack government, military, and civilian targets. A unit known as the Black Tigers specialized in terrorist attacks, often committing suicide in the process. Sinhalese forces and irregular gangs often used extreme violence to repress the Tamil uprising.

About half the members of the Tiger movement were teenagers. Indoctrination of potential Tigers included spiritual purity, nationalist militancy, a higher morality, and a glorification of death. At the conclusion of training and indoctrination, young Tiger initiates were given a vial of cyanide, which was worn around the neck to be taken if capture is inevitable. Songs, poetry, and rituals glorified the Tamil people and nation. The Tamil Tigers were very shrewd with public relations, making extensive use of the media, video, and the Internet; they also established a foreign service presence in numerous countries. They also apparently became adept at transnational organized crime, raising revenue for the cause by trading in arms and drugs.

Estimates of membership numbers ranged between 6,000 and 15,000 fighters. They were well organized and disciplined. Women, called Freedom Birds, took on important leadership positions over time as Tamil male leaders died. About one third of the movement were women.

Some Tamil Tiger attacks were spectacular. In May 1991, a young Tamil woman detonated a bomb, killing herself and Indian prime minister Rajiv Gandhi. In 1996, Tigers surrounded and annihilated a government base, killing all 1,200 troops. Also in 1996, a Tiger bomb at Colombo's Central Bank killed scores and injured 1,400 others. In 1997, the new Colombo Trade Center was bombed, causing 18 deaths and more than 100 injuries. The Tamil Tigers operated a small naval unit of speedboats (the Sea Tigers) that intercepted Sri Lankan shipping. Fighting centered repeatedly on the Jaffna peninsula in the north, with both sides capturing and losing bases.

By 1997, the war had claimed at least 58,000 military and civilian lives, including 10,000 Tigers. By 2002, the combatants had fought to a stalemate. In early 2002, both sides agreed to Norwegian mediation to negotiate terms for a lasting peace settlement. Several hundred thousand Tamils eventually fled the island, with more than 100,000 living in India and about 200,000 in the West.

Beginning in 2006, the Sri Lankan government began a massive expansion of its armed forces, doubling its size by late 2008. After a protracted and massive government offensive, the Tamil Tigers were overrun in May 2009, thus ending the 26-year conflict.

Note

a. Data mostly derived from Central Intelligence Agency, *The World Fact Book 2013–14* (Washington, DC: U.S. Central Intelligence Agency, 2014).

CHAPTER SUMMARY

This chapter provided readers with an understanding of the nature of dissident terrorism. The purpose of this discussion was to identify and define several categories of dissident behavior, to classify antistate dissident terrorism, to describe types of communal dissident terrorism, and to provide examples of these concepts.

The dissident terrorist paradigm identified several categories of dissident terrorism—revolutionary, nihilist, and nationalist. These environments were defined and discussed with the underlying recognition that they are "ideal" categorizations and that some terrorists will exhibit characteristics of several categories. It should also be understood that new models became more common as the 20th century drew to a close—the cell organizational structures and lone-wolf attacks are now integral to the modern terrorist environment.

Antistate dissident terrorism was defined as terrorism directed against existing governments and political institutions to destabilize the existing environment as a precondition to building a new society. Several antistate terrorist environments were presented as examples. The cases included the United States, several European societies, and the nexus of antistate and communal violence in Israel. The seemingly irrational faith in ultimate victory despite overwhelming odds was examined; this faith in the inevitability of success is at the center of antistate dissident campaigns.

Communal terrorism was defined as group against group terrorism, in which subpopulations of society are involved in internecine violence. Several environments were discussed to illustrate differences in motivations, manifestations of violence, and environments conducive to communal conflict. The evaluated categories were ethno-nationalist, religious, and ideological communal terrorism. Cases were identified to illustrate each concept.

KEY TERMS AND CONCEPTS

The following topics were discussed in this chapter and can be found in the Glossary:

WEB EXERCISE

Using this chapter's recommended websites listed on the student study site at **edge.sagepub.com/martiness5e**, conduct an online investigation of dissident terrorism.

1. How would you describe the self-images presented by dissident movements?

2. Based on the information given by the monitoring organizations, are some dissident movements seemingly more threatening than others? Less threatening? Why?

3. Compare the dissident websites to the monitoring agency sites. Are any of the dissident groups unfairly reported by the monitoring agencies?

For an online search of dissident terrorism, readers should enter the following keywords in their Web browser's search engine:

"Terrorist organizations (or groups)"

"Revolutionary movements"

The names of specific dissident organizations

RECOMMENDED READINGS

The following publications provide discussions on dissident activism, protest movements, and violence.

Barkan, S. E., & Snowden, L. L. (2007). *Collective violence* (2nd ed.). Cornwall-on-Hudson, NY: Sloan.

Bell, J. B. (2000). *The IRA 1968–2000: Analysis of a secret army*. London, UK: Frank Cass.

Bergen, Peter L. *Holy War, Inc.: Inside the Secret World of Osama bin Laden*. New York, NY: Simon & Schuster, 2001.

Berko, A. (2009). *The path to paradise: The inner world of suicide bombers*. Westport, CT: Praeger Security International.

Cambanis, T. (2010). *A privilege to die: Inside Hezbollah's legions and their endless war against Israel*. New York, NY: Free Press.

Cragin, K. (2007). *Sharing the dragon's teeth: Terrorist groups and the exchange of new technologies*. Santa Monica, CA: RAND.

Cromer, G. (2006). *Insurgent terrorism*. Aldershot, UK: Ashgate.

Dekker, T., & Medearis, C. (2010). *Tea with Hezbollah: Sitting at the enemies' table*. New York, NY: Doubleday.

Dolnik, A. (2007). *Understanding terrorist innovation: Technology, tactics and global trends*. London, UK: Routledge.

Follian, J. (2011). *Jackal: The complete story of the legendary terrorist, Carlos the Jackal*. New York, NY: Arcade.

Frantz, D., & Collis, C. (2007). *The nuclear jihadist: The true story of the man who sold the world's most dangerous secrets—And how we could have stopped him*. New York, NY: Twelve Books.

Glucklich, A. (2009). *Dying for heaven: Holy pleasure and suicide bombers*. New York, NY: HarperOne.

Hafez, M. (2007). *Suicide bombers in Iraq: The strategy and ideology of martyrdom*. Washington, DC: United States Institute of Peace Press.

Horne, A. (2006). *A savage war of peace: Algeria 1954–1962*. New York, NY: New York Review Books.

Hughes, J. (2007). *Chechnya: From nationalism to jihad*. Philadelphia: University of Pennsylvania Press.

Jaber, H. (1997). *Hezbollah: Born with a vengeance*. New York, NY: Columbia University Press.

Janczewski, L., & Colarik, A. (Eds.). (2008). *Cyber warfare and cyber terrorism*. Hershey, PA: Information Science Reference.

Karmon, E. (2005). *Coalitions between terrorist organizations: Revolutionaries, nationalists, and Islamists*. Boston, MA: Martinus Nijhoff.

Katz, S. M. (2001). *The hunt for the engineer: How Israeli agents tracked the Hamas master bomber*. New York, NY: Fromm International.

Levi, M. (2009). *On nuclear terrorism*. Cambridge, MA: Harvard University Press.

Mallin, J. (Ed.). (1971). *Terror and urban guerrillas: A study of tactics and documents*. Coral Gables, FL: University of Miami Press.

Mitchell, T. G. (2010). *When peace fails: Lessons from Belfast for the Middle East*. Jefferson, NC: McFarland.

Mueller, R. (2009). *Atomic obsession: Nuclear alarmism from Hiroshima to Al Qaeda*. New York, NY: Routledge.

Norton, A. R. (2009). *Hezbollah: A short history*. Princeton, NJ: Princeton University Press.

Oliver, A. M., & Steinberg, P. F. (2005). *The road to martyrs' square: A journey into the world of the suicide bomber*. New York, NY: Oxford University Press.

Pape, R. (2005). *Dying to win: The strategic logic of suicide terrorism*. New York, NY: Random House.

Powell, W. (1989). *The anarchist cookbook*. New York, NY: Barricade Books. (Original work published 1971)

Raab, D. (2007). *Terror in Black September: The first eyewitness account of the infamous 1970 hijacking.* New York, NY: Palgrave Macmillan.

Ranstorp, M., & Normark, M. (Eds.). (2009). *Unconventional weapons and international terrorism: Challenges and a new approach.* New York, NY: Routledge.

Rosen, D. M. (2005). *Armies of the young: Child soldiers in war and terrorism.* New Brunswick, NJ: Rutgers University Press.

Shay, S. (2007). *Islamic terror abductions in the Middle East.* Portland, OR: Sussex Academic Press.

Shirlow, P. (2012). *The end of Ulster loyalism?* New York, NY: Manchester University Press.

Spaaij, R. (2007). *Lone-wolf terrorism.* The Hague, Netherlands: COT Institute for Safety, Security and Crisis Management.

Stern, J. (1999). *The ultimate terrorists.* Cambridge, MA: Harvard University Press.

Thornton, R. (2007). *Asymmetric warfare: Threat and response in the twenty-first century.* Cambridge, UK: Polity Press.

Tucker, J. B. (Ed.). (2000). *Toxic terror: Assessing terrorist use of chemical and biological weapons.* Cambridge, MA: MIT Press.

Wickham-Crowley, T. P. (1993). *Guerrillas and revolution in Latin America: A comparative study of insurgents and regimes since 1956.* Princeton, NJ: Princeton University Press.

Zubay, G., et al. (Eds.). (2005). *Agents of bioterrorism: Pathogens and their weaponization.* New York, NY: Columbia University Press.

CHAPTER SEVEN

RELIGIOUS TERRORISM

Terrorism in the name of religion has become the predominant model for political violence in the modern world. This is not to suggest that it is the only model, because nationalism and ideology remain as potent catalysts for extremist behavior. However, religious extremism has become a central issue for the global community.

In the modern era, religious terrorism has increased in its frequency, scale of violence, and global reach. At the same time, a relative decline has occurred in secular terrorism. The old ideologies of class conflict, anticolonial liberation, and secular nationalism have been challenged by a new and vigorous infusion of sectarian ideologies. Grassroots extremist support for religious violence has been most widespread among populations living in repressive societies that do not permit demands for reform or other expressions of dissent.

What is religious terrorism? What are its fundamental attributes? Religious terrorism is a type of political violence motivated by an absolute belief that an otherworldly power has sanctioned—and commanded—terrorist violence for the greater glory of the faith. Acts committed in the name of the faith will be forgiven by the otherworldly power and perhaps rewarded in an afterlife. In essence, one's religious faith legitimizes violence as long as such violence is an expression of the will of one's deity.

Table 7.1 presents a model that compares the fundamental characteristics of religious and secular terrorism.

The discussion in this chapter will review the following:

Learning Objectives

This chapter will enable readers to do the following:

1. Explain the concept of primary and secondary motives for religious terrorism.

2. Understand the historical context of religious terrorism.

3. Interpret some incidents of religious-motivated political violence as state-sponsored religious terrorism.

4. Interpret some incidents of religious-motivated political violence as dissident-sponsored religious terrorism.

5. Discuss the future of religious terrorism.

Paul Souders/The Image Bank/Getty Images

▶ A ritualistic Ku Klux Klan (KKK) "cross lighting" ceremony in the United States. The KKK is a longstanding racist movement that lives according to a code of racial supremacy. Its ceremonies invoke mystical symbols such as hooded gowns and the burning cross, as well as the adoption of bizarre titles such as Imperial Wizard and Exalted Cyclops.

Table 7.1 Case Comparison: Religious and Secular Terrorism

Religious and secular terrorism have contrasting activity profiles. Both environments certainly pose threats to targeted systems, but the manifestations of dissent differ in potential scale and scope of impact.
The quality of violence, constituency profile, and relationship to the existing system are summarized in this table.

Environment	Activity Profile			
	Quality of Violence[a]	Scope of Violence	Constituency Profile	Relationship to Existing System
Religious	Unconstrained scale of terrorist violence	Expansive target definition	Narrow, insular, and isolated	Alienated "true believers"
	Result: Unconstrained choice of weapons and tactics	Result: Indiscriminate use of violence	Result: No appeals to a broader audience	Result: Completely reconfigured social order
Secular	Constrained scale of terrorist violence	Focused target definition	Inclusive, for the championed group	Liberators
	Result: Relative constraint in choice of weapons and tactics	Result: Relative discrimination in use of violence	Result: Appeals to actual or potential supporters	Result: Restructured or rebuilt society

Source: Adapted from Bruce Hoffman, *Inside Terrorism: Revised and Expanded Edition.* New York: Columbia University Press, 2006, pp. 88–89.

[a] Communal terrorism is rarely constrained and is a case in point of convergence in the quality of violence used by religious and secular terrorism.

- Historical Perspectives on Religious Violence
- The Practice of Religious Terrorism
- Trends and Projections

HISTORICAL PERSPECTIVES ON RELIGIOUS VIOLENCE

Terrorism carried out in the name of the faith has long been a feature of human affairs. The histories of people, civilizations, nations, and empires are replete with examples of extremist true believers who engage in violence to promote their belief system. Some religious terrorists are inspired by defensive motives, others seek to ensure the predominance of their faith, and others are motivated by an aggressive amalgam of these tendencies.

Religious terrorism can be communal, genocidal, nihilistic, or revolutionary. It can be committed by lone wolves, clandestine cells, large dissident movements, or governments. And, depending on one's perspective, there is often debate about whether the perpetrators should be classified as terrorists or religious freedom fighters. The following cases are historical examples of religious violence. This is a selective survey (by no means exhaustive) that demonstrates how some examples of faith-based violence are clearly examples of terrorism, how others are not so clear, and how each example must be considered within its historical and cultural context.

Judeo-Christian Antiquity

Within the Judeo-Christian belief system, references in the Bible are not only to assassinations and conquest but also to the complete annihilation of enemy nations in the name of the faith. One such campaign is described in the book of Joshua.

The story of Joshua's conquest of Canaan is the story of the culmination of the ancient Hebrews' return to Canaan (the modern-day equivalent of Israel, Palestine, and some borderlands). To Joshua and his followers, this was the Promised Land of the covenant between God and the chosen people. According to the Bible, the Canaanite cities were destroyed and the Canaanites attacked until "there was no one left who breathed."[1] Assuming that Joshua and his army put to the sword all the inhabitants of the 31 cities mentioned in the Bible, and assuming that each city averaged 10,000 people, his conquest cost 310,000 lives.[2]

Chapter Perspective 7.1 presents the passages that describe the conquest.

Christian Crusades

During the Middle Ages, the Western Christian (i.e., Roman Catholic) Church launched at least nine invasions of the Islamic east, the first one in 1095. These invasions were called the

---

CHAPTER PERSPECTIVE 7.1

The Conquest of Canaan

To the ancient Hebrews, enemy trespassers had occupied God's Promised Land of Canaan. Thus, from the Hebrews' perspective, it was rational and necessary to drive the interlopers from the land, exterminating them when necessary.

> When King Jabin of Hazor heard of this, he sent to [other kings in the region for assistance to defeat the Hebrews.] . . . They came out, with all their troops, a great army, in number like the sand on the seashore, with very many horses and chariots. All these kings joined their forces, and came and camped together at the waters of Merom, to fight with Israel.
>
> And the Lord said to Joshua, "Do not be afraid of them, for tomorrow at this time I will hand over all of them, slain, to Israel." . . . So Joshua came suddenly upon them with all his fighting force, by the waters of Merom, and fell upon them. And the Lord handed them over to Israel. . . . They struck them down, until they had left no one remaining.
>
> Joshua turned back at that time, and took Hazor, and struck its king down with the sword. . . . And they put to the sword all who were in it, utterly destroying them; there was no one left who breathed, and he burned Hazor with

fire. And all the towns of those kings, and all their kings, Joshua took, and struck them with the edge of the sword, utterly destroying them. . . .

> All the spoil of these towns, and the livestock, the Israelites took for their booty; but all the people they struck down with the edge of the sword, until they had destroyed them, and they did not leave any who breathed.[a]

Other passages in the Bible are arguably examples of religious communal violence or terrorism, such as the following story from the Book of Numbers:

> While Israel was staying at Shittim, the people began to have sexual relations with the women of Moab. . . . Just then one of the Israelites came and brought a Midianite woman into his family. . . . When Phineas . . . saw it, he got up and left the Congregation. Taking a spear in his hand, he went after the Israelite man into the temple, and pierced the two of them, the Israelite and the woman, through the belly.[b]

Notes

a. Joshua 11:1, 4–8, 10–14, *The Holy Bible, New Revised Standard Version* (Nashville, TN: Thomas Nelson, 1990).

b. Numbers 25:1, 6–8, *The Holy Bible, New Revised Standard Version* (Nashville, TN: Thomas Nelson, 1990).

Crusades because they were conducted in the name of the Cross. The purpose of the Crusades was to recapture the holy lands from the disunited Muslims, who had previously conquered these lands, and to whom Crusaders referred collectively as Saracens.

Christian knights and soldiers answered the call for many reasons. The promise of land, booty, and glory was certainly central. Another important reason was the spiritual promise, made by Pope Urban II, that fighting and dying in the name of the Cross would ensure martyrdom and thereby guarantee a place in heaven. Liberation of the holy lands would bring eternal salvation. Thus, "knights who with pious intent took the Cross would earn a remission from temporal penalties for all his sins; if he died in battle he would earn remission of his sins."[3] This religious ideology was reflected in the war cry of the early Crusades: *Deus vult!* ("God wills it!").

During the First Crusade, Western knights—primarily Frankish soldiers—captured a broad swath of biblical lands, including Jerusalem and Bethlehem. When cities and towns were captured, most of the Muslim and Jewish inhabitants were killed outright, a practice common in medieval warfare. When Jerusalem was captured in July 1099, Frankish knights massacred thousands of Muslim, Jewish, and Orthodox Christian residents. An embellished Crusader letter sent to Pope Urban II in Rome boasted that the blood of the Saracens reached the bridles of the Crusaders' horses.

Not all Christian Crusades were fought in Muslim lands. The Western Church also purged its territories of Jews and divergent religious beliefs that were denounced as heresies. The zealousness and violence of these purges became legendary. During the brutal Albigensian Crusade in southern France during the 13th century, the story was told that concerns were raised about loyal and innocent Catholics who were being killed along with targeted members of the enemy Cathar sect. The pope's representative, Arnaud Amaury, allegedly replied, "Kill them all. God will know his own."

The Church-sanctioned invasions and atrocities were deemed to be in accordance with God's wishes and therefore perfectly acceptable. An extreme and unquestioning faith in the cause led to a series of campaigns of terror against the non-Christian (and sometimes the Orthodox Christian) residents of conquered cities and territories. In a typical and tragic irony of the time, the Greek Orthodox city of Constantinople, center of the Byzantine Empire and one of the great cities of the world, was captured and sacked by Western Crusaders in 1204 during the Fourth Crusade. The Crusaders looted the city and created a short-lived Latin Empire, which lasted until 1261.

The Assassins

The Order of Assassins,[4] sometimes referred to as the Brotherhood of Assassins, was founded by Hasan ibn al-Sabbah (d. 1124) in 11th-century Persia. Al-Sabbah was a caliph (religious head) of the Ismaili sect of Islam. He espoused a radical version of Ismaili Islam and founded the Order of Assassins to defend this interpretation of the faith. Beginning in 1090, he and his followers seized a string of fortresses in the mountains of northern Persia, the first of which was the strong fortress of Alamut near Qazvin. Because of these origins, al-Sabbah was called the "Old Man of the Mountain."

The word *assassin* was allegedly derived from the drug hashish, which some commentators believe al-Sabbah's followers ate before committing acts of violence in the name of the faith.[5] They referred to themselves as *hashashins* or *hashishis*, reputedly meaning "hashish eaters," although this is widely considered by historians to be an apocryphal attribution. During the early years of the movement, Assassin followers spread out of the mountains to the cities of Persia, modern Iraq, Syria, and the Christian Crusader–occupied areas of Palestine. The Assassins killed many people, including fellow Muslims who were Sunnis along with Christians. Suicide missions were common, and some Crusader leaders went so far as to pay tribute to the Assassins so that the Assassins would leave them alone.

The Assassins were very adept at disguise, stealth, and surprise killings, and thus the word *assassination* was coined. A key component of the Assassins' beliefs was the righteousness of their cause and methodology. To kill or be killed was a good thing, because it was done in the name of the faith and ensured a place in paradise after death. This belief continues to be held by many of today's religious terrorists.

Although their political impact was negligible and the organization was eliminated in 1256, the Assassins left a profound psychological mark on their era and, in many ways, on the modern era.

A Secret Cult of Murder

In India during the 13th through the 19th centuries, the **Thuggee** cult existed among worshippers of the Hindu goddess Kali, the destroyer. They were called by various names, including Phansigars ("noose operators") and Dacoits ("members of a gang of robbers"). Thuggee comes from *thag*, Hindi for thief, from which the English word *thug* is derived. They would strangle sacrificial victims—usually travelers—with a noose called a *phansi* in the name of Kali and then rob and ritually mutilate and bury them. Offerings would then be made to Kali.

The British eventually destroyed the movement during the 19th century, but the death toll of Thuggee victims was staggering: "This secretive cult is believed to have murdered 20,000 victims a year . . . perhaps dispatching as many as several million victims altogether before it was broken up by British officials."[6] There are few debatable counterpoints to the underlying character of this cult—the Thuggees waged a campaign of religious terror for centuries.

Modern Arab Islamist Extremism

The Arab world passed through several important political phases during the 20th century. Overlordship by the Ottoman Empire ended in 1918 after World War I. It was followed by European domination, which ended in the aftermath of World War II. New Arab and North African states were initially ruled primarily by monarchs or civilians who were always authoritarian and frequently despotic. A series of military coups and other political upheavals led to the modern era of governance. These phases had a significant influence on activism among Arab nationalists and intellectuals, culminating in the late 1940s, when the chief symbol of Western encroachment became the state of Israel. Post–World War II activism in the Arab Muslim world likewise progressed through several intellectual phases, most of them secular expressions of nationalism and socialism. The secular phases included the following:

- anticolonial nationalism, during which Arab nationalists resisted the presence of European administrators and armed forces

- pan-Arab nationalism (Nasserism), led by Egyptian president Gamal Abdel-Nasser, which advocated the creation of a single dynamic United Arab Republic

- secular leftist radicalism, which activists often adopted to promote Marxist or other socialist principles of governance, sometimes in opposition to their own governments

Many activists and intellectuals became disenchanted with these movements when they failed to deliver the political reforms, economic prosperity, and desired degree of respect from the international community. In particular, several humiliating military defeats at the hands of the Israelis—and the seemingly intractable plight of the Palestinians—diminished the esteem and deference the secular movements had once enjoyed. Arab nationalists—both secular and sectarian—had struggled since the end of World War II to resist what they perceived as Western domination and exploitation, and some tradition-oriented nationalists began to interpret Western culture and values as alien to Muslim morality and values.

As a result, new movements promoting Islamist extremism began to overshadow the ideologies of the previous generation. This has placed many Islamists at odds with existing Arab governments, many of which are administered under the principles of the older ideologies.

In the post–Cold War political environment, adopting Islam as a vehicle for liberation is a logical progression. When radical secular ideologies and movements made little progress in resisting the West and Israel, and when secular Arab governments repressed any expressions of domestic dissent, many activists and intellectuals turned to radical interpretations of Islam.

There is a sense of collegiality and comradeship among many Islamists, but there are also differences within the ideologies of many leaders, as well as between the Sunni and Shi'a traditions. The Islamist movement, however, has transcended most ethnic and cultural differences and is a global phenomenon.

Cult Case: Mysticism and Rebellion in Uganda[7]

Phase 1: The Holy Spirit Mobile Force. Uganda in 1987 was a hotbed of rebellion, with several rebel groups opposing the new government of President Yoweri Museveni. One such group was the **Holy Spirit Mobile Force**, inspired and led by the mystical **Alice Auma Lakwena**. Lakwena claimed to be possessed by a spirit called Lakwena and preached that her movement would defeat Museveni's forces and purge Uganda of witchcraft and superstition. Because her followers championed the Acholi tribe, the Holy Spirit Mobile Force attracted thousands of followers, many of whom were former soldiers from previous Ugandan government armies. In late 1987, she led thousands of her followers against Museveni's army. To protect themselves from death, Holy Spirit Mobile Force fighters anointed themselves with holy oil, which they believed would ward off bullets. When they met Museveni's forces, thousands of Lakwena's followers were slaughtered in the face of automatic weapons and artillery fire. Alice Lakwena fled the country to Kenya, where she lived until her death in January 2007.

Phase 2: The Lord's Resistance Army. **Josef Kony**, either a cousin or nephew of Alice Lakwena, reorganized the Holy Spirit Mobile Force into the **Lord's Resistance Army**. Kony blended Christianity, Islam, and witchcraft into a bizarre mystical foundation for his movement. Kony proclaimed to his followers that he would overthrow the government, purify the Acholi people, and seize power and reign in accordance with the principles of the biblical Ten Commandments.

From its inception in 1987, the Lord's Resistance Army was exceptionally brutal and waged near-genocidal terrorist campaigns—largely against the Acholi people it claimed to champion. The movement destroyed villages and towns, killed thousands of people, drove hundreds of thousands more from the land, abducted thousands of children, and routinely committed acts of mass rape and banditry. With bases in southern Sudan, the Lord's Resistance Army proved extremely difficult for the Ugandan government to defeat in the field.

An estimated 30,000 children became kidnap victims, and 1.6 million Ugandans were displaced into refugee camps. These camps became regular targets of the Lord's Resistance Army, which raided them for supplies, to terrorize the refugees, and to kidnap children. Among the kidnapped children, boys were forced to become soldiers and girls became sex slaves known as bush wives. There has been some hope of ending the conflict. In 2005, a top Lord's Resistance Army commander surrendered, the government claimed a temporary cease-fire, and Sudan began to stabilize its border with Uganda after its own southern civil war ended. Unfortunately, the Lord's Resistance Army continued its pattern of violence and abductions, and from 2008 through 2011, the group conducted destructive raids into neighboring Democratic Republic of Congo. The resilience of the Lord's Resistance Army was unmistakable, as it repeatedly survived a series of operations designed to neutralize its effectiveness.

Like the Thuggees, the Lord's Resistance Army is unquestionably an example of a cultic movement that waged a campaign of religious terrorism.

Religious Scapegoating Case: The Protocols of the Learned Elders of Zion

Extremist ideologies have historically scapegoated undesirable groups. Many conspiracy theories have been invented to denigrate these groups and to implicate them in nefarious plans to destroy an existing order. Some of these conspiracy theories possess quasi-religious elements that in effect classify the scapegoated group as being in opposition to a natural and sacred order.

Among right-wing nationalists and racists, a convergence is often seen between scapegoating and mysticism. Just as it is common for rightists to assert their natural and sacred superiority, it is also common for them to demonize a scapegoated group, essentially declaring that it is inherently evil. One quasi-religious conspiracy theory is the promulgation of a document titled the *Protocols of the Learned Elders of Zion*.[8]

The *Protocols* originated in czarist Russia and were allegedly the true proceedings of a meeting of a mysterious committee of the Jewish faith, during which a plot to rule the world was hatched—in league with the Freemasons. They are a detailed record of this alleged conspiracy for world domination but were, in fact, a forgery written by the secret police (**Okhrana**) of Czar Nicholas II around 1895 and later published by Professor Sergyei Nilus. Many anti-Semitic groups have used this document to justify the repression of European Jews, and it was an ideological foundation for the outbreak of anti-Jewish violence in Europe, including massacres and **pogroms** (violent anti-Jewish campaigns in eastern Europe).

The National Socialist (Nazi) movement and Adolf Hitler used the *Protocols* extensively. Modern Eurocentric neo-Nazis and Middle Eastern extremists, both secular and religious, continue to publish and circulate the *Protocols* as anti-Semitic propaganda. In this regard, neo-Nazis and Middle Eastern extremists have found common cause in quasi-religious anti-Semitism. In 1993, a Russian court formally ruled that the *Protocols* are a forgery.[9]

Chapter Perspective 7.2 describes Holocaust denial, a conspiracy belief that claims to debunk the Nazi Holocaust. It is an example of how ideological and religious extremists perpetuate conspiratorial worldviews.

CHAPTER PERSPECTIVE 7.2

Holocaust Denial

Among the many conspiracy theories found on the far and fringe right wing and among Middle Eastern extremists is the argument that the Nazi Holocaust (genocide against European Jews) never occurred. The underlying belief is that the Holocaust is a hoax, that the Nazis never systematically murdered any ethnic group, and that death camps such as Auschwitz were merely detention or work facilities. Holocaust denial has become a fundamental tenet for many tendencies on the reactionary right and has been repeated by fairly high-profile individuals. There have been publications and websites dedicated to this theory.[a]

In the United States, this is an anti-Semitic conspiracy theory that was promulgated by two right-wing organizations—the Liberty Lobby and the Institute for Historical Review—beginning in the late 1970s and early 1980s. Neo-Nazi groups, Ku Klux Klan factions, and Patriot survivalists have all been known to cite the "hoax" of the Holocaust to justify their anti-Semitic conspiracy theories. Although Holocaust denial is mostly a white racial supremacist phenomenon in the United States, it has been endorsed by other domestic groups such as the Nation of Islam, which has historically promoted African American racial supremacy.

(Continued)

(Continued)

The conspiracy theory has found an international audience among Western neofascists, anti-Zionists, and extremist groups in the Middle East. In December 2006, a major international conference was convened in Tehran, Iran, to promote Holocaust denial.[b] It drew scholars, researchers, and anti-Semitic activists from many countries, including anti-Semitic writer Georges Thiel from France and racial supremacist David Duke from the United States. The two-day conference was sponsored by the Iranian government at the behest of President Mahmoud Ahmadinejad, who publicly called the Holocaust a myth in 2005. The United Nations General Assembly passed a resolution condemning Holocaust denial in January 2007.[c]

Holocaust denial should be considered to be a facet of broader anti-Semitic tendencies, such as the promulgation of *The Protocols of the Learned Elders of Zion*.

Notes

a. For an excellent discussion of Holocaust denial, see Deborah E. Lipstadt, *Denying the Holocaust: The Growing Assault on Truth and Memory* (New York, NY: Plume, 1994).

b. Nazila Fathi, "Holocaust Deniers and Skeptics Gather in Iran," *New York Times*, December 11, 2006.

c. Associated Press, "U.N. Condemns Holocaust Denial," *Los Angeles Times*, January 27, 2007.

THE PRACTICE OF RELIGIOUS TERRORISM

Understanding Jihad as a Primary Religious Motive:
An Observation and Caveat

Keeping the idiosyncratic quality of religious terrorism in mind, it is arguably necessary to make a sensitive observation—and caveat—about the study of religious terrorism in the modern era. The observation is that today, the incidence of religious terrorism is disproportionately committed by radical Islamists:

> Popular Western perception equates radical Islam with terrorism. . . . There is, of course, no Muslim or Arab monopoly in the field of religious fanaticism; it exists and leads to acts of violence in the United States, India, Israel, and many other countries. But the frequency of Muslim- and Arab-inspired terrorism is still striking. . . . A discussion of religion-inspired terrorism cannot possibly confine itself to radical Islam, but it has to take into account the Muslim countries' preeminent position in this field.[10]

The caveat is the degree of misunderstanding in the West about the historical and cultural origins of the growth of radical interpretations of Islam. One is the common belief that the concept of holy war is an underlying principle of the Islamic faith. Another is that Muslims are united in supporting jihad. This is simplistic and fundamentally incorrect. Although the term *jihad* is widely presumed in the West to refer exclusively to waging war against nonbelievers, an Islamic jihad is not the equivalent of a Christian Crusade, at least not as practiced by most Muslims.

Chapter Perspective 7.3 provides some clarification of the concept of jihad.

State-Sponsored Religious Terrorism

Government sponsorship of terrorism is not limited to providing support for ideological or ethno-nationalist movements. It also incorporates state sponsorship of religious revolutionary movements.

CHAPTER PERSPECTIVE 7.3

Jihad: Struggling in the Way of God

The concept of jihad is a central tenet in Islam. Contrary to misinterpretations common in the West, the term literally means a sacred "struggle" or "effort" rather than an armed conflict or fanatical holy war.[a] Although a jihad can certainly be manifested as a holy war, it more correctly refers to the duty of Muslims to personally strive "in the way of God."[b]

This is the primary meaning of the term as used in the Quran, which refers to an internal effort to reform bad habits in the Islamic community or within the individual Muslim. The term is also used more specifically to denote a war waged in the service of religion.[c]

Regarding how one should wage jihad,

> The greater jihad refers to the struggle each person has within himself or herself to do what is right. Because of human pride, selfishness, and sinfulness, people of faith must constantly wrestle with themselves and strive to do what is right and good. The lesser jihad involves the outward defense of Islam. Muslims should be prepared to defend Islam, including military defense, when the community of faith is under attack.[d] (emphasis added)

Thus, waging an Islamic jihad is not the same as waging a Christian crusade—it has a broader and more intricate meaning. Nevertheless, it is permissible—and even a duty—to wage war to defend the faith against aggressors. Under this type of jihad, warfare is conceptually defensive in nature; in contrast, the Christian Crusades were conceptually offensive in nature. Those who engage in armed jihad are known as *mujahideen,* or holy warriors. Mujahideen who receive "martyrdom" by being killed in the name of the faith will find that awaiting them in paradise are rivers of milk and honey, and beautiful young women. Those entering paradise are eventually reunited with their families and as martyrs stand in front of God as innocent as a newborn baby.[e]

The precipitating causes for the modern resurgence of the armed and radical jihadi movement are twofold: the revolutionary ideals and ideology of the 1979 Iranian Revolution and the practical application of jihad against the Soviet Union's occupation of Afghanistan.

Some radical Muslim clerics and scholars have concluded that the Afghan jihad brought God's judgment against the Soviet Union, leading to the collapse of its empire. As a consequence, radical jihadis fervently believe that they are fighting in the name of an inexorable force that will end in total victory and guarantee them a place in paradise. From their perspective, their war is a just war.[f]

Notes

a. Karen Armstrong, *Islam: A Short History* (New York, NY: Modern Library, 2000), 201.

b. Josh Burke and James Norton, "Q&A: Islamic Fundamentalism: A World-Renowned Scholar Explains Key Points of Islam," *Christian Science Monitor,* October 4, 2001.

c. Armstrong, *Islam,* 201.

d. Burke and Norton, "Q&A."

e. Walter Laqueur, *The New Terrorism: Fanaticism and the Arms of Mass Destruction* (New York, NY: Oxford University Press, 1999), 100.

f. See Evan R. Goldstein, "How Just Is Islam's Just-War Tradition?," *The Chronicle Review,* April 18, 2008.

National Case: Iran

Iran became a preeminent state sponsor of religious terrorism after the overthrow of the monarchy of **Shah Mohammad Reza Pahlavi** in 1979 and the creation of the theocratic Islamic Republic of Iran soon thereafter.

Iran has been implicated in the sponsorship of a number of groups known to have engaged in terrorist violence, making it a perennial entry on the U.S. Department of State's list of state sponsors of terrorism. The Iranian **Revolutionary Guards Corps** has a unit—the **Qods (Jerusalem) Force**—that promotes Islamic revolution abroad and the liberation of Jerusalem from non-Muslims. Members of the Revolutionary Guards have appeared in Lebanon and Sudan, and the United States designated the entire corps as a terrorist group in August 2007.[11] Significantly, Iranian officials have repeatedly announced the formation of Iranian "martyrdom" units whose members are prepared to engage in suicide attacks against American and Israeli targets.[12]

Case: Iranian Support for Lebanon's Hezbollah

An important example of Iranian support for politically sympathetic groups is the patronage and assistance Iran gives to Lebanon's Hezbollah movement. The Iran–Hezbollah relationship is important because of the central role Hezbollah has played in the region's political environment.

Hezbollah (Party of God) is a Shi'a movement in Lebanon that arose to champion the country's Shi'a population. The organization emerged during the Lebanese civil war and Israel's 1982 invasion as a strongly symbolic champion for Lebanese independence and justice for Lebanese Shi'a. It was responsible for hundreds of incidents of political violence during the 1980s and 1990s, which included kidnappings of Westerners in Beirut, suicide bombings, attacks against Israeli interests in South Lebanon, and attacks against Israel proper. Hezbollah operated under various names, such as Islamic Jihad and **Revolutionary Justice Organization**.

Hezbollah has for some time been closely linked to Iran. Hezbollah's leadership, although sometimes guarded about their identification with Iran, has said publicly that they support the ideals of the Iranian Revolution. Their ultimate goal is to create an Islamic republic in Lebanon, and they consider Israel an enemy of all Muslims. Hezbollah tends to consider Iran a "big brother" for its movement. At their root, the ideological bonds between the movement and the Iranian Revolution are strong. These bonds allowed Iran's support to extend beyond ideological identification toward overt sponsorship. Beginning in the 1980s, Iran deployed members of its Revolutionary Guards Corps into Lebanon's **Beka'a Valley**—then under Syrian occupation—to organize Hezbollah into an effective fighting force. Iran provided training, funding, and other logistical support. This was done with the acquiescence of Syria, so Hezbollah also became a pro-Syrian movement.

Case: Iranian Support for Palestinian Islamists

Iran has also promoted movements that directly confront the Israelis in Gaza, the West Bank, and inside Israel's borders. Since the early days of the Iranian Revolution, the Iranian regime has never been guarded about its goal to liberate Jerusalem. To achieve it, Iran has likewise never been guarded about its support for Palestinian organizations that reject dialogue and negotiations with the Israelis. Iran has, in fact, helped the Palestinian cause significantly by promoting the operations of religious movements. For example, two militant Islamic organizations—Palestine Islamic Jihad (PIJ) and HAMAS (Islamic Resistance Movement)—are Palestinian extremist groups that have received important support from Iran. Both groups perpetrated many acts of terrorism, including suicide attacks, bombings, shootings, and other violent assaults.

PIJ is not a single organization but instead a loose affiliation of factions, an Islamic revolutionary movement that advocates violent jihad to form a Palestinian state. Iranian support provided to PIJ includes military instruction and logistical support. PIJ members have appeared in Hezbollah camps in Lebanon's Beka'a Valley and in Iran, and planning for terrorist attacks has apparently taken place in these locations. Members who received this training were infiltrated back into Gaza and the West Bank to wage jihad against Israel.

HAMAS's roots lie in the Palestinian branch of the Muslim Brotherhood. It operates as both a social service organization and an armed resistance group that promotes jihad. Because of its social service component, Iran's **Fund for the Martyrs** has disbursed millions of dollars to HAMAS. HAMAS posted a representative to Iran who held a number of meetings with top Iranian officials. Iran has also provided HAMAS with the same type of support that it provides PIJ, including military instruction, logistical support, training in Hezbollah's Beka'a Valley camps (before the Syrian withdrawal), and training in Iran. HAMAS operatives returned from these facilities to Gaza and the West Bank.

Regional Case: Pakistan and India

India and Pakistan are seemingly implacable rivals. Much of this rivalry is grounded in religious animosity between the Hindu and Muslim communities of the subcontinent, but sponsorship of terrorist proxies has kept the region in a state of nearly constant tension. Hindus and Muslims in Southwest Asia have engaged in sectarian violence since 1947, when British colonial rule ended. During and after the British withdrawal, communal fighting and terrorism between Hindus and Muslims led to the partition of British India into mostly Muslim East Pakistan and West Pakistan (now Bangladesh) and mostly Hindu India. Since independence, conflict has been ongoing between Pakistan and India over many issues, including Indian support for Bangladesh's war of independence from Pakistan, disputed borders, support for religious nationalist terrorist organizations, the development of nuclear arsenals, and the disputed northern region of Jammu and Kashmir.

Pakistan, through its intelligence agency, the **Directorate for Inter-Services Intelligence (ISI)**, has a long history of supporting insurgent groups fighting against Indian interests. Religious terrorist groups in the Indian state of Punjab and in Jammu and Kashmir have received Pakistani aid in what has become a high-stakes conflict between two nuclear powers that can also field large conventional armies. The Pakistan-India conflict is arguably as volatile as the Arab-Israeli rivalry but with many times the manpower and firepower. This is especially noteworthy because both countries have nuclear arsenals.

Chapter Perspective 7.4 discusses the 2008 assault on Mumbai, India, by highly trained members of Lashkar-e-Taiba.

CHAPTER PERSPECTIVE 7.4

Assault on Mumbai

Mumbai (formerly Bombay) is India's largest city, the country's financial hub, and home to the famous and lucrative "Bollywood" Hindi-language film industry. Its reputation is one of prosperous cosmopolitanism, and Western tourists are drawn to reputable hotels, an active nightlife, and rich cultural history. Unfortunately, in recent years, the port city has experienced a series of lethal terrorist attacks. These incidents include the detonation of two car bombs in August 2003 that killed approximately 50 people and seven bombs aboard passenger trains that killed more than 200 in July 2006.

From November 26 through 29, 2008, Mumbai was attacked by 10 determined terrorists who entered the city from the sea aboard dinghies. The attackers spread out to assault high-profile targets throughout Mumbai's urban center, firing at victims randomly and throwing explosives. Tourist sites, hotels, and a Jewish center were specifically selected for their symbolic value and to inflict maximum casualties. The ferocity of the assault is reflected in the following events:

- More than 50 people were killed at the Taj Mahal Palace and Tower hotel. During the initial assault on the night and early morning of November 26 to 27, terrorists seized and killed hostages. A large fire broke out as they fought National Security Guard commandos and police officers when the troops and officers conducted room-to-room searches. Dozens of hostages were rescued during the operation. Firefights continued for days as the terrorists evaded the security sweep, finally ending on the morning of November 29.

- More than 30 people were killed at the Oberoi Hotel, which was attacked at the same time

(Continued)

and in a similar manner as the Taj Mahal Palace and Tower. Terrorists at the Oberoi seized and killed hostages on November 26 to 27 and began hide-and-seek gun battles with members of the National Security Guard. The Guard restored order during the afternoon of November 28.

- Eight people were killed at Nariman House, an ultra-orthodox Jewish Lubavitch-Chabad center. On the night of November 26 to 27, terrorists attacked the center and seized hostages, including the center's rabbi and his wife. As gunshots were intermittently heard inside Nariman House, commandos assaulted the building on the morning of November 28 and secured the center by nighttime. Although many hostages were freed, others were killed by the terrorists. Victims included the rabbi and his wife.

- Members of the terrorist unit struck several other targets around the city, including the Chhatrapati Shivaji Terminus (where dozens were killed), the popular Leopald Café (frequented by tourists), and the Cama and GT Hospitals.

Indian security forces were caught off guard by the scope and violence of the assault. By the time order was restored, more than 160 people had been killed and hundreds more injured. Nine terrorists and approximately 20 police officers and soldiers were killed. The lone survivor among the terrorists signed a seven-page confession approximately two weeks after the attack in which he confirmed that the men were members of Lashkar-e-Taiba (Army of the Pure), a Pakistan-based Islamist organization. He described his weapons training at several Lashkar camps in Pakistan and his indoctrination on alleged Indian atrocities against Muslims. Training in Karachi, Pakistan, included how to operate fast boats. When he and nine others embarked on a ship in late November, each man was issued an AK-47 assault rifle, hand grenades, and ammunition. They were ordered to maximize casualties on their mission.

The involvement of Lashkar-e-Taiba resulted in an escalation in tensions between India and Pakistan. Distrust was exacerbated because of Lashkar's long affiliation with Pakistan's Directorate for Inter-Services Intelligence (ISI). This affiliation was instrumental in the group's rise to prominence and viability within the Islamist movement, largely because ISI allowed the group to engage in recruitment, training, logistical support, and networking. In fact, ISI patronage allowed the group to operate rather openly in Pakistan. Lashkar's initial role as a Pakistani proxy against India in Kashmir eventually grew into a sizeable movement with wealthy patrons from Saudi Arabia and other countries. Their sophisticated use of the Internet permitted the group to communicate with fellow Islamists in Asia and the Middle East, thus enhancing its international image and contacts. Significantly, Lashkar operatives fought in Iraq against the American-led occupation.

Dissident Religious Terrorism in the Modern Era

Dissident religious terrorism is political violence conducted by groups of fervent religious true believers with faith in the sacred righteousness of their cause. Any behavior in the defense of this cause is considered not only justifiable but also blessed. As discussed, most major religions—in particular, Christianity, Islam, Judaism, and Hinduism—have extremist adherents, some of whom have engaged in terrorist violence. Smaller religions and cults have similar adherents. Among the ubiquitous principles are the convictions that they are defending their faith from attack by nonbelievers or that their faith as indisputable and a universal guiding principle must be advanced for the salvation of the faithful. These principles are manifested in various ways and to varying degrees by religious extremists but are usually at the core of the belief system.

From the perspective of religious radicals in the Middle East, violence done in the name of God is perfectly rational behavior because God is on their side. Many of the holy sites in the region are sacred to more than one faith, such as Jerusalem, where a convergence of claims exists among Muslims, Jews, and Christians. When these convergences occur, some extremists believe that the claims of other faiths are inherently blasphemous. Because of this sort of indisputable truth, some extremists believe that God wishes for nonbelievers to be driven from sacred sites or otherwise barred from legitimizing their claims.

Case: The Grand Mosque Incident

The framework for Muslim life is based on the Five Pillars of Islam. The Five Pillars are faith, prayer, charity (*zakat*), fasting during the month of Ramadan, and the *hajj* (pilgrimage) to the holy city of Mecca, Saudi Arabia. In November 1979, during their hajj, 300 radicals occupied the Grand Mosque in Mecca. Their objective was to foment a popular Islamic uprising against the ruling Saud royal family. After nearly two weeks of fighting, the Grand Mosque was reoccupied by the Saudi army, but not before the Saudis called in French counterterrorist commandos to complete the operation. More than 100 radicals were killed, and scores were later executed by the Saudi government. During the fighting, Iranian radio accused the United States and Israel of plotting the takeover, and a Pakistani mob attacked the U.S. embassy in Islamabad, killing two Americans.

Case: The Hebron Mosque Massacre

On February 25, 1994, a New York–born physician, **Baruch Goldstein**, fired on worshippers inside the Ibrahim Mosque at the Cave of the Patriarchs holy site in the city of Hebron, Israel. As worshippers performed their morning prayer ritual, Goldstein methodically shot them with an Israel Defense Forces Galil assault rifle. He fired approximately 108 rounds in about 10 minutes before a crowd of worshippers rushed him and killed him. According to official government estimates, he killed 29 people and wounded another 125;[13] according to unofficial estimates, approximately 50 people died.[14] In reprisal for the Hebron massacre, the Palestinian Islamic fundamentalist movement HAMAS launched a bombing campaign that included the first wave of human suicide bombers.

Case: The Rabin Assassination

On November 4, 1995, Israeli prime minister Yitzhak Rabin was assassinated by **Yigal Amir**, who had stalked Rabin for about a year.[15] He shot Rabin in the back with hollow-point bullets in full view of Israeli security officers. Amir was a Jewish extremist who said that he acted fully within the requirements of *Halacha*, the Jewish code.[16]

Case: Sectarian Civil War in Iraq

Iraq is a multicultural nation with significant but varying strong ethno-nationalist, tribal, and religious identities. The demography consists of the following subpopulations.[17]

- Arab: 75% to 80%
- Kurdish: 15% to 20%
- Turkoman, Assyrian, or other: 5%
- Shi'a Muslim: 60% to 65%
- Sunni Muslim: 32% to 37%
- Christian or other: 3%

Tensions that had simmered during the Hussein years led to difficulty in fully integrating all groups into accepting a single national identity. For example, many Arabs who had moved into northern Kurdish regions after native Kurds were forced out became pariahs when Kurds returned to reclaim their homes and land. Some violence was directed against the Arab migrants. More ominously, the Sunni minority—which had dominated the country under Saddam Hussein—found itself recast as a political minority when the country began to move toward democracy when an interim government was established in June 2004. Sunnis expressed their dissatisfaction when large numbers refused to participate in elections to form a Transitional National Assembly in January 2005.

Also in Iraq, religious extremists—it is unclear whether they are Sunni or Shi'a—conducted a series of attacks on non-Muslim cultural institutions. These included liquor stores (often owned by Christians) and barbershops that designed Western-style haircuts.[18]

These examples confirm that religious terrorism in the Middle East occurs between, and within, local religious groups. Radical true believers of many faiths attack not only those of other religions but also "fallen" members of their own. Attacks against proclaimed apostasies can be quite violent.

Readers should be familiar with the essential distinctions between the Sunni and Shi'a Islamic traditions, which Table 7.2 summarizes.

Movement Case: The International Mujahideen (Holy Warriors for the Faith)

The mujahideen are Islamic fighters who have sworn a vow to take up arms to defend the faith. They tend to be believers in fundamentalist interpretations of Islam that have defined their jihad, or personal struggle, to be one of fighting and dying on behalf of the faith.

The modern conceptualization of the mujahideen began during the Soviet war in Afghanistan, which dated from the Soviet invasion of the country in December 1979 to its withdrawal in February 1989. Although several Afghan rebel groups (mostly ethnically based) fought the Soviets, they collectively referred to themselves as mujahideen. To them, their war of resistance was a holy jihad. Significantly, Muslim volunteers from around the world

---

Table 7.2   Two Traditions, One Religion

Sunni and Shi'a Muslims represent the two predominant traditions in Islam. Demographically, Sunni Islam represents about 85% to 90% of all Muslims, and Shi'a Islam represents about 10% to 15%. They are distinct practices that originate from, and worship within, a core system of belief.

Unlike Christian denominations, which can diverge quite markedly, the Sunni and Shi'a traditions differ less in interpretations of religious faith and more on historical sources of religious authority. The two paths in Islam hearken back to the death of the prophet Muhammed and the question of who among his successors represented true authority within the faith.

The differences between Sunni and Shi'a beliefs are summarized in this table.

Sunni Muslims	Shi'a Muslims
Historically accept all four caliphs (successors to Muhammed) as being legitimate, including the caliph Ali, Muhammed's son-in-law and cousin.	Historically reject the first three caliphs before Ali as being illegitimate successors to Muhammed.
Only the prophet Muhammed and the holy Quran are authorities on questions of religion. The Shi'a succession of imams is rejected.	As the first legitimate caliph, Ali was also the first in a historical line of imams, or leaders within Muslim communities.
Historically, leaders within the Islamic world have been political leaders and heads of governments rather than religious leaders.	Imams serve as both political and religious leaders.
There is no strictly organized clergy. For example, no single religious leader can claim ultimate authority, and non-clergy may lead prayers.	Imams have strict authority, and their pronouncements must be obeyed. Imams are without sin, and they appoint their successors.

---

served alongside them. These so-termed **Afghan Arabs** played an important role in spreading the modern jihadist ideology throughout the Muslim world.

Reasons for taking up arms as a **jihadist** vary.[19] Some recruits answer calls for holy war from religious scholars who might declare, for example, that Islam is being repressed by the West. Others respond to clear and identifiable threats to their people or country, such as the Soviet invasion of Afghanistan, the U.S.-led occupation of Iraq, or the Israeli occupation of Gaza and the West Bank. Others may join on behalf of the cause of other Muslims, such as the wars fought by Bosnian Muslims or Algerian rebels. Following the 2011 Arab Spring protests, thousands of Islamist fighters volunteered to wage jihad against the Assad regime in Syria and the Shi'a-led government in Iraq. Several thousand of these volunteers were Westerners.

▶ Holy war against Communist invaders. Afghan mujahideen during their jihad against occupying Soviet troops.

Regardless of the precipitating event, mujahideen are characterized by their faith in several basic values. The ideology of the modern mujahideen requires selfless sacrifice in defense of the faith. Accepting the title of mujahideen means that one must live, fight, and die in accordance with religious teachings. Mujahideen believe in the inevitability of victory, because the cause is being waged on behalf of the faith and in the name of God; both the faith and God will prevail. In this defense of the faith, trials and ordeals should be endured without complaint because the pain suffered in this world will be rewarded after death in paradise. If one lives a righteous and holy life, for example, by obeying the moral proscriptions of the Quran, one can enjoy these proscribed pleasures in the afterlife.

As applied by the mujahideen, the defensive ideology of jihad holds that when one defends the faith against the unfaithful, death is martyrdom, and through death paradise is ensured.[20]

Organization Case: Al Qaeda's Religious Foundation

The most prominent pan-Islamic revolutionary organization of this era is now-deceased Saudi national **Osama bin Laden**'s cell-based Al Qaeda (the Base), which seeks to unite Muslims throughout the world in a holy war. Al Qaeda is not a traditional hierarchical revolutionary organization, nor does it call for its followers to do much more than engage in terrorist violence in the name of the faith. It is best described as a loose network of like-minded Islamic revolutionaries. Al Qaeda is different because it

- holds no territory,
- has virtually no state sponsorship,
- does not champion the aspirations of an ethno-nationalist group,
- promulgates vague political demands,
- has no top-down organizational structure, and
- has a completely religious worldview.

Al Qaeda's religious orientation is a reflection of Osama bin Laden's sectarian ideological point of view. Bin Laden's worldview was created by his exposure to Islam-motivated armed resistance. As a boy, he inherited from his father between $20 million and $80 million, with estimates ranging as high as $300 million. When the Soviets invaded Afghanistan in 1979, bin Laden eventually joined with thousands of other non-Afghan Muslims who traveled to Peshawar, Pakistan, to prepare to wage jihad. However, his main contribution to the holy war was to solicit financial and matériel (military hardware) contributions from wealthy Arab sources. He apparently excelled at this. The final leg of his journey toward international Islamic terrorism occurred when he and thousands of other Afghan veterans—the Afghan Arabs—returned to their countries to carry on their struggle in the name of Islam. Beginning in 1986, bin Laden organized a training camp that grew in 1988 into the Al Qaeda group. While in his home country of Saudi Arabia, bin Laden "became enraged when King Fahd let American forces, with their rock music and Christian and Jewish troops, wage the Persian Gulf War from Saudi soil in 1991."[21]

After the Gulf War, bin Laden and a reinvigorated Al Qaeda moved to their new home in Sudan for five years. It was there that the Al Qaeda network began to grow into a self-sustaining financial and training base for promulgating jihad. Bin Laden and his followers configured the Al Qaeda network with one underlying purpose: "launching and leading a holy war against the Western infidels he could now see camped out in his homeland, near the holiest shrines in the Muslim world."[22]

Al Qaeda has inspired Islamic fundamentalist revolutionaries and terrorists in a number of countries. It became a significant source of financing and training for thousands of jihadis. The network is essentially a nonstate catalyst for transnational religious radicalism and violence.

When Al Qaeda moved to Afghanistan, its reputation as a financial and training center attracted many new recruits and led to the creation of a loose network of cells and sleepers in dozens of countries. Significantly, aboveground radical Islamic groups with links to Al Qaeda took root in some nations and overtly challenged authority through acts of terrorism. These affiliated groups included **Laskar Jihad (Militia of the Holy War)** in Indonesia, Al Qaeda in the Islamic Maghreb (AQIM) in West Africa, and Al Qaeda in the Arabian Peninsula (AQAP) in Yemen and Saudi Arabia.

Al Qaeda and martyrdom in the new era of terrorism. Operatives of the late Osama bin Laden's Al Qaeda network have demonstrated a propensity for suicidal violence. Highly destructive attacks are most frequently targeted against American interests but not unknown against rival factions.

Interestingly, Al Qaeda apparently designed an internal consensus about how to conduct its operations. Members of the network committed to writing what are best described as operational protocols, discovered during searches of Al Qaeda hideouts in the aftermath of the September 11 attacks. Manuals—including a six-volume, 1,000-page CD-ROM version—were found in locations as diverse as Chechnya, the United States, Afghanistan, and England. Chapter Perspective 7.5 presents the case of the San Bernardino attack in the United States.

CHAPTER PERSPECTIVE 7.5

The San Bernardino Attack

On December 2, 2015, 14 people were killed and 21 injured when two armed assailants—a married couple—attacked the Inland Regional Center in San Bernardino, California. The state-run center assisted people with developmental disabilities. The assailants were Syed Rizwan Farook, who had worked at the regional center for five years, and his wife Tashfeen Malik. Farook was born and raised in the United States, and Malik was born in Pakistan. Farook previously traveled abroad to Pakistan and Saudi Arabia, where he participated in the Muslim hajj to Mecca. He returned to the United States in July 2014 with Malik, whom he subsequently married.

On the day of the attack, Farook attended a holiday party at the regional center. He left the gathering and went to his home to prepare with Malik for their assault. They left their six-month-old child with Farook's mother, advising her that they were on their way to a medical appointment. Farook and Malik then dressed in paramilitary tactical gear and armed themselves. They returned to the regional center carrying semiautomatic assault rifles and pistols while wearing masks and opened fire on celebrants at the holiday party, killing and wounding at least 35 people. They left the facility and returned home, where the police had posted a stakeout after a tip about the vehicle they were driving. Law enforcement officers identified their vehicle and gave chase when Farook and Malik took to the road. During the chase, Farook and Malik shot at police officers and tossed an inert pipe out of their vehicle, apparently as an attempted ruse that it was a pipe bomb. Both assailants were shot and killed when they stopped their vehicle and engaged in an intensive firefight with more than 20 officers.

The incident required extensive prior planning by the couple. Aside from the weapons and tactical gear in their possession during the assault and chase, a search of their home by law enforcement officers uncovered 12 functional pipe bombs, thousands of rounds of ammunition, and material for constructing more bombs. The couple had also placed an improvised explosive device (IED) at the scene of the assault. The IED consisted of three pipe bombs with a remote control detonator that would have been activated by a toy car controller. A law enforcement official reported that an unsuccessful attempt had been made to convert at least one of the semiautomatic assault rifles to fully automatic. Farook and Malik attempted to destroy computer hard drives and other electronic equipment in their home prior to the incident.

The incident also confirmed the reality of a domestic threat environment in the United States that for years had existed in Europe: mass-casualty violence emanating from homegrown terrorists inspired by international terrorist movements. During the attack, Malik posted a message, under an alias, on Facebook pledging allegiance to Abu Bakr al-Baghdadi, leader of ISIS. Two days later, a pro-ISIS broadcast declared that the couple were supporters of the movement.

Insurgency Case: The Rise of the Islamic State of Iraq and the Levant[23]

In early 2014 the international community was surprised when a little-known Sunni insurgent movement overran significant swaths of territory in northern Iraq. The international community was further alerted when these insurgents seized major population centers in Iraq—particularly the cities of Mosul and Tikrit (Saddam Hussein's home city)—as the Iraqi army and other security forces were routed. The movement was the **Islamic State of Iraq and the Levant**, also known as the Islamic State of Iraq and al-Sham, or ISIS.

ISIS was formally declared to exist in April 2013 during the Syrian civil war that began in the aftermath of the 2011 Arab Spring protests and that subsequently escalated to internecine warfare in 2012. The central tenets of ISIS are its refusal to recognize the borders of Syria, Iraq, and other Eastern Mediterranean nations and its war to achieve the avowed goal of establishing a renewed caliphate (Islamic state) transcending these borders. This doctrine brought the movement into political opposition with Al Qaeda's central leadership, in particular leader Ayman al-Zawahiri, who disavowed ISIS when the group refused to limit its operations only to Syria. This disavowal did nothing to diminish ISIS's operations on the battlefield. In Iraq, ISIS became the de facto successor to Abu Musab al-Zarqawi's Al Qaeda Organization for Holy War in Iraq (AQI), which had waged an intensive Islamist insurgency from about 2005 to 2006 against U.S.-led occupation forces, the Iraqi army, and the Shi'a Badr Brigade.

ISIS adopted brutal tactics from the beginning of its war. The movement regularly executed captured Iraqi soldiers and police officers, imprisoned and tortured Iraqi civilians, and imposed draconian shari'a law and order in the territory it occupied. ISIS routinely recorded and broadcast beheadings, crucifixions, and massacres via social networking media. As knowledge of ISIS's tactics spread, thousands of members of the Iraqi army and security forces literally shed their uniforms and abandoned weapons when relatively small numbers of ISIS fighters advanced.

ISIS successfully inspired international fighters to join the movement in Syria and Iraq, many of whom were volunteers from North Africa, Chechnya, Europe, and the United States. A stated goal of ISIS was to have these volunteers return to their home countries to wage jihad domestically.

Like Al Qaeda, the ISIS "brand" inspired other insurgent groups to profess allegiance to the ISIS cause of creating a pan-Islamic state. Boko Haram in northeastern Nigeria and bordering regions declared allegiance in 2015. The Abu Sayyaf group in the Philippines also professed allegiance to ISIS after reversing its initial allegiance to Al Qaeda.

National Case: Boko Haram in Nigeria

The **Boko Haram** organization was founded in 2002 in the city of Maiduguri in northeastern Nigeria. Originally little more than a religious complex with a school and a mosque, the organization also espoused a political agenda with the goal of establishing an Islamic state. The Islamic school actively recruited adherents for waging jihad, and in 2009 Boko Haram launched sporadic attacks against government installations and personnel in Maiduguri. Since 2009, Boko Haram has attacked military and police targets, schools, Christian churches, and gathering places such as bars. It has been responsible for thousands of casualties, kidnappings, and population displacements, with the weekly death toll sometimes exceeding 100 victims.

The term *Boko Haram* is loosely translated as "Western education is forbidden," a reference in part to the legacy of British colonial missionary work and the presence of a significant Christian population in Nigeria. The group also holds that participation in Western social or political activity is forbidden, including participating in elections and adopting Western dress.

Cult Case: Aum Shinrikyō (Supreme Truth; Aleph)

Aum Shinrikyō is a Japan-based cult founded by **Shoko Asahara** in 1987. Its goal under Asahara's leadership was to seize control of Japan and then the world. The core belief is that Armageddon is imminent. One component is that the United States will wage World War III against Japan.[24] As one top member of the cult explained, "This evil [of the modern age] will be shed in a 'catastrophic discharge' . . . [and only those who] repent their evil deeds . . . [will survive]."[25]

At its peak membership, Aum Shinrikyō had perhaps 9,000 members in Japan and 40,000 members around the world, thousands of them in Russia.[26] Asahara claimed to be the reincarnation of Jesus Christ and Buddha and urged his followers to arm themselves if they were to survive Armageddon. This apocalyptic creed led to the stockpiling of chemical and biological weapons, including nerve gas, anthrax, and Q-fever.[27] One report indicated that Aum Shinrikyō members had traveled to Africa to acquire the deadly Ebola virus. Several mysterious biochemical incidents occurred in Japan, including one in June 1994 in the city of Matsumoto, where seven people died and 264 were injured from a release of gas into an apartment building.[28]

On March 20, 1995, members of Aum Shinrikyō positioned several packages containing sarin nerve gas on five Tokyo subway trains scheduled to travel through Tokyo's Kasumigaseki train station. The containers were simultaneously punctured with umbrellas, thus releasing the gas into the subway system. Twelve people were killed and an estimated 5,000 to 6,000 were injured.[29] Tokyo's emergency medical system was unable to adequately respond to the attack, so only about 500 victims were evacuated and the remaining victims had to make their own ways to local hospitals.

The police seized tons of chemicals the cult had stockpiled. Asahara was arrested and charged with 17 counts of murder and attempted murder, kidnapping, and drug trafficking. A new leader, Fumihiro Joyu, assumed control of Aum Shinrikyō in 2000 and renamed the group Aleph (the first letter in the Hebrew and Arabic alphabets). He publicly renounced violence, and the cult enjoyed new growth in membership. A Japanese court sentenced Shoko Asahara to death by hanging on February 27, 2004. In July 2018, he and twelve other Aum members were executed.

Aum Shinrikyō is an example of the potential terrorist threat from apocalyptic cults and sects that are completely insular, segregated from mainstream society. Some cults are content to simply prepare for the End of Days, but others—like Aum Shinrikyō—are not averse to giving the apocalypse a violent push.

Table 7.3 summarizes the activity profiles of several of the terrorist groups and movements discussed in this chapter.

Table 7.3 Religious Terrorism

Although religious terrorist groups and movements share the general profile of religious identity and often are rooted in similar belief systems, they arise out of unique historical, political, and cultural environments that are peculiar to their respective countries. With few exceptions, most religious movements are grounded in these idiosyncratic influences.

Group	Activity Profile	
	Constituency	Adversary
Aum Shinrikyō	Fellow believers	The existing world order
Lord's Resistance Army	Fellow believers and members of the Acholi tribe	Ugandan government and "nonpurified" Acholis
Palestine Islamic Jihad	Palestinian Muslims	Israel
HAMAS	Palestinian Muslims	Israel
Al Qaeda	Faithful Muslims, as defined by Al Qaeda	Secular governments, nonbelievers, the West
Abu Sayyaf	Filipino Muslims	Filipino government, Western influence
Laskar Jihad	Moluccan Muslims	Moluccan Christians
Jammu-Kashmir groups	Jammu-Kashmir Muslims	India
Sikh groups	Punjabi Sikhs	India
Algerian/North African cells	Algerian Muslims and Muslims worldwide	Secular Algerian government, the West
Boko Haram	West African Muslims	Nigerian and West African nonbelievers, the West
Islamic State of Iraq and the Levant (al-Sham)	Levant Sunnis	Secular Arab nations, Shi'a, Non-believers

TRENDS AND PROJECTIONS

Religion is a central feature of the New Terrorism, which is characterized by asymmetrical tactics, cell-based networks, indiscriminate attacks against soft targets, and the threatened use of high-yield weapons technologies. Al Qaeda and its Islamist allies pioneered this strategy, and it serves as a model for similarly motivated individuals and groups. Religious extremists understand that if they take on these characteristics, their agendas and grievances will receive extensive attention and their adversaries will be sorely challenged to defeat them. It is therefore reasonable to presume that religious terrorists will practice this strategy for the near future.

Having made this observation, it is important to critically assess the following questions: What trends are likely to challenge the global community in the immediate future? Who will enlist as new **cadres** in extremist religious movements? Who will articulate the principles of their guiding ideologies? The following patterns, trends, and events are offered for critical consideration:

▶ A member of the Islamic State of Iraq and the Levant poses. From a propaganda film released by the group titled *The Flames of War.*

The Flames of War/al-Hayat Media/ISIL

- *Extremist religious propaganda cannot be prevented.* All religious extremists—Christian, Islamic, Jewish, and others—have discovered the utility of the Internet and the global media. They readily communicate with each other through the Internet, and their websites have become forums for propaganda and information.[30] Cable television and other members of the globalized media frequently broadcast interviews and communiqués. Social media are readily accessible dissemination outlets for live events as they occur in real time.

- *A new generation of Islamist extremists has been primed.* In a study reported in January 2005, the Central Intelligence Agency's National Intelligence Council concluded that the war in Iraq created a new training and recruitment ground for potential terrorists, replacing Afghanistan in this respect. As one official suggested, "There is even, under the best scenario . . . the likelihood that some of the jihadists [will go home], and will therefore disperse to various other countries."[31] This assessment accurately predicted the rise of a new generation of jihadists especially after the Arab Spring in 2011, when international fighters enlisted in newly emergent Islamist movements in Syria, Iraq, Libya, and elsewhere.

- *Al Qaeda has become more than an organization—it has evolved to become a symbol and an ideology.* Osama bin Laden, founder and leader of Al Qaeda, presented himself in a series of communiqués as an elder statesman and intellectual of Islam. He recast himself as a symbolic mentor for the next generation of fighters.[32] After his death in 2011, he was considered a martyr by many jihadists.

- *The jihadist movement has become a globalized phenomenon.* The dissemination of information and images through the media and the Internet created a global sense of solidarity among Islamists. Potential recruits easily access information, and many new volunteers are young people who live in the West, often in Europe.[33] The influx of Western volunteers who fought with Islamist movements such as ISIS confirmed the international scope and influence of the jihadist movement.

- *Christian extremists continue to promote a religious motivation for the war on terrorism.* Postings on some Christian websites and comments from some Christian leaders, usually in the United States, suggest that the Islamic faith is wrong or evil or both, and the war on terrorism is part of a divine plan pitting the "true faith" against Islam.[34]

Chapter Perspective 7.6 discusses two terrorist attacks in Paris, France. They represent an escalation of religious New Terrorism directed against domestic targets in Western democracies.

CHAPTER PERSPECTIVE 7.6

Assault on Paris

Paris, France, was the site of two significant terrorist incidents carried out by Islamist extremists in 2015. From January 7 to 9, 2015, several incidents occurred. On January 7, two brothers wielding AK-47 assault rifles opened fire inside the offices of *Charlie Hebdo*, a popular French satirical publication. *Charlie Hebdo* had published satirical cartoons of Islam and other religions, including depictions of the Prophet Muhammed, and the assault was conducted in retaliation for these depictions. The gunmen killed 12 people, including eight cartoonists and journalists and two police officers. The next day a police officer was killed outside Paris, and on January 9, the same shooter took four people hostage at a Jewish kosher market, eventually killing four hostages before being killed by French police. The kosher market shooter was an acquaintance of the two *Charlie Hebdo* attackers, who were killed on January 9 by French police.

On the night of November 13, 2015, several gunmen methodically attacked several sites in the heart of Paris. The assault began when a suicide explosion occurred near the Stade de France, where a Germany–France soccer match was being held. French president François Hollande was in attendance at the match. Elsewhere, approximately 15 people were killed at a bar and a restaurant when men opened fire from an automobile with AK-47 assault rifles. A second suicide explosion occurred outside the Stade de France, and nearly simultaneously, more people were killed in a separate attack from an automobile at another bar in Paris. A few minutes later, at least 19 people were killed at a café by gunfire from an automobile. A third suicide explosion occurred at another restaurant, and nearly simultaneously, three armed men opened fire and seized hostages during a concert at the Bataclan concert hall. The Bataclan attackers calmly and methodically executed scores of patrons with gunfire and hand grenades. As this was occurring, a fourth suicide bomb was detonated, again at the Stade de France—the third at the stadium. French police successfully stormed the Bataclan concert hall and killed all of the assailants but not before they had executed more than 100 patrons.

On November 18, 2015, French police and soldiers killed Abdelhamid Abaaoud, the alleged mastermind of the attack, during a raid conducted on a fortified dwelling in the Saint Denis neighborhood in Paris. A fifth suicide bomb was detonated during the raid.

DISCUSSION BOX

THE ONE TRUE FAITH

This chapter's Discussion Box is intended to stimulate critical debate about faith-motivated terrorism within major religions.

Most religious traditions have produced extremist movements whose members believe that their faith and value system is superior to other beliefs. This concept of the "one true faith" has been used by many fundamentalists to justify violent intolerance on behalf of their religions. Religious terrorists are modern manifestations of historical traditions of extremism within the world's major faiths. Consider these examples:

- In *Christianity*, the medieval Crusades were a series of exceptionally violent military campaigns against Muslims, Jews, and heretical Christian sects. Later, during the 16th and 17th centuries, Catholic and Protestant Christians waged relentless wars against each other, which were marked by extreme brutality. In the modern era, Christian terrorists and extremists have participated in communal fighting in numerous countries and, in the United States, have bombed abortion clinics and committed other acts of violence.

- In *Judaism,* the Old Testament is replete with references to the ancient Hebrews' faith-based mandate to wage war against non-Jewish occupiers of the Promised Land. In the modern era, the late **Rabbi Meir Kahane**'s Kach (Kahane Chai) movement in Israel has likewise advocated the expulsion of all Arabs from Israel. Two members of the **Jewish Defense League** were arrested in the United States in December 2001 on charges of conspiring to bomb Muslim mosques and the offices of a U.S. congressman in Los Angeles.

- In *Islam*, the relative religious tolerance of the 15th and 16th centuries is counterbalanced against modern intolerance among movements such as Afghanistan's Taliban, Palestine's HAMAS, and Lebanon's Hezbollah. Numerous examples exist of political and communal violence waged in the name of Islam. Overt official repression has also been imposed in the name of the Islamic faith, as in Saudi Arabia's policy of relegating women to second-class status.

(Continued)

(Continued)

Modern religious extremism is arguably rooted in faith-based natural law. Natural law is a philosophical "higher law" that is theoretically discoverable through human reason and references to moral traditions and religious texts. In fact, most religious texts have passages that can be selectively interpreted to encourage extremist intolerance. To religious extremists, it is God's law that has been revealed to—and properly interpreted by—the extremist movement.

Discussion Questions

1. Is faith-motivated activism a constructive force for change?

2. At what point does the character of faith-motivated activism become extremist and terrorist?

3. Does faith-based natural law justify acts of violence?

4. Why do religious traditions that supposedly promote peace, justice, and rewards for spiritual devotion have so many followers who piously engage in violence, repression, and intolerance?

5. What is the future of faith-based terrorism?

CHAPTER SUMMARY

Religious movements are motivated by a belief that an otherworldly power sanctions and commands their behavior. Some terrorists are motivated primarily by faith, whereas others use religion secondarily. The latter movements are motivated by nationalism or another ideology as a primary inspiration but are united by an underlying religious identity. The goals of both primary and secondary religious terrorism are to construct a new society based on a religious or ethno-nationalist identity. The terrorist behavior of both tendencies is active and public.

State-sponsored religious terrorism arises in governments that pursue international agendas by mentoring and encouraging religious proxies. The case of Iranian support for religious dissident terrorists is an example of a theocracy promoting its own revolutionary agenda. Syria is an example of a secular government that supports religious movements from a sense of common cause against a mutual enemy. Dissident religious terrorism involves attacks by self-proclaimed true believers against members of other faiths and perceived apostasies within their own faith. Some dissident groups espouse mystical or cult-like doctrines outside the belief systems of major religions.

KEY TERMS AND CONCEPTS

The following topics were discussed in this chapter and can be found in the Glossary:

WEB EXERCISE

Using this chapter's recommended websites listed on the student study site at **edge.sagepub.com/martiness5e**, conduct an online investigation of religious extremism.

1. What commonalities can you find among the religious websites? What basic values are similar? In what ways do they differ?

2. Are the religious sites effective propaganda? How would you advise the site designers to appeal to different constituencies?

For an online search of historical and cultural issues pertaining to religious extremism, readers should enter the following keywords in their Web browser's search engine:

"Christian Crusades"

"Jihad"

RECOMMENDED READINGS

The following publications discuss the motives, goals, and characteristics of religious extremism.

Allen, T. (2006). *Trial justice: The International Court and the Lord's Resistance Army*. New York, NY: Zed Books.

Bader, E. J., & Baird-Windle, P. (2002). *Targets of hatred: Anti-abortion terrorism*. New York, NY: Palgrave.

Bhutto, B. (2008). *Reconciliation: Islam, democracy, and the West*. New York, NY: Harper.

Crews, R. D., & Tarzi, A. (Eds.). (2009). *The Taliban and the crisis of Afghanistan*. Cambridge, MA: Harvard University Press.

Fishman, B. (2009). *Dysfunction and decline: Lessons learned from inside Al Qaeda in Iraq*. West Point, NY: Combating Terrorism Center, Harmony Project.

Gerges, F. A. (2006). *Journey of the jihadist: Inside Muslim militancy*. Orlando, FL: Harcourt.

Halevi, Y. K. (1995). *Memoirs of a Jewish extremist: An American story*. New York, NY: Little, Brown.

Huband, M. (1999). *Warriors of the prophet: The struggle for Islam*. Boulder, CO: Westview.

Jamal, A. (2010). *Shadow war: The untold story of jihad in Kashmir*. Hoboken, NJ: Melville.

Kelsay, J. (2007). *Arguing the just war in Islam*. Cambridge, MA: Harvard University Press.

Kepel, G., Milelli, J.-P., & Ghazaleh, P. (2008). *Al Qaeda in its own words*. Cambridge, MA: Belknap Press.

Lifton, R. J. (2000). *Destroying the world to save it: Aum Shinrikyō, apocalyptic violence, and the new global terrorism*. New York, NY: Holt.

Maszka, J. (2018). *Al-Shabaab and Boko Haram: Guerrilla insurgency or strategic terrorism?* London, UK: World Scientific.

Miniter, R. (2011). *Mastermind: The many faces of the 9/11 architect, Khalid Sheikh Mohammed*. New York, NY: Sentinel HC.

Norton, A. R. (2007). *Hezbollah: A short history*. Princeton, NJ: Princeton University Press.

Rashid, A. (2010). *Taliban: Militant Islam, oil and fundamentalism in central Asia* (2nd ed.). New Haven, CT: Yale University Press.

Reidel, B. (2010). *The search for Al Qaeda: Its leadership, ideology and future*. Washington, DC: Brookings Institution Press.

Rotberg, R. I. (Ed.). (2005). *Battling terrorism in the horn of Africa*. Washington, DC: Brookings Institution Press.

Schofield, V. (2010). *Kashmir in conflict: India, Pakistan, and the unending war*. New York, NY: I. B. Tauris.

Stern, J. (2003). *Terror in the name of God: Why religious militants kill*. New York, NY: Ecco/HarperCollins.

Tamimi, A. (2007). *Hamas: A history from within*. Northampton, MA: Olive Branch.

SAGE edge™

Want a better grade?

Get the tools you need to sharpen your study skills. Access practice quizzes, eFlashcards, video, and multimedia at **edge.sagepub.com/martiness5e**.

CHAPTER EIGHT

INTERNATIONAL TERRORISM

This chapter investigates the dimensions of international terrorism. International terrorism is terrorism that "spills over" onto the world's stage. Targets are selected because of their value as symbols of international interests and the impact that attacks will have on a global audience. Terrorism in the international arena has been a common feature of political violence since the late 1960s, when political extremists began to appreciate the value of allowing their revolutionary struggles to be fought in a global arena, primarily for its propaganda benefits. In adopting terrorism on a broader scale, revolutionary movements have been very successful in moving their underlying grievances to the forefront of the international agenda. It is not an exaggeration to conclude that "international terrorism represents one of the defining elements of politics on the world's stage today."[1]

International terrorism is one of the best examples of asymmetrical warfare—that is, unconventional, unexpected, and nearly unpredictable acts of political violence. Although it is an old practice, asymmetrical warfare has become a core feature of the New Terrorism. Practicing it, terrorists can theoretically acquire and wield new high-yield arsenals, strike at unanticipated targets, cause mass casualties, and apply unique and idiosyncratic tactics. The dilemma for victims and for counterterrorism policy makers is that by using these tactics, the terrorists can win the initiative and redefine the international security environment by overriding traditional protections and deterrent policies. In an era of immediate media attention, small and relatively weak movements have concluded that worldwide exposure is possible and worthwhile. They have discovered that politically motivated hijackings, bombings, assassinations, kidnappings, extortion, and other criminal acts conducted under an international spotlight guarantee some degree of attention and afford greater opportunities.

Chapter Perspective 8.1 summarizes the changing environments of international terrorism, presenting the predominant dissident profiles during the latter part of the 20th century and early decades of the 21st century.

Learning Objectives

This chapter will enable readers to do the following:

1. Define international terrorism.

2. Discuss the reasons for international terrorism.

3. Explain terrorist networks and environments.

4. Understand the international dimension of the New Terrorism.

CHAPTER PERSPECTIVE 8.1

The Changing Environment of International Terrorism

International terrorism is in many ways a reflection of global politics, so the international terrorist environment is dominated at different times by different terrorist typologies. Thus, one may conclude that the profile of international terrorism has progressed through several phases in the postwar era, which can be roughly summarized as follows:[a]

- From the 1960s through the early 1980s, *left-wing* terrorists figured prominently in international incidents. For example, Western European groups frequently attacked international symbols "in solidarity" with defined oppressed groups. Only a few leftist groups remain, and most of them do not often practice international terrorism.

- From the beginning of the modern era of international terrorism in the late 1960s, *Palestinian nationalists* were perhaps the leading practitioners of international terrorism. Participating in their struggle were Western European and Middle Eastern extremists who struck targets in solidarity with the Palestinian cause. By the late 1990s, with the creation of the governing authority in the West Bank and Gaza, Palestinian-initiated terrorism focused primarily on targets inside Israel and the occupied territories. Their radical Western comrades ceased their violent support by the late 1980s, but many Middle Eastern extremists continued to cite the Palestinian cause as a reason for their violent activism.

- Throughout the postwar era, *ethno-nationalist* terrorism occupied an important presence in the international arena. Its incidence has ebbed and flowed in scale and frequency, but ethno-nationalist violence has never completely disappeared. By the late 1990s, these groups operated primarily inside their home countries but continued to occasionally attack international symbols to bring attention to their domestic agendas.

- By the end of the 20th century, the most prominent practitioners of international terrorism were *religious* extremists. Although Islamic movements such as Al Qaeda–generated groups were the most prolific international religious terrorists, extremists from every major religion operated on the international stage.

- During the early decades of the 21st century, religious international terrorism firmly eclipsed international practitioners espousing other extremist causes. ISIS and Al Qaeda operatives conducted high-profile mass casualty attacks internationally, and these movements encouraged lone-wolf and small-cell attacks in Western countries.

- In the 21st century, extremist religious ideologies inspired followers via the Internet and other technologies. The Internet and social media provide robust resources for extremists to promulgate messages and to facilitate the recruitment of new adherents to their cause. No longer must movements directly communicate with sympathizers to advocate direct action; Internet- and social media–generated communiqués allow them to do so safely and remotely.

Note

a. Adapted from Paul R. Pillar, *Terrorism and U.S. Foreign Policy* (Washington, DC: Brookings Institution, 2001), 44–45.

International terrorism has two important qualities. It is both a specifically selected tactical and strategic instrument of political violence and a type of terrorism. The discussion in this chapter will review the following:

- Understanding International Terrorism
- International Terrorist Networks
- The International Dimension of the New Terrorism

UNDERSTANDING INTERNATIONAL TERRORISM

International terrorism occurs when the target is a global symbol and the political-psychological effects go beyond a purely domestic agenda. It will be recalled that state terrorism as foreign policy is often characterized by state sponsorship of dissident movements. In addition, many dissident terrorist groups and extremist movements have regularly acted in solidarity with international interests, such as class struggle or national liberation. It is also not uncommon for domestic groups and movements to travel abroad to attack targets symbolizing their domestic conflict or some broader global issue. Especially in the post–World War II world, terrorist groups have selected targets that only tangentially symbolize the sources of their perceived oppression. Links between seemingly domestic-oriented dissident terrorist groups and international terrorism are therefore not uncommon. Table 8.1 illustrates this point by reviewing the activity profiles of several dissident terrorist groups implicated in international incidents.

The Spillover Effect

Those who engage in political violence on an international scale do so with the expectation that it will have a positive **spillover effect** on their cause at home—thus reasoning that international exposure will bring about compensation for perceived injustices. Using this logic, terrorists will either go abroad to strike at targets or remain at home to strike

Table 8.1 Dissident Terrorism on the World's Stage

During the latter quarter of the 20th century, dissident terrorist groups attacked symbols of international interests many times. Some groups traveled abroad to strike at targets, whereas others attacked domestic symbols of international interests.

This table summarizes a variety of international incidents conducted by dissident terrorist groups.

Dissident Group	Activity Profile			
	Home Country	Incident	Target	International Effect
Abu Sayyaf	Philippines	April 2000 kidnapping	20 Asian and European tourists in Malaysia	Increased profile; $20 million ransom
Jemaah Islamiyah	Indonesia	October 2002 bombing	Tourist district in Bali; 202 killed, including 88 Australian tourists	International security fears of asymmetrical Islamist terrorism
Domestic cell inspired by Al Qaeda	Spain	March 2005 series of bombings	Commuter trains in Madrid; 191 killed, 1,800 injured	International security fears of asymmetrical terrorism; Spain withdrew troops from Iraq
Red Brigade	Italy	December 1981 kidnapping	U.S. Brigadier General James Dozier	Increased profile; NATO security crisis
Black September	Palestinian diaspora	Summer 1972 kidnapping	Israeli athletes at Summer Olympics	Increased profile; international crisis

internationally symbolic targets. The following characteristics distinguish international terrorism as a specific type of terrorism:

- Domestic Attacks Against Victims With an International Profile
- Operations in a Foreign Country

Domestic Attacks Against Victims With an International Profile

Most experts would agree that international terrorism by definition does not require terrorists to leave their home countries; they can strike domestically, depending on what the target represents. Examples of domestic targets with symbolic international links include diplomats, businessmen and -women, military personnel, and tourists. An important and disturbing result of these attacks has been a repeated trend in which terrorists recognize no qualitative difference between their victim group and the enemy interest it represents. Thus, innocent business travelers, civilians, academics, and military personnel are considered legitimate targets and fair game because they symbolize an enemy interest.

During the long Lebanese civil war in the 1970s and 1980s, militant Islamic groups targeted symbols of international interests with great drama. The Shi'a group Hezbollah was responsible for most of these incidents, examples of which include the bombing of the U.S. embassy in Beirut and attacks against French and American peacekeeping troops in Beirut. In addition, the kidnapping of foreign nationals by Islamic extremists became a prominent characteristic of the violence.

Operations in a Foreign Country

The history of terrorism is replete with examples of extremists who deliberately travel abroad to strike at an enemy. Their targets often include nationals that the terrorists symbolically associate with the policies of their perceived enemy. Some are representatives of these policies, such as diplomats or political officials, whereas others, such as business travelers and tourists, are only minimally linked. For example, the Algerian Armed Islamic Group launched a terrorist campaign in metropolitan France from July to October 1995. Eight people were killed and 180 injured during bombings of trains, schools, cafés, and markets. Terrorist plots today have taken on a decidedly transnational dimension, with cells linked across several countries. Extremist groups have deliberately positioned terrorist operatives and autonomous cells in foreign countries. Their purpose is to attack enemy interests with a presence in those countries. For example, during the 1990s, Latin American and U.S. security officials identified an apparent threat in South America, which indicated that Middle Eastern cells became active in the 1990s along the triangular border region where Brazil, Argentina, and Paraguay meet.

Unambiguous International Implications

Regardless of whether political violence is directed against domestic targets that are international symbols or takes place in other countries, the fundamental characteristic of international terrorism is that international consequences are clear. For example, the February 1993 attack on the World Trade Center in New York City had clear international consequences, as did the terrorist attacks of September 11, 2001. In both instances, foreign terrorist cells and the Al Qaeda network had used transnational resources to position terrorist operatives in the United States, their targets were prominent symbols of international trade and power, and their victims were citizens from many countries.

Case: Attacks on Embassies

International law recognizes embassies as legal representations of nations in foreign countries. Diplomats have special status as representatives of their governments, and because of this special status, embassies and diplomats are afforded recognized legal protections. It is therefore not uncommon that embassies and diplomats have been targets of terrorist attacks. The following plots against diplomatic missions are typical:

- India (January 21, 2002): Armed militants on motorcycles fire on the U.S. consulate in Kolkata, killing five Indian security personnel.

- Pakistan (June 14, 2002): A bomb explodes outside the American consulate in Karachi, killing 12.

- Uzbekistan (July 30, 2004): A suicide bomber detonates explosives at the U.S. embassy in Tashkent, killing two Uzbek security guards.

- Saudi Arabia (December 6, 2004): Militants storm the U.S. consulate compound in the Red Sea city of Jeddah, killing five non-American consular staff. Four of the five attackers die in the attack and a fifth is wounded and arrested.

- Pakistan (March 2, 2006): A car bomb outside the U.S. consulate in Karachi kills four people, including an American foreign service officer.

- Syria (September 12, 2006): Four Syrians try to blow up the U.S. embassy in Damascus, but the plot fails after Syrian guards kill three of the assailants in a shootout. The fourth man later dies of his wounds. A Syrian guard and bystander are also killed.

- Yemen (December 4, 2006): Yemeni security forces shoot and wound, as well as arrest, a gunman after he opens fire on the U.S. embassy in Sanaa.

- Greece (January 12, 2007): Attackers fire a rocket at the U.S. embassy in Athens. Authorities say anonymous callers claim that Greek leftists staged the attack.[2]

- Afghanistan (July 7, 2008): A large car bomb in Kabul kills more than 41 people at the gates of the Indian embassy.

- Libya (September 11, 2012): An attack on the U.S. consulate in Benghazi leaves four people dead, including the U.S. ambassador to Libya.

- Lebanon (November 19, 2013): The Iranian embassy in Beirut is bombed, killing and injuring more than 70 people.

- Ukraine (June 14, 2014): The Russian embassy in Kiev is attacked in the aftermath of the downing of a Ukrainian aircraft by pro-Russian separatists.

- Egypt (July 11, 2015): Suspected members of Islamic State attack the Italian embassy in Cairo.

- Afghanistan (November 11, 2016): The Taliban attacks the German consulate in Mazar-i-Sharif with a suicide truck bomb and firearms. The explosion causes extensive damage.

Chapter Perspective 8.2 discusses the 2012 attack on two U.S. diplomatic facilities in Benghazi, Libya. The U.S. ambassador, a foreign service officer, and two Central Intelligence Agency contractors were killed during the assault.

Case: Hijackings as International Spillovers

International passenger carriers are relatively soft targets that attract international media attention when attacked. The passengers are considered legitimate symbolic targets, so terrorizing or killing them is justifiable in the minds of the terrorists.

Beginning in the late 1960s, terrorists began attacking international ports of call used by travelers. International passenger carriers—primarily airliners—became favorite targets. In the

CHAPTER PERSPECTIVE 8.2

The Benghazi Attack

Islamist insurgents attacked two U.S. diplomatic facilities in Benghazi, Libya, on the night of September 11, 2012. U.S. ambassador John Christopher Stevens was killed during the attack, as was a foreign service officer (FSO) and two Central Intelligence Agency (CIA) security contractors. The insurgents first attacked and burned the U.S. diplomatic mission where the ambassador and FSO were killed, and later in the early morning attacked the annex where the CIA security contractors died. More than 30 American personnel were rescued from the diplomatic mission.

An international U.S. emergency response effort was activated. When the attack began, a surveillance drone was dispatched to the site. Secretary of Defense Leon Panetta and Chairman of the Joint Chiefs of Staff General Martin Dempsey met with President Barack Obama at the White House to discuss response options. Secretary Panetta ordered Marine antiterrorist teams in Spain to prepare to deploy to Benghazi and Tripoli. Special operations teams were also ordered to prepare for deployment from Croatia, the United States, and a staging area in Italy. A small security team was also deployed from the U.S. embassy in Tripoli.

Initial reports were that the attack was the work of a mob angered by the promulgation of an American-made film mocking the Prophet Muhammed and Islam. It was later determined that the attackers were armed Islamists. The political backlash about the initial assessment was intense, with calls for the resignation of the U.S. ambassador to the United Nations. Congressional hearings were held by the Senate Select Committee on Intelligence, the House Foreign Affairs Committee, the House Oversight Committee, and the Senate Foreign Relations Committee. Officials called to testify included Secretary of State Hillary Clinton. A House of Representatives Select Committee on Benghazi was established, which quickly became deeply divided along partisan political lines.

The attack and its aftermath created a partisan political crisis in the United States on the questions of what the facts of the crisis response actually were, whether information was intentionally obfuscated, and whether the Congressional investigations were motivated more by partisan politics than objective fact-finding.

---

beginning, hijackings were often the acts of extremists, criminals, or otherwise desperate people trying to escape their home countries to find asylum in a friendly country. This profile changed, however, when the Popular Front for the Liberation of Palestine (PFLP) staged a series of aircraft hijackings as a way to **publicize the cause** of the Palestinians before the world community. The first successful high-profile PFLP hijacking was Leila Khaled's attack in August 1969. The PFLP struck again in September 1970, when it attempted to hijack five airliners, succeeding in four of the attempts. These incidents certainly directed the world's attention to the Palestinian cause, but they also precipitated the Jordanian army's Black September assault against the Palestinians. Nevertheless, passenger carriers have since been frequent targets of international terrorists.

Table 8.2 summarizes the interplay between international terrorism and terrorist environments.

Reasons for International Terrorism

Extremist groups and movements resort to international terrorism for a number of reasons. Some act in cooperation with others, waging an international campaign against a perceived global enemy. France's **Direct Action**, Germany's Red Army Faction, and Italy's Red Brigade frequently attacked symbolic targets as expressions of solidarity with international causes, for

Table 8.2 International Terrorism and Terrorist Environments

Although cases of international terrorism exist for most terrorist environments, right-wing and traditional criminal terrorists tend to refrain from violence in the international arena.
This table identifies incidents of international terrorism within the framework of several terrorist environments.

Environment	Activity Profile			
	Incident	Perpetrator	Target	International Effect
State (1988)	Airline bombing over Lockerbie, Scotland	Libyan intelligence officers	Pan Am Flight 103	Significant effect; international crisis
Dissident (1994)	Bombing in Buenos Aires, Argentina	Possibly Hezbollah	Argentine Israelite Mutual Association	Medium effect; regional spillover
Left wing (2012)	Kidnapping	Colombia's FARC	France 24 journalist Romeo Langlois	Minimal effect; one of many hostages taken by FARC
Right wing (1990s–present)	Arson and other attacks in Germany	Neo-Nazis and supporters	Foreign "guest workers"; nonethnic German citizens	Minimal effect
Religious (2001)	Attacks of September 11, 2001	Al Qaeda	World Trade Center; Pentagon	Significant effect; international crisis and war
Criminal (1985)	Kidnapping and murder	Mexican narcotraficantes	U.S. DEA Special Agent Enrique Camarena	Significant effect; enhanced war on drugs

example. Other groups are motivated by idiosyncrasies unique to the group. For example, the **Armenian Secret Army for the Liberation of Armenia (ASALA)**, the **Justice Commandos of the Armenian Genocide**, and the **Armenian Revolutionary Army** waged a campaign of international terrorism against Turkish interests in Europe and the United States during the 1970s and 1980s.

The following discussion summarizes several underlying reasons extremists select international terrorism as a strategy:

- Ideological Reasons: Modern "isms" and International Revolutionary Solidarity

- Practical Reasons: Perceived Efficiency

- Tactical Reasons: Adapting Theory to Operations

- Historical Reasons: Perceptions of International Terrorism

Ideological Reasons: Modern "isms" and International Revolutionary Solidarity

Conflict in the post–World War II era was largely a by-product of resistance in many countries against former colonial powers. These indigenous wars of national liberation were global in the sense that insurgents established a common cause against what they perceived as domination by repressive and exploitative imperial powers and their local allies. Marxism and generalized leftist sentiment provided a common bond among radicals in the developing world and among Western dissidents.

Reasons for this resistance included, of course, the overt presence of foreign troops, administrators, and business interests in the newly emerging countries. From a broader global perspective, other reasons included the policies and ideologies of the Western powers. These policies and ideologies were given negative labels that insurgents affixed to the Western presence in the developing world. If one were to apply Marxist interpretations of class struggle and national liberation, these indigenous wars could easily be interpreted as representing an internationalized struggle against global exploitation by the West. The conceptual labels commonly used by violent extremists—both secular and religious—include the following:

Imperialism. Post–World War II dissidents fought against what they considered to be the vestiges of European colonial empires. Western powers had traditionally deemed empire building (**imperialism**) a legitimate manifestation of national prestige and power, an ideology that existed for centuries and was not finally ended until the latter decades of the 20th century. For example, the European scramble for Africa during the late 19th century was considered completely justifiable. During the wars of national liberation, foreign interests and civilians were attacked because they were seen as representatives of imperial powers.

Neocolonialism. **Neocolonialism** referred to exploitation by Western interests, usually symbolized by **multinational corporations**. Even when Western armies or administrators were not present and when indigenous governments existed, insurgents argued that economic exploitation still relegated the developing world to a subordinate status. From their perspective, the wealth of the developing world was being drained by Western economic interests. Domestic governments thus became targets because they were labeled as dupes of Western interests. Multinational corporations and other symbols of neocolonialism became targets around the world so that facilities and employees were attacked internationally.

Zionism. Historically an intellectual movement that sought to establish the proper means, conditions, and timing to resettle Jews in Palestine, **Zionism** was officially sanctioned by the Balfour Declaration of November 2, 1917; this was a statement by the British government that favored establishing a Jewish nation in Palestine as long as the rights of non-Jewish residents were guaranteed. The concept has become a lightning rod for resistance against Israel and its supporters. One significant difference in the international character of anti-Zionist terrorism—vis-à-vis resistance against imperialism and neocolonialism—is that international terrorists have attacked Jewish civilian targets around the world as symbols of Zionism. This adds a religious and ethno-nationalist dimension to anti-Zionist terrorism that does not necessarily exist in the other concepts discussed.

Practical Reasons: Perceived Efficiency

One basic (and admittedly simplified) reason for the high incidence of international terrorism is that it is perceived by many extremists to be "a highly efficient (if repugnant) instrument for achieving the aims of terrorist movements."[3] Using the rationale of perceived efficiency as a core motivation, practical reasons for international terrorism include several factors:

The Potential for Maximum Publicity. Terrorists practice propaganda by the deed and understand that international deeds get maximum media exposure. The media have always moved dramatic events to the top of their reporting agenda, and thus international terrorism is always depicted as important news. In November 1979, the American embassy was attacked in Tehran, Iran, and 53 Americans were held hostage until January 1981, a total of 444 days. During that time, Iran was at the center of media attention, and the revolutionaries were able to publicize their revolutionary agenda. They also embarrassed the most powerful nation in the world.

Inflicting the Potential for Maximum Psychological Anxiety. Terrorism against enemy interests on a global scale theoretically creates security problems and psychological anxiety everywhere that the target commands a political or economic presence. When travelers, airliners, and diplomats are attacked internationally, an enemy will give attention to the grievances of the movement that is the source of the violence.

Pragmatism. Demanding concessions from adversaries who become the focus of worldwide attention has occasionally been successful. Terrorists and extremists have sometimes secured ransoms for hostages, prisoner releases, and other concessions.

Thus, international terrorism is a functional operational decision that offers—from the perspective of the terrorists—greater efficiency in promoting the goals of the cause.

Tactical Reasons: Adapting Theory to Operations

One may observe that international extremists apply modern adaptations of their ideas on a global scale. It is therefore instructive to consider their theories from an international perspective.

1. *Fish swimming in the sea of the people.* With the inexorable trend toward globalization, many national, information, and communication barriers have been altered dramatically. Members of dissident movements are now able to live in multiple countries yet remain in regular contact through the Internet and other communications technologies. Adapting Mao Zedong's maxim to the international arena, terrorists can become "fish swimming in the sea of the global community." It is much more difficult to root out a movement that uses cells prepositioned in several countries, as became apparent during the post–September 11, 2001, war against terrorism.

2. *Enraging the beast.* Relatively weak groups continue to attempt to provoke governments into reacting in ways detrimental to government interests. In doing so, they almost guarantee that new supporters will arise to join the cause. Adapting Carlos Marighella's theory of provoking a powerful adversary into overreacting—and thus creating a heightened revolutionary consciousness among the people—international terrorists can now provoke a nation on a global scale. These provocations provide effective propaganda if the offending nation can be depicted as an international bully. This is not difficult to do, because modern information technology allows for dramatic images and messages to be disseminated worldwide. During the 2001–2002 coalition campaign against the Taliban in Afghanistan and the 2003 invasion of Iraq, images of dead and wounded civilians were regularly and graphically broadcast throughout the Muslim world.

U.S. Department of State

▶ The rubble of Khobar Towers. An indication of the destruction in the aftermath of a 1996 terrorist attack against the American military facility in Dharan, Saudi Arabia.

Historical Reasons: Perceptions of International Terrorism

Governments in developing countries do not always share the West's interpretations when political violence is used in the international arena. Western democracies regularly abhor and denounce international terrorism, whereas many regimes and leaders elsewhere either have been weak in their denunciations or have on occasion expressed their approval of international extremist violence.

Three factors illustrate why terrorism is unacceptable to Western governments:

1. Western governments have adopted an ideology of democratic justice as a norm. A norm is an accepted standard for the way societies ought to behave. Within the context of these norms, terrorism is perceived as inherently criminal behavior.

2. The West is often a target of terrorism. This is a practical consideration.

3. The West recognizes accepted methods of warfare. These include rules that define which modes of conflict constitute a legal manner to wage war and that only just wars should be fought. If possible, so-called collateral damage (unnecessary casualties and destruction) is to be avoided.

In the developing world, wars waged to gain independence or to suppress political rivals were commonly fought by using irregular tactics. Combatants often used guerrilla or terrorist tactics against colonial opponents or against indigenous adversaries during civil wars. In fact, many of the statesmen who rose to prominence after the formation of the new nations were former insurgents known by their adversaries as terrorists. From their perspective, terrorism and other violent methods were necessary weapons for waging poor man's warfare against enemies that were sometimes many times stronger than themselves.

Three factors demonstrate why terrorism is often acceptable to governments in the developing world:

1. Many anticolonial extremists, freedom fighters, and heroes, in the eyes of their people, became national leaders. A large number of revolutionaries became national leaders in Asia, Africa, and the Middle East.

2. Terrorism was used as a matter of practical choice during insurgencies. It provided **armed propaganda**, sowed disorder, and demoralized their adversaries. At some point in many post–World War II conflicts, the cost of war simply became unacceptable to the colonial powers.

3. Many developing world insurgents crafted an effective fusion of ideology and warfare. Terrorism was a justifiable and legitimate method of warfare as long as the cause was just and the fighters were cadres who understood why they were fighting.

INTERNATIONAL TERRORIST NETWORKS

Historically, many revolutionary movements have proclaimed their solidarity with other movements. In some cases, these movements engaged in coordinated attacks or other behaviors that intimated the existence of terrorist networks. In the modern era, radical Islamists from many nations have found common cause on the international stage. Adherents have been active in nations and regions far from their home countries and have carried out attacks in Europe, Africa, Asia, and the Middle East in the name of Islamist solidarity.

The concept of an international terrorist network naturally presumes one or more of the following environments:

- Terrorist groups talk to each other.

- The international terrorist environment is basically conspiratorial.

- Terrorist groups support each other.

- Governments sponsor terrorists.

CHAPTER PERSPECTIVE 8.3

A Remarkable Example of International Terrorism: The Japanese Red Army and the Lod (Lydda) Airport Massacre

The Japanese Red Army (JRA) was a nearly fanatical international terrorist organization founded in about 1970. It participated in a series of terrorist incidents, including assassinations, kidnappings, and airline hijackings. The JRA on one occasion tried to occupy the U.S. Embassy in Kuala Lumpur, Malaysia. On another occasion, the group bombed a United Service Organizations club in Naples, Italy. Members have been arrested in a number of countries, including one who was caught with explosives on the New Jersey Turnpike. Others who were not arrested were thought to have joined Latin American revolutionaries in Colombia and Peru.

The JRA committed a number of terrorist acts in cooperation with other terrorist groups. On May 30, 1972, three members of the organization fired assault rifles into a group of religious pilgrims and other travelers at Israel's Lod (Lydda) Airport. The death toll was high—26 people were killed and about 80 were wounded. Most of the injured were travelers from Puerto Rico on a religious pilgrimage. During the firefight that ensued, two of the terrorists were killed by security guards, and one was captured. The Japanese terrorists had been retained by the Popular Front for the Liberation of Palestine (PFLP) for the attack, and the PFLP had sent the three operatives on their mission on behalf of the Palestinian cause.

The attack is a remarkable example of international terrorism in its purest form: Leftist Japanese terrorists killed Christian pilgrims from Puerto Rico arriving on a U.S. airline at an Israeli airport on behalf of the nationalist Popular Front for the Liberation of Palestine.

As a postscript, the one survivor of the Lod attack—Kozo Okamoto—was tried and sentenced to life imprisonment in Israel but was later released in a 1985 prisoner exchange with other Palestinian prisoners. He lived in Lebanon's Beka'a Valley until 1997 but was arrested by the Lebanese with four other members of the JRA. After serving three years in prison, all five members were freed in 2000.

Chapter Perspective 8.3 discusses a noteworthy example of cooperation between Japanese Red Army terrorists and the Popular Front for the Liberation of Palestine.

International Terrorist Environments

Several terrorist environments are theoretically possible at different times and in different regional contexts. These are not, of course, exclusive descriptions of every aspect of international terrorism. They are, however, useful models for framing a generalized interpretation of international terrorism. The following discussion summarizes four environments that range in structure and cohesion from tightly knit single-sourced threats to loosely linked multiple-source threats:[4]

- Monolithic Terrorist Environments

- Strong Multipolar Terrorist Environments

- Weak Multipolar Terrorist Environments

- Cell-Based Terrorist Environments

Monolithic Terrorist Environments

The emphasis in the **monolithic terrorist environment** model is on state-centered behavior. The old model of a global Soviet-sponsored terrorist threat described an environment in which terrorism was a single threat from a single source. This presupposed that Soviet assistance and Marxist ideology were binding motivations for international terrorism. As a matter of counterterrorism policy, if this had been correct, combating the threat would have been uncomplicated because, in theory, the source (i.e., the Soviets) might have been induced or co-opted to reduce or end their sponsorship.

Strong Multipolar Terrorist Environments

In the **strong multipolar terrorist environment** model the emphasis is also on state-centered behavior. This model presumes that state sponsorship guides terrorist behavior but that several governments support their favored groups. It also presumes that there are few truly autonomous international terrorist movements; they all have a link to a state sponsor. Unlike the theory of a monolithic Soviet-sponsored threat, this scenario suggests that regional powers use terrorism to support their agendas and that many proxies exist. To counter this type of environment, the several sources would theoretically each have to be co-opted independently of the others.

Weak Multipolar Terrorist Environments

The model of the **weak multipolar terrorist environment** shifts the emphasis away from the state toward the terrorist movements. It presupposes both state sponsorship and more autonomous terrorist groups. Under this scenario, several governments support their favored groups, but many of the groups are relatively independent. The terrorist groups would be content with any state sponsor as long as they received enough assistance to continue their revolutionary struggle. Countering this environment is more difficult than countering the monolithic or strong multipolar models because the dissident movements are more flexible and adaptable. Cutting off one source of assistance would theoretically have little more effect than a temporary disruption in operations.

Cell-Based Terrorist Environments

In the model of the **cell-based terrorist environment**, the emphasis is centered on the terrorist movement. This model presumes that state sponsorship may exist to some extent but that the revolutionary movement is independent of governmental constraints, a kind of free-floating

Table 8.3   Understanding International Terrorist Environments

International terrorism occurs within the context of international social and political environments. These environments are not static and can vary from time to time and region to region.

This table suggests a model for understanding the features of several international terrorist environments.

Environment	Activity Profile			
	Foremost Participant	State Control	Group Autonomy	Difficulty in Countering
Monolithic	Single state sponsor	Strong and direct	Minimal	Clear options; easiest to counter
Strong multipolar	Several state sponsors	Strong and direct	Minimal	Clear options
Weak multipolar	Dissident groups; several state sponsors	Weak and insecure	Strong	Problematic and unpredictable
Cell-based	Dissident groups	Weak	Strong	Problematic and unpredictable; most difficult to counter

revolution that maintains its autonomy through its own resources. In this kind of environment, the movement is based on the viability of small cells loosely affiliated with one another. Thus, the movement will prevail even when some of its cells are destroyed or otherwise compromised. Because of its fluid organizational structure, this environment is the most difficult to counter.

Table 8.3 summarizes the activity profiles for these terrorist environments.

THE INTERNATIONAL DIMENSION OF THE NEW TERRORISM

Movement Case: The Afghan Arabs at War

The series of wars in Afghanistan, which began with the 1979 Soviet invasion, produced a large cadre of hardened Islamic fighters and led to a sustained guerrilla insurgency that eventually forced the occupying Soviet army to withdraw after losing 15,000 personnel killed in action. The war was considered a jihad in the eyes of the insurgents, who declared themselves mujahideen in a holy war against nonbelievers.

Muslims from around the world volunteered to fight alongside or otherwise support the Afghani mujahideen. This created a pan-Islamic consciousness that led to the creation of the Al Qaeda network and domestic jihadi movements as far afield as the Philippines, Malaysia, Central Asia, and Algeria. The Muslim volunteers—Afghan Arabs—became a legendary fighting force among Muslim activists. It is not known exactly how many Afghan Arabs fought in Afghanistan during the anti-Soviet jihad. However, reasonable estimates have been calculated:

> [A former] senior CIA official claims the number is close to 17,000, while the highly respected British publication *Jane's Intelligence Review* suggests a figure of more than 14,000 (including some 5,000 Saudis, 3,000 Yemenis, 2,000 Egyptians, 2,800 Algerians, 400 Tunisians, 370 Iraqis, 200 Libyans, and scores of Jordanians).[5]

After the Soviet phase of the war, many of the Afghan Arabs carried on their jihad in other countries, becoming **international mujahideen**. Dozens of Islamist movements grew in the aftermath of the anti-Soviet jihad, and a new generation of dedicated Islamists tactically adopted the model of international solidarity begun by the Afghan Arabs. International mujahideen regularly fight far from their home countries alongside indigenous Islamists on behalf of their common cause.

The Afghan Arabs symbolize a phenomenon that carried on well into the second decade of the 21st century. They represent the "first generation" of international Islamist fighters who inspired younger mujahideen recruits to join the cause, a process that continued on in the post-2011 Arab Spring conflicts.

Case: Mujahideen in Bosnia

The first wars that were fought after the breakup of Yugoslavia were between the Serbs, Croatians, and Bosnian Muslims. When Bosnia declared independence, it precipitated a brutal civil war that at times had all three national groups fighting against each other simultaneously. The war between the Bosnians and Serbs was particularly violent and involved genocidal ethnic cleansing that was initiated by the Serbs and imitated later by other national groups. From the beginning, the Bosnian Muslims were severely pressed by their adversaries and were nearly defeated as town after town fell to the Serbs. Overt international arms shipments were prohibited, although some Islamic countries did provide covert support. Into this mix came Muslim volunteers who fought as mujahideen on behalf of the Bosnians. Most were Middle Eastern Afghan Arabs. An estimated 500 to 1,000 mujahideen fought alongside the Bosnians, coming from nearly a dozen countries. Many came from Afghanistan, Algeria, Egypt, Tunisia, and Yemen. Although the international mujahideen were motivated by religious zeal, the Bosnians are traditionally secular Muslims, so they were motivated by nationalist zeal.[6] This was a cause for some friction, but a handful of Bosnians also took an oath to become mujahideen.

Organization Case: Al Qaeda and International Terrorism

Al Qaeda is a transnational movement with members and supporters from throughout the Muslim world. It is, at its very core, an international revolutionary movement that uses terrorism as a matter of routine. Al Qaeda has two overarching goals: to link together Muslim extremist groups throughout the world into a loose pan-Islamic revolutionary network and to expel non-Muslim (especially Western) influences from Islamic regions and countries.

▶ Death in Kenya: A Kenyan man is lifted out of the rubble of the American embassy in Nairobi, Kenya. On August 7, 1998, the U.S. Embassy in Nairobi was bombed by an Al Qaeda cell, which coordinated the assault with an attack conducted by another cell against the American Embassy in Dar es Salaam, Tanzania.

Despite the deaths of Osama bin Laden and other central leaders, Al Qaeda continues to serve as an internationalist model for regional Islamist insurgencies. This has been a dynamic feature of the modern terrorist environment, giving rise to movements such as Al Qaeda in Iraq, Al Qaeda in the Islamic Maghreb, and Al Qaeda in the Arabian Peninsula. Indigenous Islamist insurgencies inspired by the internationalist model were also formed, including Al Shabaab in East Africa and Boko Haram in Nigeria.

Case: International Cells

Operatives who were trained or inspired by Al Qaeda established cells in dozens of countries and regions. For instance, cells and larger groups became resident in the following predominantly Muslim countries and regions: Afghanistan, Algeria, Bosnia, Chechnya, Indonesia, Iraq, Kosovo, Lebanon, Malaysia, Pakistan, the southern Philippines, Somalia, Sudan, the West Bank, and Yemen. Other cells were covertly positioned in the following Western and non-Muslim countries: Britain, France, Germany, Israel, Spain, the United States, and the border region of Argentina, Brazil, and Paraguay.

Members communicate with each other using modern technologies, such as faxes, the Internet, cell phones, and e-mail. Most Al Qaeda cells are small and self-sustaining and apparently receive funding when activated for specific missions. For example, the bombings of the American embassies in Kenya and Tanzania may have cost $100,000.[7] Not all cells are **sleeper cells**, defined as groups of terrorists who take up long-term residence in countries prior to attacks. For example, most of the September 11, 2001, hijackers entered the United States for the express purpose of committing terrorist acts; they were never prepositioned as sleepers to be activated at a later date. Al Qaeda has been rather prolific in its direct and indirect involvement in international terrorism.

The following cases of international Al Qaeda terrorist activity illustrate the scope, skill, and operational design of the network.

The Hijacking of Air France Flight 8969

In December 1994, **Air France Flight 8969** was hijacked in Algeria by an Algerian Islamic extremist movement, the **Armed Islamic Group (GIA)**. The GIA apparently has ties to Al Qaeda, and many members of its movement are Afghan Arab war veterans. After hijackers killed three passengers, the plane was permitted to depart the Algerian airfield and made a refueling stop in Marseilles. Intending to fly to Paris, the hijackers demanded three times the amount of fuel needed to make the journey. The reason for this demand was that they planned to blow up the aircraft over Paris—or possibly crash it into the Eiffel Tower—thus killing themselves and all of the passengers as well as raining flaming debris over the city. French commandos disguised as caterers stormed the plane in Marseilles, thus bringing the incident to an end. The assault was played out live on French television.

The Singapore Plot

During December 2001 and January 2002, security officers in Singapore, Malaysia, and the Philippines arrested more than three dozen terrorist suspects. Thirteen were arrested in Singapore, 22 in Malaysia, and four in the Philippines. The sweep apparently foiled a significant plot by Al Qaeda to attack Western interests in Singapore. The arrests were made after anti-Taliban Northern Alliance coalition forces in Afghanistan captured a Singaporean of Pakistani descent who was fighting for the Taliban. The prisoner gave details about "plans to bomb U.S. warships, airplanes, military personnel and major U.S. companies in Singapore [as well as] American, Israeli, British and Australian companies and government offices there."[8]

Members of the Singaporean cell had been trained by Al Qaeda in Afghanistan, and Al Qaeda operatives had traveled to Singapore to advise some of the suspects about bomb construction and other operational matters. During their preparations for the strike, the cell had sought to purchase 21 tons of ammonium nitrate—by comparison, **Timothy McVeigh's ammonium nitrate and fuel oil (ANFO)** truck bomb had used only two tons of ammonium nitrate. The Singaporean cell organized itself as the Islamic Group (Jemaah Islamiah). The Malaysian cell called itself the Kumpulan Militan Malaysia. In an interesting twist, the Malaysian group apparently had indirect ties to the October 2000 bombing of the USS *Cole* in Yemen, the September 11 attacks, and perhaps to **Zacarias Moussaoui**, the French Moroccan implicated as affiliated with the September 11 terrorists.[9]

▶ U.S. Marshals Service handout image of Umar Farouk Abdulmutallab, who pled guilty in 2011 of attempting to destroy Northwest Airlines Flight 253 near Detroit, Michigan, in 2009 with a bomb embedded in his underwear.

Northwest Airlines Flight 253 in Detroit

On December 25, 2009, Nigerian national Umar Farouk Abdulmutallab ignited explosive chemicals aboard Northwest Airlines Flight 253 with approximately 290 people aboard as it approached Detroit, Michigan, in the United States. According to a federal criminal complaint and FBI affidavit, Abdulmutallab attempted to detonate an improvised explosive containing PETN (pentaerythritol tetranitrate) which had been attached to his leg. He used a syringe to detonate the PETN, but fortunately the device merely caught fire and did not fully detonate. Passengers reported that immediately prior to the incident, Abdulmutallab had been in the restroom for approximately 20 minutes. He pulled a blanket over himself, and passengers heard cracking sounds comparable to firecrackers, sensed an odor, and observed Abdulmutallab's pant leg and the airplane wall on fire. Abdulmutallab was subdued by passengers and members of the crew, who also extinguished the fire. He was calm throughout the incident, and replied "explosive device" when asked by a flight attendant what he had in his pocket.

Abdulmutallab had recently associated with religious militants in Yemen and visited there from August to December 2009. He said to officials that he had been trained in Yemen to make explosives; he also claimed that Yemenis had given him the chemicals used on Flight 253. His name had been listed in a U.S. terrorism database during November 2009 after his father reported to the U.S. embassy in Nigeria that his son had been radicalized and was associating with religious extremists. However, Abdulmutallab was not placed on an airlines watch list for flights entering the United States because American authorities concluded they had insufficient information to do so. In fact, Abdulmutallab possessed a two-year tourist visa that he received from the U.S. embassy in London in June 2008, and he had traveled to the United States on at least two occasions. In October 2011, Abdulmutallab pleaded guilty to eight counts of terrorism-related criminal charges.

Chapter Perspective 8.4 explores the bona fide threat from terrorist organizations that have been inspired by the Al Qaeda model.

Wartime Case: Terrorist Violence in Iraq

The U.S.-led invasion of Iraq, designated Operation Iraqi Freedom, commenced on March 20, 2003, with an early morning decapitation air strike intended to kill Iraqi leaders. Ground forces crossed into Iraq from Kuwait the same day. During the drive toward Baghdad from March 21 to April 5, coalition forces encountered stiff resistance from regular and irregular Iraqi forces, but this opposition was overcome or bypassed. American armored units swept through Baghdad on April 5, British troops overcame resistance in Basra on April 7, and Baghdad fell on April 9. On May 1, the coalition declared that major combat operations had ended.

CHAPTER PERSPECTIVE 8.4

Beyond Al Qaeda

It is well known that the idea of Al Qaeda was born in the crucible of the anti-Soviet jihad in Afghanistan. International fighters were brought together under the banner of jihadist solidarity, and those who passed through the Al Qaeda network became imbued with a global and extreme belief system.

Because Al Qaeda's belief system is grounded in fundamentalist religious faith, the organization evolved into an ideology and an exemplar for other radical Islamists.[a] In a sense, Al Qaeda "franchised" its methods, organizational model, and internationalist ideology.[b] As the original leadership and Afghan Arabs were killed, captured, or otherwise neutralized, new personnel stepped to the fore, many of whom had minimal contacts with the original Al Qaeda network. New Islamist terrorist movements inspired by Al Qaeda's ideology and reputation were formed, and new extremists thus became affiliated with Al Qaeda by virtue of their replication of the Al Qaeda model.[c]

Although Al Qaeda remains actively engaged in its war against Western influence and perceived Muslim apostasies, its role has in part become that of an instigator and mentor. For example, the Islamists who joined the anticoalition resistance in Iraq became an Al Qaeda–affiliated presence. Jordanian-born Abu Musab al-Zarqawi was an important symbol of Islamist resistance in Iraq, and Osama bin Laden communicated with him. Al-Zarqawi and his followers eventually claimed credit for terrorist attacks under the banner of a hitherto unknown group called Al Qaeda Organization for Holy War in Iraq. This example is not unique, as evidenced by Al Qaeda–affiliated movements in Yemen, North Africa, and Syria.

In effect, a robust pattern of terrorist behavior arose, involving claims of responsibility for terrorist attacks around the world by Al Qaeda–inspired or loosely affiliated groups.

One scenario offered by experts during the height of the U.S.-led wars in Iraq and Afghanistan was that the unanticipated resistance resulted in a new generation of extremists with a similar internationalist mission as the original Afghan Arabs.[d] It is plausible that this occurred, as the global jihad evolved beyond the Al Qaeda network into a formidable web of similar organizations and networks such as Islamic State in Iraq and the Levant (ISIS).

Notes

a. Sebastian Rotella and Richard C. Paddock, "Experts See Major Shift in Al Qaeda's Strategy," *Los Angeles Times*, November 19, 2003.

b. Douglas Farah and Peter Finn, "Terrorism, Inc.," *Washington Post*, November 21, 2003.

c. Josh Meyer, "Al Qaeda 'Co-Opts' New Affiliates," *Los Angeles Times*, September 16, 2007.

d. Dana Priest, "Report Says Iraq Is New Terrorist Training Ground," *Washington Post*, January 14, 2005.

Unfortunately for the coalition and the people of Iraq, the security environment and quality of life in Iraq became progressively poorer in the immediate aftermath of the fall of Saddam Hussein's government. Crime became widespread, and provision of basic services such as electricity and water became sporadic. Most ominously, an insurgency took root.

The insurgency spread and increased in intensity during the first year of the occupation. The insurgents engaged in classic guerrilla attacks, some of them professionally and intricately planned, against occupation troops and Iraqi security forces. Roadside bombs, ambushes, harassing mortar fire, and firefights occurred in many areas. Insurgents also used terrorism and assassinations against foreign contract workers and those they defined as collaborators—police officers, Iraqi soldiers, moderate leaders, election workers, and many others.

This early and politically motivated insurgency was the first phase of violence in post-invasion Iraq. A decidedly communal quality of violence also spread, primarily between Shi'a and Sunni Iraqis, but also within these communities. Bombs were indiscriminately detonated in Shi'a neighborhoods in Baghdad, mosques were attacked, Sunni and Shi'a leaders were assassinated, and hundreds of bodies were found in rivers, mass graves, and other locations. These incidents were the result of intracommunal power struggles and tit-for-tat revenge killings. Thousands of Iraqis died.

The insurgency in Iraq had international implications from the outset because the intensity of the noncommunal resistance was widely admired throughout the Arab and Muslim worlds, from which international volunteers came to participate in the insurgency. In addition, disaffected individuals in Muslim communities in Europe sympathized with the resistance in Iraq, and a few Western Muslims declared their solidarity. These individuals became active in the United Kingdom, Spain, and elsewhere.

The insurgency also became a focal point for debate about the prosecution of the war against terrorism. For example, some leaders and supporters of the occupation reasoned that terrorists were being "flushed out" and that it would be better to fight them in Iraq than elsewhere. Others maintained that Iraq had never posed a direct threat of Al Qaeda–style terrorism, that resources were needlessly expended in an unnecessary war, and that a significant number of new extremists became inspired by the Iraqi insurgency.

Table 8.4 summarizes the activity profiles of secular, sectarian, and ethno-nationalist stateless revolutions.

Table 8.4 The Stateless Revolutions

Some movements operate almost exclusively in the international arena. The reasons for this include ideologies of transnational revolution, global spiritual visions, or simple practicality brought on by their political environment. This table describes the activity profiles of three such radical movements.

Political Orientation	Activity Profile				
	Group	Constituency	Adversary	Benefactor	Goal
Secular	Japanese Red Army	Oppressed of the world	Capitalism, imperialism, Zionism	Unclear; probably PFLP, maybe Libya	International revolution
Sectarian	Al Qaeda	Muslims of the world	Foes of Islam	Self-supporting; maybe radical states	International Islamic revolution
Ethno-nationalist	Popular Front for the Liberation of Palestine—General Command	Palestinians	Israel; mainline PLO groups	Government sponsor (Syria)	Palestinian state

DISCUSSION BOX

UNDERSTANDING TERRORIST "SPILLOVERS": MIDDLE EASTERN AND NORTH AFRICAN SPILLOVERS IN EUROPE

This chapter's Discussion Box is intended to stimulate critical debate about whether spillover incidents are a legitimate expression of grievances.

Terrorist spillovers have occurred regularly since the 1960s. The most common sources of spillovers since that time have been from the Middle East and North Africa, and the most frequent venue for these spillovers has been Western Europe. For example, during the 1980s, hundreds of Middle Eastern and North African terrorist incidents occurred in more than a dozen countries, causing hundreds of deaths and hundreds of people wounded. Outside of the Middle East and North Africa, Europe is the favored theater of operations.

There are several types of Middle Eastern and North African spillovers in Europe: Some result from the foreign policies of governments, others are PLO-affiliated groups, and others are attacks by Islamist revolutionaries.

The motives behind these incidents have included the following:

- the silencing or intimidating of exiles
- attempts to influence European policies
- retaliation against a person or state
- "solidarity" attacks by indigenous European groups

Europe has been an attractive target for many reasons, including the following:

- the presence of large Middle Eastern and North African communities
- many "soft" targets
- immediate publicity
- open borders and good transportation
- proximity to the Middle East and North Africa

These attacks have been widespread geographically, and many have been indiscriminate.

Discussion Questions

1. Is the international arena a legitimate option for the expression of grievances?

2. Is Europe an appropriate venue for conflicts originating in the Middle East or North Africa?

3. Are some grievances more legitimate, or more acceptable, for spillovers?

4. What is the likely future of spillover attacks in Europe?

5. Since Europe has historically been perceived to be an easy battlefield with soft targets, should the European Union "harden" itself?

CHAPTER SUMMARY

This chapter provided readers with a critical assessment of international terrorism, which was defined from the motives of the perpetrators and the symbolism of their selected targets; terrorists who choose to operate on an international scale select targets that symbolize an international interest. Readers were reintroduced to the terrorist environments discussed in previous chapters. These environments were evaluated from the perspective of the international venue.

Within the framework—ideological, practical, tactical, and historical—of the reasons identified for international terrorism, readers were asked to apply adaptations of revolutionary theory to international operations. Recalling previous discussions about Mao's doctrine for waging guerrilla warfare as fish swimming in the sea of the people and Marighella's strategy for destabilizing established governments, it is no surprise that modern terrorists would carry variations of these themes onto the international stage.

International terrorist networks have been a facet of international terrorism since the 1960s. The models presented in this chapter are useful in understanding the networking features of terrorist environments. The cases of Al Qaeda and the international mujahideen illustrate the nature of modern terrorist networks.

KEY TERMS AND CONCEPTS

The following topics were discussed in this chapter and can be found in the Glossary:

WEB EXERCISE

Using this chapter's recommended websites listed on the student study site at **edge.sagepub.com/martiness5e**, conduct an online investigation of international terrorism.

1. From your review of these websites, how significant do you think the threat is from international terrorist groups?

2. Which groups do you think pose a serious threat of international terrorism? Which groups do you think present less serious threats?

3. Critique the websites of the international monitoring organizations. Are some more helpful than others?

For an online search of international terrorism, readers should enter the following keywords in their Web browser's search engine:

"International terrorism" (or "international terrorists")

"Global terrorism"

RECOMMENDED READINGS

The following publications provide discussions about the nature of international terrorism and cases in point about international terrorists.

Follain, J. (2011). *Jackal: The complete story of the legendary terrorist, Carlos the Jackal.* New York, NY: Arcade.

Gartenstein-Ross, D., & Grossman, L. (2009). *Homegrown terrorists in the U.S. and U.K.* Washington, DC: FDD Press.

Gerges, F. A. (2009). *The far enemy: Why jihad went global*. Cambridge, UK: Cambridge University Press.

Gunaratna, R. (2002). *Inside Al Qaeda: Global network of terror.* New York, NY: Columbia University Press.

Herman, E. S. (1982). *The real terror network: Terrorism in fact and propaganda.* Boston, MA: South End Press.

Kegley, C. W., Jr. (Ed.). (2002). *The new global terrorism: Characteristics, causes, controls.* New York, NY: Prentice Hall.

Lutz, J. M., & Lutz, B. (2008). *Global terrorism* (2nd ed.). New York, NY: Routledge.

Perkins, S. (2011). *Homegrown terror and American jihadists: Assessing the threat.* Hauppauge, NY: Nova.

Pillar, P. R. (2001). *Terrorism and U.S. foreign policy.* Washington, DC: Brookings Institution.

Reeve, S. (1999). *The new jackals: Ramzi Yousef, Osama bin Laden and the future of terrorism.* Boston, MA: Northeastern University Press.

Sageman, M. (2008). *Leaderless jihad: Terror networks in the twenty-first century.* Philadelphia: University of Pennsylvania Press.

Siniver, A. (Ed.). (2010). *International terrorism post-9/11: Comparative dynamics and responses.* London, UK: Routledge.

CHAPTER NINE

DOMESTIC TERRORISM IN THE UNITED STATES

The quality of post–World War II ideological extremism in the United States reflects the characteristics of the classical ideological continuum. Readers may recall that the classical ideological continuum, discussed in Chapter 2, incorporates political tendencies that range from the fringe left to the fringe right, but many examples of nationalist and religious terrorism do not fit squarely within the continuum categories. However, the United States is an idiosyncratic subject, and most terrorism in the post–World War II era did originate from the left- and right-wing spectrums of the continuum.

The discussion in this chapter will review the following:

- Left-Wing Extremism in the United States
- Left-Wing Terrorism in the United States
- Right-Wing Extremism in the United States
- Right-Wing Terrorism in the United States
- Understanding the Persistence of Violent Ideologies in the United States

Table 9.1 summarizes and contrasts the basic characteristics of contemporary left-wing, right-wing, and international political violence in the United States.[1] This is not an exhaustive profile, but it is instructive for purposes of comparison.

Table 9.2 shows groups responsible for the most terrorist incidents in the United States from 2001 to 2011.

Unlike many terrorist environments elsewhere in the world, where the designations of left and right are not always applicable, most political violence in the United States falls within them. Even nationalist and religious sources of such incidents have tended to reflect the attributes of leftist or rightist movements. Among outliers of this profile are violent religious cults in the United States. Chapter Perspective 9.1 discusses this phenomenon.

Learning Objectives

This chapter will enable readers to do the following:

1. Describe the general attributes of the American ideological left and right wings.

2. Understand the attributes of left-wing activism and ideological extremism in the United States.

3. Discuss left-wing terrorism in the United States.

4. Understand the attributes of right-wing activism and ideological extremism in the United States.

5. Discuss right-wing terrorism in the United States.

Table 9.1   Attributes of Terrorism in the United States

In the United States, terrorism has typically been conducted by groups and individuals espousing leftist or rightist ideologies or those who engage in international "spillover" conflicts. These interests are motivated by diverse ideologies, operate from different milieus, possess distinctive organizational profiles, and target a variety of interests. This table summarizes these profiles.

Environment	Ideological Profile	Activity Profile		
		Bases of Operation	Organizational Profile	Typical Targets
Leftist	Marxist; left-wing nationalist	Urban areas; suburbs	Clandestine groups; movement-based	Symbolic structures; avoidance of human targets
Rightist	Racial supremacist; antigovernment; religious	Rural areas; small towns	Self-isolated groups; cells; lone wolves	Symbolic structures; human targets
"Old" international terrorism	Ethno-nationalist	Urban areas	Clandestine groups	Symbols of enemy interest
"New" international terrorism	Religious	Urban areas	Cells; lone wolves	Symbolic structures; human targets

Table 9.2   Groups Responsible for Most Terrorist Attacks in the United States, 2001–2011[a]

Rank	Organization	Number of Attacks	Number of Fatalities
1	Earth Liberation Front (ELF)	50	0
2	Animal Liberation Front (ALF)	34	0
3	Al-Qa'ida	4	2,996
4	Coalition to Save the Preserves (CSP)	2	0
4	Revolutionary Cells-Animal Liberation Brigade	2	0
5	Al-Qa'idain the Arabian Peninsula (AQAP)	1	0
5	Ku Klux Klan	1	0
5	Minutemen American Defense	1	2
5	Tehrik-i-Taliban Pakistan (TTP)	1	0
5	The Justice Department	1	0

Source: LaFree, Gary, Laura Dugan and Erin Miller, "Integrated United States Security Database (IUSSD): Data on the Terrorist Attacks in the United States Homeland, 1970 to 2011," Final Report to the Resilient Systems Division, DHS Science and Technology Directorate, U.S. Department of Homeland Security. College Park, MD: START, 2012, p. 26 (table 9).

Note: These are all groups attributed responsibility for attacks in the Global Terrorism Database between 2001 and 2011. If responsibility for an attack was attributed to more than one group, then both are listed. The total number of attacks with attributed groups is 90. Seven of those attacks list a second perpetrator, resulting in 97 attributions of responsibility.

[a]Federal Bureau of Investigation.

CHAPTER PERSPECTIVE 9.1

American Cults and Terrorist Violence

Cults are self-isolated mystical communities that claim to have definitive answers for societal and personal problems. They are usually tightly knit groups of people who follow a spiritual belief, often based on extreme interpretations of existing religions, that is a product of some higher mystical insight. Many cults are led by a single charismatic leader. The Tokyo subway terrorist attack by the Japanese cult Aum Shinrikyō was discussed in Chapter 7.

Most American cults have not directed violence against nonmembers. However, some—such as the apocalyptic People's Temple of the Disciples of Christ—have committed acts of extreme violence against their own members as well as nonmembers who challenged their authority. Founded and led by Jim Jones, the People's Temple was originally based in California. In the late 1970s, hundreds of its members migrated to Guyana to establish a compound called Jonestown after Jones and others became obsessed with conspiracy theories about government oppression and the imminence of the Apocalypse (a time of global trial and warfare). In November 1978, during a visit to Jonestown by a delegation led by U.S. Congressman Leo Ryan, a number of cult members decided to leave the People's Temple. They accompanied Ryan's party to an airfield, where they were assaulted by heavily armed members of the People's Temple; Ryan and several others were killed. Jones and hundreds of his followers committed suicide—mostly by drinking flavored sugar water that had been poisoned, although some shot themselves. A number of members were apparently murdered by gunshots or injections of the poison. Jim Jones audiotaped the episode, in which 914 people died, including more than 200 children.

Another cult—the Black Hebrew Israelites—is a counterpart to the neo-Nazi Christian Identity faith, with the distinction that it promotes African racial supremacy. Branches of the cult have called themselves the Tribe of Judah, Nation of Yahweh, and Temple of Love. Black Hebrew Israelites believe that the ancient Hebrews were Africans and that these chosen people migrated to West Africa during the Diaspora (scattering) of the ancient Jewish people. The descendants of these migrants were brought to the Western hemisphere as slaves by Europeans during the 400-year African slave trade. Thus, Africans in general—and African Americans in particular—are the true Chosen People of God. This "truth" has been rediscovered by followers of the Black Hebrew Israelite movement. One branch was established in Miami in 1979 by Hulon Mitchell Jr., who adopted the name of Yahweh Ben Yahweh (God, Son of God). This branch became highly insular, and members followed Mitchell's authority without question. Disobedience was dealt with harshly, so that when some members tried to leave the group, they were assaulted, and some were beheaded. Mitchell also taught that whites are descendants of the devil and worthy of death. Mitchell and some of his followers were eventually prosecuted and imprisoned after the group dispatched death squads known as the Death Angels to murder whites in the Miami area. The group was linked to at least 14 murders.

In the Pacific Northwest, followers of the Bhagwan Shree Rajneesh committed at least one act of biological terrorism. The group occupied a rural area in Oregon where their leader—the Bhagwan—was revered as the source of ultimate spiritual truth and enlightenment. Their mystical belief system was loosely based on Hinduism. Cult members, known as Rajneeshees, were expected to renounce their previous lifestyles and totally devote themselves and their livelihoods to their group and the Bhagwan. For example, they expressed great pride in the Bhagwan's fleet of Rolls Royce sedans. In September 1984, the group poisoned the salad bars of 10 Oregon restaurants with *Salmonella* bacteria. More than 700 people fell ill. The incident had been an experiment to test options for how the group could influence a local election in which the Rajneeshees hoped to elect members of the cult.

LEFT-WING EXTREMISM IN THE UNITED STATES

The modern American left is characterized by several movements that grew out of the political fervor of the 1960s. They were fairly interconnected, so understanding their origins provides instructive insight into the basic issues of the left. One should bear in mind that none was fundamentally violent and that they were not terrorist movements. However, extremist trends within them led to factions that sometimes espoused violent confrontation, and a few engaged in terrorist violence.

The Rise of Black Power[2]

The modern civil rights movement initially centered on the struggle to win equality for African Americans in the South. During the early 1950s, the movement—at first led by the National Association for the Advancement of Colored People (NAACP)—forced an end to segregation on trains and interstate buses by successfully appealing several federal lawsuits to the U.S. Supreme Court. Despite these victories, southern state laws still allowed segregation on intrastate transportation.

In 1955 and 1956 in Birmingham, Alabama, the Reverend Martin Luther King Jr. led a bus boycott that lasted for 13 months. A Supreme Court decision forced the bus company to capitulate. This was the beginning of the application of civil disobedience using a strategy known as **collective nonviolence**. The theory was that massive resistance, coupled with moral suasion and peaceful behavior, would lead to fundamental change. Unfortunately, official and unofficial violence was directed against the movement. There were numerous anti–civil rights bombings, shootings, and beatings in the South during this period. For this reason, not every member of the civil rights movement accepted collective nonviolence as a fundamental principle, and the strategy was not particularly effective outside of the southern context.

As a direct result of the violence directed against the nonviolent movement, an emerging ideology of African American empowerment took root among many activists. It began in June 1966, when civil rights activist **James Meredith** planned to walk through Mississippi to demonstrate that African Americans could safely go to polling places to register to vote. When Meredith was ambushed, shot, and wounded early in his walk, King and other national civil rights activists traveled to Mississippi to finish Meredith's symbolic march. One of the leaders was **Stokely Carmichael**, chairman of the Student Nonviolent Coordinating Committee (SNCC).

Carmichael renounced collective nonviolence. At a rally in Mississippi, he roused the crowd to repeatedly shout "Black power!" and adopted the clenched fist as a symbol of defiance. The slogan caught on, as did the clenched-fist symbol, and the **Black Power** movement began. It is important to note that the movement occurred at a time when the violence in the South was paralleled by urban activism, unrest, and rioting in the impoverished African American ghettos of the North, Midwest, and West.

The ideology of Black Power advocated political independence, economic self-sufficiency, and a cultural reawakening. It was expressed in Afrocentric political agendas, experiments in economic development of African American communities, and cultural chauvinism that was expressed in music, art, and dress (the **Black Pride** movement). Some members of the movement were radicalized by the violence in the South and began to advocate Black Nationalism. This led to the formation of overtly nationalist and militant organizations such as the **Black Panther Party for Self-Defense**.

Growth of the New Left

The so-called old left was characterized by orthodox Marxist ideologies and political parties dating from the Russian Revolution. However, new issues galvanized a new movement among educated young activists, primarily on the nation's university campuses. The **New Left** arose in the mid-1960s when a new generation of activists rallied around the antiwar movement, the civil rights movement, women's rights, and other political and social causes. New student organizations, such as **Students for a Democratic Society (SDS)**, advocated a philosophy of **direct action (action directe)** to confront mainstream establishment values. In the fall of 1964, participants in the Free Speech Movement at the University of California, Berkeley, seized an administration building on the campus. This was a wakeup call for adopting direct action as a central tactic of the fledgling New Left.

The New Left adapted its ideological motivations to the political and social context of the 1960s. It championed contemporary revolutionaries and movements, such as the Cuban, Palestinian, and Vietnamese revolutionaries. At its core, "the [American] New Left was a mass movement that led, and fed upon, growing public opposition to U.S. involvement in Vietnam."[3] Many young Americans experimented with alternative lifestyles, drugs, and avant-garde music. They also challenged the values of mainstream American society, questioning its fundamental ideological and cultural assumptions. This component of the New Left was commonly called the **counterculture**. The period was marked by numerous experiments in youth-centered culture.

▶ National Guard soldiers advance at Kent State University, in Ohio, on May 4, 1970. Four students were slain when troops fired into a crowd of some 600 antiwar demonstrators.

Howard Ruffner/Archive Photos/Getty Images

LEFT-WING TERRORISM IN THE UNITED STATES

As New Left and Black Power movements and organizations became radicalized, many individuals and groups began to advocate active resistance against **the Establishment**—defined as mainstream American political and social institutions. This resistance included explicit calls for civil disobedience and confrontation with the authorities. Many within these movements referred to themselves as revolutionaries, and some advocated the overthrow of the military-industrial complex. Prototypical revolutionary organizations began to form in the late 1960s, and a few groups produced factions that became terrorist organizations. All of this occurred in a generalized environment of activism and direct action. A large number of politically motivated bombings, shootings, and assaults occurred during this period. The Senate Committee on Government Operations reported the following statistics:[4]

    1969: 298 explosive and 243 incendiary bombings

    January to July 1970: 301 explosive and 210 incendiary bombing incidents

    January 1968 to June 1970: 216 ambushes against law enforcement personnel and headquarters

    January 1968 to June 1970: 359 total assaults against police, causing 23 deaths and 326 injuries

Chapter Perspective 9.2 presents two examples of radicalized organizations—one from the New Left (Students for a Democratic Society) and the other from the Black Power movement (the Black Panthers). The stories of both groups illustrate the evolutionary process of left-wing revolutionary cadres and factions that eventually advocated political violence.

CHAPTER PERSPECTIVE 9.2

Seeds of Terrorism: Radicals on the American Left

Two militant case studies are discussed here: the Black Panthers and the radicalized Students for a Democratic Society. Within each movement were groups or cadres who advocated violent revolution.

Case: The Black Panthers

The Black Panther Party for Self-Defense was organized in 1966 in Oakland, California. The name was selected from an African American organization founded in Alabama called the Lowndes County Freedom Organization. The Lowndes County group had used the symbol of a black panther on voter ballots, ostensibly so that illiterate voters would know who their candidates were.

The Oakland Black Panthers initially imitated a tactic that had been used by the Los Angeles–based Community Alert Patrol, which had formed after the Watts riot in August 1965.[a] The Community Alert Patrol would dispatch observers to scenes of suspected harassment by the Los Angeles Police Department and observe police stops. In Oakland, the Black Panthers took this tactic one step further and arrived on the scene openly carrying law books and shotguns or rifles (legal at the time in California).[b] The symbolism of young African Americans projecting a paramilitary image in poor urban ghettos attracted members to the Black Panthers around the country. More than 40 chapters were formed, with a total of more than 2,000 members. By 1968, the group made worldwide headlines and came to symbolize the Black Power movement. Public demonstrations by the Black Panthers maximized the use of paramilitary symbolism, with members marching and chanting slogans in precision and wearing black berets and black leather jackets.

Ideologically, the Black Panthers were inspired by Malcolm X,[c] Frantz Fanon, and Mao Zedong. They were advocates of Black Nationalism and encouraged economic self-sufficiency and armed self-defense in the Black community. Black Panther self-help initiatives included free breakfasts for poor schoolchildren in urban areas. The police (at that time all male and mostly white in most cities) were especially singled out and labeled as a kind of "occupation" force in African American communities.

The group's militancy attracted the attention of federal and local law enforcement agencies, who considered the organization to be a threat to national security. The revolutionary and antipolice rhetoric of Black Panther leaders and the militant articles in its newspaper *The Black Panther* increased their concern. Federal Bureau of Investigation (FBI) director J. Edgar Hoover stated that the Black Panthers were the most significant threat to domestic security in the United States. A series of arrests and shootouts at Black Panther offices occurred. The leadership of the organization was decimated by arrests, police raids, and a successful disinformation campaign that sowed distrust among central figures. Internal feuds between leaders Huey Newton and Eldridge Cleaver also disrupted the group. Although the Black Panthers continued to be active into the late 1970s—after significantly moderating its militancy by the mid-1970s—its heyday as a paramilitary symbol of Black Nationalism was during the late 1960s and early 1970s. As it declined under relentless internal and external pressures, some of its more radical members joined the revolutionary underground.

Case: Students for a Democratic Society

In June 1962, a group of liberal and mildly leftist students, known as Students for a Democratic Society (SDS), many from the University of Michigan, met to draft a document that became known as the Port Huron Statement. In this document, SDS harshly criticized the values of mainstream American society and called for the establishment of a "new left" movement in the United States. The Port Huron Statement was a critique and a call for action directed to middle-class students. At this time, SDS was liberal and leftist but hardly revolutionary. SDS espoused direct action, which originally referred to peaceful and nonviolent confrontation.

By 1965, SDS had moved to the radical left, and when the bombing of North Vietnam began, its national membership soared. By 1966, its focal point was the war in Vietnam and support for the Black Power movement (SDS's membership mostly comprised white students). In 1967, SDS cast activist American youth as a "new working class" oppressed by the military-industrial complex. This was a classic Marcuse-like interpretation of capitalist "manacles" of privilege used to co-opt middle-class youth to keep them docile and content (discussed further in Chapter 2). By 1968, SDS's leadership was revolutionary. An SDS-led takeover of Columbia University occurred during the 1968 spring term, when students seized five buildings for five days. When the police were called in, a riot ensued; more than 700 people were arrested, and nearly 150 were injured. A student strike—again led by SDS—closed Columbia. SDS also led dozens of other campus disturbances in 1968.

In June 1968, SDS factionalized because of ideological tensions within the group. Some members formed a prototypical Revolutionary Youth Movement, others aligned themselves with developing world revolutionary heroes, and others (sometimes called Crazies) espoused violent revolution. At its next meeting in June 1969 in Chicago,

SDS split along doctrinal and tactical lines into the Maoist Progressive Labor Party (also known as the Worker-Student Alliance), Revolutionary Youth Movement II, and the violent revolutionary Weathermen group.

Notes

a. The toll for the Watts disturbance was high; 34 people were killed, more than 1,000 injured, and nearly 4,000 arrested. Approximately 200 businesses were destroyed and about 700 were damaged. For a study of the Watts riot, see Robert Conot, *Rivers of Blood, Years of Darkness* (New York, NY: Bantam, 1967).

b. The armed patrols ended when California passed a law prohibiting the open display of firearms.

c. For more information about Malcolm X, see Malcolm X, *The Autobiography of Malcolm X* (New York, NY: Grove, 1964).

The following discussion evaluates four trends on the violent left:

- Generational Rebellion: New Left Terrorism
- Civil Strife: Ethno-nationalist Terrorism on the Left
- The Revolution Continues: Leftist Hard Cores
- Single-Issue Violence on the Left

Generational Rebellion: New Left Terrorism

The New Left was deeply affected by the war in Vietnam, the civil rights movement, and the turmoil in inner-city African American communities. A number of terrorist groups and cells grew out of this environment. Although the most prominent example was the Weatherman group, other groups such as the Symbionese Liberation Army also engaged in terrorist violence. The United Freedom Front proved to be the most enduring of all terrorist groups of the era.

The Weatherman/Weather Underground Organization

The Weatherman group—known as the Weathermen—jelled at the June 1969 Students for a Democratic Society national convention in Chicago, Illinois, when SDS splintered into several factions. The Weathermen were mostly young, white, educated members of the middle class. They represented—starkly—the dynamic ideological tendencies of the era as well as the cultural separation from the older generation. Although they and others were sometimes referred to collectively as the Crazies, they operated within a supportive cultural and political environment.

From the beginning, the Weathermen were violent and confrontational. In October 1969, they distributed leaflets in Chicago announcing what became known as their Days of Rage action. The Days of Rage lasted for four days and consisted of acts of vandalism and running street fights with the Chicago police. In December 1969, the Weathermen held what they called a war council in Michigan. Its leadership, calling itself the **Weather Bureau**, advocated bombings, armed resistance, and assassinations. In March 1970, an explosion occurred in a Greenwich Village townhouse in New York City that was being used as a bomb factory. Three Weathermen were killed, several others escaped through the subway system, and hundreds of members went underground to wage war.

By the mid-1970s, the Weathermen—renamed the Weather Underground Organization—had committed at least 40 bombings. Aside from these actions, the Weather Underground also freed counterculture guru Timothy Leary from prison,[5] published a manifesto called *Prairie Fire*, and distributed an underground periodical called *Osawatomie*. By the mid-1970s, members of the Weather Underground began to give up their armed struggle and returned to aboveground activism—a process that they called inversion. Those who remained underground (mostly the East Coast wing) committed acts of political violence into the 1980s. Others joined other terrorist organizations.

The Symbionese Liberation Army

The Symbionese Liberation Army (SLA) was a violent terrorist cell that gained notoriety for several high-profile incidents in the mid-1970s. The core members were led by **Donald DeFreeze**, who took the nom de guerre **Cinque** (named for the leader of a 19th-century rebellion aboard the slave ship *Amistad*). Members trained in the Berkeley Hills of California near San Francisco, rented safe houses, and obtained weapons. In November 1973, the Oakland school superintendent was assassinated when he was shot eight times; five of the bullets were cyanide tipped. In a communiqué, the SLA took credit for the attack, using a rhetorical phrase that became its slogan: "Death to the fascist insect that preys upon the people!"

In February 1974, newspaper heiress Patricia Hearst was kidnapped by the cell. She was kept bound and blindfolded in a closet for more than 50 days under constant physical and psychological pressure, including physical abuse and intensive political indoctrination. She broke down under the pressure, and a tape recording was released in which she stated that she had joined the SLA. In April 1974, Hearst participated in a bank robbery in San Francisco.

In May 1974, five of the SLA's core members, including DeFreeze, were killed in a shootout in a house in the Watts neighborhood of Los Angeles, California.

Patricia Hearst was a fugitive for approximately a year. She was hidden by activists in the radical underground and traveled across the country with compatriots. By 1975, the SLA had a rebirth with new recruits and was responsible for several bank robberies and bombings in California. They and other violent leftists referred to themselves as the **New World Liberation Front**. Hearst was captured in September 1975 in San Francisco, along with another underground fugitive.

Civil Strife: Ethno-nationalist Terrorism on the Left

Ethno-nationalist violence—which is distinguishable from racial supremacist violence—has been rare in the United States. This is primarily because activist environments have not historically supported nationalist terrorism. Exceptions grew out of the political environment of the 1960s, when nationalist political violence originated in African American and Puerto Rican activist movements.

The Black Liberation Movement

Racial tensions in the United States were extremely high during the 1960s. African Americans in the South directly confronted southern racism through collective nonviolence and the burgeoning Black Power ideology. In the urban areas of the North and West, cities became centers of confrontation between African Americans, the police, and state National Guards. When President Lyndon Johnson and the U.S. Senate organized inquiries into the causes of

Table 9.3 Racial Conflict in America: The "Long Hot Summers" of the 1960s

The urban disturbances in the United States during the 1960s caused a major period of communal discord, sometimes referred to as the **long hot summers**. The disturbances were widespread and violent and were a culmination of many factors. One factor was the deeply rooted racial polarization in American society. The presidential-appointed National Advisory Commission on Civil Disorders (known as the **Kerner Commission**) reported in 1968 that

segregation and poverty have created in the racial ghetto a destructive environment totally unknown to most white Americans. What white Americans have never fully understood—but what the Negro can never forget—is that white society is deeply implicated in the ghetto. White institutions created it, white institutions maintain it, and white society condones it.[a]

This table reports data from a Senate Permanent Subcommittee on Investigations inquiry into urban rioting after the serious disturbances in the summer of 1967.[b] The table summarizes the environment during three years of civil disturbances.[c]

Incident Report	Activity Profile		
	1965	1966	1967
Number of urban disturbances	5	21	75
Casualties			
Killed	36	11	83
Injured	1,206	520	1,897
Legal sanctions			
Arrests	10,245	2,298	16,389
Convictions	2,074	1,203	2,157
Costs of damage (in millions of dollars)	$40.1	$10.2	$664.5

[a]Report of the National Advisory Commission on Civil Disorders. New York: Bantam Books, 1968, p. 2.
[b]In 1967, the Senate passed a resolution ordering the Senate Permanent Subcommittee on Investigations to study what had caused the 1967 rioting and to recommend solutions.
[c]Senate Permanent Subcommittee on Investigations. Data reported in Ebony Pictorial History of Black America, vol. 3. Chicago: Johnson, 1971, p. 69.

these disorders, their findings were disturbing. Table 9.3 describes the quality of these findings, which indicate the severity of tensions in urban areas during the mid-1960s.

Within this environment grew cadres of African American revolutionaries dedicated to using political violence to overthrow what they perceived to be a racist and oppressive system.

The Black Liberation Army

The **Black Liberation Army (BLA)** was an underground movement whose membership included Vietnam veterans, former members of the Black Panthers, and other radical activists. BLA members were nationalists who were inspired in part by the 1966 film *Battle of Algiers*, a semidocumentary of an urban terrorist uprising in the city of Algiers against the French during their colonial war in Algeria. In the film, Algerian rebels organized themselves into many autonomous cells to wage urban guerrilla warfare against the French. There were at least two centers (likely consisting of groups of cells) of the BLA: the East Coast and West Coast groups. Although the BLA was active in late 1970 and early 1971, both centers became known later, and in similar fashion, to law enforcement agencies and the media:

- *East Coast cells.* In May 1971, two New York City police officers were ambushed and killed by .45-caliber fire. A package delivered to the *New York Times* containing, among other items, a communiqué and a .45 bullet claimed credit for the shootings on behalf of the BLA. This was the beginning of a number of known and suspected BLA attacks in the New York City region.

- *West Coast cells.* In August 1971, similar attacks were made against police officers in San Francisco. In one ambush, the police were attacked by .45-caliber machine gun fire; two BLA "soldiers" were captured after a shootout in this incident.

The BLA is suspected to have committed a number of attacks in New York and California prior to and after these incidents. They are thought to have been responsible for numerous bombings, ambushes of police officers,[6] and bank robberies to "liberate" money to support their cause. Their primary areas of operation were California and New York City, though some cells were active in the South and Midwest.

Most members of the BLA were eventually captured or killed. Those who escaped the FBI net re-formed to join other radical organizations. Interestingly, the only known white member of the BLA, Marilyn Buck, was a former member of the radicalized SDS who had disappeared into the revolutionary underground.

Puerto Rican *Independencistas*

Puerto Rico is a commonwealth of the United States, meaning that it is self-governed by a legislature and an executive (a governor) and has a nonvoting delegate to Congress. Those who desire independence are nationalists called *independencistas*, most of whom use democratic institutions to promote the cause of independence; they are activists but not prone to violence. The Puerto Rico Independence Party, for example, is a fairly mainstreamed leftist political movement in Puerto Rico.

Some *independencistas* are revolutionaries, and a few have resorted to violence. Modern violent nationalists pattern themselves after Cuban nationalism and view the United States as an imperial and colonial power. This is an understandable tendency, because some Puerto Rican nationalists fought alongside Cuban revolutionaries during the Cuban revolution. Cuba has historically provided support for violent *independencista* groups, especially during the 1980s.

The FALN

The **Armed Forces for National Liberation (Fuerzas Armadas de Liberación Nacional, or FALN)**[7] was a particularly active terrorist organization that concentrated its activities on the U.S. mainland, primarily in Chicago, Illinois, and New York City. One important fact about the FALN stands out: It was the most prolific terrorist organization in U.S. history. The group became active in 1974, and from 1975 to 1983, approximately 130 bombings were linked to it. Most attacks were symbolic, directed against buildings, but some were deadly. For example, in January 1975, the FALN detonated a bomb at the trendy restaurant Fraunces Tavern in New York City, killing four people and wounding more than 50. In another incident, in 1983, three New York City police officers were maimed while trying to defuse explosives at the New York police headquarters. FALN was also responsible for armored car and bank robberies.

In 1980, more than a dozen FALN members were convicted of terrorist-related crimes. Sentences were imposed for seditious conspiracy, possession of unregistered firearms, interstate transportation of a stolen vehicle, interference with interstate commerce by violence, and interstate transportation of firearms with intent to commit a crime. None of the charges were linked to homicides. FALN members' sentences ranged from 15 to 90 years, and they considered themselves prisoners of war.

The Revolution Continues: Leftist Hard Cores[8]

The left-wing revolutionary underground re-formed after the decline of groups such as the Weather Underground and the BLA. These new groups were made up of die-hard former members of the Weather Underground and BLA, as well as former activists from other organizations such as the radicalized SDS and the Black Panthers. Two cases illustrate the character of the reconstituted revolutionary left in the 1980s.

May 19 Communist Organization

The **May 19 Communist Organization (M19CO)** derives its name from the shared birthdate of Malcolm X and Vietnamese leader Ho Chi Minh. The symbolism of this designation is obvious—it combines domestic and international examples of resistance against self-defined U.S. racism and imperialism. The group was composed of remnants of the **New African Freedom Fighters**, the BLA, the Weather Underground, and the Black Panthers. These cadres included the founders of the **Republic of New Africa (RNA)** and the most violent members of the Weather Underground. Many of its members were individuals who had disappeared for years into the revolutionary underground.

M19CO was active during the late 1970s and early 1980s, engaging in bank and armored car robberies, bombings, and other politically motivated actions. The group adopted several different names when claiming responsibility for its attacks. These aliases included Red Guerrilla Resistance, **Resistance**, **Revolutionary Fighting Group**, and **Armed Resistance Unit**. Four M19CO members were captured in October 1981 after an automobile chase and shootout following a violent attempted robbery of a Brinks armored car in suburban Nyack, New York. After the Nyack incident, M19CO remained active for several years and engaged in several bombings, but the group was finally broken when its remaining members were arrested in May 1985.

The United Freedom Front[9]

Formed in 1975, the **United Freedom Front (UFF)** was underground and active for approximately 10 years. In 1975, it detonated a bomb at the State House in Boston, Massachusetts, under the name of the **Sam Melville–Jonathan Jackson Unit**, named for two imprisoned revolutionaries. The group was never large but was active, peaking during the early 1980s. The UFF is suspected of committing at least 25 bombings and robberies in New York and New England. The attacks were primarily intended to exhibit anticorporate or antimilitary symbolism. A group calling itself the Armed Resistance Unit detonated a bomb on the Senate side of the U.S. Capitol building on November 6, 1983, to protest the U.S. invasion of Grenada. It is possible that the Armed Resistance Unit was in fact the UFF operating under another name. The UFF was broken when its members were arrested in late 1984 and early 1985. Few leftist groups had survived by remaining both underground and active for as long as the UFF.

Single-Issue Violence on the Left

The left has produced violent single-issue groups and individuals who focus on one issue to the exclusion of others. To them, their championed issue is the central point—arguably the political crux—for solving many of the world's problems. For example, Ted Kaczynski, also known as the Unabomber, protested the danger of technology by sending and placing bombs that killed three people and injured 22 others during a 17-year campaign.

Typical of leftist single-issue extremism is the fringe environmental movement. Groups such as the **Animal Liberation Front (ALF)** and the **Earth Liberation Front (ELF)** have committed numerous acts of violence, such as arson and vandalism.

The ALF and ELF have coordinated their activities. Several joint claims have been made about property damage and other acts of vandalism, and it is likely that the two groups share members. For the most part, both have been nonviolent toward humans, but they are responsible for many incidents of property destruction. ALF and ELF targets include laboratories, facilities where animals are kept, and sport utility vehicles (SUVs). Some of these incidents are vandalism sprees. The FBI estimates that the ELF alone has engaged in 1,200 criminal acts and caused more than $100 million in property damage since 1996. In 2001, an ELF firebomb destroyed the University of Washington's Center for Urban Horticulture, which was rebuilt at a cost of $7 million. In one particularly destructive incident in August 2003, the group caused approximately $50 million in damages when it set fire to a condominium complex under construction in San Diego, California. The ELF has also targeted suburban property developments, as occurred in 2008 when four luxury homes were burned in a suburb north of Seattle, Washington. In September 2009, members of the ELF toppled two radio towers near Seattle, Washington.

RIGHT-WING EXTREMISM IN THE UNITED STATES

Extremist tendencies within the modern American right are characterized by self-defined value systems. This tendency is rooted in emerging trends, such as antigovernment and evangelical religious activism, as well as in historical cultural trends such as racial supremacy. The following discussion surveys the modern (post–World War II) characteristics of these trends, which provide a useful background to contemporary terrorism on the right.

Religious Politics and the Christian Right

The movement commonly termed the **Christian Right** is a mostly Protestant fundamentalist movement that links strict Christian values to political agendas. Its modern origins lie in the conservative political environment of the 1980s. It is not an inherently violent movement, and some activists have practiced variations of collective nonviolence and direct action by blockading and protesting at the offices of abortion providers. The ultimate goal of the Christian Right is to make Christian religious values (primarily evangelical Christian values) an integral part of the nation's social and political framework.

Far- and fringe-right members of the Christian Right have adopted a highly aggressive and confrontational style of activism. One significant aspect of the more **reactionary** tendency within the movement is the promotion of a specifically evangelical Christian agenda, thus rejecting agendas that are secular, non-Christian, or nonfundamentalist Christian.

Rise of the Antigovernment Patriots

The Patriot movement came to prominence during the early 1990s. The movement considers that it represents the true heirs of the ideals of the framers of the U.S. Constitution. For many Patriots, government in general is not to be trusted, the federal government in particular is to be distrusted, and the United Nations is a dangerous and evil institution. The Patriot movement is not ideologically monolithic, and numerous tendencies have developed, such as the Common Law Courts and Constitutionalists.

Two events from the 1990s served to invigorate paranoid political activism on the Patriot right, giving rise to new conspiracy theories. These events were the tragedies at **Ruby Ridge**, Idaho, and **Waco**, Texas.

- *Ruby Ridge.* In August 1992 at Ruby Ridge, Idaho, racial supremacist Randy Weaver and his family, with compatriot Kevin Harris, were besieged by federal agents for Weaver's failure to reply to an illegal weapons charge. Two members of the Weaver family were killed during the standoff, as was a U.S. marshal. Weaver's teenage son,

Sammy, and Marshal William Degan were killed during a shootout that occurred when Sammy, Randy, and Harris were confronted as they walked along a path. Weaver's wife, Vicky, was later fatally shot by an FBI sniper as she held her baby in the doorway of the Weaver home. The sniper had previously fired shots at Randy Weaver and Harris. Members of the Patriot movement and other right-wing extremists cite this incident as evidence of a broad government conspiracy to deprive freedom-loving "true" Americans of their right to bear arms and other liberties. Randy Weaver's story has inspired Patriots and other members of the extreme right.

- *Waco.* In early 1993 at Waco, Texas, federal agents besieged the Branch Davidian cult's compound after a failed attempt in February to serve a search warrant for illegal firearms had ended in the deaths of four federal agents and several cult members. On April 19, 1993, during an assault led by the FBI, about 80 Branch Davidians—including more than 20 children—died in a blaze that leveled the compound. As with Ruby Ridge, Patriots and other rightists consider this tragedy to be evidence of government power run amok.

Conspiracy theories abound within the Patriot movement. Some have long and murky origins, having been developed over decades. Other theories appear and disappear during periods of political or social crisis. Patriots cite evidence that non-American interests are threatening to take over—or have already taken over—key governmental centers of authority. This is part of an international plot to create a one-world government called the **New World Order**.

Chapter Perspective 9.3 summarizes several conspiracy theories from the right.

CHAPTER PERSPECTIVE 9.3

Conspiracy Theories on the American Right

The modern far and fringe right have produced a number of conspiracy theories and rumors. Although they may seem fantastic to people who are not members of the Patriot (and other) movements, many adherents of these theories live their lives as if the theories were an absolute reality. Three phases of modern conspiracy beliefs may be identified.

Phase 1: Communist Invaders During the Cold War

- Rumors "confirmed" that Soviet cavalry units were preparing to invade Alaska across the Bering Strait from Siberia.

- Thousands of Chinese soldiers (perhaps an entire division) had massed in tunnels across the southwestern border of the United States in Mexico.

- Thousands of Viet Cong and Mongolian troops had also massed in Mexico across the borders of Texas and California.

Phase 2: The New World Order Replaces the Communist Menace

- Hostile un-American interests (which may already be in power) include the United Nations, international Jewish bankers, the Illuminati, the Council on Foreign Relations, and the Trilateral Commission.

- Assuming it is Jewish interests who are in power, the U.S. government has secretly become the Zionist Occupation Government (ZOG).

- The government has constructed concentration camps that will be used to intern Patriots and other loyal Americans after their weapons have all been seized (possibly by African American street gangs).

- Invasion coordinates for the New World Order have been secretly stuck to the backs of road signs.

- Sinister symbolism and codes have been found in the Universal Product Code (the bar lines

(Continued)

(Continued)

on consumer goods), cleaning products, cereal boxes, and dollar bills (such as the pyramid with the eyeball).

- Sinister technologies exist that will be used when ZOG or the New World Order makes its move. These include devices that can alter the weather and scanners that can read the plastic strips in American paper currency.

- FEMA (Federal Emergency Management Agency) has built concentration camps for the day when patriotic Americans will be interned.

With these and other conspiracy theories as an ideological foundation, many within the Patriot movement organized themselves into citizens' militias. Scores of militias were organized during the 1990s, and at their peak, it is estimated that 50,000 Americans were members of more than 800 militias, drawn from five to six million adherents of the Patriot movement.[a] Some members joined to train as weekend "soldiers," whereas other militias organized themselves as paramilitary survivalists. Survivalism originated during the Cold War, when many people believed that a nuclear exchange between the superpowers was inevitable. They moved into the countryside, stocked up on food and weapons, and prepared for the nuclear holocaust. Many militias adapted this expectation to the New World Order conspiracy theory. Militia members who became survivalists went off the grid by refusing to have credit cards, driver's licenses, Social Security numbers, or government records. The purpose of going off the grid was to disappear from the prying eyes of the government and the New World Order or ZOG. Several principles are common to most Patriot organizations and militias:

- The people are sovereign. When necessary, they can resist the encroachment of government into their lives. They can also reject unjust government authority.

- Only an armed citizenry can counterbalance the authority of an oppressive government.

- The U.S. government has become oppressive, so the time is right to organize citizens' militias.

- It is necessary for citizens' militias to train and otherwise prepare for the day when an oppressive government or the New World Order moves in to take away the sovereignty of the people.

The potential for political violence from some members of the armed, conspiracy-bound Patriot movement has been cited by experts and law enforcement officials as a genuine threat.

Phase 3a: 9/11 "Truther" Conspiracy Theories

A number of conspiracy theories emerged in the aftermath of the September 11, 2001, terrorist attacks, part of the so-called truther movement. These include the following theories:

- The U.S. government allowed the attacks to happen.

- Explosives destroyed the Twin Towers in a controlled detonation, as evidenced by the vertical fall of the towers and debris that was pushed through the windows.

- A missile hit the Pentagon, as evidenced by the small size of two holes in the building.

- World Trade Center Building 7 was brought down by controlled explosions.

Phase 3b: Post-9/11 Conspiracy Theories

Other conspiracy theories gained traction in the years following the September 11 attacks. These include the following theories:

- President Barack Obama was not born in the United States (so-called birther conspiracies), was a socialist, and was secretly a Muslim.

- The New World Order is spraying toxic chemicals in the atmosphere. These may be seen in the contrails of aircraft.

- The Federal Reserve System will be used to create a one-world banking system.

- Military training exercises such as Jade Helm 15 in 2015 are actually preludes for seizing firearms, declaring martial law, and (in the case of Jade Helm 15) invading Texas.

Note

a. Bruce Hoffman, *Inside Terrorism* (New York: Columbia University Press, 1998), 107. These numbers declined during the late 1990s and then rebounded after the September 11, 2001, attacks on the U.S. homeland. For annual reports on the status of the Patriot militia movement, see Southern Poverty Law Center. *Intelligence Report*, https://www.splcenter.org/intelligence-report.

Racial Supremacy: An Old Problem With New Beginnings

The history of racial supremacy in the United States began during the period of African chattel slavery and continued with the policy to remove Native Americans from ancestral lands. The racial dimensions of these practices became norms of the early American nation. After the Civil War and prior to World War II, the United States became a highly segregated country. After World War II, though, the tide turned against overt and unquestioned racial supremacy. Supremacist beliefs, however, continued to win adherents.

Modern organized racial supremacist groups include the modern Ku Klux Klan, neo-Nazi movements, racist skinhead youth gangs, and some adherents of the Neo-Confederate movement. New non-Klan groups came into their own during the 1980s, when supremacist groups created their own mythologies and conspiracy theories. For example, many neo-Nazis considered the novel *The Turner Diaries*[10] a blueprint for the Aryan revolution in America. Also on the racist right, the **Fourteen Words** have become a rallying slogan. Originally coined by David Lane, a convicted member of the terrorist group the Order, the Fourteen Words are "We must secure the existence of our people and a future for White children." The Fourteen Words have been incorporated into the Aryan Nations' "declaration of independence" for the white race, and the slogan is often represented by simply writing or tattooing the number 14.

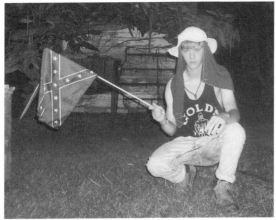

Dylann Roof/www.lastrhodesian.com

▶ Racial supremacist Dylann Roof poses prior to his attack at a Charleston, South Carolina, church. One of several provocative photographs posted by Roof on his website that he titled "The Last Rhodesian."

Racial Mysticism

Neofascist movements and political parties in Europe are decidedly secular. They reference religion and the organized Christian church only to support their political agendas; they do not adopt Christian or cult-like mystical doctrines to justify their legitimacy. In the United States, members of far- and fringe-right movements frequently justify their claims of racial supremacy and cultural purity by referencing underlying spiritual values—essentially claiming that they have a racial mandate from God. Racial supremacists in particular have developed mystical foundations for their belief systems, many of which are cult-like.

The Creativity Movement

Creativity is premised on a rejection of the white race's reliance on Christianity, which adherents believe Jews created in a conspiracy to enslave whites. According to movement adherents, the white race itself should be worshipped.

Ásatrú

A neopagan movement, **Ásatrú** venerates the pantheon of ancient Norse (Scandinavian) religions. In its most basic form, which is not racial in conviction, Ásatrú adherents worship the Norse pantheon of Odin, Thor, Freyr, Loki, and others. A minority of Ásatrú believers have adopted an activist and racist belief system, linking variants of Nazi ideology and racial supremacy to the Nordic pantheon.

Race and the Bible: The Christian Identity Creation Myth

Christian Identity is the Americanized strain of an 18th-century quasi-religious doctrine called **Anglo-Israelism** developed by **Richard Brothers**. Believers hold that whites are descended from Adam and are the true chosen people of God, that Jews are biologically descended from Satan, and that nonwhites are soulless beasts, also called the **Mud People**. Christian Identity adherents have developed two cultish creation stories loosely based on the Old Testament. The theories are called **One-Seedline Christian Identity** and **Two-Seedline Christian Identity**.

One-Seedline Identity accepts that all humans regardless of race are descended from Adam. However, only Aryans (defined as northern Europeans) are the true elect of God. Two-Seedline Identity rejects the notion that all humans are descended from Adam. Instead, their focus is on the progeny of Eve. Two-seedline adherents believe that Eve bore Abel as Adam's son but Cain as the son of the Serpent (that is, the devil). Outside of the Garden of Eden lived nonwhite, soulless beasts that are a separate species from humans. They are the modern nonwhite races of the world and are often referred to by Identity believers as Mud People. When Cain slew Abel, he was cast out of the Garden to live among the soulless beasts. Those who became the descendants of Cain are the modern Jews.

Chapter Perspective 9.4 summarizes several examples of racial supremacist activity on the right in the modern era. These examples illustrate how potentially violent members of the right wing can find organizations to provide direction and structure for their underlying animosity toward target groups.

CHAPTER PERSPECTIVE 9.4

Seeds of Terrorism: Reactionaries on the American Right

Three reactionary case studies are discussed here: White Aryan Resistance (WAR), Aryan Nations, and the National Alliance. Each case has directly or indirectly influenced activists on the racial supremacist right.

White Aryan Resistance

White Aryan Resistance (WAR) is an overtly racist organization founded and led by Tom Metzger. Based in California, WAR publishes neo-Nazi propaganda, manages an active website, and has tried to recruit and organize racist skinheads. Implicit in its message is the notion that skinheads should be mobilized as Aryan shock troops in the coming Racial Holy War. WAR has used popular culture and music to appeal to potential skinhead recruits, and its website is largely marketed to racist youth. In October 1990, WAR lost a $12.8 million verdict after the Southern Poverty Law Center litigated a case on behalf of the family of an Ethiopian immigrant who was beaten to death by WAR-inspired racist skinheads.

Aryan Nations

The "Reverend" Richard Butler established the Aryan Nations organization as a political counterpart to his Christian Identity sect, called the Church of Jesus Christ Christian. Aryan Nations established its spiritual and political headquarters in a compound at Hayden Lakes, Idaho. Residents of the compound were overtly neo-Nazi. They adopted a rank hierarchy, established an armed security force, trained as survivalists, worshipped as Identity believers, and took to wearing uniforms. A number of people who passed through the Aryan Nations group eventually engaged in political and racial violence, a pattern that included violence by the Order and Buford Oneal Furrow. This pattern led to its financial ruin. In a celebrated lawsuit brought by the Southern Poverty Law Center, Aryan Nations lost its title to the Hayden Lakes property in September 2000 when a $6.3 million verdict was decided. During the trial, the Southern Poverty Law Center successfully linked Aryan Nations security guards to the terrorizing of a family who had driven to the compound's entrance.

National Alliance

The National Alliance is historically linked to the now-defunct American Nazi Party, which had been founded and led by George Lincoln Rockwell prior to his assassination. William Pierce, the founder and leader of the National Alliance, was long considered by experts and members of the neo-Nazi movement to be the most prominent propagandist of the movement. Prior to his death in July 2002, Pierce authored *The Turner Diaries* (under the nom de plume Andrew MacDonald), published a magazine called the *National Vanguard*, made regular radio broadcasts, and managed an active website. The National Alliance's original headquarters is a compound in rural Hillsboro, West Virginia, where Pierce's followers try to carry on his tradition. Although some violent neo-Nazis or other reactionaries may have been inspired by the National Alliance's message (recall that *The Turner Diaries* was found in the possession of Timothy McVeigh), no acts of terrorism or hate crimes were directly linked to the original group.

Postscript: Aryan Nations and National Alliance in Disarray

Two of the most active and influential neo-Nazi organizations were thrown into disarray when their founders and longtime leaders died in the early years of the new millennium. National Alliance's William Pierce died in July 2002, and Aryan Nations' Richard Butler died in September 2004. With the deaths of these leaders, both organizations engaged in bitter infighting over who would assume leadership and whose ideology most reflected the ideologies of the founding leaders. Infighting led to splits within the organizations, and factions formed claiming to be the heirs of the original groups. Membership declined significantly because of the leadership crisis and internal quarreling, eventually marginalizing both organizations by the end of the first decade of the 21st century.

RIGHT-WING TERRORISM IN THE UNITED STATES

Right-wing terrorism in the United States is usually motivated by racial supremacist and antigovernment sentiment. Unlike the violent left, terrorist campaigns by underground rightist organizations and networks have been rare, as have massive bombings such as the Oklahoma City attack. It is more common for the right to be characterized by small-scale, cell-based conspiracies within the Patriot and neo-Nazi movements. In comparison with the left, the violent right has been less organized and less consistent.

This discussion explores the terrorist right by investigating the following subjects:

- Homegrown Racism: The Legacy of the Ku Klux Klan

- Racial Mysticism: Neo-Nazi Terrorism

- Patriot Threats

- Case in Point: Moralist Terrorism

Homegrown Racism: The Legacy of the Ku Klux Klan

The **Ku Klux Klan (KKK)** is a racist movement with no counterpart among international right-wing movements—it is a purely American phenomenon. Its name comes from the Greek word **kuclos**, or circle. The KKK is best described as an enduring movement that developed the following ideology:

- racial supremacy

- violent assertion of Klan racial doctrine

- Protestant Christian supremacy

- ritualistic symbolism, greetings, and fraternal behavior

- American cultural nationalism (also known as nativism)

Klan terminology in many ways is an exercise in racist secret fraternal bonding. Table 9.4 samples the exotic language of the KKK.

There have been several manifestations of the KKK, which most experts divide into five eras.

First-Era Klan

The KKK was founded in the immediate aftermath of the Civil War. Some sources date its origin to Christmas Eve 1865, whereas others cite 1866. According to most sources, the KKK was first convened in Pulaski, Tennessee, by a group of Southerners who initially formed the group as a fraternal association. Its first imperial wizard, or national leader, was former Confederate general and slave trader Nathan Bedford Forrest. Military-style rankings were established, and by 1868, the KKK was a secretive and politically violent organization. Its targets included African Americans, Northerners, and Southern collaborators. The KKK was suppressed by the Union Army and the anti-Klan "Ku Klux laws" were passed by Congress. Imperial Wizard Forrest ordered the KKK to be officially disbanded, and its robes and regalia were ceremoniously burned. It has been estimated that the Klan had about 400,000 members during its first incarnation.

Second-Era Klan

After the Reconstruction era—that is, after the gradual departure of the Union Army from the South and the final repeal of martial law in 1877—the KKK re-formed into new secret societies and fraternal groups. It wielded a great deal of political influence and successfully helped

Table 9.4 The Fraternal Klan

From its inception in 1866, the Ku Klux Klan has used fraternity-like greetings, symbolism, and rituals. These behaviors promote secrecy and racial bonding within the organization. Examples of Klan language include the following greeting: *Ayak*? (Are you a Klansman?) and *Akia*! (A Klansman I am!). The language used for regional offices is also unique, as indicated in the following examples:

Invisible Empire	National
Realm	State
Klavern	Local

This table summarizes the activity profiles of official Klan organizational designations.

Klan Official	Duties	Scope of Authority	Symbolic Identification
Imperial Wizard	National leader	Invisible Empire	Blue stripes or robe
Grand Dragon	State leader	Realm	Green stripes or robe
Exalted Cyclops	County leader	Klaverns within county	Orange stripes or robe
Nighthawk	Local security and administration	Klavern	Black robe
Klonsel	General counsel	Invisible Empire	White robe
Citizen	Member	Klan faction	White robe

restore racial supremacy and segregation in the South. Racial supremacy was violently enforced and officially sanctioned by the passage of racial legislation often referred to as "Black Codes." As a result, African Americans in the South lost most political and social rights after 1877, thus inaugurating a long period of legally sanctioned racial subjugation that did not end until the passage of federal legislation and Supreme Court decisions during the civil rights movement in the mid-20th century. The targets of Klan violence during this period were African Americans, immigrants, Catholics, and Jews.

Lawrence Beitler/Hulton Archive/Getty Images

▶ Communal terrorism in America. The lynchings of Tommy Shipp and Abe Smith in Marion, Indiana, on August 7, 1930. The crowd is in a festive mood, including the young couple holding hands in the foreground.

Third-Era Klan

During the early part of the 20th century and continuing into the 1920s, the KKK became a broad-based national movement. In 1915, members gathered at Stone Mountain, Georgia, and formed a movement known as the Invisible Empire. The Klan was glorified in the novel *The Clansman* and in the 1915 film *The Birth of a Nation*, which was shown in the White House during the administration of President Woodrow Wilson. During this period, the Invisible Empire had between three and four million members. In 1925 in Washington, D.C., 45,000 Klansmen and Klanswomen paraded down Pennsylvania Avenue. Also during this period, Klan and Klan-inspired violence was widespread. Thousands of people—mostly African Americans—were victimized by the KKK. Many acts of terrorism were ritualistic communal lynchings.

Fourth-Era Klan

After a decline because of revelations about Third-Era violence and corruption, the Klan was reinvigorated in 1946—once again at Stone Mountain, Georgia. At this gathering, the Invisible Empire disbanded, and new independent Klans were organized at local and regional levels. There was no longer a single national Klan but rather autonomous Klan factions. During the civil rights movement of the 1950s and 1960s, some Klan factions became extremely violent. The White Knights of Mississippi and the United Klans of America (mostly in Alabama) committed numerous acts of terrorism to try to halt progress toward racial equality in the American South. This era ended after several successful federal prosecutions during the 1960s on criminal civil rights charges, though the Klan itself endured.

Fifth-Era Klan

Violence during the Fifth Era has been committed by lone wolves rather than as organized Klan action. The modern era of the Ku Klux Klan began to emerge during the 1980s and is characterized by two trends:

The moderate Klan. Some Klansmen and Klanswomen have tried to moderate their image by adopting more mainstream symbolism and rhetoric. Rather than advocating violence or paramilitary activity, they have projected an image of law-abiding activists working on behalf of white civil rights and good moral values. Those who promote this trend have eschewed the prominent display of Klan regalia and symbols.

The purist Klan. During the 1990s a traditional and "pure" Klan emerged that hearkens back to the original traditions and ideology of the KKK. This movement has held a number of aggressive and vitriolic rallies—many in public at county government buildings. Its rhetoric is unapologetically racist and confrontational. Some factions of the purist trend prohibit the display of Nazi swastikas or other non-Klan racist symbols at KKK gatherings.

KKK membership has ebbed and flowed in the Fifth Era, in part because of competition from other racial supremacist movements, such as racist skinhead and neo-Nazi groups. There was also fresh competition beginning in the late 1990s from the neo-Confederate movement.

Racial Mysticism: Neo-Nazi Terrorism

In the modern era, most non-Klan terrorism on the right wing has come from the neo-Nazi movement. Neo-Nazi terrorism is predicated on varying mixes of religious fanaticism, political violence, and racial supremacy. Its worldview is predicated on the superiority of the Aryan race, the inferiority of non-Aryans, and the need to confront an evil global Jewish conspiracy. Another common theme is the belief that a **racial holy war**—called **Rahowa**—is inevitable.

Although most violence emanating from these beliefs has been expressed as lone-wolf terrorism and **hate crimes**, several groups have embarked on violent sprees. For example, a group calling itself the **Aryan Republican Army (ARA)** operated in the Midwest from 1994 to 1996.[11]

The Order

The Order was a covert, underground, and violent group that was inspired by a fictional secret organization depicted in the novel *The Turner Diaries*. In the book, the Order was a heroic inner circle and vanguard for the Aryan revolution in the United States. **Robert Jay Mathews**, a racial supremacist activist, was the founder of the actual Order in 1983.

The Order's methods for fighting the war against the Zionist Occupation Government were counterfeiting, bank and armored car robberies, and occasional murders.[12] Its area of operation was primarily in the Pacific Northwest. In April 1984, the group bombed a synagogue in Boise, Idaho. In March 1984, members of the Order seized $500,000 from a parked armored car in Seattle, Washington; the group detonated a bomb at a theater as a diversion. In June 1984, Alan Berg, a Jewish talk-radio host, was murdered in Denver; he had regularly lambasted the neo-Nazi movement. Also in June, a Brinks armored car was robbed near Ukiah, California, with disciplined precision, and the Order made off with $3.6 million. The end of the Order came when more than 20 of its members were prosecuted and imprisoned in December 1985.

Patriot Threats

Although the Patriot movement attracted a significant number of adherents during the 1990s, and militias at one point recruited tens of thousands of members, no underground similar to that of the radical left was formed. Few terrorist movements or groups splintered from the Patriot movement. Thus, despite many implicit and explicit threats of armed violence from Patriots, terrorist conspiracies were rarely carried to completion.

In 1992, former KKK member Louis Beam began to publicly advocate **leaderless resistance** against the U.S. government. Leaderless resistance is a cell-based strategy based on forming **phantom cells** to wage war against the government and enemy interests. Dedicated Patriots and neo-Nazis believe that leaderless resistance and the creation of phantom cells will prevent infiltration from federal agencies. The chief threat of violence came from the armed militias, which peaked in membership immediately before and after the Oklahoma City bombing. In the wake of that incident, federal authorities broke up at least 25 Patriot conspiracies.

The number of militias declined between the April 1995 Oklahoma City bombing and the attacks of September 11, 2001.[13] By 2000, the number of Patriot organizations was only one fourth of the 1996 peak,[14] and this decline continued after September 11, 2001.[15] Experts have noted, however, that the most militant and committed Patriot adherents remain in the movement and that these dedicated members constitute a core of potentially violent true believers.[16]

The Oklahoma City Bombing

On April 19, 1995, Timothy McVeigh drove a rented Ryder truck to the Alfred P. Murrah Federal Building in Oklahoma City. He deliberately chose April 19 as a symbolic date for the attack—it was the 220th anniversary of the battles of Lexington and Concord and the second anniversary of the law enforcement disaster in Waco, Texas.

McVeigh was a hard-core devotee of the Patriot movement and a believer in New World Order conspiracy theories. He was almost certainly a racial supremacist, having tried to solicit advice from the neo-Nazi National Alliance and the racial separatist Elohim City group about going underground after the bombing. McVeigh had also visited the Branch Davidian site at Waco, Texas, approximately one month before the compound was burned.[17] About 80 members of the Branch Davidian cult died in that fire ignited during a paramilitary raid by federal law enforcement officers.

McVeigh had converted the Ryder truck into a powerful mobile ammonium nitrate and fuel oil (ANFO)–based bomb. He used "more than 5,000 pounds of ammonium nitrate fertilizer mixed with about 1,200 pounds of liquid nitromethane, [and] 350 pounds of Tovex."[18] When he detonated the truck bomb at 9:02 a.m., it destroyed most of the federal building and killed 168 people, including 19 children. More than 500 other people were injured.

McVeigh's attack was in large part a symbolic act of war against the federal government. He had given careful consideration to achieving a high casualty rate, just as "American bombing raids were designed to take lives, not just destroy buildings."[19]

The deaths of the 19 children were justified in his mind as the unfortunate "collateral damage" against innocent victims common to modern warfare.[20] Timothy McVeigh was tried and convicted, and he was executed in a federal facility in Terre Haute, Indiana, on June 11, 2001. His execution was the first federal execution since 1963.

Case in Point: Moralist Terrorism

Moralist terrorism refers to acts of political violence motivated by a moralistic worldview. Most moralist terrorism in the United States is motivated by an underlying religious doctrine, which is usually a fringe interpretation of Christianity. Abortion clinics and gay bars have been the most frequent targets of moralist violence.

Examples of violent moralist movements include the **Army of God** and the **Phineas Priesthood**. They are both shadowy movements that apparently have little or no organizational structure, operate as lone wolves or cells, and answer to the so-called higher power of their interpretations of God's will. They seem to be belief systems in which like-minded activists engage in similar behavior. The Phineas Priesthood is apparently a calling (divine revelation) for Christian Identity fundamentalists, and the Army of God membership is perhaps derived from fringe evangelical Christian fundamentalists. These profiles are speculative. Both groups may simply be manifestations of terrorist contagion (copycatting). There has also been speculation that both movements are linked.

UNDERSTANDING THE PERSISTENCE OF VIOLENT IDEOLOGIES IN THE UNITED STATES

Leftist activism has certainly not disappeared in the United States. New symbols have attracted the attention of a renewed far-left movement. For example, the "Battle of Seattle" in November 1999 (protesting globalization) is typical of an ongoing pattern of left-wing activism. Adherents of the far-left are also increasingly opposed to perceived right-wing politics in the United States. Some leftists have violently challenged what they define as rightist policies such as anti-immigration and austerity programs. For example, in early 2017 in the United States, far-left activists confronted police and engaged in vandalism in Portland, Oregon, and Washington, D.C., to protest the presidential election of businessman Donald Trump. In January 2017, black-clad protesters committed acts of vandalism in Berkeley, California, to challenge a planned speech by a right-wing journalist at the University of California. Some members of the far-left employ a tactic popularly dubbed "Black Bloc" to engage in confrontational street protests. Widely considered to be an anarchistic tactic, it occurs when street protesters dress in black and mask their faces en masse at demonstrations. They find other black-clad protesters, form a Black Bloc at the demonstration site, and confront the authorities and engage in acts of vandalism.

Similarly, trends suggest that extremists on the fringe and far right persist in promulgating conspiracy theories and attracting true believers to their causes. Reactionary activists continued to attract a number of people to their causes during the 1990s and 2000s. For example, racial supremacist and Patriot political sentiment morphed into White nationalist and alternative right (so-called alt-right) political movements. Also, some extremist anti-abortion activism continued sporadically, sustained by a core of dedicated true believers. There continues to be sporadic violence from militia members, racial supremacists, and single-issue terrorists. Members of militias, racial supremacist groups, and religious terrorists occasionally target government symbols, ethnic and religious minority groups, and single-issue victims.

DISCUSSION BOX

DOMESTIC TERRORISM IN THE AMERICAN CONTEXT

This chapter's Discussion Box is intended to stimulate critical debate about the idiosyncratic nature of domestic terrorism in the United States.

The subject of domestic terrorism in the United States is arguably a study in idiosyncratic political violence. Indigenous terrorist groups reflected the American political and social environments during historical periods when extremists chose to engage in political violence.

In the modern era, left-wing and right-wing political violence grew from very different circumstances. Leftist violence evolved from a uniquely American social environment that produced the civil rights, Black Power, and New Left movements. Rightist violence grew out of a combination of historical racial and nativist animosity, combined with modern applications of religious and antigovernment ideologies.

In the early years of the new millennium, threats continued to emanate from right-wing antigovernment and racial supremacist extremists. Potential violence from leftist extremists remained low in comparison with the right. When the September 11, 2001, attacks created a new security environment, the question of terrorism originating from domestic sources remained uncertain; this was especially true after the anthrax attacks on the U.S. East Coast.

CHAPTER SUMMARY

This chapter investigated domestic political violence in the United States, the sources of which were identified as extremist tendencies that grew out of movements and cultural histories.

On the left, modern terrorism originated in the social and political fervor of the 1960s and 1970s. Some members of activist movements became radicalized by their experiences within this environment. A few became dedicated revolutionaries and chose to engage in terrorist violence. Members of New Left and nationalist terrorist groups waged terrorist campaigns until the mid-1980s. Single-issue and nascent anarchist tendencies have replaced the now-defunct Marxist and nationalist movements on the left.

On the right, the long history of racial violence continued into the 21st century. The Ku Klux Klan is a uniquely American racist movement that has progressed through five eras, with terrorist violence occurring in each. Modern Klansmen and Klanswomen, neo-Nazis, and moralists have also engaged in terrorist violence.

Threats of potential political violence come from antigovernment movements and emerging "heritage" movements. The activity profile of the modern era is primarily either lone wolf or cell based. It has become rare for racial supremacist and moralist terrorists to act as members of established organizations.

KEY TERMS AND CONCEPTS

The following topics were discussed in this chapter and can be found in the Glossary:

WEB EXERCISE

Using this chapter's recommended websites listed on the student study site at **edge.sagepub.com/martiness5e**, conduct an online investigation of terrorism in the United States.

1. How would you describe the typologies of terrorist groups that predominate in the United States?

2. Conduct a Web search of American monitoring organizations, read their mission statements, and assess their services. Which organizations do you think provide the most useful data? Why?

3. If you were an American dissident extremist (leftist or rightist), how would you design your own website?

   For an online search of terrorism in the United States, readers should enter the following keywords in their Web browser's search engine:

   "Homeland security"

   "Domestic terrorism"

RECOMMENDED READINGS

The following publications discuss the nature of terrorism in the United States and the root causes of political violence in American society.

Burrough, B. (2015). *Days of rage: America's radical underground, the FBI, and the forgotten age of revolutionary violence*. New York, NY: Penguin Press.

Dunbar, D., & Reagan, B. (Eds.). (2006). *Debunking 9/11 myths: Why conspiracy theories can't stand up to the facts*. New York, NY: Hearst Books.

Emerson, S. (2002). *American jihad: The terrorists living among us*. New York, NY: Free Press.

Emerson, S. (2006). *Jihad incorporated: A guide to militant Islam in the US*. Amherst, NY: Prometheus.

George, J., & Wilcox, L. (1996). *American extremists: Militias, supremacists, Klansmen, communists, and others*. Amherst, NY: Prometheus.

German, M. (2007). *Thinking like a terrorist: Insights of a former FBI undercover agent*. Washington, DC: Potomac Books.

Graebmer, W. (2008). *Patty's got a gun: Patricia Hearst in 1970s America*. Chicago, IL: University of Chicago Press.

Kurst-Swanger, K. (2008). *Worship and sin: An exploration of religion-related crime in the United States*. New York, NY: Peter Lang.

MacDonald, A. (1978). *The Turner diaries*. New York, NY: Barricade.

McCann, J. T. (2006). *Terrorism on American soil: A concise history of plots and perpetrators from the famous to the forgotten*. Boulder, CO: Sentient.

McCarthy, T. P., & McMillan, J. (2003). *The radical reader: A documentary history of the American radical tradition*. New York, NY: New Press.

Michel, L., & Herbeck, D. (2001). *American terrorist: Timothy McVeigh and the Oklahoma City bombing*. New York, NY: Regan Books.

Ogbar, J. O. G. (2004). *Black power: Radical politics and African American identity*. Baltimore, MD: Johns Hopkins University Press.

Ridgeway, J. (1995). *Blood in the face: The Ku Klux Klan, Aryan Nations, Nazi skinheads, and the rise of a new white culture* (2nd ed.). New York, NY: Thunder's Mouth.

Ronczkowski, M. (2006). *Terrorism and organized hate crime: Intelligence gathering, analysis, and investigations* (2nd ed.). Boca Raton, FL: CRC Press.

Sargent, L. T. (Ed.). (1995). *Extremism in America: A reader*. New York, NY: New York University Press.

Smith, B. L. (1994). *Terrorism in America: Pipe bombs and pipe dreams*. Albany: State University of New York Press.

Stern, K. S. (1997). *A force upon the plain: The American militia movement and the politics of hate*. New York, NY: Simon & Schuster.

Wilkerson, C. (2007). *Flying close to the sun: My life and times as a Weatherman*. New York, NY: Seven Stories Press.

Zakin, S. (2002). *Coyotes and town dogs: Earth First! and the environmental movement*. Tucson: University of Arizona Press.

Zeskind, L. (2009). *Blood and politics: The history of the white nationalist movement from the margins to the mainstream*. New York, NY: Farrar, Straus and Giroux.

PART THREE

THE TERRORIST BATTLEGROUND

AF archive/Alamy Stock Photo

▶ Osama Bin Laden's compound in Abbottabad, Pakistan, where he was killed by a U.S. naval Special Forces unit in May 2011.

CHAPTER TEN

COUNTERTERRORISM AND THE WAR ON TERRORISM

Learning Objectives

This chapter will enable readers to do the following:

1. Classify the scope of counterterrorist options.

2. Discuss counterterrorism and the use of force.

3. Explain repressive options for operations other than war.

4. Explain conciliatory options for operations other than war.

5. Discuss counterterrorism and legalistic options.

This chapter reviews policy options for responding to acts of political violence. **Counterterrorism**, as it has come to be known, refers to proactive policies that specifically seek to eliminate terrorist environments and groups. Regardless of which policy is selected, the ultimate goal is clear: to save lives by preventing or decreasing the number of terrorist attacks. There is consensus among policy makers that several basic counterterrorist options and suboptions are available. For the purposes of our discussion, this chapter reviews the following classifications of counterterrorist options and suboptions:

The Use of Force

This policy classification allows policy makers to use the force of arms against terrorists and their supporters. The following are examples of military and **paramilitary repressive options**:

- *Suppression campaigns* are military strikes against targets affiliated with terrorists.

- *Coercive covert operations* are secretive operations that include assassinations, sabotage, kidnapping, extraordinary renditions, and other quasi-legal methods.

- *Special operations forces* are highly trained military and police units that are deployed to conduct unconventional operations.

Operations Other Than War: Repressive Options

This policy classification allows policy makers to disrupt and deter terrorist behavior without resorting to military options. The following are examples of nonmilitary repressive options:

- *Nonviolent covert operations* are secretive operations that include a number of possible counterterrorist measures, such as infiltration, disinformation, and cyberwar.

- *Intelligence* refers to collecting data about terrorist movements and to predict their behavior.

- *Enhanced security* refers to the hardening of targets to deter or prevent terrorist attacks.

- *Economic sanctions* are used to punish or disrupt state sponsors of terrorism.

Operations Other Than War: Conciliatory Options

This policy classification allows policy makers to develop a range of options that do not involve force or other repressive methods. The following are examples of conciliatory options:

- *Diplomatic options* refer to engaging with the terrorists to negotiate an acceptable resolution to a conflict. Diplomatic solutions can be incident specific, or they can involve sweeping conditions that may completely resolve the conflict.

- *Social reform* is an attempt to address the grievances of the terrorists and the group they champion.

- *Concessionary options* refer to different degrees of capitulation to the terrorists. Concessions can be incident specific, in which immediate demands are met, or generalized, in which broad demands are accommodated.

Legalistic Responses

The overall objective of **legalistic responses** is to promote the rule of law and regular legal proceedings. The following are examples of these responses:

- *Law enforcement and counterterrorism* refers to the use of law enforcement agencies and criminal investigative techniques in the prosecution of suspected terrorists.

- *Domestic laws* attempt to criminalize terrorist behavior within nations.

- *International law* relies on cooperation among states who are parties to international agreements.

Table 10.1 summarizes activity profiles for these counterterrorist policy categories.

Table 10.1 Counterterrorist Options: General Policy Classifications

Experts have developed categories for counterterrorist options. These policy classifications have been given a variety of labels, but they refer to similar concepts. Each of the categories has been divided into subcategories. This table illustrates the activity profiles of general counterterrorist policy classifications.

Counterterrorist Policy Classification	Activity Profile		
	Rationale	Practical Objectives	Typical Resources Used
Use of force	Symbolic strength	Punish or destroy the terrorists	Military assets Paramilitary assets Covert operatives
Operations other than war: repressive options	Deterrence Prediction Destabilization	Disruption of the terrorists Intelligence Coercion of supporters	Technologies Intelligence operatives Covert operatives
Operations other than war: conciliatory options	Resolve underlying problems	End immediate crises Forestall future crises	Social resources Economic assets Negotiators
Legalistic options	Rule of law	International cooperation Prosecution, conviction, and incarceration of terrorists	International organizations Law enforcement agencies Domestic legal establishments

THE USE OF FORCE

The use of force is a hardline policy approach that states and their proxies use to violently suppress terrorist environments. The goals of this approach are case specific, so the decision to use violent suppression is based on policy calculations peculiar to each terrorist environment. When states decide to use force against terrorists and their supporters, coercion and violence are considered to be justifiable and desirable policy options.

This policy option requires the deployment of military or paramilitary assets to punish, destabilize, or destroy terrorists and their supporters. Military assets are defined as the recognized and official armed forces of a nation. Paramilitary assets are defined as irregular armed units or individuals supported or organized by regimes.

States have waged military and paramilitary counterterrorist operations domestically and internationally. Domestic operations involve coercive use of military, police, and other security forces against domestic threats. International operations involve overt or covert deployment of security assets abroad. These deployments can include ground, air, or naval forces in large or very small operational configurations.

The following discussion explores several use-of-force options that nations commonly adopt.

Maximum Use of Force: Suppression Campaigns

Military and paramilitary forces can undertake counterterrorist campaigns, that is, long-term operations against terrorist cadres, their bases, and support apparatuses. **Suppression campaigns** are uniquely adapted to the conditions of each terrorist environment. They are launched within the policy contexts of war or quasi-war and are generally waged with the goal of defeating rather than simply suppressing the terrorist movement.

For example, in 2002 and 2003, Israel began a concerted effort to disrupt HAMAS and destroy its capability to indefinitely sustain its trademark suicide bombing campaign. Israeli policy included assassinations, military incursions, and a series of raids that resulted in arrests and gunfights with HAMAS operatives as well as many deaths. By 2004, the Israeli government credited these operations and other measures with weakening HAMAS's infrastructure and reducing the incidence of HAMAS bombings.

Military Suppression Campaigns

Nations sometimes resort to using conventional units and special operations forces to wage war against terrorist movements. The goal is to destroy their ability to use terrorism to attack the nation's interests. Military campaigns require that troops be deployed to bases in friendly countries or, in the case of nations with significant seaborne capability,[1] offshore aboard naval vessels. The following case illustrates the nature of military suppression campaigns:

Case: Operation Enduring Freedom. The United States declared itself at war against global terrorism after the attacks of September 11, 2001. It was joined by a number of allies who agreed to commit their armed forces and domestic security services to the new war. Dubbed **Operation Enduring Freedom**, the operation began with the October 2001 invasion of Afghanistan and was defined from the beginning as a long-term suppression campaign. It was also made clear from the outset that the war against terrorism would require extended deployments of U.S. and allied troops around the world, as well as an intensive use of special operations forces, commandos, marines, and other elite units. The immediate objectives were to destroy Al Qaeda's safe havens in Taliban-controlled Afghanistan, collect intelligence, disrupt the terrorist network around the world, and capture or kill as many cadres as possible. The long-term goal of the campaign—which policy makers stated would take years to achieve—was to degrade or destroy the operational capabilities of international terrorists. Interestingly, Operation Enduring Freedom was allegedly first called **Operation Infinite Justice** but renamed after a negative reaction in the Muslim world.[2]

Paramilitary Suppression Campaigns

In some suppression campaigns, military and paramilitary units actively coordinate their operations. A typical government policy has been to arm and support paramilitaries in areas where the military does not have a strong presence. The following example illustrates the nature of such campaigns:

Case: Paramilitary Suppression in Algeria. During the 1990s, Algeria was beset by intensive terrorist violence from jihadis belonging to several radical Islamic groups. The Algerian government was unable to suppress the rebels and was accused of committing human rights violations. Many thousands of civilians were killed, mostly at the hands of the jihadis. During the suppression campaign, the government organized and armed paramilitary home guard units.[3] These units, which were used as local self-defense forces, effectively staved off attacks from the rebels, thus reducing their operational effectiveness in the countryside. In part because of the paramilitary policy, as well as government-initiated programs and brutal suppression, the rebellion eventually ended in a negotiated amnesty settlement in 1999.

Punitive and Preemptive Strikes

Short-duration military and paramilitary operations are usually conducted for a specific purpose under specific rules of engagement. These actions are designed to send a clear symbolic message to terrorists. The following two types have been used:

> **Punitive strikes** are launched as reprisals against terrorists for incidents that have already taken place. Successful punitive strikes require the attacker to symbolically and politically link the attacks to the terrorist incident.
>
> **Preemptive strikes** are undertaken to hurt terrorists before a terrorist incident. Preemptive operations are launched as a precautionary measure to degrade the terrorists' ability to launch future attacks. Symbolic and political linkage between the attacks and a real threat is often difficult.

Punitive strikes are more common than preemptive strikes. These attacks can be justified to some extent, as long as links can be established between the attacks and a terrorist incident. Linkage must also be made between the specific targets of the reprisal and the alleged perpetrators of the incident. This latter consideration sometimes goes awry. Preemptive strikes are less frequent than punitive strikes, partly because preemption by definition means that the attack is a unilateral action conducted in response to a perceived threat. Such attacks are therefore not as easily justified as punitive operations, which is an important consideration for regimes concerned about world opinion. Unless a threat can be clearly defined, it is unlikely that preemptive actions will receive widespread support. Nevertheless, some nations have adopted preemptive operations as a regular counterterrorist method. Israel has for some time preemptively attacked neighboring countries that harbor anti-Israeli terrorists and dissidents. Chapter Perspective 10.1 presents an example of a large punitive operation that the United States launched against Libya in 1986.

CHAPTER PERSPECTIVE 10.1

Operation El Dorado Canyon

On April 14, 1986, the United States bombed targets in Libya using Air Force bombers based in Great Britain and Navy carrier-borne aircraft based in the Mediterranean. The attacks occurred at the height of tensions between the United States and Libya, which were precipitated by a radically activist Libyan government and its partnership with the Soviet Union.

Background

During the 1980s, Libya established strong ties with the Communist Eastern bloc (Soviet-dominated Eastern Europe). It also declared itself to be a champion of people "oppressed" by the West and Israel. Libyan leader Muammar el-Qaddafi permitted the Libyan government to build camps to train terrorists from around the world, to stockpile weapons far in excess of Libya's needs, to acquire large amounts of plastic explosives (including powerful Czech-made Semtex), and to directly engage in state-sponsored international terrorism.

In March 1986, the U.S. Mediterranean fleet sailed into a disputed exclusionary zone off the coast of Libya. Qaddafi responded to the American show of force by declaring that a "line of death" had been drawn in the disputed waters—which the U.S. Sixth Fleet then purposefully crossed. Two terrorist bombings blamed on Libya subsequently occurred in Europe. The first bomb killed four Americans aboard a TWA airliner in Greece,

and the second bomb killed one U.S. serviceman at La Belle Discothèque in West Berlin. The American punitive raids—dubbed **Operation El Dorado Canyon**—were ostensibly in retaliation for these bombings, but they probably would have occurred in any event.

Aftermath

More than 100 Libyans were killed in Benghazi and Tripoli, including Qaddafi's young adopted daughter. American policy makers considered the attacks to be successful because Libya thereafter temporarily scaled back its international adventurism, and Qaddafi reduced his inflammatory rhetoric. Libya then entered a second, shorter period of international activism and then pulled back—this time for an extended period of time.

It should be noted that the strike force based in Britain was forced to detour around France and the Iberian Peninsula (Spain and Portugal) and enter the Mediterranean through the Straits of Gibraltar, which separate Europe and Africa. This was necessary because the French and Spanish governments refused to permit the bombers to fly over their airspace.

The American air strike was unpopular in Europe. After the attack, demonstrations occurred in several countries, and many Europeans expressed outrage over the bombings. In Beirut, one American and two British hostages were murdered in retaliation for the attack on Libya.

War in the Shadows, Part 1: Coercive Covert Operations

Coercive covert operations seek to destabilize, degrade, and destroy terrorist groups. Targets include individual terrorists, terrorist networks, and support apparatuses. Although covert assets have been developed by nations to wage so-called shadow wars using special operatives, conventional forces have also been used to surreptitiously resolve terrorist crises.

Case: Assassinations

The underlying rationale for using assassination as a counterterrorist option is uncomplicated: The terrorism will end or diminish if the terrorists and their supporters are eliminated. The argument is that those targeted for assassination will, as a threat, be permanently removed. It is debatable whether this assumption is accurate because little evidence supports the supposition that assassinations have ever had an appreciable deterrent effect on determined terrorists—new recruits continue to enlist in movements worldwide. As discussed in previous chapters, symbolic martyrdom is actively manipulated by terrorist movements to rally their followers and recruit new fighters. Assassinations can have the effect of sending a symbolic message of reprisal and retribution. In this regard, Israel has used assassinations repeatedly in its war against terrorism, primarily targeting Palestinian nationalists. For example, a covert Israeli unit known as **Wrath of God** (Mivtzan Elohim) was responsible for tracking and assassinating Black September terrorists after the 1972 Munich Olympics massacre. At least 20 Palestinians were assassinated in Europe and the Middle East. The Wrath of God program went awry in 1973 when Israeli agents mistakenly shot and killed a North African waiter in Norway while his wife looked on; they had mistaken him for a Black September operative. Assassinations can also have the effect of "decapitating" a vertically integrated extremist movement. For example, in August 2009, the United States successfully deployed a drone aircraft in Pakistan's tribal region to assassinate Baitullah Mahsud, the leader of Pakistan's Taliban movement. Mahsud was the putative leader of the coalitional movement, and his death had the immediate effect of causing the Pakistan Taliban to fracture along tribal lines. And in October 2011, American-born cleric Anwar al-Awlaki was killed by a drone strike.

Case: Armed Drone Aircraft

Armed remotely controlled drone aircraft became fixtures in the United States' arsenal during the post-9/11 era. Operated by military and Central Intelligence Agency personnel from remote locations, armed drones proved to be a deadly counterpart to other options involving targeted killings of terrorists. The deployment and use of drones was relatively modest in years immediately following the September 11, 2001, attacks but increased markedly in 2008. From 2008, armed drone aircraft were deployed extensively in Pakistan and Afghanistan. Hundreds of drone airstrikes occurred. Within three years, the United States had launched lethal drone attacks in six countries: Afghanistan, Iraq, Libya, Pakistan, Somalia, and Yemen. Targeted assassinations of members of Al Qaeda and other organizations occurred with regularity, resulting in the deaths of dozens of upper- and middle-echelon commanders. In 2011, the United States began a campaign targeting the leadership of the Al Shabaab Islamist militia in Somalia. The purpose of the attacks was to disrupt reportedly growing ties between Al Shabaab and Al Qaeda, which intelligence reports indicated had been established to enhance Al Shabaab's capability to launch international attacks.

In essence, drone attacks have become a commonly used lethal option during operations against terrorist havens and individuals. From 2009 to 2014, approximately 2,400 people were killed, and U.S. officials reported most were militants.[4] Between 2004 and 2017, nearly 3,000 Taliban or Al Qaeda militants were killed in known drone attacks and airstrikes in Pakistan.[5]

Surgical Use of Force: Special Operations Forces

Special operations forces are defined here as highly trained military and police units that specialize in unconventional operations. These units are usually not organized the same way as conventional forces because their missions require them to operate quickly and covertly in hostile environments. Operations are frequently conducted by small teams of operatives, though fairly large units can be deployed if circumstances require. Depending on their mission, special operations forces are trained for long-range reconnaissance, surveillance, surgical punitive raids, hostage rescues, abductions, and liaisons with allied counterterrorist forces. Their training and organizational configurations are ideally suited to counterterrorist operations.

Special Operations Forces: Military Units

Special operations forces today have become fully integrated into the operational commands of national armed forces worldwide. Their value in counterterrorist operations has been proved many times in the post–World War II era. The following examples illustrate the mission and configuration of special operations forces commands.

United Kingdom. The **Special Air Service (SAS)** is a secretive organization in the British army that has been used repeatedly in counterterrorist operations. Organized at a regimental level but operating in very small teams, the SAS is similar to the French **1st Navy Parachute Infantry Regiment** and the American Delta Force (discussed later in the chapter). The SAS has been deployed repeatedly to assignments in Northern Ireland and abroad, as well as to resolve domestic terrorist crises such as rescuing hostages in May 1980 inside the Iranian embassy in London. The **Special Boat Service (SBS)** is a special unit under the command of the Royal Navy. It specializes in operations against seaborne targets and along coastlines and harbors. The SBS is similar to the French Navy's special assault units and the American SEALs (discussed later in the chapter). The **Royal Marine Commandos** are rapid-reaction troops that deploy in larger numbers than the SAS and SBS. They are organized around units called commandos, which are roughly equivalent to a conventional battalion.

France. The 1st Navy Parachute Infantry Regiment (1RPIMa) is similar to the British SAS and American Delta Force. Within the 1RPIMa, small RAPAS (intelligence and special operations) squads are trained to operate in desert, urban, and tropical environments. Along with the special police unit GIGN (discussed later in the chapter), they form the core of French counterterrorist special operations forces. 1RPIMa has been deployed to crises around the world, particularly in Africa. Five **French Navy Special Assault Units** have been trained for operations against seaborne targets, coastlines, and harbors. Their mission is similar to those of the British SBS and American SEALs. When large elite combat forces must be deployed, the French use their all-volunteer **11th Parachute Division (Paras)** and the commando or parachute units of the famous French Foreign Legion.[6]

Israel. The **Sayaret** are reconnaissance units that were organized early in the history of the Israel Defense Force (IDF). Several Sayaret exist within the IDF, the most noted of which is **Sayaret Matkal**, a highly secretive formation that is attached to the IDF General Headquarters. The **Parachute Sayaret** has been deployed in small and large units, often using high mobility to penetrate deep into hostile territory. These units participated in the Entebbe operation (discussed in Chapter Perspective 10.2) and were used extensively in Lebanon against Hezbollah. The IDF has also deployed undercover agents against suspected terrorist cells. **Duvdevan** is a deep-cover unit that conducts covert special operations in urban areas against suspected militants. These agents are noted for dressing as Arabs during these operations, and among other specialized operations they are known for rendering (kidnapping) specific individuals. When large elite combat forces must be deployed, the **Golani Brigade** and its Sayaret are frequently used. The Golani Brigade was used extensively against Hezbollah in South Lebanon.

United States. U.S. Special Operations Forces are organized under the U.S. **Special Operations Command.** The **Delta Force (1st Special Forces Operational Detachment-Delta)** is a secretive unit that operates in small teams. Similar in mission to the British SAS and French 1RPIMa, Delta Force operates covertly outside of the United States. Its missions probably include abductions, reconnaissance, and punitive operations. **Green Berets (Special Forces Group)** usually operate in units called A Teams. These teams comprise specialists whose skills include languages, intelligence, medicine, and demolitions. The traditional mission of the A Team is force multiplication; that is, they are inserted into regions to provide military training to local personnel, thus multiplying their operational strength. They also participate in reconnaissance and punitive raids. U.S. Navy **Sea Air Land Forces (SEALs)** are similar to the British SBS and the French Navy's Special Assault Units. Their primary mission is to conduct seaborne, riverine, and harbor operations, though they have also been used extensively on land. When large elite combat units must be deployed, the United States relies on the army's **75th Ranger Regiment** and units from the U.S. Marine Corps. The marines have formed their own elite units, which include force reconnaissance and long-range reconnaissance units (referred to as Recon). These units are organized into teams, platoons, companies, and battalions.

Qassem Zein/AFP/Getty Images

▶ Iraqi special forces police unit on parade during a ceremony in the city of Najaf.

Special Operations Forces: Police Units

Many nations have special units within their police forces that participate in counterterrorist operations. In several examples, these units have been used in a semimilitary role.

France. The **GIGN (Groupe d'Intervention Gendarmerie Nationale)** is recruited from the French gendarmerie, the military police. GIGN is a counterterrorist unit with international operational duties. In an operation that foiled what was arguably a precursor to the September 11 attacks, the GIGN rescued 173 hostages from an Air France Airbus in December 1994. Four Algerian terrorists had landed the aircraft in Marseilles, intending to fly to Paris to crash or blow up the plane over the city.

Germany. **GSG-9 (Grenzschutzgruppe 9)** was organized after the disastrous failed attempt to rescue Israeli hostages taken by Black September at the 1972 Munich Olympics. It is a paramilitary unit that has been used domestically and internationally as a counterterrorist and hostage rescue unit. GSG-9 first won international attention in 1977, when the group freed hostages held by Palestinian terrorists in Mogadishu, Somalia.

Israel. The **Police Border Guards** are an elite force that is frequently deployed as a counterterrorist force. Known as the **Green Police**, it operates in two subgroups. **YAMAS** is a covert group that has been used extensively during the Palestinian intifada to neutralize terrorist cells in conjunction with covert IDF operatives. **YAMAM** was specifically created to engage in counterterrorist and hostage rescue operations.

United States. At the national level, the United States has organized several units that have counterterrorist capabilities, all paramilitary groups that operate under the administrative supervision of federal agencies and perform traditional law enforcement work. Perhaps the best known is the Federal Bureau of Investigation's **Hostage Rescue Team**. Not as well known but very important is the Department of Energy's **Emergency Search Team**. Paramilitary capabilities have also been incorporated into the Treasury Department's Bureau of Alcohol, Tobacco, Firearms and Explosives and Secret Service. At the local level, American police forces also deploy units that have counterterrorist capabilities. These units are known by many names, but the most commonly known designation is Special Weapons and Tactics (SWAT).

Both military and police special units have been deployed to resolve hostage crises. Chapter Perspective 10.2 summarizes several famous hostage incidents in which special operations forces were used—usually with success, but not always.

Table 10.2 summarizes the activity profile of counterterrorist options that sanction the use of force.

CHAPTER PERSPECTIVE 10.2

Hostage Rescues

When hostage rescue operations succeed, they seem to be almost miraculous victories against terrorism. There have been a number of hostage rescue operations in which well-trained elite units have dramatically resolved terrorist crises. However, there have also been cases when elite units have failed because of poor planning or overly complicated scenarios. The fact is that when they fail, the consequences have been disastrous.

The following cases illustrate the inherently risky nature of hostage rescue operations.

Successful Operations

The Betancourt Rescue ("Operation Jaque"). In July 2008, Colombian special forces rescued 15 hostages held by Revolutionary Armed Forces of Colombia (Fuerzas Armados Revolucionarios de Colombia, or FARC) rebels. Prominent among the hostages, which included three Americans, was former presidential candidate Ingrid Betancourt. Betancourt, who held dual French-Colombian citizenship, had been taken hostage in 2002 while campaigning in rebel-held territory in Colombia's interior region. The three Americans, who were contractors, were captured in 2003 when their antinarcotics surveillance plane went down. The operation, which was accomplished with exceptional stealth and deception, resulted in no casualties. Colombian military intelligence had previously identified the location of the hostages, infiltrated a FARC unit that controlled a group of hostages, and designed an intricate rescue plan. The leader of the FARC unit (nom de guerre Cesar) had been told that the hostages were to be flown to a meeting with another FARC leader aboard a helicopter operated by a human rights organization. The helicopter arrived, the crew assisted in binding over the prisoners, and the aircraft departed. In fact, the story was a ruse. After the hostages and FARC guards entered the helicopter, the guards were overcome and the group was flown to freedom.

Entebbe. In June 1977, an Air France Airbus was hijacked in Athens while en route from Tel Aviv to Paris. Seven terrorists—two West Germans and five PFLP members—forced the plane to fly to Entebbe, Uganda. There were 248 passengers, but 142 were released. The remaining 106 passengers were Israelis and Jews, who were kept as hostages. Israeli troops, doctors, and nurses flew 2,620 miles to Entebbe, attacked the airport, killed at least seven of the terrorists and 20 Ugandan soldiers, and rescued the hostages. Three hostages and one Israeli commando died. One British-Israeli woman who had become ill was moved to a Ugandan hospital, where she was murdered by Ugandan personnel after the rescue.

Mogadishu. In October 1977, a Lufthansa Boeing 737 was hijacked in midair while en route from Mallorca, Spain, to Frankfurt. The hijackers took the aircraft on an odyssey to Rome, the Persian Gulf, the Arabian Peninsula, and East Africa. The four Palestinian terrorists demanded a ransom[a] and the release of imprisoned Palestinian and West German terrorists. The plane eventually landed in Mogadishu, Somalia. Throughout its odyssey, the aircraft had been shadowed by a plane bearing elite West German GSG-9 police commandos. In Mogadishu, the unit landed, attacked the hijacked aircraft, killed three of the terrorists, and rescued the hostages. None of the hostages or rescuers was killed, and only one person was injured. As a postscript, several imprisoned West German terrorists committed suicide when they learned of the rescue.

Unsuccessful Operations

Operation Eagle Claw. During the consolidation of the Iranian Revolution in November 1979, Iranian radicals seized the American embassy in Tehran. Some hostages were soon released, but more than 50 were held in captivity. In April 1980, the United States launched a rescue attempt, called Operation Eagle Claw, that was led by the Delta Force but included units from all branches of the military. The plan was to establish a base in the Iranian desert, fly commando teams into Tehran, assault the embassy compound, ferry the hostages to a soccer field, have helicopters land to pick them up, shuttle them to an airfield secured by Army Rangers, and then fly everyone to safety. Gunships and other aircraft would provide air cover during the operation. The operation did not progress beyond its first phase. As helicopters approached the desert site—dubbed Desert One—they flew into a massive dust storm. Because they were under orders to not exceed 200 feet, they tried to fly through the storm; two helicopters were forced out of the operation, as was a third helicopter that later malfunctioned. On the ground, a helicopter drove into one of the airplanes, and both exploded. Eight soldiers were killed, and the mission was ordered to be cancelled.

The Munich Olympics. In September 1972, members of the Black September terrorist organization captured nine Israeli athletes and killed two others at the Olympic Village during the Munich Olympics. They demanded the release of Palestinian and Red Army Faction prisoners as well as one Japanese Red Army member. West German officials permitted the terrorists to transport their hostages to an airport, using the ruse that they would be flown out of the country. In reality, the plan called for five Bavarian police snipers to shoot the terrorists when they were in the open. At the airport, five terrorists, one police officer, and all of the hostages were killed in a firefight with the Bavarian police. Three terrorists were captured and imprisoned in West Germany, but they were later released and flown to Libya. Israel's Wrath of God program later hunted down and assassinated two of the terrorists.

Force 777. In 1977, Egypt organized Force 777 as a small elite counterterrorist special operations unit. Soon after its creation, Force 777 was twice used to assault aircraft hijacked to other countries by Palestinian terrorists. In the first incident, the PFLP landed a hijacked Cyprus Airways airliner in Nicosia, Cyprus. The Egyptian government dispatched Force 777 but neglected to inform Cypriot authorities. When the Egyptians landed and rushed the hijacked airliner, Cypriot police and other security personnel opened fire, thinking that the commandos were reinforcements for the terrorists. During an 80-minute firefight, more than 15 Egyptians and Cypriots were killed. In the second incident, Abu Nidal Organization terrorists landed Egyptair Flight 648 in Malta in retaliation for the Egyptian government's failure to protect the *Achille Lauro* terrorists.[b] The Egyptian government again dispatched Force 777, this time in larger numbers and after notifying Maltese officials. Unfortunately, the assault plan called for explosive charges to blow a hole in the aircraft's roof so that Force 777 commandos could jump into the cabin. The charges were much too strong, and the explosion immediately killed approximately 20 passengers. During the ensuing six-hour firefight, a total of 57 passengers were killed. Reports alleged that Egyptian snipers shot at passengers as they fled the aircraft.

Notes

a. The ransom demand was directed to the son of industrialist Hanns-Martin Schleyer, who was in the hands of West Germany's Red Army Faction.

b. During the *Achille Lauro* crisis, Flight 648 was the same aircraft that had transported the PLF terrorists when it was diverted by U.S. warplanes to Sicily.

Table 10.2 Counterterrorist Options: The Use of Force

The purpose of violent responses is to attack and degrade the operational capabilities of terrorists. This can be done by directly confronting terrorists or destabilizing their organizations.

The following table summarizes basic elements of the use of force.

Counterterrorist Option	Activity Profile		
	Rationale	Practical Objectives	Typical Resources Used
Suppression campaigns	Symbolic strength Punitive measures Preemption	Destruction of the terrorists Disruption of the terrorists	Military assets Paramilitary assets
Coercive covert operations	Symbolic strength Destabilization Preemption	Disruption of the terrorists Deterrent effect on potential terrorists	Military assets Paramilitary assets
Special operations forces	Coercive covert operations Destabilization Preemption	Disruption of the terrorists Deterrent effect on potential terrorists	Military and police assets

Source: Created from Ripley, Amanda, "Why Suicide Bombing Is Now All the Rage," *Time*, April 15, 2002.

OPERATIONS OTHER THAN WAR: REPRESSIVE OPTIONS

Nonmilitary and nonparamilitary **repressive responses** can be effective in suppressing terrorist crises and terrorist environments. The purpose is to disrupt and deter terrorist behavior. They are unlikely to bring a long-term end to terrorism but can reduce the scale of violence by destabilizing terrorist groups and forcing them to be on the run.

War in the Shadows, Part 2: Nonviolent Covert Operations

Nonviolent covert operations encompass a number of options, are often quite creative, and are inherently secretive. Their value lies in manipulating terrorist behavior and taking terrorist groups by surprise. For example, covert operations can create internal distrust, fear, infighting, and other types of discord. The outcome might also be a reduction in operational focus, momentum, and effectiveness. Typical covert operations include the following options:

Infiltration

Ideally, infiltration will improve the quality of intelligence prediction, as well as the possible betrayal of cadres to counterterrorist forces. However, in New Terrorism, infiltration of terrorist organizations is more difficult because of their cell-based organizational profiles.

Disinformation

Disinformation uses information to disrupt terrorist organizations. It is used to selectively create and deliver data that are calculated to create disorder within the terrorist group or its support apparatus. It can also be used to spread damaging propaganda about terrorist organizations and cadres.

Cyberwar

Bank accounts, personal records, and other data are stored no longer on paper but instead in digital formats. **Cyberwar** uses this electronic information against adversaries. Terrorist movements that maintain or send electronic financial and personal information run the risk of having that information intercepted and compromised. In June 2011, U.S. president Barack Obama signed executive orders approving guidelines for military applications of computer-initiated actions against adversaries. The guidelines governed a range of options, including espionage and aggressive cyberattacks.

Rob Jensen/U.S. Air Force/Getty Images

▶ A Predator drone aircraft departs on a mission.

Modern Surveillance Technologies

Surveillance technologies are central components of counterterrorist systems. It is technologically feasible to access private electronic transactions, including telephone records and conversations, computer transactions and communications (such as e-mail), social media, and credit card records. Digital fingerprinting and facial imaging permit security agencies to access records virtually instantaneously. The Federal Bureau of Investigation (FBI) has used **biometric technologies** to collect and analyze unique human traits. These technologies permit the storage of data such as iris scans, facial recognition, fingerprints, hand geometry, speech verification, and vascular recognition.

Chapter Perspective 10.3 explores the utility of monitoring private social media by homeland security and emergency response authorities.

CHAPTER PERSPECTIVE 10.3

The Utility of Monitoring Social Media

Modern social media technologies allow users to upload and post information electronically on provider websites. Popular providers include Twitter, Facebook, and dating enterprises, and users typically use provider websites as social networking resources. Users upload information about themselves that may be accessed by other users and the public. Information typically includes photographs, videos, statements of interest, and personal information.

Social media have proven to be very useful systems for disseminating information when natural or intentional disasters occur. Real-time information about the effect of hurricanes, tornadoes, and other natural events has assisted the media and emergency responders in assessing the magnitude and geographic location of critical incidents. Similarly, social media have alerted the public to unfolding terrorist events, such as what occurred in the aftermath of the 2013 Boston Marathon bombing.

Unfortunately, criminals also use social media technologies. For example, confidence artists and child sexual predators have been known to target unknowing potential victims.

Social media provide intelligence and law enforcement officials with resources to monitor individuals and investigate crimes. Law enforcement agencies have found social media information to be a useful forensic tool for pursuing active investigations and for framing sting operations to take criminals into custody. For example, undercover law enforcement officers posing as children online have successfully captured adult predators. Similarly, intelligence analysts are able to examine the use of Web-based social media by extremist individuals and organizations. This can be useful for projecting the intentions of violent extremists. For example, increased "chatter" could suggest an increased likelihood of actual activity by extremists, especially when combined with increased activity on social media websites.

Knowing the Enemy: Intelligence

Intelligence agencies involve themselves with collecting and analyzing information. The underlying goal is to develop an accurate activity profile of terrorists. Data are collected from overt and covert sources and evaluated by expert intelligence analysts. This process is at the heart of counterterrorist intelligence gathering. The outcome can range from having profiles of terrorist organizations to tracking the movements of terrorists. An optimal outcome is to be able to anticipate the behavior of terrorists and thus to predict terrorist incidents.

SIGINT—Signal Intelligence

Intelligence collection and analysis in the modern era require the use of sophisticated technological resources. These technological resources are used primarily for the interception of electronic signals—known as SIGINT. **Signal intelligence** is used for a variety of purposes, such as interceptions of financial data, monitoring communications such as cell phone conversations, and reading e-mail messages. The use of satellite imagery is also commonly used by intelligence agencies, and sophisticated computers specialize in code breaking. However, the practicality of these technologies as counterterrorist options is limited in the era of the New Terrorism. Because of the cellular organizational structure of terrorist groups and their insular interactions (i.e., based on personal relationships), technology cannot be an exclusive counterterrorist resource. Human intelligence is also a critical component. Prominent SIGINT centers include the United Kingdom's Government Communications Headquarters (GCHQ) and the National Security Agency (NSA) in the United States.

HUMINT—Human Intelligence

The collection of **human intelligence**, also referred to as HUMINT, is often a cooperative venture with friendly intelligence agencies and law enforcement officials. This sharing of information is a critical component of counterterrorist intelligence gathering. Circumstances may also require the covert manipulation of individuals affiliated with terrorist organizations or their support groups, with the objective of convincing them to become intelligence agents. The manipulation process can include making appeals to the sense of justice or patriotism of potential spies, paying them with money and other valuables, or offering them something that they would otherwise be unable to obtain (such as asylum for their family in a Western country). One significant problem with finding resources for human intelligence is that most terrorist cells are made up of individuals who know one another very well. Newcomers are not openly welcomed, and those who may be potential members are usually expected to commit an act of terrorism or other crime to prove their commitment to the cause. In other words, intelligence agencies must be willing to use terrorists to catch terrorists. This has been a very difficult task, and groups such as Al Qaeda have proven very difficult to penetrate with human assets.[7]

OSINT—Open Source Intelligence

Open source intelligence is information collected from publicly available electronic and print outlets. It is information that is readily available to the public but used for intelligence analysis. Examples of open sources include newspapers, the Internet, journals, radio, videos, television, and commercial outlets.

IMINT—Imagery Intelligence

Images are regularly collected to provide actionable intelligence. Collection technologies range from relatively routine handheld equipment to very sophisticated means. IMINT includes "intelligence information derived from the collection by visual photography, infrared sensors, lasers, electro-optics, and radar sensors."[8]

MASINT—Measurements and Signatures Intelligence

The use of a broad array of technical and scientific disciplines to measure the characteristics of specified subjects. For example, tracking communications signatures or measuring water and soil samples. MASINT is "intelligence information obtained by quantitative and qualitative analysis of data derived from specific technical sensors for the purpose of identifying any distinctive features associated with the source, emitter, or sender."[9]

GEOINT—Geospatial Intelligence

The collection and assessment of topography and geographical features can provide actionable intelligence regarding locations, time frames, and other information. GEOINT is "the all-source analysis of imagery and geospatial information to describe, assess, and visually depict physical features and geographically referenced activities on earth."[10]

Intelligence Agencies

In many democracies, intelligence collection is traditionally divided between agencies that are separately responsible for domestic and international intelligence collection. This separation is often mandated by law. For example, the following agencies roughly parallel each other's missions:

- In Great Britain, the Security Service (**MI-5**) is responsible for domestic intelligence and the Secret Intelligence Service (**MI-6**) is responsible for international collection. GCHQ provides SIGINT support for both MI-5 and MI-6.

- In the United States, the FBI performs domestic intelligence collection, and the **Central Intelligence Agency (CIA)** operates internationally. The NSA is responsible for international SIGINT collection but does not have authorization to collect SIGINT domestically.

- In Germany, the **Bureau for the Protection of the Constitution** shares a mission similar to MI-5 and the FBI, and the **Military Intelligence Service** roughly parallels MI-6 and the CIA. SIGINT support is provided by several centers, including the Military Intelligence Service and the Bundeswehr's (united armed forces) Strategic Reconnaissance Command.

Hardening the Target: Enhanced Security

Target hardening is an antiterrorist measure that makes potential targets more difficult to attack. This is a key component of **antiterrorism**, which attempts to deter or prevent terrorist attacks. **Enhanced security** is also intended to deter would-be terrorists from selecting hardened facilities as targets. These measures are not long-term solutions for ending terrorist environments but do provide short-term protection for specific sites. Target hardening includes increased airport security, the visible deployment of security personnel, and the erection of crash barriers at entrances to parking garages beneath important buildings. In the United States, technologies permit digital screening of fingerprints and other physical features as one enhancement at ports of entry.[11]

Typical examples of target hardening include the following:

- Vehicular traffic was permanently blocked on Pennsylvania Avenue in front of the White House because of the threat from high-yield vehicular bombs in the aftermath of the 1993 New York City World Trade Center and 1995 Oklahoma City bombings. The area became a pedestrian mall.

- During the 1990s, Great Britain began to make widespread use of closed-circuit surveillance cameras in its urban areas. The police maintain these cameras on city streets, at intersections, and on highways. The purpose of this controversial policy is to monitor suspicious activities, such as abandoned packages or vehicles.

Long-Term Coercion: Economic Sanctions

Economic sanctions are a precedented counterterrorist method directed against governments. They are defined as trade restrictions and controls that are imposed to pressure sanctioned governments to moderate their behavior. Used as a counterterrorist option, sanctions serve several purposes:

- Sanctions symbolically demonstrate strong condemnation of the behavior of the sanctioned regime.

- Sanctions are an exercise of the power of the sanctioning body.

- Sanctions potentially bring to bear considerable pressure on the sanctioned regime.

Unlike many other counterterrorist options, sanctions inherently require sanctioning nations to commit to a long timeline to ensure success. The reason for this commitment is straightforward: Economic pressure is never felt immediately by nations, unless they are already experiencing dire economic conditions. Trade restrictions require time to be felt in a domestic market, particularly if the nation produces a commodity that is desired on the international market.

Problems can include the following:

- Sanctioned regimes rarely suffer—it is their people who suffer. Sanction coalitions do not always remain firm.

- Leaks in trade embargoes are difficult to control, and sanctioning policies sometimes become quite porous.

Table 10.3　Economic Sanctions: Conditions for Success and Problems

Economic sanctions can theoretically pressure state sponsors of terrorism to moderate their behavior. However, successful sanctions require certain conditions to be in place and to remain firm during the sanctioning process. This table summarizes several conditions, problems, and case studies.

Conditions for Success	Common Problems	Cases
Bring pressure to bear on sanctioned regime.	Economic pressure is passed on to a politically powerless population.	Sanctions against Iraq beginning in the early 1990s; regime remained strong
Maintain strong international cooperation.	International cooperation can weaken or dissolve.	U.S. sanctions against Cuba; perceived by world community to be a relic of the Cold War
Control leaks in the sanctioning policy.	When leaks occur, they cannot be controlled.	Uncoordinated sanctions movement against South Africa during apartheid era; failed to affect South African policy

Table 10.4　Operations Other Than War: Repressive Options

The purpose of repressive responses other than war is to degrade the operational capabilities of terrorists. This table summarizes basic elements of repressive options.

| Counterterrorist Option | Activity Profile | | |
	Rationale	Practical Objectives	Typical Resources Used
Nonviolent covert operations	Deterrence Destabilization Prediction	Deterrent effect on potential terrorists Disruption of the terrorists	Covert operatives Technology
Intelligence	Prediction	Calculating the activity profiles of terrorists	Technology Covert operatives
Enhanced security	Deterrence	Hardening of targets	Security personnel Security barriers Security technology
Economic sanctions	Deterrence Destabilization	Long-term destabilization and deterrence of sanctioned states	National economic resources Coalitional diplomacy

Table 10.3 summarizes the conditions for success, and problems that commonly arise, when attempting to impose economic sanctions. Table 10.4 summarizes the activity profiles of repressive counterterrorist options other than war.

OPERATIONS OTHER THAN WAR: CONCILIATORY OPTIONS

Conciliatory responses are soft-line approaches for ending terrorist environments. They apply policies designed to resolve underlying problems that cause people to resort to political violence. Diplomatic options such as negotiations and social reform are typical policy options and can be very effective. **Concessionary options** are also an alternative, but these are more problematic.

Reasoned Dialogue: Diplomatic Options

Diplomatic options, or **diplomacy**, refer to the use of channels of communication to secure a counterterrorist objective. These channels range in degree from direct talks with dissidents to formal diplomatic overtures with nations that can influence the behavior of terrorist groups. The characteristics of these overtures are case specific, so the style of interaction and communication between the parties are unique to each example. Peace processes and negotiations are typical diplomatic options used to establish channels of communication.

Peace Processes

In regions with ongoing communal violence, long-term diplomatic intervention has sought to construct mutually acceptable terms for a cease-fire. **Peace processes** often involve long, arduous, and frustrating proceedings. Contending parties are always suspicious of each other and do not always represent all of the factions within their camps. The Northern Ireland peace process is instructive.

The peace process in Northern Ireland enjoyed a significant turning point in May 1998, when the so-called **Good Friday Agreement** of April 10, 1998 (also known as the Belfast Agreement), was overwhelmingly approved by voters in the Irish Republic and Northern Ireland. It signaled the mutual acceptance of a Northern Ireland assembly and the disarmament, or **decommissioning**, of all paramilitaries. In July 2002, the Irish Republican Army (IRA) surprised all parties in the peace process by issuing a formal apology for all of the people it killed during **the Troubles**.[12] Although the IRA and paramilitaries failed to disarm by the May 2000 deadline, the scale of violence markedly decreased. Nevertheless, in May 2005, the Independent Monitoring Commission—a watchdog group established by the British and Irish governments—reported that the IRA and Protestant paramilitaries continued to maintain weapons caches and recruit members. These caches, which con-

▶ A lost chance for peace? U.S. president Bill Clinton with Israeli prime minister Benjamin Netanyahu and PLO chairman Yasir Arafat. Clinton had hoped to establish a framework for an ongoing peace process, but the process collapsed amid the fighting of the Palestinian *intifada*.

Ron Sachs/Consolidated News Pictures/Hulton Archive/Getty Images

tained tons of weapons, became a major hindrance to the peace process. The peace process did not collapse, however, because the IRA maintained as its official position a shift from violence to political struggle.[13] In July 2005, the leadership of the IRA announced an end to armed struggle and ordered its paramilitary units to cease engaging in political violence. For the first time in three decades, and after more than 3,000 deaths, the Troubles were officially declared ended.[14]

Negotiations

Conventional wisdom in the United States and Israel holds that one should never negotiate with terrorists, never consider their grievances as long as they engage in violence, and never concede to any demand. Nevertheless, history has shown that case-specific negotiations can resolve immediate crises. Not all negotiations end in complete success for either side but sometimes do provide a measure of closure to terrorist crises. The following cases are examples of negotiations between states, terrorists, and third parties that successfully secured the release of hostages:

- The OPEC hostage crisis of December 1975 in Vienna, Austria, was resolved when the terrorists were permitted to fly to Algiers, Algeria, with a few hostages in tow. The hostages were released when a $5 million ransom was paid for Palestinian causes, and the terrorists were permitted to escape.

- The odyssey of TWA Flight 847 in June 1985 ended with the release of the remaining hostages after negotiations were conducted through a series of intermediaries. The Lebanese Shi'a hijackers used the media and the Lebanese Shi'a Amal militia as intermediaries to broadcast their demands. The hostages were freed after the United States negotiated with Israel the release of more than 700 Shi'a prisoners.

The following cases are examples of negotiations (and bribery) between states that successfully secured the capture of terrorist suspects:

- Ilich Ramirez Sanchez, better known as Carlos the Jackal, was "purchased" by the French government from the government of Sudan in August 1994. When the French learned that the Sudanese had given Carlos refuge, they secretly negotiated a bounty for permission to capture him, which they did from a Khartoum hospital room. Sanchez was eventually sentenced to life imprisonment for murdering two French gendarmes.

- **Johannes Weinrich**, a former West German terrorist, was also purchased—this time by the German government from the government of Yemen. Weinrich was sent to Germany in June 1995 to stand trial for the 1983 bombing of a French cultural center in Berlin, in which one person was killed and 23 others were wounded. Weinrich, who had been a very close associate of Carlos, was convicted in January 2000 and sentenced to life imprisonment. The bounty paid for his capture was presumed to be $1 million.

Responding to Grievances: Social Reform

Social reform attempts to undercut the precipitating causes of national and regional conflicts. Reforms can include improved economic conditions, increased political rights, government recognition of ethno-nationalist sentiment, and public recognition of the validity of grievances.

The following case is an example of social reforms that successfully reduced the severity of a terrorist environment.

Case: Spain and ETA

Ethno-nationalist sentiment in the Basque region had been repressed during the regime of Francisco Franco. After his death in 1975, Spanish democracy was restored, and Basque semi-autonomy was granted. Open discussion of nationalism was permitted, political groups were recognized, labor organizations became independent, and civil liberties were protected. ETA's political party was legalized. Nevertheless, ETA's most violent period occurred immediately after the restoration of democracy. ETA has since continued to strike from time to time, but Basque sentiment turned against the group during the 1980s. In addition, many ETA members returned to civilian life after accepting the terms of a reintegration program during the mid-1980s. Over time, Spanish commitment to social reforms undercut Basque support for ETA.

Giving Them What They Want: Concessionary Options

Granting concessions to terrorists is widely viewed as a marginally optimal counterterrorist response. The reason for this is obvious: Giving terrorists what they want is likely to encourage them to repeat their successful operation or perhaps to increase the stakes in future incidents. In other words, many extremists and those in the general population should be expected to conclude that concessions simply reward extremist behavior. Concessions include the following policy decisions:

- payment of ransoms

- broadcasts or other publications of extremist propaganda

- releases of imprisoned comrades

- political amnesty for dissidents

An interesting example of concessionary behavior is the Iran-Contra scandal. It is a study in how a nation with a publicly strong counterterrorist position (the United States) secretly tried to appease a country that it had defined as a state sponsor of terrorism (Iran).[15]

Case: Iran-Contra Revisited

The United States was embarrassed in November 1986 when a Lebanese magazine revealed that high-ranking officials in the Reagan administration had secretly agreed to sell arms to Iran. The operation, which was under way in August 1985, involved the sale of arms to Iran in exchange for help from the Iranian government to secure the release of American hostages held by Shi'a terrorists in Lebanon. Profits from the sales (reportedly $30 million) were used to support Nicaraguan Contras in their war against the Sandinista government. This support was managed by National Security Adviser John Poindexter and Lieutenant Colonel Oliver North. The administration's embarrassment was aggravated by the fact that the United States had previously adopted a get-tough policy against what it deemed to be terrorist states, and Iran

Table 10.5   Operations Other Than War: Conciliatory Options

The purpose of conciliatory options is to resolve the underlying grievances of the terrorists, which can be done by addressing immediate or long-term threats. This table summarizes basic elements of conciliatory options.

Counterterrorist Option	Activity Profile		
	Rationale	Practical Objectives	Typical Resources Used
Diplomatic options	Resolve terrorist crises	Negotiate case-specific agreements Negotiate long-term agreements	Direct contacts Intermediary contacts
Social reform	Degrade terrorist environments	Win support from potential terrorist supporters Decrease effectiveness of terrorist propaganda	Targeted economic programs Intensive political involvement
Concessionary options	Resolve terrorist crises Degrade terrorist environments	Satisfy the demands that motivate the terrorists	Negotiators Economic concessions Political concessions

had been included in that category. Soon after American captives were released (apparently as a result of the weapons deal), Lebanese terrorists seized more hostages.

Table 10.5 summarizes the activity profile of conciliatory counterterrorist options.

LEGALISTIC RESPONSES

The **law enforcement** approach to combating terrorism has had some success in disrupting conspiratorial networks and has brought closure to criminal cases arising out of terrorist attacks. For example, in the aftermath of the September 11 attacks, European and Southeast Asian police uncovered a number of Al Qaeda and other jihadi cells in Spain, Germany, Singapore, and elsewhere.

Law Enforcement and Counterterrorism

International Cooperation

Internationally, there is no enforcement mechanism for violations of international criminal law other than treaties and other voluntary agreements between nations. Nevertheless, many nations have become members of the **International Criminal Police Organization**, more commonly known as **INTERPOL**. An international association of more than 140 nations that agree to share intelligence and provide assistance in the effort to suppress international crime, INTERPOL is based in Ste. Cloud, France, and each member nation has a bureau that serves as a liaison. INTERPOL is more of an investigative consortium than a law enforcement agency. Its value lies in the cooperative sharing of information between members as well as the coordination of counterterrorist and criminal investigations. Similarly, the **European Police Office (EUROPOL)** is a cooperative investigative consortium of members of the European Union.

The Police and Terrorist Environments

Before the terrorist environments became so prevalent, the primary mission of police agencies was to serve as law enforcement. Today, the mission has refocused onto internal security. In these cases, the police become responsible for day-to-day civil protection operations. Internal security missions require law enforcement units to be stationed at strategic locations and to perform security-focused (rather than crime-focused) patrols. These responsibilities are sometimes threat specific and mirror the terrorist environment of the times. Other security duties include promoting airport security, securing borders, tracking illegal immigrants, looking out for fugitives and other suspects, and conducting surveillance of groups and people who fit **terrorist profiles**. The police are also the first to stabilize the immediate vicinity around attack sites and are responsible for maintaining long-term order in cities suffering under terrorist campaigns. Thus, the role of law enforcement agencies varies in scale and mission depending on the characteristics of the environment and can include the following.

Police Repression

Ideally, the security role of the police will be carried out professionally, within the context of constitutional constraints, and with respect for human rights. However, the reality is that many police agencies around the world are highly aggressive and sometimes abusive—particularly those in authoritarian and weakly democratic countries. They are less concerned with human rights than with maintaining order. The consequences are that police agencies in authoritarian environments perform a very different mission than the professionalized police forces in most stable democracies. For example, police in Brazil and Colombia have been implicated in practicing social cleansing against undesirables. Social cleansing involves intimidating a range of people defined as undesirable, including political dissidents, supporters of political dissidents, morals criminals (such as prostitutes and drug users), and marginal demographic groups (such as homeless children). Deaths and physical abuse have been documented during social cleansing campaigns.

Domestic Laws and Counterterrorism

An important challenge for lawmakers in democracies is balancing the need for counterterrorist legislation against the protection of constitutional rights. In severely strained terrorist environments, it is not uncommon for nations—including democracies—to pass authoritarian laws that promote social order at the expense of human rights. Policy makers usually justify these measures by using a balancing argument, in which the greater good is held to outweigh the suspension of civil liberties. As illustrated in the following examples, severe threats to the state are sometimes counteracted by severe laws.

Counterterrorist Courts in Algeria

During the 1990s, several Islamic terrorist movements waged a campaign of terror against the Algerian government. By the time the most severe fighting ended in 1999 (when an amnesty was offered), about 150,000 Algerians had died. During the emergency, special courts were established by the government to prosecute suspected Islamic terrorists and their supporters. The purpose of these courts was to establish a nonmilitary option in their war against terrorism.

The special courts and special prosecutions were used in conjunction with a brutal suppression campaign. It can be argued that the Islamic rebels had been forced into an untenable no-win situation by the time the 1999 amnesty was offered. In March 2006, the Algerian government freed a group of Islamic militants as part of a program to pardon or end legal processing for more than 2,000 convicted or suspected terrorists.

Qualified Amnesty in Italy

Italy suffered thousands of terrorist attacks during the heyday of the Red Brigade terrorist campaign in the 1970s and 1980s. As part of its effort to combat the Red Brigade, the so-called **repentance laws** offered Red Brigade members qualified amnesty for demonstrations of repentance for their crimes. Repentance could be established by cooperating within a sliding scale of collaboration. Thus, those who collaborated most generously had a proportionally large amount of time removed from their sentences, whereas those whose information was less useful had less time removed. A significant number of the roughly 2,000 imprisoned Red Brigade terrorists accepted repentance reductions in their sentences.

▶ Torture or not? An Iraqi detainee is forced by American captors to stand in a "stress position" in Abu Ghraib prison in Baghdad.

International Law: Legalistic Responses by the World Community

International law is based on tradition, custom, and formal agreements between nations. It is essentially a cooperative concept because there is no international enforcement mechanism comparable to domestic courts, law enforcement agencies, or crimes codes. All of these institutions exist in some form at the international level, but it should be remembered that nations voluntarily recognize their authority. They do this through formal agreements. Bilateral and multilateral agreements are used to create an environment conducive to maintaining legal order.

Nations enter into treaties to create predictability and consistency in international relations. When threats to international order arise—such as hijackings, kidnappings, and havens for wanted extremists—the international community often enters into multilateral agreements to manage the threat. The following examples illustrate the nature of multilateral counterterrorist agreements.

International Conventions on Hijacking Offenses

In response to the spate of airline hijackings that occurred in the late 1960s and early 1970s, the world community enacted a number of international treaties to promote cooperation in combating international terrorism directed against international travel services. These included the following:

> *Tokyo Convention on Offences and Certain Other Acts Committed on Board Aircraft.* Enacted in 1963 as the first airline crimes treaty, it required all signatories to "make every effort to restore control of the aircraft to its lawful commander and to ensure the prompt onward passage or return of the hijacked aircraft together with its passengers, crew, and cargo."[16]

> **Hague Convention of 1970.** This required signatories to extradite "hijackers to their country of origin or to prosecute them under the judicial code of the recipient state."[17]

> **Montreal Convention of 1971.** This extended international law to cover "sabotage and attacks on airports and grounded aircraft, and laid down the principle that all such offenses must be subject to severe penalties."[18]

Protecting Diplomats

In reply to the spate of attacks on embassies and assaults on diplomats in the late 1960s and early 1970s, several international treaties were enacted to promote cooperation in combating international terrorism against diplomatic missions. These included the following:

> **Convention to Prevent and Punish Acts of Terrorism Taking the Form of Crimes Against Persons and Related Extortion That Are of International Significance.** A treaty among members of the Organization of American States, this "sought to define attacks against internationally protected persons as common crimes, regardless of motives."[19]

> **Prevention and Punishment of Crimes Against Internationally Protected Persons, Including Diplomatic Agents.** This sought to establish a common international framework for suppressing extremist attacks against those who are protected by internationally recognized status.[20]

Extradition Treaties

Nations frequently enter into treaties that allow law enforcement agencies to share intelligence and operational information that can be used to track and capture terrorists. An example is **extradition treaties**, which require parties to bind over terrorist suspects at the request of fellow signatories. Strong extradition treaties and other criminal cooperation agreements are powerful tools in the war against terrorism and, when properly implemented, can be quite effective. However, these treaties are collaborative and not easily enforceable when one party declines to bind over a suspect or is otherwise uncooperative. In this event, there is little recourse other than to try to convince the offending party to comply with the terms of the treaty.

International Courts and Tribunals

The United Nations (UN) has established several institutions to address the problems of terrorism, genocide, torture, and international crime and to bring the perpetrators of crimes against humanity to justice. They are international courts, and their impact can be significant when nations agree to recognize their authority. Examples of UN authority include the following institutions:

The **International Court of Justice** is the principal judicial arm of the United Nations.

The **International Criminal Court (ICC)** was established to prosecute crimes against humanity, such as genocide.

The **International Criminal Tribunal for the Former Yugoslavia (ICTY)** has investigated allegations of war crimes and genocide arising out of the wars that broke out after the fragmentation of Yugoslavia during the 1990s.

The **International Criminal Tribunal for Rwanda (ICTR)** has investigated allegations of war crimes and genocide that resulted from the breakdown of order in Rwanda during the 1990s.

Table 10.6 summarizes the activity profile of legalistic counterterrorist options.

Table 10.6 Counterterrorist Options: Legalistic Responses			
The purpose of legalistic responses is to provide protection to the general public, protect the interests of the state, and criminalize the behavior of the terrorists. The following table summarizes basic elements of legalistic responses.			
Counterterrorist Option	**Activity Profile**		
	Rationale	**Practical Objectives**	**Typical Resources Used**
Law enforcement	Enhancement of security apparatus Demilitarization of counterterrorist campaign	Day-to-day counterterrorist operations Bringing terrorists into the criminal justice system	Police personnel Specialized personnel
Domestic laws	Criminalization of terrorist behavior	Enhancement of criminal penalties for terrorist behavior Bringing terrorists into the criminal justice system	Criminal justice system Legislative involvement
International law	International consensus and cooperation	Coalitional response to terrorism	International organizations State resources

DISCUSSION BOX

THE UTILITY OF ELITE COUNTERTERRORIST UNITS

This chapter's Discussion Box is intended to stimulate critical debate about the purpose of elite antiterrorism units.

Elite military and police counterterrorism units have been mustered into the security establishments of many nations. Many of these units include highly trained professionals who can operate in a number of environments under extremely hazardous conditions. Their missions include hostage rescues, punitive strikes, abductions, and reconnaissance operations.

When elite units perform well, the outcomes include rescued hostages, resolved crises, and disrupted terrorist environments. However, these units sometimes find themselves involved in ambiguous political situations or tenuous operational conditions. In other words, special operations are often high-risk, high-gain situations.

Nevertheless, proponents of elite counterterrorist units argue that conventional forces are not trained or configured to fight "shadow wars"—only special operations forces can do so. Critics of these units argue that conventional forces can accomplish the same objectives and goals and that, aside from the very good special operations units, other elite units have not proven themselves to be very effective.

Discussion Questions

1. How necessary are elite counterterrorism units? Why?

2. How effective do you think these elite units are?

3. What other counterterrorist options do you think can be effective without resorting to the deployment of elite units?

4. Which counterterrorist options work most efficiently in conjunction with elite units? Which options work least efficiently?

5. In the long term, what impact will elite units have in the war against international terrorism?

CHAPTER SUMMARY

This chapter discussed options for responding to terrorism within the context of several categories and subcategories. The decision-making process for selecting counterterrorist options is predicated on several key factors:

- the characteristics of the terrorist movement
- the nature of the overall terrorist environment
- the political goals of the counterterrorist actor

When assessing the practical utility of resorting to the use of force, it is important to remember that many of these responses are inconsistently effective against determined terrorists in the long term. Successes have been won against domestic terrorists—especially when governments have been unconstrained in their use of force and coercion—but this is not a universal outcome. Internationally, short-term successes have resulted in the resolution of specific terrorist incidents. Long-term successes, however, have sometimes been difficult to achieve. Nevertheless, the use of force has produced some success in disrupting terrorist groups and reducing the intensity of terrorist environments.

Repressive operations other than war include a number of options. Intelligence collection and analysis are extremely useful in building activity profiles of terrorist groups and in understanding the dynamics of terrorist environments. Intelligence is also useful for generalized prediction but less so in predicting the precise location and timing of specific terrorist attacks. Regarding enhanced security, because target hardening usually involves establishing fixed barriers, surveillance technologies, and security posts, determined terrorists can design methods to circumvent these precautions. Nevertheless, there is an increased potential for failure from the terrorists' perspective, and it should be presumed that enhanced security deters less determined and less resourceful terrorists.

Conciliatory responses have achieved both short-term and long-term success in ending terrorist environments. There have also been a number of failed conciliatory operations. Diplomatic options have enjoyed marked success in some cases but have been frustrated by entrenched hostilities and uncooperative parties in others. Social reforms have enjoyed long-term success when reforms are gradually accepted as legitimate by target populations. Concessionary options are risky because of the perception of appeasement of the terrorists but are nonetheless sometimes successful.

Legalistic responses are in many ways the front line for counterterrorist policies. Law enforcement agencies are usually the first responders to incidents, and they are responsible for ongoing civil security and investigations. Problems arise when repression or miscarriages of justice discredit police agencies. Nevertheless, security-oriented police duties have successfully resolved or controlled terrorist environments. Domestic laws are adaptations of legal systems to domestic terrorist crises. Some of these adaptations—both authoritarian and democratic—have been quite successful. International laws and institutions have likewise enjoyed some success, but because they are inherently cooperative, parties to treaties and other agreements must comply with their terms. Otherwise, international laws and institutions have very little enforcement authority.

KEY TERMS AND CONCEPTS

The following topics were discussed in this chapter and can be found in the Glossary:

WEB EXERCISE

Using this chapter's recommended websites listed on the student study site at **edge.sagepub.com/martiness5e**, conduct an online investigation of counterterrorism.

1. Compare and contrast the services described online by the referenced organizations. How do their services differ?

2. How important are the services provided by organizations that monitor terrorist behavior and fugitives? Why?

3. In what ways do you think the Internet will contribute to the counterterrorist effort in the future?

For an online search of counterterrorism, readers should enter the following keywords in their Web browser's search engine:

"Terrorism and counterterrorism"

"Antiterrorism"

RECOMMENDED READINGS

The following publications provide information about counterterrorist units and intelligence agencies.

Andrew, C. (1987). *Her majesty's secret service: The making of the British intelligence community*. New York, NY: Penguin.

Bamford, J. (2001). *Body of secrets: Anatomy of the ultra-secret national security agency, from the Cold War through the dawn of a new century*. New York, NY: Doubleday.

Begg, M., & Brittain, V. (2006). *Enemy combatant: My imprisonment at Guantánamo, Bagram, and Kandahar*. New York, NY: New Press.

Berentsen, G. (2008). *Human intelligence, counterterrorism, and national leadership: A practical guide*. Dulles, VA: Potomac Books.

Betancourt, I. (2010). *Even silence has an end: My six years of captivity in the Colombian jungle*. New York, NY: Penguin.

Beyer, C., & Bauer, M. (Eds.). *Effectively countering terrorism: The challenges, prevention, preparedness and response*. Eastbourne, UK: Sussex Academic Press.

Biersteker, T. J., & Eckert, S. E. (Eds.). (2008). *Countering the financing of terrorism*. London, UK: Routledge.

Bowden, M. (2012). *The finish: The killing of Osama bin Laden*. New York, NY: Atlantic Monthly Press.

Coulson, D. O., & Shannon, E. (1999). *No heroes: Inside the FBI's secret counter-terror force*. New York, NY: Pocket.

Crank, J. P., & Gregor, P. E. (2005). *Counter-terrorism after 9/11: Justice, security and ethics reconsidered*. New York, NY: Anderson.

Daalder, I. H. (Ed.). (2007). *Beyond preemption: Force and legitimacy in a changing world*. Washington, DC: Brookings Institution.

Dolnik, A., & Fitzgerald, K. M. (2007). *Negotiating hostage crises with the new terrorists*. Westport, CT: Praeger.

Donahue, L. K. (2008). *The cost of counterterrorism: Power, politics, and liberty*. Cambridge, UK: Cambridge University Press.

Gardner, H. (2007). *American global strategy and the "War on Terrorism."* Aldershot, UK: Ashgate.

Ginbar, V. (2008). *Why not torture terrorists?* Oxford, UK: Oxford University Press.

Grey, S. (2006). *Ghost plane: The inside story of the CIA's secret rendition program*. New York, NY: St. Martin's.

Harclerode, P. (2000). *Secret soldiers: Special forces in the war against terrorism*. London, UK: Cassel.

Howard, R. D., & Sawyer, R. L. (2004). *Defeating terrorism: Shaping the new security environment*. New York, NY: McGraw-Hill.

Klein, A. J. (2007). *Striking back: The 1972 Munich Olympics massacre and Israel's deadly response*. New York, NY: Random House.

Maras, M. (2013). *Counterterrorism*. Burlington, MA: Jones & Bartlett Learning.

Mazzetti, M. (2013). *The way of the knife: The CIA, a secret army, and a war at the ends of the earth*. New York, NY: Penguin.

Pedahzur, A. (2010). *The Israeli secret services and the struggle against terrorism*. New York, NY: Columbia University Press.

Reeve, S. (2000). *One day in September: The full story of the 1972 Munich Olympics massacre and the Israeli revenge operation "Wrath of God."* New York, NY: Arcade.

Rich, P., & Duyvesteyn, I. (Eds.). (2012). *The Routledge handbook of insurgency and counterinsurgency*. New York, NY: Routledge.

Rid, T., & Keaney, T. (Eds.). (2010). *Understanding counterinsurgency: Doctrine, operations, and challenges*. New York, NY: Routledge.

Shah, N. A. (2008). *Self-defense in Islamic and international law*. New York, NY: Palgrave Macmillan.

Suskind, R. (2006). *The one percent doctrine: Deep inside America's pursuit of its enemies since 9/11*. New York, NY: Simon & Schuster.

Thomas, G. (2009). *Gideon's spies: The secret history of the Mossad* (5th ed.). New York, NY: St. Martin's.

Tophoven, R. (1984). *GSG 9: German response to terrorism*. Koblenz, Germany: Bernard and Graefe.

Warrick, J. (2011). *The triple agent: The Al-Qaeda mole who infiltrated the CIA*. New York, NY: Doubleday.

CHAPTER ELEVEN

HOMELAND SECURITY

Learning Objectives

This chapter will enable readers to do the following:

1. Explain the conceptual and national contexts of homeland security.

2. Describe the American approach to homeland security.

3. Explain civil liberties challenges that occur when implementing homeland security policies.

4. Discuss balancing the need for security and civil liberties protections.

The term *homeland security* is common to the modern political lexicon and security environment. Although the term is relatively new, and originated within the context of the September 11, 2001, attacks and American policy adaptations, the underlying concept has been periodically applied during historical periods of national security and political crises. In order to understand the modern conceptualization of homeland security, it is necessary to evaluate this concept within the context of several historical, administrative, and theoretical perspectives.

The discussion in this chapter will review the following subjects:

- Homeland Security in Perspective

- Homeland Security in the United States

- Civil Liberties and Securing the Homeland

JEWEL SAMAD/AFP/Getty Images

▶ Diagram of a vehicular bomb found in Times Square, New York City, in May 2010.

HOMELAND SECURITY IN PERSPECTIVE

On October 8, 2001, President George W. Bush issued Executive Order 13228, titled "Establishing the Office of Homeland Security and the Homeland Security Council." The Executive Order stated "the functions of the Office [of Homeland Security] shall be to coordinate the executive branch's efforts to detect, prepare for, prevent, protect against, respond to, and recover from terrorist attacks within the United States."[1] This statement of purpose by the United States was the first to result from the September 11 crisis and continues to guide the implementation of the concept of homeland security in relation to counterterrorist policies. Post-9/11 homeland security has been adapted conceptually to the unique domestic environments of Western democracies. In the European context, the concept has historically been framed under the concept of security and (recently) "interoperability" among partners in the European Union. Nevertheless, and regardless of adopted phraseology in the West, the homeland security concept expanded considerably during the post–September 11 era.

Homeland security is a dynamic concept that constantly evolves with the emergence of new terrorist threats. This evolution is necessary because counterterrorist policies must adapt to ever-changing political environments and new threat scenarios. Factors that influence the conceptualization and implementation of homeland security include changes in political leadership, demands from the public, and the discovery of serious terrorist plots (both successful and thwarted). Keeping this in mind, the following statement by the U.S. Department of Homeland Security exemplifies the conceptual framework for homeland security in the United States:

> Protecting the American people from terrorist threats is the reason the Department of Homeland Security was created, and remains our highest priority. Our vision is a secure and resilient nation that effectively prevents terrorism in ways that preserve our freedom and prosperity. . . . Terrorist tactics continue to evolve, and we must keep pace. Terrorists seek sophisticated means of attack, including chemical, biological, radiological, nuclear and explosive weapons, and cyber attacks. Threats may come from abroad or be homegrown. We must be vigilant against new types of terrorist recruitment as well, by engaging communities at risk being targeted by terrorist recruiters. . . . The Department's efforts to prevent terrorism are centered on a risk-based layered approach to security in our passenger and cargo transportation systems and at our borders and ports of entry. It includes new technologies to: Detect explosives and other weapons; Help protect critical infrastructure and cyber networks from attack; Build information-sharing partnerships. We do this work cooperatively with other federal, state, local, tribal and territorial law enforcement as well as international partners.[2]

The discussion in this section will review homeland security from the following perspectives:

- The Threat From Homegrown Jihadists
- Crisis and Homeland Security

The Threat From Homegrown Jihadists

A significant threat to homeland security in Europe and the United States arose from an unanticipated source—homegrown sympathizers of the international jihadist movement. Domestic security became increasingly challenged in the aftermath of high-casualty terrorist incidents carried out by extremists who resided in Western democracies. Such incidents were particularly problematic because many of the perpetrators were seamlessly woven into the fabric of mainstream society. The following incidents are instructive case studies of this phenomenon.

The Madrid Train Bombings. Spain suffered its worst terrorist incident on March 11, 2004, when terrorists detonated 10 bombs on several commuter trains in Madrid. Terrorists had delivered the explosives in backpacks, which they dropped at key locations. The explosions were synchronized, occurring within a span of 20 minutes, at the height of rush hour when the trains were certain to be crowded with commuters. Casualties were high: 191 people were killed and more than 1,500 were injured. Casualties could have been more severe, but fortunately three additional bombs (also in backpacks) failed to explode and were later detonated by Spanish authorities.

A group calling itself the **Abu Hafs al-Masri Brigades** claimed credit for the attack. In a statement faxed to the Reuters press agency, the group said, "We have succeeded in infiltrating the heart of Crusader Europe and struck one of the bases of the crusader alliance" and referred to the attack as **Operation Death Trains**.[3] The Abu Hafs al-Masri Brigades have also been implicated in the August 2003 bombing of the United Nations headquarters in Baghdad, Iraq, and the November 2003 bombings of two synagogues in Istanbul, Turkey.

The operation is an excellent example of how terrorist attacks can be carried out with considerable effect. Prior to the attack, Spain had been a staunch partner in the U.S.-led invasion of Iraq. Along with the United States and United Kingdom, Spain committed a sizable contingent of combat forces—1,300 Spanish troops actively participated in Operation Iraqi Freedom. The government of Prime Minister Jose Maria Aznar had strongly advocated a central role for Spain, even though many Spaniards had opposed such participation, particularly the deployment to Iraq. The bombings occurred three days before national elections in Spain, and Spanish officials initially blamed the Basque terrorist group ETA for the attack. When this allegation proved to be false, and it was shown that the attacks were linked to Aznar's policies, his government was voted out of power. Spain quickly withdrew all 1,300 soldiers from Iraq.

The Abu Hafs al-Masri Brigades are an example of how Al Qaeda–affiliated cells operate as prepositioned "sleepers" in foreign countries. It was estimated that 12 to 30 terrorists may have participated in the delivery of the bombs.[4] Fifteen suspects, 11 of them Moroccans, were arrested within several weeks of the attack. It was believed that some of the suspects were members of the Moroccan Islamic Combatant Group, another Al Qaeda–affiliated group. When Spanish police prepared to storm an apartment in the town of Leganes near Madrid, three terrorists and a police officer were killed when the suspects detonated explosives and blew themselves up.

In October 2007, three men were convicted of the attack and received maximum 40-year sentences. Eighteen others were sentenced for lesser charges, and seven others were acquitted of charges.[5]

The London Transportation System Attacks. On July 7, 2005, four bombs exploded in London, three simultaneously aboard London Underground trains and one aboard a double-deck bus. The attacks, carried out by suicide bombers, killed more than 50 people and injured more than 700.[6] The attack was well synchronized by suicide bombers so that the three Underground bombs exploded within 50 seconds of each other. Several days later, on July 21, an identical attack was attempted but failed when the explosives misfired. Four bombs—three aboard Underground trains and one aboard a bus—failed to detonate because the explosives had degraded over time. Investigators quickly identified four suspects from video surveillance cameras, all of whom were residents of London. A fifth bomb was found in a London park on July 23, abandoned by a fifth bomber. Authorities were acutely concerned because British-based cells—sympathizers of Al Qaeda—were responsible for both attacks.

Other plots were later uncovered in the United Kingdom. In August 2006, British police thwarted a plot to blow up several transatlantic airliners using liquid explosives. In June 2007, authorities discovered two car bombs in London. One day later, an attempted car-bombing plot went awry when two men crashed a vehicle into the departure doors of Glasgow Airport in Scotland; the vehicle caught on fire but did not explode.

Politically and in terms of policy, the London case is a counterpoint to the March 2004 attacks in Madrid. Unlike the case of the Madrid attacks, which led to significant political turmoil, Britons rallied around the slogan of "We are not afraid" and supported the government of Prime Minister Tony

Blair. Blair's popularity rose, and the three main British political parties (the Labor, Conservative, and Liberal Democratic Parties) agreed to collaborate on passing stricter antiterrorism laws.[7]

The Fort Hood Incident. On November 5, 2009, a gunman opened fire in the sprawling military base at Fort Hood, Texas, killing 13 people and wounding 29. The attack occurred inside a Fort Hood medical center, and the victims were four officers, eight enlisted soldiers, and one civilian. The shooter was Army Major Nidal Malik Hasan, a psychiatrist at the base who treated returning veterans for combat stress.

Hasan is an interesting profile in how someone born and raised in the West can eventually adopt an ideology that advocates violent resistance to Western governments and policies. He was born in Virginia to Palestinian parents. He received an undergraduate degree from Virginia Tech University and eventually graduated from medical school with a specialization in psychiatry. Hasan was a devout Muslim who eventually became outspoken about his opposition to the wars in Afghanistan and Iraq. He also had a history of expressing himself provocatively. For example, at a public health seminar he presented a PowerPoint presentation titled "Why the War on Terrorism is a War on Islam." At another presentation to medical colleagues, Hasan detailed the torments awaiting non-Muslims in hell. On other occasions, he proselytized his patients on behalf of Islam, argued that he believed Islamic law (*shari'a*) is paramount to the U.S. Constitution, and publicly identified himself as a Muslim first and an Army officer second.

After the Fort Hood attack, investigators uncovered connections between Hasan and an openly radical cleric named Anwar al-Awlaki. Like Hasan, Awlaki grew up in the United States, having been born in New Mexico. He eventually became a dedicated jihadi who specialized in recruiting English-speaking Muslims and Muslims who were raised in the West, the rationale being that such recruits would be able to blend in more easily. Awlaki also became known as a propagandist who maintained a website with his writings about how to wage jihad. He was believed to operate from Yemen.

The cases of Major Hasan and Anwar al-Awlaki are two examples of an increasing pattern of homegrown jihadists in Western countries. In the United States, for example, federal prosecutors in December 2009 charged David Coleman with conspiring to assist the Pakistani terrorist group Lashkar-e-Taiba with planning the November 2008 assault in Mumbai, India, as well as another planned attack in Denmark. There are also cases of Americans leaving the country to join radical jihadi groups, including Somali Americans recruited to fight with Al Qaeda–affiliated groups in Somalia and five Americans arrested by Pakistani authorities who proudly proclaimed their dedication to waging holy war.

The Boston Marathon Bombing. On April 15, 2013, two bombs were detonated at the crowded finish line of the Boston Marathon. Three people were killed and more than 260 were wounded, many severely. The devices were constructed from pressure cookers and were detonated 13 seconds apart within approximately 210 yards of each other. They were packed with nails, ball bearings, and possibly other metal shards. Emergency response occurred swiftly, in part because medical personnel and emergency vehicles were already on hand to assist runners at the finish line. Law enforcement officers were also present as members of the race's security detail.

Two brothers, Dzokhar and Tamerlan Tsarnaev, were responsible for the attack. The Tsarnaevs were young immigrants from Chechnya who had resided in the United States since about 2002. Tamerlan, the elder brother, became radicalized during a visit to Chechnya when he became a committed Islamist. His and Dzokhar's underlying motive for the attack was to condemn the United States' interventions in the Middle East. It was reported that they downloaded instructions on how to construct pressure cooker bombs from the online Al Qaeda magazine *Inspire.*

FBI analysis of video and photographic evidence from the scene of the attack eventually focused on images of two men whose behavior and demeanor differed from that of others in the crowd. Images of the men, one wearing a black baseball cap (Tamerlan) and the other wearing a white cap backward (Dzokhar), were disseminated to law enforcement officials, the media, and the public. During the manhunt, the Tsarnaevs shot and killed a Massachusetts Institute of

Figure 11.1 The U.S. Department of Homeland Security Advisory System

BULLETIN	ELEVATED ALERT	IMMINENT ALERT
Describes current developments or general trends regarding threats of terrorism	Warns of a credible terrorism threat against the United States	Warns of a credible, specific and impending terrorism threat against the United States

The U.S. Department of Homeland Security Advisory System was developed after the September 11, 2001, attacks. This system was replaced in 2011 with the National Threat Advisory System, a more nuanced warning system that indicates whether threats are Elevated or Imminent.

Source: U.S. Department of Homeland Security, National Terrorism Advisory System Awareness Poster.

Technology police officer. They also carjacked a vehicle and forced its occupant to withdraw money from an ATM. When the Tsarnaevs stopped the car at a gas station, the victim escaped, ran to another station, and notified the authorities. The victim left his cell phone in the car, which was used by the authorities to track the Tsarnaevs. They were later observed driving a stolen sport utility vehicle and were confronted by the police. An intense gunfight ensued, and Tamerlan Tsarnaev was killed when he was run over by the SUV driven by his brother. Dzokhar Tsarnaev temporarily evaded the police, but he was eventually captured after an intense door-to-door manhunt while hiding in a boat parked in a backyard.

Crisis and Homeland Security

The European Context

West European countries have not established centralized ministries or agencies similar to the U.S. Department of Homeland Security. Most homeland security and counterterrorism functions are designed to be administered across multiple ministries and agencies. This approach is derived from Europe's historical experience with terrorism in the modern era. As discussed previously, modern terrorist activity in Europe was characterized by ideological, nationalist, and international spillover political violence. The intensity of this violence was often rather high and sustained over several decades. In essence, the European approach to the homeland security concept has evolved in a unique manner during decades of security challenges from organizations such as the IRA, Red Brigade, Red Army Faction, ETA, Direct Action, individuals like Carlos the Jackal, and nationalist spillovers from around the globe.

Most European nations allocated increased resources to counterterrorist law enforcement and intelligence efforts in response to the September 11 attacks in the United States and the transportation system attacks in Spain and the United Kingdom. However, the primary focus has been on counterterrorist law enforcement and multiagency cooperative approaches. This is in contrast to the drastic reorganization and nearly total centralization of federal homeland security bureaucracies in the United States. Thus, although the American approach has been to create a sweeping homeland security apparatus, the European approach has been to operate from within existing bureaucracies.

The American Context

Strong proposals were made to revamp the American homeland security community within nine months of the September 11, 2001, attacks. This occurred because of the apparent failure of the pre–September 11 domestic security community to adapt to the new terrorist environment and because of highly publicized operational problems.

Prior to the domestic attacks of September 11, the United States had relied on administratively separated federal law enforcement and services agencies to provide homeland security. These agencies are defined as follows:

Law Enforcement Agencies. These are bureaus within large cabinet agencies charged with enforcing federal criminal laws. The Federal Bureau of Investigation (FBI), Drug Enforcement Administration, and Bureau of Alcohol, Tobacco, Firearms, and Explosives are examples of federal law enforcement agencies. Prior to the September 11, 2001, attacks, these agencies investigated security threats in the same manner that they investigated crimes—by working cases and making arrests.

Services Agencies. These agencies regulate and manage services for the general population. Service agencies include large cabinet agencies, regulatory agencies, and independent agencies. The Departments of Health and Human Services, Energy, and Defense and the Central Intelligence Agency (CIA) are examples of services agencies. Prior to the September 11 attacks, these agencies had a variety of missions, including regulating immigration, inspecting nuclear facilities, and responding to emergencies.

Interagency Challenges

Among law enforcement agencies, the FBI was one of the few agencies that performed a quasi-security mission, explicitly adopting as one of its primary missions the protection of the United States from foreign intelligence and terrorist threats. The FBI did this through one of its five functional areas, foreign counterintelligence. The FBI also established missions in several U.S. embassies to coordinate its investigations of cases with international links. Among the services agencies, several bureaus performed a variety of security missions. For example, the Secret Service (part of the Department of the Treasury) protected the president, and the Federal Emergency Management Agency responded to natural and human disasters.

An ideal policy framework would have required the FBI and CIA to coordinate and share counterterrorist intelligence in a spirit of absolute cooperation. In theory, the FBI would focus on investigating possible domestic security threats, and the CIA would pass along foreign intelligence that might affect domestic security. Table 11.1 summarizes the pre–September 11, 2001, security duties of several U.S. federal agencies.

One problem that became quite clear during the year following the September 11, 2001, homeland attacks was that the old organizational model did not adapt well to the new security crisis. This failure to adapt proved to be operationally damaging; it was politically embarrassing, and it projected an image of disarray. A series of revelations and allegations called into question previous assertions by the FBI and CIA that neither agency had prior intelligence about the September 11 homeland attacks. For example, it was discovered that

- the FBI had been aware for years prior to September 2001 that foreign nationals were enrolling in flight schools, and

- the CIA had compiled intelligence data about some members of the Al Qaeda cell that carried out the attacks.

These allegations were compounded by a leak to the press of a memorandum from an FBI field agent that strongly condemned the FBI director's and headquarters' handling of field

Table 11.1 Federal Agencies and Homeland Security: Before the September 11, 2001, Organizational Crisis

Prior to the September 11, 2001, organizational crisis, homeland security was the responsibility of a number of federal agencies. These agencies were not centrally coordinated, and they answered to different centers of authority. Cooperation was theoretically ensured by liaison protocols, special task forces, and oversight. In reality, there was a great deal of functional overlap and bureaucratic "turf" issues.

This table summarizes the activity profiles of several bureaus prior to the post–September 11 organizational crisis.

Agency	Activity Profile		
	Parent Organization	Mission	Enforcement Authority
Central Intelligence Agency	Independent agency	Collection and analysis of foreign intelligence	No domestic authority
Coast Guard	Department of Transportation	Protection of U.S. waterways	Domestic law enforcement authority
Customs	Department of the Treasury	Examination of people and goods entering the United States	Domestic inspection, entry, and law enforcement authority
Federal Bureau of Investigation	Department of Justice	Investigating and monitoring criminal and national security threats	Domestic law enforcement authority
Federal Emergency Management Agency	Independent agency	Responding to natural and human-made disasters	Coordination of domestic emergency responses
Immigration and Naturalization Service	Department of Justice	Managing the entry and naturalization of foreign nationals	Domestic inspection, monitoring, and law enforcement authority
Secret Service	Department of the Treasury	Establishing security protocols for president, vice president, and special events	Domestic protection of president and vice president and special law enforcement authority (including counterfeiting)

Source: U.S. Department of Justice, Federal Bureau of Investigation, *Terrorism 2002–2005* (Washington, DC: U.S. Department of Justice, 2007), 11.

intelligence reports about Zacarias Moussaoui. Moussaoui was alleged to have been a member of the September 11, 2001, Al Qaeda cell; he had been jailed prior to the attacks. Moussaoui had tried to enroll in flying classes, in which he was apparently interested only in how to *fly* airplanes and uninterested in the *landing* portion of the classes.

Policy makers and elected leaders wanted to know why neither the FBI nor the CIA had "connected the dots" to create a single intelligence profile. Serious interagency and internal problems became publicly apparent when a cycle of recriminations, press leaks, and congressional interventions damaged the "united front" image projected by the White House. Policy makers determined that problems in the homeland security community included the following:

- long-standing interagency rivalries

- entrenched and cumbersome bureaucratic cultures and procedures

- no central coordination of homeland security programs

- fragmentation of counterterrorist operations

- poor coordination of counterterrorist intelligence collection and analysis

- disconnect between field offices and Washington headquarters

- turf-based conflict between the FBI and CIA

Table 11.2 summarizes the security duties of several U.S. federal agencies immediately after the creation of the new department.

To remedy the highly publicized political and operational disarray of the domestic security effort, President George W. Bush in June 2002 initiated a process that completely reorganized the American homeland security community. The process led to the enactment of the **Department of Homeland Security Act of 2002**, which was signed into law by President Bush on November 25, 2002. The new law created a large cabinet-level **Department of Homeland Security**. Because of the operational fragmentation of homeland intelligence and security—and the important fact that the original **Office of Homeland Security** had no administrative authority over other federal agencies—the new department absorbed the functions of several

Table 11.2 Federal Agencies and Homeland Security: After the September 11, 2001, Organizational Crisis

In the wake of the post–September 11 organizational crisis, the Bush administration subsumed the homeland security duties of several federal agencies under the jurisdiction of a new Department of Homeland Security. The goal was to coordinate operations and to end overlapping duties.

This table is a good snapshot of a nation's reorganization of national security in response to a significant shift in a terrorist environment. It is also an example of how two security agencies that arguably precipitated the organizational crisis—the FBI and CIA—were able to maintain their independence.

Agency	Activity Profile		
	New Parent Organization	New Directorate	New Directorate's Duties
Central Intelligence Agency	No change: independent agency	No change	No change: collection and analysis of foreign intelligence
Coast Guard	Department of Homeland Security	Border and Transportation Security	Coordination of all national entry points
Customs	Department of Homeland Security	Border and Transportation Security	Coordination of all national entry points
Federal Bureau of Investigation	No change: Department of Justice	No change	No change: investigating and monitoring criminal and national security threats
Federal Emergency Management Agency	Department of Homeland Security	Emergency Preparedness and Response	Coordination of national responses to terrorist incidents
Immigration and Naturalization Service (some functions)	Department of Homeland Security	Border and Transportation Security	Coordination of all national entry points
Secret Service	Department of Homeland Security	Secret Service	Establishing security protocols for president and special events

Source: U.S. Department of Justice, Federal Bureau of Investigation, *Terrorism 2002–2005* (Washington, DC: U.S. Department of Justice, 2007).

Figure 11.2 Organization Chart of the U.S. Department of Homeland Security

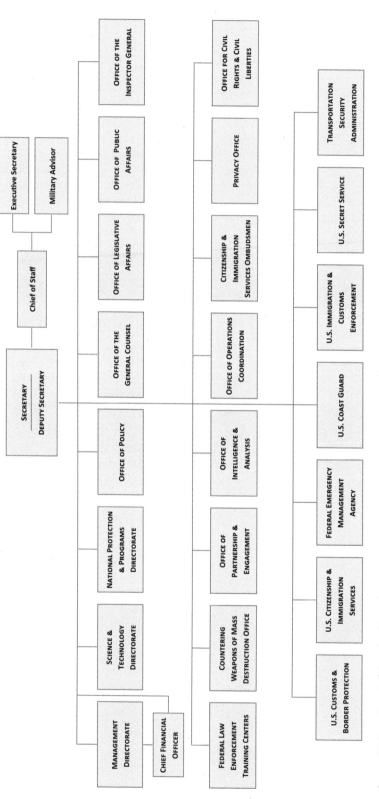

Source: U.S. Department of Homeland Security.

CHAPTER PERSPECTIVE 11.1

DHS Areas of Responsibility

The U.S. Department of Homeland Security (DHS) has been tasked with five main areas of responsibility, which reflect the underlying missions of the former emergency response and security agencies that were subsumed under the authority of DHS. The five areas of responsibility are classified as follows:

Prevent terrorism and enhance security.

Secure and manage our borders.

Enforce and administer our immigration laws.

Safeguard and secure cyberspace.

Ensure resilience to disasters.

Thus, the concept of homeland security has expanded far beyond counterterrorism. The Department of Homeland Security's mission evolved from a primarily counterterrorist function to encompass a large number of domestic emergency response and security functions.

Source: U.S. Department of Homeland Security.

---

large federal agencies.[8] The result of this massive reorganization was the creation of the third largest federal agency, behind only the Department of Veterans Affairs and the Department of Defense in size.

Figure 11.2 shows the organization chart of the U.S. Department of Homeland Security.

Subsequent commission reports led to sweeping changes in the U.S. intelligence community. These reports included the following:

- In July 2004, the National Commission on Terrorist Attacks on the United States, also known as the 9/11 Commission, issued a detailed report on the September 11, 2001, attacks.[9]

- In March 2005, the Commission on the Intelligence Capabilities of the United States Regarding Weapons of Mass Destruction issued a detailed report on intelligence failures regarding the possession and proliferation of weapons of mass destruction.

A **National Counterterrorism Center (NCTC)** was established to integrate the counterterrorism efforts of the intelligence community. Although some jurisdictional tension existed between the NCTC and the CIA's Counterterrorism Center, the NCTC became an important component of the new homeland security culture in the United States. Clearly, the attacks of September 11, 2001, were the catalyst for a broad and long-needed reconfiguration of the American security environment. Chapter Perspective 11.1 summarizes the areas of responsibility for the U.S. Department of Homeland Security.

HOMELAND SECURITY IN THE UNITED STATES

The discussion in this section reviews the following components of the homeland security environment in the United States:

- Counterterrorist Laws
- Homeland Security Agencies

- Law Enforcement and Bureaucracy: The Federal Context
- The U.S. Intelligence Community: Mission and Challenges

Counterterrorist Laws

The United States designed and adopted counterterrorist laws and law enforcement policies as adaptations to the modern terrorist environment. These laws and policies serve as broad law-related approaches for controlling emerging terrorist environments. Norms of criminal justice and legal procedures are used to investigate and punish those who commit acts of political violence. Legislation, criminal prosecutions, and incarceration are typical policy measures.

Table 11.3 summarizes domestic antiterrorism laws in the United States.

The Anti-Terrorism and Effective Death Penalty Act of 1996

In 1996, during the administration of President Bill Clinton, the United States passed its first comprehensive counterterrorism legislation, the **Anti-Terrorism and Effective Death Penalty Act.** The purpose of the Anti-Terrorism Act was to regulate activity that could be used to mount a terrorist attack, provide resources for counterterrorist programs, and punish terrorism. The act included the following provisions:

- a federal death penalty for deaths that result from acts of terrorism
- inclusion of so-called taggant agents in plastic explosives, which mark the time and place of their manufacture
- the ability to prosecute crimes against federal employees while on duty as federal (rather than state) offenses
- funding for terrorism prevention, counterterrorism, and counterintelligence

Table 11.3 Domestic Laws on Terrorism

Domestic terrorist incidents often result in legislative responses and the enactment of new laws. This table summarizes selected domestic antiterrorist laws.

Perceived Threat	Response and Purpose	
	Domestic Legal Response	**Purpose**
Domestic Terrorism	Anti-Terrorism and Effective Death Penalty Act of 1996	First omnibus anti-terrorist legislation
The New Terrorism	USA PATRIOT Act of 2001	Comprehensive omnibus antiterrorist legislation
	Department of Homeland Security Act of 2002	Remedy political and operational disarray for domestic security
	USA PATRIOT Improvement and Reauthorization Act of 2005	Renewal and amendment of 2001 USA PATRIOT Act
	USA FREEDOM Act of 2015	Limited data collection by intelligence agencies; reauthorized key provisions of USA PATRIOT Act

- stronger procedural controls on asylum, deportation, and entry into the country

- a prohibition on government and private business financial transactions with terrorist states

- authority for the secretary of state to designate private groups as terrorist organizations and forbid them from raising funds in the United States

The Anti-Terrorism and Effective Death Penalty Act was passed after the terrorist attack at Centennial Park during the Atlanta Olympics and the explosion of TWA Flight 800 near Long Island, New York. Although the Flight 800 disaster was later concluded not to be an act of terrorism, officials considered the Anti-Terrorism Act to be a milestone in responding to domestic terrorism.

The USA PATRIOT Act of 2001

In the aftermath of the September 11, 2001, homeland attacks, the U.S. Congress quickly passed legislation with the intent to address the new security threat. On October 26, 2001, President George W. Bush signed this legislation into law. It was labeled the Uniting and Strengthening America by Providing Appropriate Tools Required to Intercept and Obstruct Terrorism Act of 2001, commonly known as the **USA PATRIOT Act.** Examples of USA PATRIOT Act provisions include the following:

- revisions of the standards for government surveillance, including federal law enforcement access to private records

- enhancement of electronic surveillance authority, such as tapping into e-mail, electronic address books, and computers

- use of "roving wiretaps" by investigators, which permit surveillance of an individual's telephone conversations on any phone anywhere in the country

- requiring banks to identify sources of money deposited in some private accounts and requiring foreign banks to report on suspicious transactions

- use of nationwide search warrants

- deportation of immigrants who raise money for terrorist organizations

- detention of immigrants without charge for up to one week on suspicion of supporting terrorism

Debate about these and other provisions came from across the ideological spectrum. Civil liberties watchdog organizations questioned whether these provisions would erode constitutional protections. At the same time, conservatives questioned the possibility of government intrusion into individuals' privacy. To address some of these concerns, lawmakers included a sunset provision mandating that the USA PATRIOT Act's major provisions would automatically expire unless periodically extended. Lawmakers also required the Department of Justice to submit reports on the impact of the act on civil liberties. In early 2005, the House of Representatives and U.S. Department of Justice advocated restricting the act's ability to access certain personal records without a warrant.

The Department of Homeland Security Act of 2002

In the immediate aftermath of the September 11 terrorist attacks, early efforts to establish a homeland security enterprise quickly revealed a relatively fractured and turf-oriented federal bureaucracy. To remedy what quickly became highly publicized reporting of political and operational disarray within the domestic security effort, in June 2002, President George W. Bush completely reorganized the American homeland security community by initiating a process that led to the enactment of the Department of Homeland Security Act of 2002. The act was signed into law by President Bush on November 25, 2002. A large, cabinet-level Department of Homeland Security was created by the new law.

The USA PATRIOT Improvement and Reauthorization Act of 2005

Sunset provisions were created as an integral component of congressional oversight and proactive management of renewal processes for the USA PATRIOT Act. The purpose of the sunset provisions was to counterbalance enhanced authority granted to the executive branch under the USA PATRIOT Act. Congress first renewed the USA PATRIOT Act in March 2006 after passage of the **USA PATRIOT Improvement and Reauthorization Act of 2005**. After intensive political debate, it incorporated compromise provisions that included the following:

- restrictions on federal agents' access to library records

- enhanced penalties for financial support of terrorism

- improved organizational coordination of criminal prosecutions against accused terrorists with the creation of the new position of assistant attorney general for national security in the Department of Justice

- enhanced standards for the protection of mass transportation

- improved information flow between law enforcement and intelligence officers

Subsequent to passage of the USA PATRIOT Improvement and Reauthorization Act of 2005, reauthorization legislation was regularly considered and passed by Congress and signed into law by sitting presidents. For example, reauthorization proposals were considered in 2006, 2010, and 2011.

The USA FREEDOM Act of 2015

The USA PATRIOT Act was reauthorized, with modifications, in June 2015 with the passage of the USA FREEDOM Act. Key provisions of the USA PATRIOT Act were restored, and other provisions were either modified or eliminated. USA FREEDOM is a colloquial acronym for Uniting and Strengthening America by Fulfilling Rights and Ending Eavesdropping, Dragnet-collection and Online Monitoring.

Initial introduction of the USA FREEDOM Act in October 2013 was a reaction to the publication of classified National Security Agency memoranda by defector Edward Snowden earlier in the year. The Snowden document leak revealed that the NSA engaged in bulk data collection of telecommunications records, including telephone records and Internet metadata. The NSA's program was perceived by many in Congress and elsewhere to be an example of unacceptable surveillance by intelligence agencies on the private communications of everyday Americans. The USA FREEDOM Act imposed strict limits on bulk data collection of telephone records and Internet metadata by intelligence agencies. It also limited government collection of data from specific geographic locations and specific telecommunications service providers. The Act continued the practice of authorizing roving wiretaps and efforts to track possible lone-wolf terrorists.

Homeland Security Agencies

The federal homeland security bureaucracy is a network of specialized agencies that contribute to the overall mission of securing the United States from terrorist threats. Many of these agencies are subsumed under the direction of the secretary of homeland security, while others are directed by Cabinet-level or independent officials. The *National Strategy for Homeland Security* established priorities for coordinating the protection of critical domestic infrastructures.

Law Enforcement and Bureaucracy: The Federal Context

The Law Enforcement Context

Law enforcement agencies often take the lead in investigating incidents of domestic terrorism, with other agencies performing a support role to assist in resolving cases. There is no national police force in the United States similar to the French *gendarmerie*, but many federal agencies are charged with law enforcement jurisdictions that concur with their specified missions.

At the federal level, the FBI has primary jurisdiction over domestic counterintelligence and counterterrorist surveillance and investigations. The CIA is not a law enforcement agency and therefore officially performs a supportive role in domestic counterterrorist investigations. Other federal agencies, such as the U.S. Diplomatic Security Service, also assist in tracking suspects wanted for acts of terrorism. The Diplomatic Security Service is a security bureau within the U.S. Department of State that manages an international bounty program called the Rewards for Justice Program. The program offers cash rewards for information leading to the arrest of wanted terrorists. These bounty programs are sometimes successful. For example, a cash bounty led to the capture and arrest of Mir Aimal Kansi, a Pakistani terrorist who attacked CIA employees in 1993 outside the CIA's headquarters in Northern Virginia.

The Bureaucratic Context

Ideally, governments act rationally and efficiently to resolve problems. In order to do so, government functions are organized in operational arrangements known as a bureaucracy. Max Weber invented the term to describe and explain rationality and efficiency in managing governments—a field of public administration known as organizational theory. It should be obvious that many functions of government require professional bureaucracies and trained managers to ensure social stability and the delivery of critical services. For example, efficiency in regulating interstate commerce permits the delivery of essential commodities throughout the nation. Many of these bureaucratic functions are literally life-and-death missions, such as emergency preparedness and disaster response. In terrorist environments, the consequences can be quite dire if homeland security bureaucracies are not flexible, efficient, and collaborative.

Homeland security's counterterrorist bureaucracy is conceptually an amalgamation of many functions of law enforcement and intelligence agencies, as well as branches of the military. The bureaucratic ideal of rationality and efficiency requires that these sectors of the government coordinate their counterterrorist missions to promote homeland security. For example, domestic law enforcement agencies must be kept apprised of terrorist threats that may be discovered abroad by intelligence agencies or the military—the challenge is how to implement this communication to promote interagency coordination.

The U.S. Department of Homeland Security and several sector-specific agencies carry out homeland security–related bureaucratic duties assigned to them.

Federal Bureau of Investigation

▶ A comparison of the sketched witness description of Oklahoma City bomber Timothy McVeigh to his mug shot—an excellent example of the value of cooperation between witnesses and law enforcement officials.

The Department of Homeland Security (DHS)

DHS is an extensive department in the federal government whose secretary holds cabinet-level authority. The major components of the department are a result of the consolidation of agencies with critical domestic missions in the aftermath of the September 11, 2001, attacks. Homeland security is a new concept and a new mission for the federal government. DHS is by far the largest and most mission-diverse department in the homeland security bureaucracy. Broadly defined, its mission is to secure the nation from the many threats we face. This requires the dedication of more than 240,000 employees in jobs that range from aviation and border security to emergency response, from cybersecurity analyst to chemical facility inspector. Our duties are wide-ranging, but our goal is clear—keeping America safe.[10]

The many missions of DHS's components include the following:

- The *Directorate for National Protection and Programs* works to advance the Department's risk-reduction mission. Reducing risk requires an integrated approach that encompasses both physical and virtual threats and their associated human elements.

- The *Directorate for Science and Technology* is the primary research and development arm of the department. It provides federal, state, and local officials with the technology and capabilities to protect the homeland.

- The *Directorate for Management* is responsible for DHS budgets and appropriations, expenditure of funds, accounting and finance, procurement, human resources, information technology systems, facilities and equipment, and the identification and tracking of performance measurements.

- The *Office of Policy* is the primary policy formulation and coordination component for the Department of Homeland Security. It provides a centralized, coordinated focus to the development of department-wide, long-range planning to protect the United States.

- The *Office of Health Affairs* coordinates all medical activities of the Department of Homeland Security to ensure appropriate preparation for and response to incidents having medical significance.

- The *Office of Intelligence and Analysis* is responsible for using information and intelligence from multiple sources to identify and assess current and future threats to the United States.

- The *Office of Operations Coordination* is responsible for monitoring the security of the United States on a daily basis and coordinating activities within DHS and with governors, homeland security advisers, law enforcement partners, and critical infrastructure operators in all 50 states and more than 50 major urban areas nationwide.

- The *Federal Law Enforcement Training Center* provides career-long training to law enforcement professionals to help them fulfill their responsibilities safely and proficiently.

- The *Domestic Nuclear Detection Office* works to enhance the nuclear detection efforts of federal, state, territorial, tribal, and local governments and the private sector and to ensure a coordinated response to such threats.

- The *Transportation Security Administration* protects the nation's transportation systems to ensure freedom of movement for people and commerce.

- *U.S. Customs and Border Protection* is responsible for protecting our nation's borders to prevent terrorists and terrorist weapons from entering the United States, while facilitating the flow of legitimate trade and travel.

- *U.S. Citizenship and Immigration Services* is responsible for the administration of immigration and naturalization adjudication functions and establishing immigration services policies and priorities.

- *U.S. Immigration and Customs Enforcement*, the largest investigative arm of the Department of Homeland Security, is responsible for identifying and shutting down vulnerabilities in the nation's border, economic, transportation, and infrastructure security.

- The *U.S. Coast Guard* protects the public, the environment, and U.S. economic interests in the nation's ports and waterways, along the coast, on international waters, or in any maritime region as required to support national security.

- The *Federal Emergency Management Agency* prepares the nation for hazards, manages federal response and recovery efforts following any national incident, and administers the National Flood Insurance Program.

- The *U.S. Secret Service* protects the president and other high-level officials and investigates counterfeiting and other financial crimes, including financial institution fraud, identity theft, computer fraud, and computer-based attacks on our nation's financial, banking, and telecommunications infrastructure.

Sector-Specific Agencies

In order to ensure the implementation of protective priorities, sector-specific homeland security missions were identified for federal agencies in addition to establishing the Department of Homeland Security. These agencies are known as sector-specific agencies, and they have been tasked with protecting critical infrastructure in the United States from terrorist attacks. Key U.S. government responsibilities for critical infrastructure are summarized as follows:

Department of Agriculture (USDA). Agricultural and food security are critical to the nation. The primary mission of the USDA is to "provide leadership on food, agriculture, natural resources, rural development, nutrition, and related issues based on public policy, the best available science, and effective management."[11] USDA's critical infrastructure responsibility is securing the nation's food supply and agricultural infrastructure.

Department of Defense (DOD). Defending the homeland from foreign threats is paramount to the overall security of the nation. The mission of DOD "is to provide the military forces needed to deter war and protect the security" of the United States.[12] Its critical infrastructure responsibility is to secure DOD installations, military personnel, and defense industries.

Department of Energy (DOE). Securing energy resources, transportation, and markets requires an overarching national agenda. The "mission of the Energy Department is to ensure America's security and prosperity by addressing its energy, environmental and nuclear challenges through transformative science and technology solutions."[13] Within this context, DOE's critical infrastructure responsibility is to secure power plants, weapons production facilities, oil and gas facilities, and research laboratories.

Department of Health and Human Services (HHS). Protecting and monitoring the health of the nation is a fundamental mission of HHS. It is "the United States government's principal agency for protecting the health of all Americans and providing essential human services."[14] The critical infrastructure responsibility of HHS is to secure the nation's health care and public health system.

Department of the Interior. Per its primary mission, the Department of the Interior "protects America's natural resources and heritage, honors our cultures and tribal communities, and supplies the energy to power our future."[15] The department's critical infrastructure responsibility is to protect national monuments and lands under its jurisdiction.

Department of the Treasury. The nation's wealth and treasure are hallmarks of the United States. The overarching mission of the Department of the Treasury is to "maintain a strong economy and create economic and job opportunities by promoting the conditions that enable economic growth and stability at home and abroad, strengthen national security by combating threats and protecting the integrity of the financial system, and manage the U.S. Government's finances and resources effectively."[16] Its critical infrastructure mission is to secure the U.S. financial and banking system.

Environmental Protection Agency (EPA). Securing and preserving the nation's environment and resources is a critical component of homeland security. The overarching mission of the EPA "is to protect human health and the environment."[17] EPA's critical infrastructure responsibility is to secure the nation's drinking water and water treatment infrastructure.

The U.S. Intelligence Community: Mission and Challenges

Intelligence collection and analysis are important components of the homeland security mission. The intelligence mission is unique in the sense that it is responsible for securing the American homeland from external threats. That is, although intelligence operations have a significant effect on domestic security, their scope of operations is also outside the borders of the nation.

Chapter Perspective 11.2 discusses the subject of waging war in the era of the New Terrorism.

CHAPTER PERSPECTIVE 11.2

Waging War in the Era of the New Terrorism

A war on terrorism was declared in the aftermath of the September 11, 2001, attacks on the United States. This is a new kind of conflict against a new form of enemy. From the outset, policy makers understood that this war would be fought in an unconventional manner, primarily against shadowy terrorist cells and elusive leaders. It is not a war against a nation, but rather against ideas and behavior.

The mobilization of resources in this war necessitated the coordination of law enforcement, intelligence, and military assets in many nations across the globe. Covert operations by special military and intelligence units became the norm rather than the exception. Suspected terrorist cells were identified and dismantled by law enforcement agencies in many countries, and covert operatives worked secretly in other countries. Although many suspects were detained at the U.S. military base in

Guantánamo Bay, Cuba, other secret detention facilities were also established.

However, the war has not been fought solely in the shadows. In contrast to the deployment of small law enforcement and covert military or intelligence assets, the U.S.-led invasions of Afghanistan and Iraq involved the commitment of large conventional military forces. In Afghanistan, reasons given for the invasion included the need to eliminate state-sponsored safe havens for Al Qaeda and other international mujahideen (holy warriors). In Iraq, reasons given for the invasion included the need to eliminate alleged stockpiles of weapons of mass destruction and alleged links between the regime of Saddam Hussein and terrorist networks. The U.S.-led operation in Iraq was symbolically named Operation Iraqi Freedom.

One significant challenge for waging war against extremist behavior—in this case, against terrorism—is that victory is not an easily definable condition. For example, on May 1, 2003, U.S. president George W. Bush landed on the aircraft carrier *Abraham Lincoln* to deliver a speech in which he officially declared that the military phase of the Iraq invasion had ended and that the overthrow of the Hussein government was "one victory in a war on terror that began on September 11, 2001, and still goes on."[a] Unfortunately, President Bush's declaration was premature. A widespread insurgency took root in Iraq, with the resistance employing both classic hit-and-run guerrilla tactics and terrorism. Common cause was found between remnants of the Hussein regime and non-Iraqi Islamist fighters. Thousands of Iraqis and occupation troops became casualties during the insurgency. In particular, the insurgents targeted foreign soldiers, government institutions, and Iraqi "collaborators" such as soldiers, police officers, election workers, and interpreters. Sectarian violence also spread, with Sunni and Shi'a religious extremists killing many civilians.

Is the war on terrorism being won? How can victory reasonably be measured? Assuming that the New Terrorism will continue for a period of time, perhaps the best measure for progress in the war is to assess the degree to which terrorist behavior is being successfully *managed*—in much the same manner that progress against crime is assessed. As the global community continues to be challenged by violent extremists during the new era of terrorism, the definition of victory is likely to continue to be refined and redefined by nations and leaders.

Note

a. David E. Sanger, "In Speech, Bush Focuses on Conflicts Beyond Iraq," *New York Times*, May 1, 2003.

U.S. Intelligence Community: Mission

In the United States, intelligence collection is divided between agencies that are separately responsible for domestic and international intelligence collection. This separation is mandated by law. For example, the FBI performs domestic intelligence collection, and the CIA operates internationally. This separation of missions is similar to the distinctive roles of the United Kingdom's MI-5 (domestic intelligence) and MI-6 (international intelligence).

The United States has attempted to coordinate intelligence collection and analysis by creating a cooperative **intelligence community**. This philosophy of cooperation is the primary conceptual goal of the American counterterrorist intelligence effort. In practice, of course, there have been very serious bureaucratic rivalries. To reduce the incidence of these rivalries, in December 2004, the intelligence community was reorganized with the passage of the Intelligence Reform and Terrorism Prevention Act. Members of the community were subsumed under the direction of a new Office of the Director of National Intelligence. President George W. Bush nominated John Negroponte, former U.S. ambassador to Iraq, as the United States' first director of national intelligence (DNI). Officially confirmed by the Senate in April 2005, the DNI is responsible for coordinating the various components of the intelligence community. Members of the American intelligence community include the following agencies:

National Security Agency. The **National Security Agency (NSA)** is the technological arm of the U.S. intelligence community. Using state-of-the-art computer and satellite technologies, the NSA's primary mission is to collect communications and other signal intelligence. It also devotes a significant portion of its technological expertise to code-making and code-breaking activities. Much of this work is done covertly from secret surveillance facilities positioned around the globe.

Central Intelligence Agency. The CIA is an independent federal agency. It is the theoretical coordinator of the intelligence community. The agency is charged with collecting intelligence outside of the borders of the United States, which is done covertly using human and technological assets. The CIA is legally prohibited from collecting intelligence inside the United States.

Defense Intelligence Agency. The **Defense Intelligence Agency (DIA)** is a bureau within the Department of Defense. It is the central intelligence bureau for the U.S. military. Each branch of the military coordinates its intelligence collection and analysis with the other branches through the DIA.

Federal Bureau of Investigation. The FBI is a bureau within the Department of Justice. It is a law enforcement agency that is charged in part with conducting domestic surveillance of suspected spies and terrorists. The agency also engages in domestic intelligence collection and has been deployed to American embassies around the world. Foreign counterintelligence investigations have included an FBI presence at the sites of the 1998 bombings of the U.S. embassies in Kenya and Tanzania.

U.S. Intelligence Community: Challenges

Problems of Intelligence Coordination. The collection and analysis of intelligence are covert processes that do not lend themselves easily to absolute cooperation and coordination between countries or between members of domestic intelligence communities. National intelligence agencies do not readily share intelligence with allied countries; they usually do so only after careful deliberation. The same is true of intelligence communities within countries. For example, prior to the September 11, 2001, homeland attacks, dozens of federal agencies were involved in the collection of intelligence about terrorism. This led to overlapping and competing interests. A case in point is the apparent failure by the FBI and CIA to collaboratively process, share, and evaluate important intelligence between their agencies. In the case of the FBI, there was also an apparent failure of coordination between the agency's field and national offices. These problems precipitated a proposal in June 2002 by President George W. Bush to completely reorganize the American homeland security community.

An example of successful international intelligence cooperation occurred in May 2002 between American and Moroccan intelligence agencies. In February 2002, Moroccan intelligence officers interrogated Moroccan Al Qaeda prisoners held by the Americans at their naval base in Guantánamo Bay, Cuba. They received information from one of the prisoners about an Al Qaeda operative in Morocco and also received information about the operative's relatives. Moroccan officials obtained a sketched description of the man from the relatives and showed the sketch to the Guantánamo prisoner, who confirmed his likeness. The Moroccans located the suspect (a Saudi), followed him for a month, and eventually arrested him and two Saudi accomplices. The suspects eventually told the Moroccans that they were Al Qaeda operatives trained in Afghanistan and that they had escaped during the anti-Taliban campaign after receiving orders to engage in suicide attacks against maritime targets in Gibraltar. They had begun the process of inquiring about speedboats, and their ultimate targets were to be U.S. navy ships passing through the Strait of Gibraltar.[18]

Problems of Collection and Analysis. Intelligence collection and analysis is not always an exact or low-risk science. It can reflect only the quality and amount of data that are available. Because of the nature of counterterrorist intelligence collection and analysis, some experts in the United States have concluded that

> the inherent difficulties in both collection and analysis of intelligence on terrorism mean that there will never be tactical warning of most attempted terrorist attacks, or even most major attempted attacks against U.S. targets.[19]

This observation became controversially apparent on July 7, 2004, when the U.S. Select Committee on Intelligence issued an extensive report titled *Report on the U.S. Intelligence Community's Prewar Intelligence Assessments on Iraq.*[20] The 521-page report's findings were a scathing critique of intelligence failures regarding Iraq. For example, its first conclusion found the following:

> Most of the major key judgments in the Intelligence Community's October 2002 National Intelligence Estimate (NIE), Iraq's Continuing Programs for Weapons of Mass Destruction, either overstated, or were not supported by, the underlying intelligence reporting. A series of failures, particularly in analytic trade craft, led to mischaracterization of the intelligence.[21]

In another highly critical report, the presidential Commission on the Intelligence Capabilities of the United States Regarding Weapons of Mass Destruction essentially labeled the American intelligence community as being dysfunctional.[22] It also said that the causes for the failure in the Iraq case continued to hinder intelligence on other potential threats, such as the nuclear programs of adversaries. The commission's 601-page report was delivered in March 2005.

▶ The aftermath of September 11, 2001. Rescue workers amid the smoke and debris of the World Trade Center in New York City.

Jim Watson/AFP/Getty Images

CIVIL LIBERTIES AND SECURING THE HOMELAND

The discussion in this section addresses the difficult balance between securing the homeland and protecting civil liberties from the following perspectives:

- Security and Liberty

- Balancing Civil Liberties and Homeland Security

- Achieving Security

Security and Liberty

Historical Perspective: Suppressing the IRA in the United Kingdom

In the United Kingdom, where factions of the Irish Republican Army were highly active in London and other cities, the British police were considered to be the front line against IRA terrorism. They usually displayed a high degree of professionalism without resorting to repressive tactics and consequently enjoyed widespread popular support. For example, London's Metropolitan Police (also known as the Met) became experts in counterterrorist operations when the IRA waged a terrorist campaign during the 1970s. The Met's criminal investigations bureau generally used high-quality detective work rather than authoritarian techniques to investigate terrorist incidents. The British criminal justice system also generally protected the rights of the accused during trials of IRA suspects. However, in the rush to stop the IRA's terrorist campaign (especially during the 1970s), miscarriages of criminal justice did occur. Examples of these miscarriages include the following examples:

> Four people were wrongfully convicted of an October 1974 bombing in Guildford, England. Two of them were also wrongfully sentenced for a bombing attack in Woolwich.

The **Guildford Four** served 15 years in prison before being released in 1989, when their convictions were overturned on appeal. The group received a formal apology from Prime Minister Tony Blair in June 2000 and received monetary awards as compensation. The case was made famous by the American film *In the Name of the Father.*

Six men were convicted for the November 1974 bombings of two pubs in Birmingham, England, that killed 21 people and injured 168. On appeal, the court ordered the release of the **Birmingham Six** after it ruled that the police had used fabricated evidence. The men were released in 1991 after serving 16 years in prison.

Chapter Perspective 11.3 discusses the suspension of civil liberties in Northern Ireland during the height of the Troubles.

Historical Perspective: Red Scares and Internment in the United States

The United States has experienced several periods of crisis when the American public and political leaders perceived a need for enacting legally based guidelines on how to manage the crisis. Laws were passed because of fear and uncertainty precipitated by domestic or foreign threats. At the time, these measures were deemed necessary and were therefore often quite popular. However, the constitutionality and ethics of these laws were frequently called into question during reflection in post-crisis years. Examples of these laws and crises include the following:

Red Scares. In the United States, periodic anticommunist "Red Scares" occurred when national leaders reacted to the perceived threat of communist subversion. Government

CHAPTER PERSPECTIVE 11.3

The United Kingdom: Suspending Civil Liberties in Northern Ireland

After the British Army was deployed to Northern Ireland, it became severely pressed by an IRA terrorist campaign. In response to repeated intimidation of jurors by paramilitaries, the government in Northern Ireland established special courts without jury trial. These Diplock Courts, so-named after Lord Diplock who reported to Parliament on the problem, held trial before a single judge without recourse to jury trial. In such cases, all defendants were tried as criminals under the same laws rather than differentiating between political and criminal suspects.

Another program aimed at prosecuting and imprisoning Irish terrorists was implemented during the 1980s. This was the supergrass program, which was a policy of convincing members of the Provisional IRA (Provos) and members of the Irish National Liberation Army (INLA) to defect from their movements and inform on their former comrades (*supergrass* is a slang term for an informer). Many decided to participate in supergrass. With these informants, British-led authorities were able to successfully prosecute and imprison a number of Provos and INLA members. However, many of these dissidents were released in the late 1980s when cases taken up on appeal successfully challenged the admissibility of supergrass testimony. In the end, supergrass disrupted Irish militant groups during the 1980s (particularly the INLA) but did not have a long-term impact on Northern Ireland's terrorist environment.

The Northern Ireland Act, passed in 1993, created conditions of quasi-martial law. The act suspended several civil liberties. It empowered the British military to engage in warrantless searches of civilian homes, temporarily detain people without charge, and question suspects. The military could also intern (remove from society) suspected terrorists and turn over for prosecution those for whom enough evidence had been seized. Nearly a quarter of a million warrantless searches were conducted by the army, which resulted in the seizure of thousands of arms and the internment or imprisonment of hundreds of suspects.

officials reacted by adopting authoritarian measures to end the perceived threats. Red Scares occurred during three periods in American history: first in the aftermath of the Bolshevik Revolution in Russia, again during the 1930s, and finally during the height of the Cold War.

The first Red Scare occurred after the founding of the Communist Party USA in 1919 and a series of letter bombs were intercepted. Other bombs were detonated in several cities, including one directed against Attorney General A. Mitchell Palmer. On September 16, 1920, a bomb was detonated in the Wall Street financial district in New York City, killing 38 people and seriously injuring 143. President Woodrow Wilson allowed Palmer to conduct a series of raids—the so-called Palmer Raids—against labor unions, socialists, Communists, and other leftist and labor groups. Offices of many organizations were searched without warrants and shut down; thousands of people were arrested. Leaders were arrested and put on trial, and hundreds of people were deported. The legal foundations for the law enforcement crackdown against leftists were the Espionage Act of 1917 and the Sedition Act of 1918. An interesting postscript is that Palmer was eventually prosecuted and convicted for misappropriation of government funds.

The second Red Scare began during the 1930s at the height of the Great Depression. Communists and socialists enjoyed a measure of popularity during this period of crisis, and fears grew that the uncertainty of the Depression would lead to mass subversive unrest. Congress reacted by establishing the House Un-American Activities Committee and passing the Smith Act in 1940, which made advocacy of the violent overthrow of the government a federal crime. In the late 1940s, high-profile investigations, such as that of Alger Hiss, were common and a number of Communists were prosecuted.

The third Red Scare occurred during the 1950s, when Senator Joseph McCarthy of Wisconsin held a series of hearings to counter fears of spying by Communist regimes (China and the Soviet Union) and a general fear that Communists were poised to overthrow the government and otherwise subvert the "American way of life." McCarthy sought to expose Communist infiltration and conspiracies in government, private industry, and the entertainment industry. McCarthy publicly interrogated people from these sectors in a way that had never been done before—on television. Hundreds of careers were ruined and many people were blacklisted, that is, barred from employment. McCarthy was later criticized for overstepping the bounds of propriety, and the term **McCarthyism** has come to mean a political and ideological witch hunt.

Wartime Internment Camps. The attack on Pearl Harbor on December 7, 1941, by the Empire of Japan created a climate of fear in the United States against ethnic Japanese. Conspiracy scenarios held that sympathizers would begin a campaign of sabotage and subversion on behalf of Japan. This would, in theory, be done in preparation for a Japanese invasion of the West Coast. Unfortunately, a prewar backdrop of prejudice against Asians in general became a focused animosity toward Asians of Japanese heritage. The administration of President Franklin Delano Roosevelt established a War Relocation Authority and the U.S. Army was tasked with moving ethnic Japanese to **internment camps** on the West Coast and elsewhere. More than 100,000 ethnic Japanese, most of whom were American citizens, were forced to relocate to the camps. Internment camps were operational until 1945. Most internees lost their property and businesses, and in 1988 the U.S. government passed the Civil Liberties Act, which formally apologized for the internments and declared the internment program as being unjust.

Balancing Civil Liberties and Homeland Security

Terrorist Profiling

European approaches to domestic counterterrorism were security-focused long prior to September 11, 2001. These approaches reflected European experience with domestic extremists such as the Red Brigade, IRA, and Red Army Faction, as well as many incidents of international terrorism. In contrast, the American approach to domestic counterterrorism prior to the September 11 attacks was a law enforcement approach; after the attacks, the new terrorist environment called for a more security-focused approach. The FBI and other agencies created a terrorist profile that was similar to standard **criminal profiles** used in law enforcement investigations. Criminal profiles are descriptive composites that include the personal characteristics of suspects, such as their height, weight, race, gender, hair color, eye color, and clothing. Suspects who match these criminal profiles can be detained for questioning. The composite of the new terrorist profile included the following characteristics: Middle Eastern heritage, temporary visa status, Muslim faith, male gender, and young adult age. Based on these criteria—and during a serious security crisis—the FBI and Immigration and Naturalization Service (INS) administratively detained hundreds of men fitting this description. Material witness warrants were used from the outset to detain many of these men for questioning. The INS was disbanded in 2003 when its duties were transferred to three new agencies: Citizenship and Immigration Services, Immigration and Customs Enforcement, and Customs and Border Protection.

As the investigations continued, and in the wake of several warnings about possible terrorist threats, the U.S. Department of Justice expanded the FBI's surveillance authority. New guidelines were promulgated in May 2002 that permitted field offices to conduct surveillance of religious institutions, websites, libraries, and organizations without an a priori (before the fact) finding of criminal suspicion.

These detentions and guidelines were criticized. Critics argued that the detentions were improper because the vast majority of the detainees had not been charged with violating the law. Critics of the surveillance guidelines contended that it gave too much power to the state to investigate innocent civilians. Many also maintained that there was a danger that these investigations could become discriminatory **racial profiling**, involving the detention of people because of their ethno-national or racial heritage. Nevertheless, the new security policies continued to use administrative detentions and enhanced surveillance as counterterrorist methods.

The Problem of Labeling the Enemy

When formulating counterterrorist policies, Western homeland security experts are challenged by two problems: first, the problem of defining terrorism, and second, the problem of labeling individual suspects. Although defining terrorism can be an exercise in semantics, and is often shaped by subjective political or cultural biases, certain fundamental elements are objective. In comparison, official designations (labels) used to confer special status on captured suspects have become controversial.

After September 11, it became clear to Western experts and the public that official designations and labels of individual suspected terrorists are a central legal, political, and security issue. The question of a suspect's official status when he or she is taken prisoner is central. It determines whether certain recognized legal or political protections are or are not observed.

When enemy soldiers are taken prisoner, they are traditionally afforded legal protections as *prisoners of war*. This is well recognized under international law. During the war on terrorism, many suspected terrorists were designated by the United States as *enemy combatants* and were not afforded the same legal status as prisoners of war. Such practices have been hotly debated among proponents and opponents.

According to the protocols of the third Geneva Convention, prisoners who are designated as prisoners of war, and who are brought to trial, must be afforded the same legal rights in the same courts as soldiers from the country holding them prisoner. Thus, prisoners of war held by the United States would be brought to trial in standard military courts under the Uniform Code of Military Justice and would have the same rights and protections (such as the right to appeal) as all soldiers.

Suspected terrorists have not been designated as prisoners of war. Official and unofficial designations such as enemy combatants, unlawful combatants, and battlefield detainees have been used by American authorities to differentiate them from prisoners of war. The rationale is that suspected terrorists are not soldiers fighting for a sovereign nation and are therefore not eligible for prisoner of war status. When hundreds of prisoners were detained by the United States at facilities such as the American base in Guantánamo Bay, Cuba, the United States argued that persons designated as enemy combatants were not subject to the Geneva Conventions. Thus, such individuals could be held indefinitely, detained in secret, transferred at will, and sent to allied countries for more coercive interrogations. Under enemy combatant status, conditions of confinement in Guantánamo Bay included open-air cells with wooden roofs and chain-link walls. In theory, each case was to be reviewed by special military tribunals, and innocent prisoners would be reclassified as nonenemy combatants and released. Civil liberties and human rights groups disagreed with the special status conferred by the labeling system on prisoners. They argued that basic legal and humanitarian protections should be granted to prisoners regardless of their designation.

Extraordinary Renditions

In many ways, the war on terrorism is a "shadow war" that is fought covertly and beyond the attention of the public. It is also a war that employs unconventional tactics and uses resources that were hitherto either uncommon or unacceptable. One unconventional tactic is known as **extraordinary renditions**, and it has been adopted by the United States as a method to covertly abduct and detain suspected terrorists or affiliated operatives.

Extraordinary renditions were initially sanctioned during the Reagan administration in about 1987, as a measure to capture drug traffickers, terrorists, and other wanted persons. It involves an uncomplicated procedure: Find suspects anywhere in the world, seize them, transport them to the United States, and force their appearance before a state or federal court. Such compulsory appearances before U.S. courts (after forcible abductions) have long been accepted as procedurally valid and do not violate one's constitutional rights. The doctrine that permits these abductions and appearances is an old one, and it has come to be known as the Ker-Frisbie Rule.[23]

This practice was significantly expanded after the September 11, 2001, terrorist attacks. It became highly controversial because, unlike previous renditions in which suspects were seized and brought into the U.S. legal system, most antiterrorist abductions placed suspects in covert detention. Many abductions have been carried out by CIA operatives, who transported a number of abductees to allied countries for interrogation. The CIA also established secret detention facilities and maintained custody of suspects for extended periods of time.[24] Allegations have arisen that these suspects were tortured.

Western governments such as Italy, Sweden, and Germany launched investigations into alleged CIA-coordinated extraordinary renditions from their countries. In June 2005, Italy went so far as to order the arrests of 13 alleged CIA operatives for kidnapping an Egyptian cleric from the streets of Milan.[25]

The Torture Debate

Few counterterrorist methods garner such passionate debate as the issue of inflicting physical and psychological pressure on terrorist suspects. In the United States, the debate was joined in the aftermath of the invasion of Iraq. From October through December 2003, Iraqi detainees held at the U.S.-controlled Abu Ghraib prison near Baghdad were abused by American guards. The abuse included sexual degradation, intimidation with dogs, stripping prisoners naked, forcing them into "human pyramids," and making them stand in extended poses in so-called stress positions. The U.S. Congress and the global community became aware of these practices in April 2004 when graphic photographs were published in the media, posted on the Internet, and shown to Congress. Criminal courts-martial were convened, and several guards were convicted and sentenced to prison.

Unfortunately for the United States, not only was its image tarnished, but further revelations about additional incidents raised serious questions about these and other practices. For example, in March 2005, U.S. army and navy investigators alleged that 26 prisoners in American custody had possibly been the victims of homicide.

A debate about the definition and propriety of torture ensued.

Torture is a practice that is officially eschewed by the United States, both morally and as a legitimate interrogation technique. Morally, such practices are officially held to be inhumane and unacceptable. As an interrogation method, American officials have long argued that torture produces bad intelligence because victims are likely to admit whatever the interrogator wishes to hear. However, during the war on terrorism, a fresh debate began about how to define torture and whether physical and psychological stress methods that fall outside of this definition are acceptable.

Assuming that the application of coercion is justifiable to some degree in order to break the resistance of a suspect, the question becomes whether physical and extreme psychological coercion are also justifiable. For instance, do the following techniques constitute torture?

- waterboarding, in which prisoners believe that they will drown

- sexual degradation, whereby prisoners are humiliated by stripping them or forcing them to perform sex acts

Figure 11.3 Waterboarding

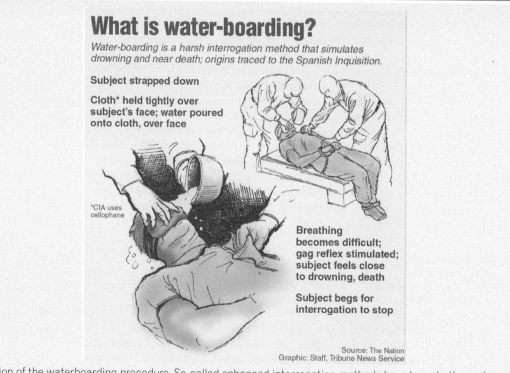

A depiction of the waterboarding procedure. So-called enhanced interrogation methods have been both condemned as unethical torture and supported as a hard necessity in the war on terror.

- stress positions, whereby prisoners are forced to pose in painful positions for extended periods

- creating a chronic state of fear

- environmental stress, accomplished by adjusting a detention cell's temperature

- sleep deprivation

- disorientation about one's whereabouts or the time of day

- sensory deprivation, such as depriving suspects of sound or light

When images such as those from Abu Ghraib became public, the political consequences were serious. Nevertheless, policy makers continued their debate on which practices constitute torture and whether some circumstances warrant the imposition of as much stress as possible on suspects—up to the brink of torture. In May 2008, the U.S. Department of Justice's inspector general released an extensive report that revealed that FBI agents had complained repeatedly since 2002 about harsh interrogations conducted by military and CIA interrogators.

Achieving Security

Government Responses

Homeland security experts must concentrate on achieving several counterterrorist objectives. These objectives can realistically, and in a practical sense, only minimize rather than eliminate terrorist threats, but they must be actively pursued. Objectives include the following:

- disrupting and preventing domestic terrorist conspirators from operationalizing their plans

- deterring would-be activists from crossing the line between extremist activism and political violence

- implementing laws and task forces to create a cooperative counterterrorist environment

- minimizing physical destruction and human casualties

It is clear that no single model or method for achieving security will apply across different scenarios or terrorist environments. Because of this reality, the process for projecting counterterrorist models must include a longitudinal framework based on both theory and practical necessity. The theoretical models used must reflect respect for human rights protections and balance this against options that may include the use of force and law enforcement options. The practicality of these models requires them to be continually updated and adapted to emerging terrorist threats. With these adaptations, perhaps terrorism can be controlled to some degree by keeping extremists and violent dissidents off balance—thereby preventing them from having an unobstructed hand in planning and carrying out attacks or other types of political violence.

Assuming that homeland security policy makers grasp the constitutional and practical parameters of counterterrorist options, it is clear that there must be a balance between coercive methods and preventive options. Preventive options may provide long-term solutions to future extremism and terrorism. If skillfully applied, adaptations of these options present potential (or actual) domestic extremists with options other than political violence. This would also have the effect of protecting civil liberties.

Countering Extremism Through Reform

Extremist ideologies and beliefs are fertile soil for politically violent behavior. Ethnocentrism, nationalism, ideological intolerance, racism, and religious fanaticism are core motivations for terrorism. History has shown that coercive measures used to counter these tendencies are often only marginally successful. The reason is uncomplicated: A great deal of extremist behavior is rooted in passionate ideas, recent historical memories of conflict, and cultural tensions. It is difficult to forcibly reverse these tendencies, and although coercion can eliminate cadres and destroy extremist organizations, sheer repression is a risky long-term solution. Because extremism has historically originated primarily from domestic conflict (sometimes from national traumas such as invasions), efforts to counter domestic extremism must incorporate societal and cultural responses. A central factor is that new societal and cultural norms often reflect demographic changes and political shifts. Dissent can certainly be repressed, but it is rarely a long-term solution absent preventive measures such as social reforms, political inclusion, and protecting constitutional rights.

The United States is a good subject for evaluating these concepts. In the aftermath of the political turmoil of the 1960s and 1970s, the United States underwent a slow cultural and ideological shift that began to promote concepts such as multiculturalism and diversity. These concepts were adaptations to the fact that the United States has gradually become a country in which no single demographic group will be a majority of the population in the near future, probably by the mid-21st century. This is a significant ideological shift from the "melting pot" ideology of previous generations, when new immigrants, racial minorities, and religious minorities were expected to accept the cultural values of the American mainstream.

In the United Kingdom, United States, and elsewhere, grassroots efforts to promote inclusion became common features of the social and political environment (although not without political opposition). For example, private "watchdog" organizations monitor extremist tendencies such as right-wing and neofascist movements. Some of these organizations, such as the Southern Poverty Law Center and the Anti-Defamation League in the United States, have implemented programs to promote community inclusiveness. In the public sector, government agencies have long been required to monitor and promote inclusion of demographic minorities and women in government-funded programs. Also in the public sector, the trend among local police forces shifted toward practicing variants of community-oriented policing, which in practice means that the police operationally integrate themselves as much as possible within local communities.

The theoretical outcome of these cultural tendencies would be an erosion of the root causes of extremist sentiment.

DISCUSSION BOX

AFTER THE NEXT 9/11

This chapter's Discussion Box is intended to stimulate critical debate about the aftermath of another catastrophic terrorist attack on the American homeland.

The September 11, 2001, attacks on the U.S. homeland produced the most sweeping reorganization of the American security culture in history. The fear that arose following the attacks was matched by concerns that the United States was ill-prepared to prevent or adequately respond to determined terrorists. Homeland security became a part of everyday life and culture because of 9/11. Although some degree of terrorist violence is likely to occur domestically, the possibility of another catastrophic attack leaves open the question of what impact such an event would have on society.

Discussion Questions

1. How serious is the threat of catastrophic terrorism?

2. Can catastrophic attacks be prevented?

3. How would a catastrophic terrorist attack affect American homeland security culture?

4. How will society in general be affected by a catastrophic attack?

5. What is the likelihood that homeland security authority will be expanded in the future?

CHAPTER SUMMARY

This chapter discussed homeland security within the contexts of its conceptual foundation, the need to reorganize security and law enforcement agencies in the aftermath of the September 11 attacks, the homeland security bureaucracy in the United States, the role of intelligence agencies and special operations forces, and the problem of balancing civil liberties and domestic security during periods of crisis.

Because of revelations about bureaucratic inefficiency in the aftermath of the September 11 attacks, the United States implemented a restructuring of its homeland security community. When examining homeland security agencies and missions, it is important to consider that they operate within the context of counterterrorist and antiterrorist options. Many federal agencies are participants in the overall homeland security network, with the Department of Homeland Security as the largest and most mission-diverse federal organization. Intelligence agencies and the military perform a critical international role that helps to secure the domestic homeland security environment. The intersection of their missions with those of domestic agencies creates a large and intricate establishment for combating terrorism domestically and internationally.

There is often a natural tension between preserving human rights and securing the homeland. This tension is reflected in political and philosophical debates about how to accomplish both goals. Nevertheless, during historical periods when threats to national security existed, sweeping measures were undertaken as a matter of perceived necessity. The implementation of these measures was often politically popular at the time but questioned in later years. The modern homeland security environment exists because of the attacks of September 11, 2001, and has resulted in the creation of bureaucracies, the passage of new security-related laws, and the implementation of controversial counterterrorist measures.

An underlying theme throughout this discussion has been that homeland security is an evolving concept. Organizational cooperation and coordination are certainly desirable, but it must be remembered that these can occur only if political and policy responses are able to adapt to changes in the terrorist environment. Homeland security in the post–September 11 era has adapted to new and emerging threats. These threats reflect the creativity and determination of those who wage terrorist campaigns against the United States and its allies. Disruption of terrorist operations requires broad cooperation and commitment to protecting the homeland from these adversaries.

KEY TERMS AND CONCEPTS

The following topics were discussed in this chapter and can be found in the Glossary:

Abu Hafs al-Masri Brigades   232
Anti-Terrorism and Effective Death
   Penalty Act   240
Birmingham Six   250

Bureaucracy   243
Criminal profiles   252
Defense Intelligence Agency
   (DIA)   248

Department of Homeland
   Security   237
Department of Homeland Security
   Act of 2002   237

WEB EXERCISE

Using this chapter's recommended websites listed on the student study site at **edge.sagepub.com/martiness5e**, conduct an online investigation of the missions of homeland security agencies and organizations. Compare and contrast these agencies and organizations.

1. What are the primary missions of these organizations?

2. How would you describe the differences between sector-specific agencies?

3. In your opinion, are any of these organizations more effective than other organizations? Less effective?

 For an online search of research and monitoring organizations, readers should enter the following keywords in their Web browser's search engine:

 "Homeland Security Agencies"

 "Homeland Security Threats"

RECOMMENDED READINGS

The following publications are good analyses of the concept of homeland security and the homeland security bureaucracy.

Aronowitz, S., & Gautney, H. (Eds.). (2003). *Implicating empire: Globalization and resistance in the 21st century world order*. New York, NY: Basic Books.

Beckman, J. (2007). *Comparative legal approaches to homeland security and anti-terrorism*. Aldershot, UK: Ashgate.

Booth, K., & Dunne, T. (Eds.). *Worlds in collision: Terror and the future of global order*. New York, NY: Palgrave Macmillan.

Borrelli, J. V. (2007). *Bioterrorism: Prevention, preparedness, and protection*. New York, NY: Nova Science.

Clark, R. (2014). *Intelligence collection*. Thousand Oaks, CA: CQ Press.

Coen, B., & Nadler, E. (2009). *Dead silence: Fear and terror on the anthrax trail*. Berkeley, CA: Counterpoint.

CQ Researcher. (2010). *Issues and homeland security: Selections from* CQ Researcher. Thousand Oaks, CA: Sage.

CQ Researcher. (2011). *Issues in terrorism and homeland security: Selections from* CQ Researcher (2nd ed.). Thousand Oaks, CA: Sage.

Elias, B. (2010). *Airport and aviation security: U.S. policy and strategy in the age of global terrorism*. Boca Raton, FL: Auerbach/Taylor & Francis.

Graff, G. M. (2011). *The threat matrix: The FBI at war in the age of global terror*. New York, NY: Little, Brown.

Kamien, D. G. (2006). *The McGraw-Hill homeland security handbook*. New York, NY: McGraw-Hill.

Kremling, J., & Sharp Parker, A. M. (2018). *Cyberspace, cybersecurity, and cybercrime*. Thousand Oaks, CA: Sage.

Monje, S. C. (2008). *The Central Intelligence Agency: A documentary history*. Westport, CT: Greenwood.

Purpura, P. P. (2007). *Terrorism and homeland security: An introduction with applications*. New York, NY: Butterworth-Heinemann.

Pushies, F. J. (2009). *Deadly blue: Battle stories of the U.S. Air Force Special Operations Command.* New York, NY: American Management Association.

Sauter, M. A., & Carafano, J. J. (2005). *Homeland security: A complete guide to understanding, preventing, and surviving terrorism.* New York, NY: McGraw-Hill.

Schawb, S. I. M. (2009). *Guantánamo, USA: The untold history of America's Cuban outpost.* Lawrence: University Press of Kansas.

Smith, C. S. (2010). *The Patriot Act: Issues and controversies.* Springfield, IL: Charles C Thomas.

Stritzke, W. G. K., Lewandowsky, S., Denemark, D., Clare, J., & Morgan, V. (2009). *Terrorism and torture: An interdisciplinary approach.* New York, NY: Cambridge University Press.

Tsang, S. (2007). *Intelligence and human rights in the era of global terrorism.* Westport, CT: Praeger Security International.

Walker, C. (2011). *The law and terrorism.* Oxford, UK: Oxford University Press.

Wilson, R. A. (Ed.). (2005). *Human rights in the War on Terror.* New York, NY: Cambridge University Press.

Worthington, A. (2007). *The Guantánamo files.* Ann Arbor, MI: Pluto Press.

CHAPTER TWELVE

FUTURE TRENDS AND PROJECTIONS

Learning Objectives

This chapter will enable readers to do the following:

1. Discuss theoretical projections for the future of terrorism.

2. Discuss possible terrorist environments in the 21st century.

3. Identify types of possible new threats posed by violent extremists.

4. Explain theoretical and plausible scenarios for ending terrorist campaigns.

5. Describe plausible scenarios for future terrorism in the United States.

Previous chapters provided a great deal of information about the causes of terrorism, the motives behind political violence, terrorist environments, and counterterrorist responses. Many examples of post–World War II terrorist movements and environments were presented to illustrate theoretical concepts and trends. The discussion in this chapter synthesizes many of these concepts and trends and projects emerging trends likely to characterize terrorist environments in the near future.

One concept must be understood at the outset: Projecting future trends is not synonymous with predicting specific events, and the two should be differentiated as follows:

- Projections involve theoretical constructs of trends based on available data.

- Predictions are practical applications of data (that is, intelligence) to anticipate specific behaviors by extremists.

One must develop a logical longitudinal framework to evaluate the future of political violence. A longitudinal framework uses past history, trends, and cycles to project future trends. It allows scholars, students, and practitioners to "stand back" from immediate crises and contemporary terrorist environments to try to construct a reasonable picture of the near future. These projections must be made with the understanding that the more near-term a forecast is, the more likely it is to be realistic. Conversely, far-term forecasts are less likely to be realistic because projections must be consistently updated using contemporary data.

The discussion in this chapter reviews the future of political violence from the following perspectives:

- What Does the Future Hold?

- Revisiting the War on Terrorism

Figure 12.1 Tactics Used in Terrorist Attacks in the United States, 1970–2011

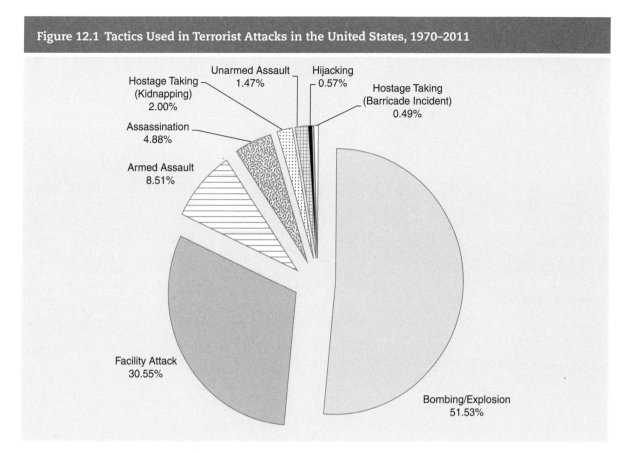

Source: LaFree, Gary, Laura Dugan and Erin Miller, "Integrated United States Security Database (IUSSD): Data on the Terrorist Attacks in the United States Homeland, 1970 to 2011," Final Report to the Resilient Systems Division, DHS Science and Technology Directorate, U.S. Department of Homeland Security. College Park, MD: START, 2012, p. 18 (figure 7).

Note: This figure includes up to three tactics per case. "Unknowns" are excluded. The total number of tactics included is 2,645.

WHAT DOES THE FUTURE HOLD?

Professor David C. Rapoport's theory of terrorist "waves" was first introduced in Chapter 2.[1] If Rapoport's theory is correct, the current terrorist environment will be characterized by the New Terrorism for the immediate future. That said, it can also be argued that the sources of extremist behavior in the modern era will generally remain unchanged in the near future. The modern era of terrorism is likely to continue to occur for the following reasons:

- People who have been relegated to the social and political margins—or who believe that they have been so relegated—often form factions that resort to violence.

- Movements and nations sometimes adopt religious or ethno-nationalist supremacist doctrines that they use to justify aggressive political behavior.

- Many states continue to value the "utility" of domestic and foreign terrorism.

▶ Indoctrinating the young. A Palestinian boy wearing a HAMAS headband attends a pro-Islamist demonstration at a refugee camp in Nuseirat, central Gaza Strip.

These factors have precipitated new trends in terrorist behavior that began to spread during the 1990s and early 2000s, including the following:

- increased use of communications and information technologies by extremists

- adaptations of cell-based organizational and operational strategies by global revolutionary movements

- continued use of relatively low-tech tactics such as suicide bombers

- efforts to construct or obtain relatively high-tech weapons of mass destruction or, alternatively, to convert existing technologies into high-yield weapons

Whither the "Old" Terrorism?

Traditional terrorism was characterized by the following commonalities:

- leftist ethno-nationalist motives

- relatively low casualty rates

- leftist ideological motives

- identifiable organizational profile

- surgical and symbolic selection of targets

- hierarchical organizational profile

- deliberate media manipulation

- full-time professional cadres and publicized incidents

Although this model did not become a relic in the 1990s, it did stop being the primary model in the 2000s. There is today in the West no single binding or common ideological foundation for political violence—no modern equivalent to revolutionary Marxism. Religious extremism is self-isolating, and there is no longer an international solidarity movement in the West for ethno-nationalist or religious violence. It remains to be seen what the long-term impact will be on actual religious terrorist violence, but it is unlikely that there will be an ideological glue to bind extremist sentiment in the West in the near future.

Many of today's terrorists have begun to promote vaguely articulated objectives and motives. They have also become cell-based **stateless revolutionaries**, unlike their predecessors, who tended to organize themselves hierarchically and had state sponsors. Even though the number of international incidents has declined during the New Terrorism, casualty rates have been higher. This is not to say that the old terrorism has disappeared or will do so in the near future. It will continue alongside a growing—and more aggressive—threat from the New Terrorism.

Table 12.1 Supplanting the Old With the New

The "old" terrorism was, in many ways, symmetrical and predictable. It was not characterized by terrorist environments exhibiting massive casualty rates or indiscriminate attacks. Its organizational profile was also characterized by traditional organizational configurations.

This table contrasts selected attributes of the activity profiles for the "old" terrorism and the New Terrorism.

Terrorist Environment	Activity Profile				
	Target Selection	Casualty Rates	Organizational Profile	Tactical/ Weapons Selection	Typical Motives
The "old" terrorism	Surgical and symbolic	Low and selective	Hierarchical and identifiable	Conventional and low to medium yield	Leftist and ethnocentric
New Terrorism	Indiscriminate and symbolic	High and indiscriminate	Cellular and lone wolf	Unconventional and high yield	Sectarian

Table 12.1 compares several key characteristics of the old and new terrorisms.

New Threats

The sources of extremist behavior have not changed in the recent past and will not change in the near future. Intense expressions of intolerance and resentment are likely to continue to motivate many extremists to blame entire systems, societies, and groups of people for their problems. Under these conditions, many people will continue to see political violence as a justifiable option. The likelihood of political violence will remain high as long as intolerance and blaming are motivated by passionate feelings of national identity, racial supremacy, religious dogma, or ideological beliefs. Both state and dissident terrorists will continue to exploit these tendencies for their own purposes.

Terrorist Environments in the 21st Century

State-Sponsored Terrorism

State-sponsored terrorism is not likely to soon disappear. It will remain a feature of future terrorist environments. Authoritarian states will continue to use terrorism as domestic policy, and aggressive states will continue to foment acts of international terrorism as foreign policy.

Domestically, political repression is—and long has been—a common practice of regimes more interested in protecting the authority of the state than human rights. The old instruments of repression will continue to be common tools of authoritarian government. These include security institutions such as police, military, and paramilitary forces. One should expect the pervasiveness of security institutions to be augmented by the continued improvement of surveillance and communications technologies. One should also expect that some of the world's more ruthless regimes will occasionally deploy weapons of mass destruction against dissident ethno-nationalist groups, as the regime of Saddam Hussein did against Iraqi Kurds and the regime of Syria's Bashar al-Assad did against civilian opponents.

Internationally, aggressive regimes in the post–World War II era frequently supported sympathetic proxies to indirectly confront their adversaries. Doing so was often a safe and low-cost alternative to overt conflict. It is reasonable to assume that some regimes will continue the practice in the near future, especially in regions where highly active proxies have the opportunity to severely press their sponsoring regime's rivals. For example, in early 2002, a ship bearing Iranian arms was intercepted by Israeli security forces before it could off-load the arms. The weapons, which were bound for Palestinian nationalist fighters, were almost certainly part of a Tehran proxy operation.

One issue that became prominent during the 2000s was nuclear proliferation among activist and authoritarian regimes. The West became particularly concerned about nuclear weapons development in Iran and North Korea, especially after Iran aggressively pursued a nuclear enrichment program. North Korea repeatedly claimed that it had manufactured nuclear weapons and subsequently conducted numerous tests of ballistic missiles. These examples are of continuing concern for the international community.

Dissident Terrorism

Patterns of dissident terrorism during the 1990s and 2000s were decreasingly ideological and increasingly cultural. Ethno-nationalist terrorism continued to occur on a sometimes grand scale, and religious terrorism spread among radical Islamic groups. In addition, stateless international terrorism began to emerge as the predominant model in the global arena. These trends are likely to continue as vestiges of the East–West ideological competition give way to patterns of religious extremism and seemingly interminable communal conflicts. This clash-of-civilizations scenario has been extensively debated since it was theorized by Samuel Huntington.[2]

Religious Terrorism

Terrorism motivated by religion has become a global problem. Religious terrorism spread during the 1980s and grew to challenge international and domestic political stability during the 1990s and early 2000s. The frequency of, and casualties from, sectarian attacks grew quickly during this period. Religious terrorists also became adept at recruiting new members and organizing themselves as semiautonomous cells across national boundaries.

The trends that developed toward the end of the 20th century suggest that religious violence will continue to be a central aspect of terrorism in the 21st century. Internationally, religious terrorists of many nationalities have consistently attacked targets that symbolize enemy interests. Unlike the relatively surgical strikes of secular leftists in previous years, religious terrorists have proved particularly homicidal. Al Qaeda, for example, was responsible in April 2002 for the explosion of a fuel tanker truck at a synagogue in Tunisia that killed 17 people, 12 of them German tourists. This kind of lethality has become a central element in international religious terrorism. Domestically, terrorist movements in Pakistan, Israel, Malaysia, the Philippines, and elsewhere have actively sought to overthrow or destabilize their governments and damage symbols representing foreign interests. For example, Western civilians were taken as hostages by radical Islamic, antigovernment Abu Sayyaf terrorists in the Philippines during 2001 and 2002.

Ideological Terrorism

Few ideologically motivated insurgencies survived into the 2000s because most ideological terrorist environments and wars of national liberation were resolved during the 1980s and 1990s. Nevertheless, a few Marxist insurgencies persisted, and Western democracies witnessed the growth of neofascist and anarchistic movements. Violence from neofascists tended to consist of relatively low-intensity hate crimes, mob brawls, and occasional low-yield bombings. Violence from the new anarchists usually involved brawls with the police at international conferences or occasional confrontations with racist skinheads. Right-wing movements and groups are likely to persist and grow in the near term. With the growth of aboveground neofascist parties in Europe, they could become a vanguard or armed wing of a renewed fascist movement.

The World in Conflict: Future Sources of Terrorism

During the 20th century, seemingly unmanageable regional and internal conflicts raged for years, and often decades, before the warring parties made peace with each other. Enormous carnage occurred during communal conflicts, and millions of people died. Terrorism on a massive scale was not uncommon. It was also during this period that high-profile acts of international terrorism became a familiar feature of the international political environment.

In the 1990s and 2000s, contending nations and communities continued to engage in significant violence. Terrorism and violent repression were used by many adversaries, who claimed them as necessary methodologies to resolve the problems of their political environments. This trend is unlikely to abate in the near future, and it is reasonable to project that some conflicts may increase in intensity.

The following cases are projected sources and targets of terrorist violence in the near future.

The Middle East

The 2011 Arab Spring demonstrations revealed widespread popular dissatisfaction with longstanding authoritarian regimes. Whether such dissatisfaction will produce long-term stability is an open question because several of the uprisings led to chronic discord, primarily in Syria, Libya, and Egypt. Political, religious, and ethno-nationalist conflicts have been endemic to the Middle East for decades and will continue for the near future. Many of these conflicts are longstanding and seemingly intractable, at least for the short term. Fundamentalist movements have also captured the imaginations of the many young Arabs disenchanted with the perceived failures of Arab nationalism and socialism. Large numbers of foreign fighters found their call to action after the U.S.-led invasion of Iraq and rallied to the side of the Iraqi insurgents. As a result, many international targets were attacked throughout the Middle East, a trend that will likely continue. For example, in August 2003, Iraqi insurgents bombed the United Nations headquarters in Iraq, killing UN High Commissioner for Human Rights Sergio Vieira de Mello. Religious tensions between Shi'a and Sunni Muslims also increased after sectarian violence erupted in Iraq. At the same time, Al Qaeda morphed into a model for other Islamists, a phenomenon that is likely to continue to be replicated by other movements and cells. In a sense, the organization of Al Qaeda became an ideology of Al Qaeda. Al Qaeda's evolution engendered new Islamist movements and organizations that proved to be extremely proficient in recruiting dedicated fighters, funding their cause, and effectively waging war. ISIS, Boko Haram, and others are typical of this new generation of Islamist insurgencies.

Palestine and Israel

Palestinian nationalism entered its second generation during the intifada. The intifada also became a war fought by young gunmen, terrorists, and suicide bombers who grew up amid the turmoil of the 1960s, 1970s, and 1980s. Black September, the Palestine Liberation Organization's expulsion from Lebanon, the airline hijackings, and many other incidents occurred when members of the new generation were children and teenagers. The new generation unhesitatingly began a new round of violence against Israel, one that was to prove more lethal and more pervasive.

Latin America

Most of the communal and ideological conflicts in Central and South America were resolved by the late 1990s. Violent leftist dissidents and repressive rightist regimes were no longer prominent features of the Latin American political environment. Some conflicts remained unresolved in the early 2000s, however. The worst scenario for near-term terrorism is in Colombia, where a weak central government has long exercised minimal control over a society beset by leftist rebels, rightist paramilitaries, and unchecked *narcotraficantes*. Aside from this and a few pockets of political violence, near-term indigenous terrorist violence (as opposed to international threats) will likely be sporadic and less intense than between the end of World War II and the early 1990s.

Europe

International terrorists have long used Europe as a battleground, as proved by the attacks in Madrid, Spain, on March 11, 2004, and in London, England, on July 7, 2005. This is unlikely to change, particularly in light of the discovery of Islamist cells and arrests of suspected Al Qaeda operatives in several Western European countries.

Domestically, there is a possibility that followers of neofascist movements may target immigrant workers or other people they define as undesirables. There are also pockets of ethnonationalist conflict that linger in Spain and the United Kingdom, though the likelihood that these conflicts will escalate is almost zero. The Balkans remains the most unstable region in Europe, and sporadic violence is likely to occur there from time to time. However, the large-scale communal conflicts and genocidal behavior that resulted from the breakup of Yugoslavia have been suppressed by the North Atlantic Treaty Organization (NATO) and UN intervention. Russia's conflict in Chechnya will continue to be a source of terrorism as well as a possible source of radical Islamist activism.

Africa

Ethno-nationalist communal conflict has long been a recurring feature in Africa. In East Africa, periodic outbreaks of violence have claimed hundreds of thousands of lives. Similar outbreaks have occurred in West Africa. Another pattern of conflict in sub-Saharan Africa has been the use of state-sponsored domestic terrorism by authoritarian regimes to suppress dissident ethnonationalist and political sentiment. Some internal conflicts—such as in Sudan, Somalia, Liberia, and Sierra Leone—are likely to flare up periodically in the near future. These conflicts have been characterized by many examples of terrorism on a large scale. In North Africa, radical Islamist movements have proven themselves motivated to commit acts of terrorism, and they are very capable of doing so. Algerian, Moroccan, and Egyptian affiliates of Al Qaeda, ISIS, and other fundamentalist movements have attacked foreign interests, religious sites, and government officials as part of a vaguely defined international jihad. Armed Islamist movements such as Boko Haram in Nigeria provide a particularly troublesome model for future Islamist insurgencies.

Asia

Established patterns of ethno-nationalist conflict and domestic terrorism suggest that some Asian nations and regions will continue to experience outbreaks of political violence. These outbreaks are likely to range from small-scale attacks to large-scale conflicts. Ethno-nationalist groups continue to wage war in Sri Lanka, Kashmir, the Caucasus, and elsewhere. Terrorism is an accepted method of armed conflict among many of these groups. Ideological rebellions are less common than during the post–World War II era, but pockets of Marxist rebellion are still to be found, in Nepal and the Philippines, for example. These leftist remnants have occasionally used terrorist tactics rather effectively. Radical Islamic movements, inspired in part by Al Qaeda and ISIS internationalism, have appeared in several Asian countries, including Indonesia, the Philippines, Malaysia, India, Pakistan, and the Central Asian republics. Some of these movements have demonstrated their willingness to engage in terrorism.

Case: The United States and the West

During the Cold War, the United States and its Western allies were frequent targets of leftist terrorism. In the modern era, the United States and the West have become targets of the New Terrorism. International terrorists still associate them with international exploitation but add other dimensions to the new environment, such as fundamentalist religion, anti-Semitism, and a willingness to use new technologies and weapons of mass destruction. Symbolic targets—embassies, military installations, religious sites, tourists, and business visitors to foreign countries—have been attacked worldwide. Table 12.2 summarizes several examples of ongoing conflict likely to result in terrorist violence in the near future.

Table 12.2 A World Still in Conflict: Projected Sources of Political Violence

Regional and domestic conflicts are certain to engender terrorist movements in the near future. Some of these conflicts are long-term disputes that have been ongoing for decades and that are often characterized by international spillovers.

This table summarizes several long-term conflicts that have increased and diminished in scale and intensity during decades of confrontation.

Conflict	Opposing Parties	Activity Profile	
		Contending Issues	Duration
Palestinians/Israelis	Palestinian nationalists, Palestinian fundamentalists, Israelis	Palestinian state, Israeli security	Decades, from late 1940s and Israeli independence
Northern Ireland	Catholic Unionists, Protestant Loyalists, British administration	Union with Irish Republic, loyalty to United Kingdom	Decades, from late 1960s and first Provo campaign
India/Pakistan	Kashmiri jihadis, India, Pakistan	Status of Kashmir, jihadi terrorism, border disputes	Decades, from late 1940s and end of British Empire
Colombia	Marxist rebels, narcotraficantes, paramilitaries, Colombian government	Social revolution, drug trade, state authority	Decades, from 1960s
Stateless New Terrorism	Internationalist terrorists, targeted interests	Vague goals, international stability	New model, from 1990s

▶ The aftermath of a vehicular bomb in Beirut, Lebanon.

High-Tech Terrorism

New technologies allow terrorists to communicate efficiently, broaden their message, and wield unconventional weapons in unexpected ways—all central characteristics of asymmetrical warfare. Because of incremental improvements in communications and computer technologies, it is reasonable to conclude that the trend among terrorists and their supporters will be to use them extensively. This is also true of the increasing availability of weapons components for weapons of mass destruction as well as the continuing softening of terrorists' reluctance to use them.

Information Technologies

The Internet and social media provide opportunities for commercial, private, and political interests to spread their message and communicate with outsiders. The use of the Internet and social media by extremists has already become a common feature of the modern era. Information technologies are being invented and refined constantly and will continue to be central to the New Terrorism. These technologies facilitate networking between groups and cells and permit propaganda to be spread widely and efficiently. The Internet and other communications technologies are certain to be used to send instructions about overall goals, specific tactics, new bomb-making techniques, and other facets of the terrorist trade. Both overt and covert information networks permit widely dispersed cells to exist and communicate covertly.

Information and computer technologies, of course, can also be used offensively. It is quite possible, even probable, that extremists will adopt cyberwar techniques to try to destroy information and communications systems. **Cyberterrorism** may very well become a central facet of the terrorist environment in the near future.

Weapons of Mass Destruction

The scenario of terrorists acquiring **weapons of mass destruction** is no longer the stuff of novels and films. The possibility that terrorists may use such weapons on a previously unimaginable scale is very real indeed.

Terrorists are not without incentives to construct and use weapons of mass destruction in lieu of conventional weapons. The psychological and economic impact of such devices, for example, can easily outweigh the destructive effect of the initial attack (which might be relatively small).

Experts have argued that terrorists are making concerted efforts to acquire the requisite components to develop weapons of mass destruction and that their doing so is probably just a matter of time. Terrorists who are motivated by race or religion (or both) are likely to have little compunction about using chemical, biological, or radiological weapons against what they define as subhumans or nonbelievers.

As an alternative to producing weapons of mass destruction, terrorists have demonstrated their ability to convert available technologies into high-yield weapons. The destructive and psychological consequences of such potential have not been lost on modern terrorists. Passenger airliners, to take the most obvious example, were used effectively indeed as ballistic missiles in the September 11 attacks. In another case, a precursor to 9/11, elite French GIGN counterterrorist police thwarted Algerian terrorists from using an airliner as a missile over Paris in December 1994.

Case: Exotic Technologies

Some technologies can theoretically be converted into weapons by terrorists who have a high degree of scientific knowledge and training. These exotic technologies include the following:

Electromagnetic Pulse Technologies. **Electromagnetic pulse (EMP) technologies** use an electromagnetic burst from a generator that can disable electronic components such as microchips. If used on a sizable scale, EMP could destroy large quantities of military or financial information. High-energy radio frequency devices are another type of generator that can disable electronic components.

Plastics. Weapons constructed from plastics and other materials such as ceramics could possibly thwart detection from metal detectors. Handguns, rifles, and bullets can be constructed of these materials.

Liquid Metal Embrittlement. Some chemicals can theoretically weaken metals when applied. They can embrittle, or make rigid, various metals. Were motivated extremists to obtain **liquid metal embrittlement** technology, they would find it relatively easy to transport and could conceivably apply it to commercial vehicles and aircraft.

Tech Terror: Feasibility and Likelihood

The feasibility of terrorists' acquiring and using emerging technologies must be calculated by addressing the availability of these technologies. This has occurred in part because the scientific knowledge needed for assembling these weapons is available from a number of sources, including the Internet. Some weapons assembly requires expertise but not necessarily extensive scientific training. Radiological weapons, for example, are relatively unsophisticated devices and require only toxic radioactive materials and a dispersion device. Other devices, such as nuclear weapons components, have so far been exceedingly difficult to assemble or steal. Nevertheless, the feasibility of obtaining weapons of mass destruction has increased not only because of the dissemination of technical know-how but also because terrorists do not necessarily need to acquire new or exotic technologies. Older technologies and materials—such as pesticides, carbon monoxide, and ammonium nitrate and fuel oil (ANFO)—can be used to construct high-yield weapons. Aerosols and other devices can also be used as relatively unsophisticated delivery systems.

The likelihood that new technologies will be acquired and used is moot: Many have already been acquired and used. For example, apparently apolitical and anarchistic hackers—some of them teenagers—have vandalized information and communications systems, demonstrating that cyberwar is no longer an abstract concept. There is little reason to presume that this trend will diminish and many good reasons to presume that it will increase. The increasing availability of new technologies, when combined with the motivations and morality of the New Terrorism, suggests very strongly that technology will be an increasingly potent weapon in terrorist arsenals.

Soft Targets and Terrorist Symbolism

Terrorists throughout the post–World War II era tended to select targets that were both symbolic and soft. Soft targets include civilians and passive military figures, both unlikely to offer resistance until after the terrorists have inflicted casualties or other destruction. Attacks against soft targets were sometimes quite effective in the short term and occasionally forced concessions from interests symbolized by these targets. Those who practice New Terrorism have regularly selected soft targets that symbolize enemy interests. These targets are chosen in part because of their symbolic value but also because they are likely to result in significant casualties. Suicide bombers have become particularly adept at maximizing casualties. Thus, regardless of terrorist motives or environments, it is highly likely that violent extremists will continue to attack passive symbolic targets.

▶ Pakistani demonstrators burn U.S. flags.

The Future of International Terrorism in the United States

With the turn of the 21st century, it has become very clear that the near future of international terrorism in the United States will be considerably threatening. Trends suggest that the United States will be a preferred target for international terrorists both domestically and abroad. This is not a new phenomenon. What is new is that the American homeland is vulnerable to attack for the first time in its history. International terrorism on U.S. soil is also not new. Many of these incidents were discussed in other chapters. The asymmetrical nature of the New Terrorism and the destructive magnitude of newly obtainable weapons and technology, however, are unlike any previous threats.

The Future of the Violent Left in the United States

Single-issue extremism is certain to be a feature of the radical left. Radical environmentalists have attracted a small but loyal constituency. New movements have also shown themselves adept at attracting new followers. For example, a nascent anarchist movement has taken root in the United States and other Western democracies. This movement is loosely rooted in an anti-globalist ideology that opposes alleged exploitation by prosperous nations of poorer nations in the new global economy. It remains to be seen whether violent tendencies will develop within this trend. Sporadic incidents from single-issue terrorists are likely to occur from time to time.

The Future of the Violent Right in the United States

The future of the politically violent right lies in a possible weak network–weak sponsor scenario. In advocating leaderless resistance, for example, the violent Patriot and neo-Nazi right proved that they had learned from the 1980s and terrorist groups such as the Order. Conspiracies uncovered by law enforcement authorities beginning in the mid-1990s thus exhibited a covert and cell-based organizational philosophy. Threats are also possible from religious extremists who might reinvigorate the violent moralist movement. An extremist pool also lingers within the Patriot and neo-Confederate movements, as well as newer movements such as the white nationalist and alt-right movements. Antigovernment and racial conspiracy theories continue to proliferate. Publications such as *The Turner Diaries*[3] and *The Myth of the Six Million*[4] continue to spread racial and anti-Semitic extremism. Promulgating these theories keeps reactionary tendencies alive on the right.

REVISITING THE WAR ON TERRORISM

Counterterrorist experts in the modern terrorist era will be required to concentrate on achieving several traditional objectives. These can realistically, and in a practical sense, only minimize the terrorist threats of the near future, not eliminate them. Objectives include the following:

- disrupting and preventing terrorist conspiracies from operationalizing their plans
- deterring would-be terrorist cadres from crossing the line between extremist activism and political violence

- implementing formal and informal international treaties, laws, and task forces to create a cooperative counterterrorist environment

- minimizing physical destruction and human casualties

It is clear that no single model or method for controlling terrorism will apply across timelines or environments. Because of this reality, projecting counterterrorist models must include a longitudinal framework based on theory and practical necessity. The models used in the near future will continue to reflect the same categories of responses of the recent past, such as the use of force, operations other than war, and legalistic measures. To be practicable, however, these models will have to be updated and adapted to emerging threats continually. If they are, perhaps terrorism will be controlled to some degree—by keeping dissident terrorists off balance and state terrorists isolated, thereby preventing them from having an unobstructed hand in planning and carrying out attacks or other political violence.

A Theoretical Model for Ending Terrorist Campaigns

In her seminal publication, *How Terrorism Ends: Understanding the Decline and Demise of Terrorist Campaigns*,[5] Professor Audrey Kurth Cronin explicated a theoretical model for evaluating why terrorist campaigns end. Analyzing the history of terrorism, Professor Cronin identified six patterns commonly found in the decline and ending of terrorist campaigns:

- *Decapitation*. Capturing or killing the movement's leader.

- *Negotiations*. Integrating the extremist movement into a legitimate political process.

- *Success*. When the movement achieves its goals, and thereby its definition of success.

- *Failure*. Group implosion because of mistakes, burnout, or collapse; or marginalization, when the group loses popular support.

- *Repression*. Defeat of the movement with force.

- *Reorientation*. The transitioning of a movement from terrorism to another form of violence.

Professor Cronin concluded that, historically, terrorist campaigns end when they undergo one or more of the foregoing patterns. Assuming the applicability of her model, it poses important analytical considerations for the ongoing conceptualization of counterterrorist policies—not the least of which is how counterterrorist policies may be designed to hasten the demise of Al Qaeda, ISIS, and other movements by triggering one or more of these patterns.

Government Responses

Assuming that policy makers grasp the limitations of relying exclusively on coercive methods, it is likely that they will develop alternative measures. Operations other than war include conciliatory options, which may provide long-term solutions to future extremism. Conciliatory options of the past—such as peace processes, negotiations, and social reforms—did have some success in resolving both immediate and longstanding terrorist crises. If skillfully applied, future adaptations of such options could help avoid political violence. In the past, these options were usually undertaken with the presumption that some degree of coercion would be kept available should the conciliatory options fail. This is a pragmatic consideration that is likely to continue.

Societal Responses

Because extremism has historically originated primarily from domestic conflict (though sometimes from national traumas such as invasion), it is important that future efforts to counter extremist ideas incorporate societal and cultural responses. It is also important that new societal and cultural norms reflect demographic changes and political shifts. As discussed in previous chapters, dissent can certainly be repressed, but repression is rarely a long-term solution absent social reforms and political inclusion. This in turn is an ideal more likely to succeed in democratic systems than under authoritarian regimes.

Societal responses must, of course, be adapted to the idiosyncrasies of each nation and region. This is difficult in many cases—and seemingly nothing more than impossibly idealistic in others—because many if not most regimes and contending groups have little interest in reducing social tensions. More often than not, they simply try to manipulate such tensions to their benefit.

Countering Extremism

Extremist ideologies and beliefs are the fertile soil for politically violent behavior. Ethnocentrism, nationalism, ideological intolerance, racism, and religious fanaticism are core motivations for terrorism. History has shown that coercive measures used to counter these tendencies are often only marginally successful. The reason is uncomplicated: A great deal of extremist behavior is rooted in passionate ideas, long histories of conflict, and codes of self-sacrifice (explored in Chapter 3). It is difficult to forcibly reverse these tendencies, and although coercion can eliminate cadres and destroy extremist organizations, sheer repression is a risky long-term solution.

New Fronts in a New War

One projection for near-term counterterrorism stands out: Models must be flexible enough to respond to new environments and must avoid stubborn reliance on methods that "fight the last war." This reality is particularly pertinent to the war against terrorism. It, unlike previous wars, was declared against behavior as much as against terrorist groups and revolutionary cadres. The fronts in the new war are amorphous and include the following:

U.S. Department of Defense

▶ The war on terrorism continues.

Covert shadow wars are fought outside public scrutiny using unconventional methods. **Shadow wars** require deploying military, paramilitary, and coercive covert assets to far regions of the world.

Domestic (homeland) security measures are required to harden targets, deter attacks, and thwart conspiracies. Internal security requires the extensive use of nonmilitary security personnel, such as customs officials, law enforcement agencies, and immigration authorities.

Counterterrorist financial operations are directed against bank accounts, private foundations, businesses, and other potential sources of revenue for terrorist networks. Intelligence agencies can certainly hack into financial databases, but a broad-based coalition of government and private financial institutions is necessary for this task.

Global surveillance of communications technologies requires tracking telephones, cell phones, browser traffic, and e-mail. Agencies specializing in electronic surveillance, such as the National Security Agency (NSA) in the United States, are the most capable institutions to carry out this mission.

Identifying and disrupting transnational terrorist cells and support networks requires international cooperation to track extremist operatives and "connect the dots" on a global scale. Primary responsibility for this task lies with intelligence communities and law enforcement agencies.

The new fronts in the new war clearly highlight the need to continuously upgrade physical, organizational, and operational counterterrorist measures; flexibility and creativity are essential. Failure in any regard will hinder adaptation to the terrorist environment of the 21st century. The inability to control and redress longstanding bureaucratic and international rivalries, to take one example, could be disastrous.

Continued Utility of Force

Violent coercion will continue to be a viable counterterrorist option. Terrorist cells, especially in disputed regions where they enjoy popular support, cannot be dismantled solely with law enforcement, intelligence, or nonmilitary assets. Situations sometimes require a warlike response with military assets, from small special operations units to large deployments of significant air, naval, and ground forces. Traditional military force has a demonstrated record against terrorist efforts that is relevant to coercive counterterrorist policies in the near future.

History has shown, of course, that military and paramilitary operations are not always successful. As discussed in previous chapters, some of these operations have ended in disaster. Others have been marginally successful. It is therefore likely that future use of force will likewise fail on occasion. Nevertheless, the past utility of this option and its symbolic value are certain to encourage its continued use. Absent a viable threat of force, states are highly unlikely to dissuade committed revolutionaries or aggressive states from acts of political violence.

Countering Terrorist Financial Operations

Mohammed Atta, the leader of the September 11 cell, was closely affiliated with Al Qaeda members in several countries. He apparently received wire transfers of money in Florida from operatives in Egypt and was in close contact with Syrians who managed financial resources in Hamburg, Germany.[6] Estimates suggest that the total cost of the 9/11 attack was $300,000, a small sum for the destruction and disruption that resulted.[7] Very few if any of these funds came from state sponsors. They instead came from private accounts run by Al Qaeda operatives. It is very clear from the Atta example that Al Qaeda and, logically, other practitioners of the New Terrorism have successfully established themselves as stateless revolutionaries. This profile is unlikely to change in the near future.

Finding Hidden Fortunes

Terrorists and their extremist supporters have amassed sizable funds from a variety of sources, including the following:

- transnational crime—the trafficking and smuggling activities of Colombian and Sri Lankan groups, for example

- personal fortunes—such as Osama bin Laden's personal financial resources

- extortion—for example, the criminal profits of Abu Sayyaf

- private charities and foundations—such as those that support Hezbollah and HAMAS[8]

Large portions of these assets were deposited in anonymous bank accounts, enabling funds to be electronically transferred between banking institutions and other accounts internationally in minutes. During the months following the September 11 attacks, government agencies from a number of countries made a concerted effort to identify and trace the terrorists' banking accounts. Law enforcement and security agencies also began to closely scrutinize the activities of private charities and foundations in an attempt to determine whether they were front groups secretly funneling money to supporters of terrorist organizations.

One problem encountered on a global scale involved the tradition and policy of **customer anonymity** found in some banking systems, such as those of the Cayman Islands and Switzerland. Many mainstream executives and policy makers were very hesitant to endorse an abrogation of the sanctity of customer anonymity. Their rationale was straightforward: Individual privacy and liberty could be jeopardized if security officers were permitted to peruse the details of hundreds of thousands of bank accounts looking for a few terrorist accounts that might or might not exist. From a practical business perspective, customers were likely to reconsider doing business with financial institutions that could no longer guarantee their anonymity.

A Resilient Adversary

Terrorists have adapted quickly to the new focus on financial counterterrorist measures. Implementing a process that apparently began during the global crackdown after September 11, 2001, terrorists and their supporters removed assets from financial institutions and began investing in valuable commodities such as gold, diamonds, and other precious metals and gems.[9] From the counterterrorist's perspective, this tactic might cripple the global effort to electronically monitor, track, and disrupt terrorist finances. From the terrorist's perspective, the chief encumbrance is the literal burden of transporting precious commodities. Such an encumbrance, however, is acceptable in light of the difficulty for counterterrorist agents in identifying and interdicting couriers or to locate and raid repositories. It is thus likely that this adaptation will continue to be made as circumstances require, perhaps making it virtually impossible to trace skillfully hidden terrorist assets.

Another adaptation is an ancient practice known as hawala, a transnational system of brokers who know and trust each other. Persons wishing to transfer money approach hawala brokers and, for a fee, ask the broker to transfer money to another person. Using the name and location of the recipient, the initial broker will contact a broker in the recipient's country. The recipient contacts the local broker, who delivers the money. To prevent fraud, the sending broker gives the recipient broker a code number (such as the string of numbers on a $20 bill). The recipient (who receives the code from the sender) must give the broker this code number before picking up the funds. No records are kept of the transaction, thus ensuring anonymity. It is a useful system because it relies on honor to succeed and money is never physically moved.

Counterterrorist Surveillance Technologies

It is technologically feasible to access virtually every private electronic transaction, including telephone records and conversations, computer transactions and communications (such as e-mail), and credit card records. Digital fingerprinting and facial imaging permit security agencies to access records virtually instantaneously. Because these technologies are inherently intrusive, they have been questioned by political leaders and civil libertarian organizations. Nevertheless, surveillance technologies are considered invaluable counterterrorist instruments.

Case: Carnivore (DCS-1000)

In July 2000, it was widely reported that the Federal Bureau of Investigation (FBI) had a surveillance system that could monitor Internet communications. Called Carnivore, the system was said to be able to read Internet traffic moving through cooperating Internet service providers. All that was required was for Carnivore to be installed on an Internet provider's network at the provider's facilities. Under law, the FBI could not use Carnivore without a specific court order under specific guidelines, much like other criminal surveillance orders.

The FBI received a great deal of negative publicity, especially after it was reported that the agency had evaded demands for documents under a Freedom of Information Act (FOIA) request filed by the Electronic Privacy Information Center (EPIC), a privacy rights group.[10] Concern was also raised by critics when it was reported in November 2000 that Carnivore had been successfully tested and exceeded expectations. This report was not entirely accurate. In fact, Carnivore did not operate properly when it was used in March 2000 to monitor a criminal suspect's e-mail; it had inadvertently intercepted the e-mail of innocent Internet users. This glitch embarrassed the Department of Justice (DOJ) and angered the DOJ's Office of Intelligence Policy and Review.

By early 2001, the FBI gave Carnivore a less ominous-sounding new name, redesignating the system DCS-1000. Despite the political row, which continued well into 2002, in part because of the continued FOIA litigation, Carnivore was cited as a potentially powerful tool in the new war on terrorism. The use of DCS-1000 after 2003 was apparently reduced markedly, allegedly because Internet surveillance was outsourced to private companies.

Case: Echelon

In the United States, the NSA manages a satellite surveillance network called Echelon, apparently in cooperation with NSA counterparts in Australia, Canada, Great Britain, and New Zealand. Its purpose is to monitor voice and data communications.

A kind of global wiretap that filters through communications using antennae, satellite, and other technologies, Echelon can reportedly intercept Internet transfers, telephone conversations, and data transmissions. It is not publicly known how much traffic can be intercepted or how it is done, but the network is apparently very capable.

The Case for International Cooperation

Cooperation between nations has always been essential to counterterrorist operations. International treaties, laws, and informal agreements were enacted during the post–World War II era to create a semblance of formality and consistency to global counterterrorist efforts. However, cooperation at the operational level was not always consistent or mutually beneficial. With the advent of the New Terrorism and international counterterrorist warfare, international cooperation at the operational level has become a priority for policy makers. A good example is the new frontline missions of intelligence and criminal justice agencies.

Intelligence and Law Enforcement

The world's intelligence communities and criminal justice systems have always been important counterterrorist instruments. After the September 11 attacks, these institutions were tasked with increased responsibilities—largely because of their demonstrated ability to incapacitate and punish terrorists. These institutions, perhaps more than military institutions, are also able to apply steady and long-term pressure on terrorist networks. They are in many cases more adept than military assets at keeping terrorists on the run over time. This is not to say that they are a panacea for future terrorism, but international cooperation between intelligence and law enforcement agencies does provide the means to track operatives, identify networks, and interdict other assets on a global scale.

International law enforcement cooperation in particular provides worldwide access to extensive criminal justice systems and their well-established **terminal institutions** (such as prisons). Such institutions—under the jurisdiction of criminal justice and military justice systems—can house individual terrorists after they have been captured, prosecuted, and convicted. These institutions can also effectively end terrorist careers. When faced with the prospect of lifelong incarceration, terrorists are also likely to be willing, for example, to exchange favors for intelligence. In a cooperative environment, of course, such data may be or would be shared among allied governments.

DISCUSSION BOX

TOWARD BIG BROTHER?

This chapter's Discussion Box is intended to stimulate critical debate about the possible use, by democracies and authoritarian regimes, of antiterrorist technologies to engage in surveillance.

Electronic surveillance has become a controversial practice in the United States and elsewhere. The fear is that civil liberties can be jeopardized by unregulated interception of telephone conversations, e-mail, and fax transmissions. Detractors argue that government use of these technologies can conceivably move well beyond legitimate application against threats from crime, espionage, and terrorism. Absent strict protocols to rein in these technologies, a worst-case scenario envisions state intrusions into the everyday activities of innocent civilians. Should this happen, critics foresee a time when privacy, liberty, and personal security become values of the past.

Discussion Questions

1. How serious is the threat from abuses in the use of new technologies?

2. How should new technologies be regulated? Can they be regulated?

3. Is it sometimes necessary to sacrifice a few freedoms to protect national security and to ensure the long-term viability of civil liberty?

4. Should the same protocols be used for domestic electronic surveillance and foreign surveillance? Why?

5. What is the likelihood that new surveillance technologies will be used as tools of repression by authoritarian regimes in the near future?

CHAPTER SUMMARY

This chapter explored trends that suggest the near-term future of terrorism. An underlying theme throughout this discussion was that the near future will reflect the emerging profile of the New Terrorism. Traditional terrorism is certainly still a factor but is no longer an exclusive or predominant model. These trends can be analyzed within the context of previous terrorist environments, with the caveat that these will continue to adapt to emerging political environments. The near future of terrorism will be shaped by ongoing regional conflicts, new technologies, and renewed attacks against symbolic soft targets.

Counterterrorism in the post–September 11 era will have to adapt to new fronts. These fronts require creative use of overt and covert operations, homeland security measures, intelligence, and cooperation among counterterrorist agencies. Disruption of terrorist financial operations will prove one of the most important and challenging priorities in the new war. Most threats in the near future for the United States will come from international religious extremists, domestic rightists, and single-issue leftists. Because of revelations about bureaucratic inefficiency in the aftermath of the September 11 attacks, the United States implemented a restructuring of its homeland security community.

KEY TERMS AND CONCEPTS

The following topics were discussed in this chapter and can be found in the Glossary:

Carnivore 275

Customer anonymity 274

Cyberterrorism 268

DCS-1000 275

Echelon 275

Electromagnetic pulse (EMP)
technologies 269

Liquid metal embrittlement 269

Narcotraficantes 266

Shadow wars 272

Stateless revolutionaries 262

Terminal institutions 276

Weapons of mass
destruction 268

RECOMMENDED READINGS

The following publications project challenges facing the world community in the present and in the near future.

Heiberg, M., O'Leary, P., & Tirman, J. (Eds.). (2007). *Terror, insurgency, and the state: Ending protracted conflicts*. Philadelphia: University of Pennsylvania Press.

Holmes, J. S. (2008). *Terrorism and democratic stability revisited*. Manchester, UK: Manchester University Press.

Weimann, G. (2015). *Terrorism in cyberspace: The next generation*. New York, NY: Columbia University Press.

The following publications are an eclectic assortment of recommendations that provide classic—and arguably timeless— insight into the nature of dissident resistance, ideologies of liberty, state manipulation, and revolution.

Hamilton, A., Jay, J., & Madison, J. (1937). *The Federalist: A commentary on the Constitution of the United States*. New York, NY: Modern Library.

Koestler, A. (1963). *Darkness at noon*. New York, NY: Macmillan.

Mill, J. S. (1975). *On liberty* (D. Spitz, Ed.). New York, NY: Norton.

Moore, B., Jr. (1966). *Social origins of dictatorship and democracy: Lord and peasant in the making of the modern world*. Boston, MA: Beacon.

Orwell, G. (1946). *Animal farm*. New York, NY: Harcourt Brace Jovanovich.

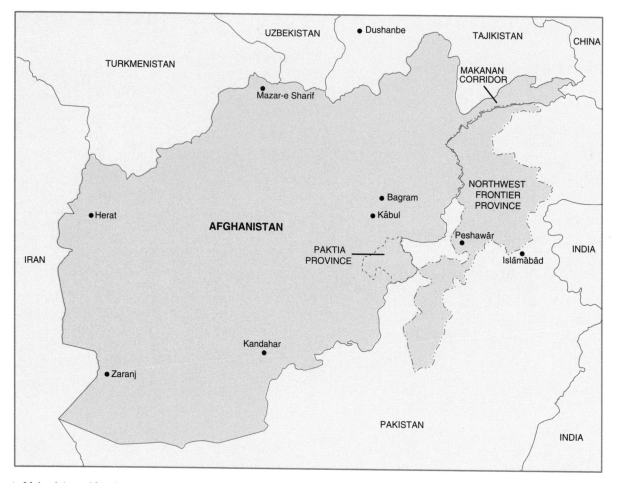

▶ **Afghanistan.** After the invasion of the country by the Soviet Union, a jihad was waged to drive out the Soviet Army. Muslims from throughout the world joined the fight, forming prototypical revolutionary movements that culminated in the creation of organizations such as Al Qaeda. Following the war against the Soviets, the Taliban seized control in most of the country. Intervention by the United States and NATO began a new phase in which the coalition and new Afghan government vied with the Taliban for control of the country. Al Qaeda remained active in the region bordered by Pakistan's Northwest Frontier province and along the border in Afghanistan's Paktia region.

▶ **Africa.** Africa has been home to many terrorist typologies. For example, Libya practiced state terrorism as foreign policy, and the apartheid government in South Africa practiced state terrorism as domestic policy. Religious dissident terrorism occurred in Algeria. Communal terrorism broke out in Rwanda, Somalia, Liberia, and Sierra Leone after the breakdown of government authority. International terrorist attacks occurred in Kenya, Tanzania, and elsewhere.

▶ **Central America and the Caribbean.** Most terrorist violence originated in Cold War proxy conflicts and was waged by rebels, paramilitaries, and state security forces. Civil wars in El Salvador and Guatemala were markedly brutal, as was the Contra insurgency in Nicaragua. The Zapatista insurgency in Mexico championed Chiapas Indians. Cuba was an active partner with the Soviet Union, fomenting and participating in conflicts in Africa and Latin America. The American base at Guantánamo Bay, Cuba, became the primary venue of detention by the United States of suspected members of Islamic terrorist groups.

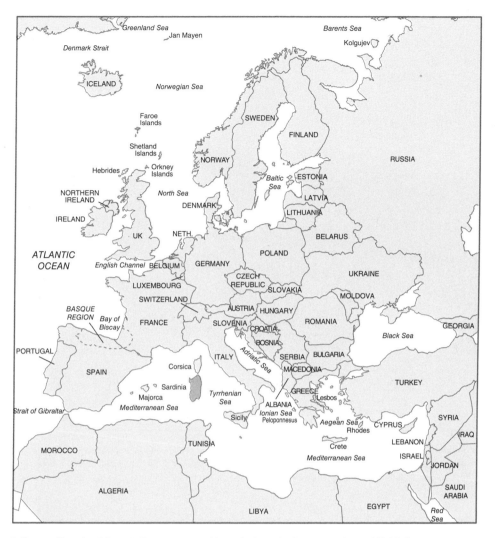

▶ **Europe.** Terrorist violence in Europe originated from ideological, ethno-nationalist, and Middle Eastern sources. The Balkans, Northern Ireland, and the Basque region of Spain have been sources of ethno-nationalist terrorism. Ideological terrorism peaked in Germany and Italy during the 1970s, while Middle Eastern spillovers continued into the 21st century.

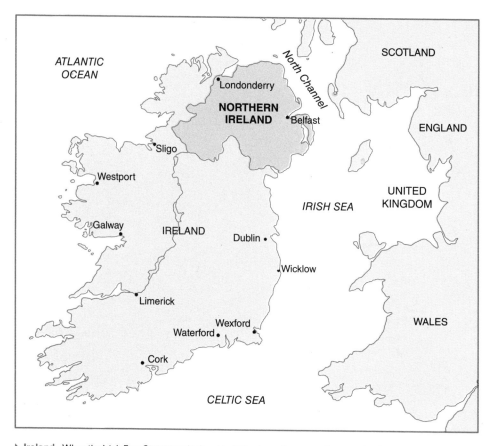

▶ **Ireland.** When the Irish Free State was declared in 1921, six northern counties remained under British Rule. The modern politics of these counties, known as Northern Ireland, were marked by violent conflict between Protestant unionists and Catholic nationalists. This conflict was termed the Troubles.

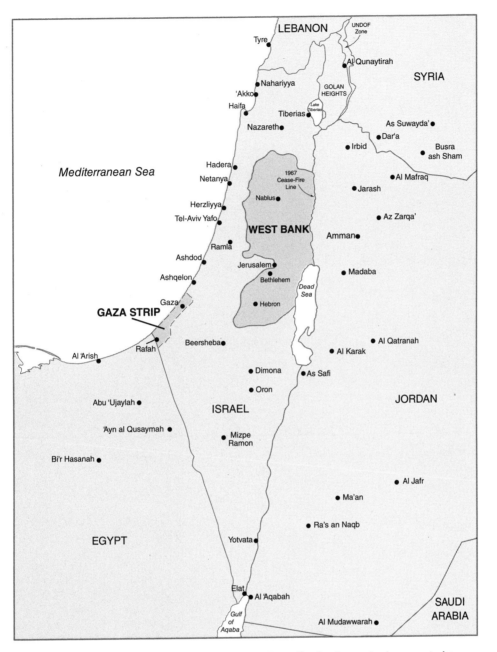

▶ **Israel, the West Bank, and Gaza.** Although a geographically small region, the area has been a center for communal and religious conflict that has frequently spilled over into the international domain and brought nations to the brink of war.

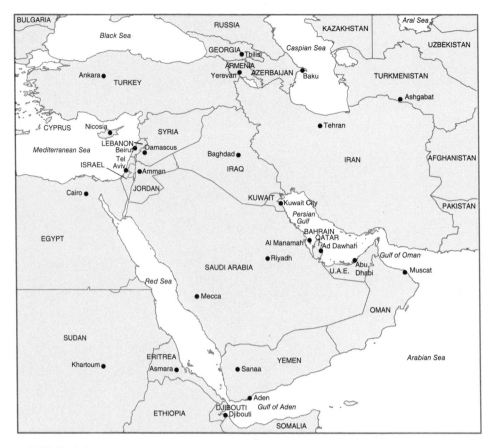

▶ **Middle East.** Religious, ethno-nationalist, and state terrorism have occurred frequently.

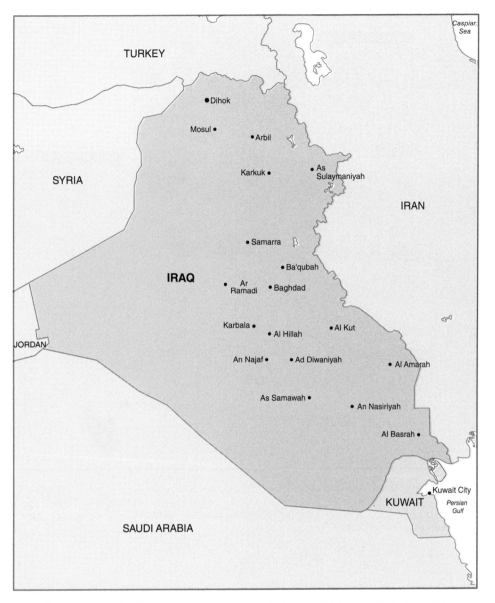

▶ **Iraq.** The regime of Saddam Hussein used terror as a regular instrument of state policy. During the Anfal campaign against ethnic Kurds in northern Iraq, the Iraqi army used chemical weapons against civilians. Iraq also invaded Iran and Kuwait and provided safe haven for secular terrorist operatives. However, the 2003 invasion of Iraq discovered no arsenals of weapons of mass destruction and no links to international Islamist terrorist networks such as Al Qaeda.

▶ **Distribution of Ethno-religious Groups in Iraq.** Iraq is a diverse nation of several ethnicities and faiths. Although the predominant groups are Shi'a and Sunni Arabs, there are also sizable populations of Kurdish, Turkoman, Assyrian, and Christian Iraqis. After the 2011 Arab Spring demonstrations in the region, Iraq became fragmented along religious and ethno-nationalist lines.

▶ **Syria.** The al-Assad regime has used terror as a regular instrument of state policy, first under the father Hafez, and then under his son Bashar. During the civil war that ensued after the 2011 Arab Spring, Syrian government forces used barrel bombs and chemical weapons against civilians and engaged in widespread human rights violations. The antigovernment insurgency included Islamist factions such as the pro–Al-Qa'ida Al Nusra Front (renamed Jabhat Fateh al-Sham in 2016). It also led to the rise of the independent Islamic State of Iraq and the Levant, which became a viable movement in both Syria and Iraq. The Assad regime demonstrated significant resilience, with active support from Russia and Iran.

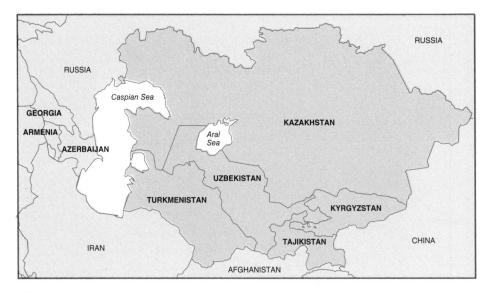

▶ **Central Asia.** The five countries of Central Asia gained their independence after the collapse of the Soviet Union. The region is predominantly Muslim. It became an important focus during the U.S.-led war on terrorism.

▶ **The Caucasus.** Strong nationalist sentiment grew in the Caucasus with the collapse of the Soviet Union, leading to ethnonationalist violence in regions such as Nagorno-Karabakh. The war in Chechnya became particularly violent, often spilling across its borders. Chechen terrorist incidents in Russia were highly destructive.

▶ **Indian Subcontinent.** Several areas of confrontation resulted in terrorist violence. Conflicts in Sri Lanka, Kashmir, and Afghanistan have been particularly active, with ethnic and religious violence taking many thousands of lives.

▶ **Southeast Asia.** Terrorism has typically originated from ethno-nationalist, ideological, state, and religious sources. Significant cases of dissident and state conflict occurred during and after the Cold War era. Religious terrorism became prominent in the Philippines and Indonesia in the aftermath of the September 11, 2001, attacks. The killing fields of Cambodia are a special case of exceptional state-sponsored violence.

▶ **South America.** This continent has been a source for many case studies on terrorist environments. Cases include urban guerrillas in Montevideo and Buenos Aires; state repression in Chile, Argentina, and Uruguay; dissident terrorism in Peru; and criminal dissident terrorism in Colombia. The tri-border region became a center of suspected radical Islamist activism.

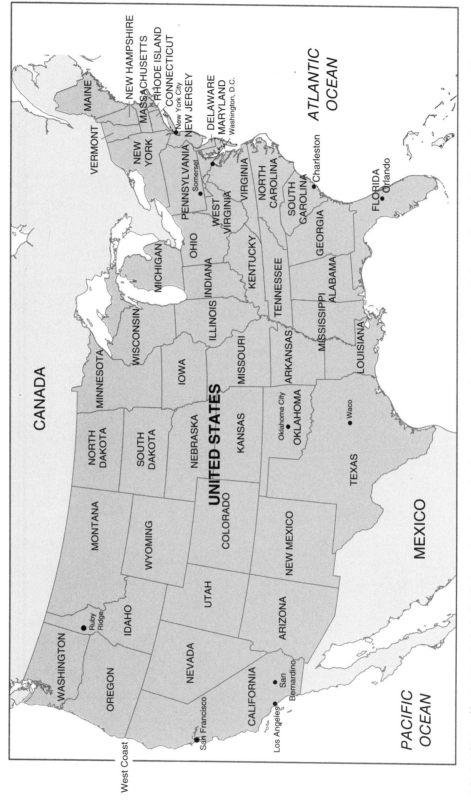

▲ **United States.** Most terrorism in the United States has been characterized by low-intensity violence in urban areas, with the exceptions of the Oklahoma City bombing and the September 11, 2001, attacks. Lone-wolf terrorism occurs periodically, usually motivated by racial and religious bias.

GLOSSARY

The glossary summarizes terms used in this textbook. Readers should refer to the glossary to refresh their knowledge of discussions and case studies explored in chapters, tables, and chapter perspectives.

1st Navy Parachute Infantry Regiment An elite French unit that is similar to the British Special Air Service and the American Delta Force. It deploys small intelligence and special operations squads that are trained to operate in desert, urban, and tropical environments. They are part of the core of French counterterrorist special operations forces.

11th Parachute Division (Paras) An elite French army unit that can deploy as a quick-reaction force to deal with terrorist threats.

75th Ranger Regiment An elite combat unit of the U.S. Army that can deploy large formations for counterterrorist missions.

Abbas, Abu The leader of the Palestine Liberation Front.

Absolute deprivation A sociological term that indicates the lack of basic human needs for survival.

Abu Hafs al-Masri Brigades An Al Qaeda–affiliated group that claimed responsibility for several significant terrorist attacks. These included the August 2003 bombing of the United Nations headquarters in Baghdad, Iraq, and the November 2003 bombings of two synagogues in Operation Death Trains.

Abu Nidal Organization (ANO) The designation given to Abu Nidal's movement.

Abu Sayyaf A Muslim insurgency on the island of Basilan in the Philippines; the group has ideological and other links to Al Qaeda. Founded by Abdurajak Janjalani, who was killed by Filipino police in 1998.

Achille Lauro A cruise ship that was hijacked by members of the Palestine Liberation Front. During the incident, the terrorists murdered a wheelchair-bound Jewish American.

Act of political will The notion that one can force change by an absolute commitment to a cause. All that is required is complete and uncompromising dedication to achieving one's goals.

Afghan Arabs A term given to foreign volunteers, mostly Arabs, who fought as mujahideen during the war against the occupation of Afghanistan by the Soviet Army.

African National Congress (ANC) The principal anti-apartheid movement in predemocracy South Africa.

Air France Flight 8969 An airliner hijacked in December 1994 by the Algerian Armed Islamic Group. After the hijackers killed three passengers, the plane was permitted to depart the Algerian airfield and made a refueling stop in Marseilles. Intending to fly to Paris, the hijackers demanded three times the amount of fuel needed to make the journey. The reason for this demand was that they planned to blow up the aircraft over Paris or possibly crash it into the Eiffel Tower. French commandos disguised as caterers stormed the plane in Marseilles, thus bringing the incident to an end.

AK-47 A durable assault rifle designed by Mikhail Kalashnikov in the Soviet Union in 1947. It became a common weapon among conventional and irregular forces around the world.

Al-Aqsa Martyr Brigades A Palestinian nationalist movement affiliated with the Palestine Liberation Organization. Noted for its use of suicide bombers, it has committed terrorist violence against Israelis.

Albigensian Crusade A Christian Crusade in southern France during the 13th century. Legend holds that concerns were raised about loyal and innocent Catholics who were being killed along with members of the enemy Cathar sect. The pope's representative, Arnaud Amaury, allegedly replied, "Kill them all. God will know his own."

Al Fatah The largest and most influential organization within the Palestine Liberation Organization. It formed the political foundation for PLO leader Yasir Arafat.

Al Jazeera An independent news service based in the Persian Gulf state of Qatar.

al-Megrahi, Abdel Basset An alleged agent of Libya's security service who was convicted and sentenced to life imprisonment by a Scottish court sitting near the Hague, Netherlands, for his participation in the bombing of Pan Am Flight 103 over Lockerbie, Scotland.

Al Qaeda An international network of Islamic mujahideen organized by Osama bin Laden in the aftermath of the anti-Soviet jihad in Afghanistan. Responsible for many acts of international and domestic terrorism.

Al Qaeda Organization for Holy War in Iraq A movement led by Abu Musab al-Zarqawi that waged holy war in Iraq against foreign interests, Shi'a organizations, and "apostate" Iraqis.

al-Sabbah, Hasan ibn The founder and leader of the Assassin movement during the 11th century.

Amal A pro-Syrian Lebanese Shi'a paramilitary movement.

Amir, Yigal A Jewish extremist who assassinated Israeli prime minister Yitzhak Rabin on November 4, 1995.

Ammonium nitrate and fuel oil (ANFO) A powerful explosive compound made from ingredients easily obtained from fertilizers and common gasoline.

Anarchism A political ideology developed during the 19th century that championed the working class and opposed central control by governments.

Anfal campaign A genocidal campaign waged by the Iraqi army in 1988 against its Kurdish population. Mustard gas and nerve agents were used against civilians.

Anglo-Israelism A mystical ideology developed by Richard Brothers during the 18th century. It posited that the Lost Ten Tribes of ancient Israel migrated through Europe and settled in the British Isles. Thus, the British were God's chosen people. The theory was adapted to the American context as the Christian Identity cult.

Animal Liberation Front (ALF) An American-based single-issue movement that protests animal abuse. Responsible for committing acts of violence such as arson and vandalism.

Anthrax A disease afflicting farm animals that can also be contracted by humans. A possible ingredient for biological weapons.

Antistate terrorism Dissident terrorism directed against a particular government or group of governments.

Antiterrorism Official measures that seek to deter or prevent terrorist attacks. These measures include target hardening and enhanced security.

Anti-Terrorism and Effective Death Penalty Act Passed by the U.S. Congress in 1996, it was the first comprehensive American counterterrorism law. The purpose of the Anti-Terrorism Act was to regulate activity that can be used to mount a terrorist attack, provide resources for counterterrorist programs, and punish terrorism.

Apartheid The former policy of racial separation and white supremacy in South Africa.

Arafat, Yasir The founder and leader of the Palestine Liberation Organization until his death on November 11, 2004.

Armed Forces for National Liberation (Fuerzas Armadas de Liberación Nacional, or FALN) A Puerto Rican *independencista* terrorist group active during the 1970s and 1980s. Responsible for more bombings than any other single terrorist group in American history.

Armed Islamic Group (GIA) An Algerian Islamic resistance movement responsible for terrorist violence in Algeria and France.

Armed propaganda The use of symbolic violence to spread propaganda about an extremist movement.

Armed Resistance Unit A cover name used by the leftist May 19 Communist Organization in the United States.

Armenian Revolutionary Army One of several Armenian terrorist groups active in the postwar era that targeted Turkish interests to avenge the Turkish genocide of Armenians.

Armenian Secret Army for the Liberation of Armenia (ASALA) One of several Armenian terrorist groups active in the postwar era that targeted Turkish interests to avenge the Turkish genocide of Armenians.

Army of God A shadowy and violent Christian fundamentalist movement in the United States that has attacked moralistic targets such as abortion providers.

Aryan Nations A racial supremacist hate group founded in the mid-1970s by Richard Butler. Originally based in Idaho, the group is organized around Christian Identity mysticism.

Aryan Republican Army (ARA) A neo-Nazi terrorist group that operated in the midwestern United States from 1994 to 1996. Inspired by the example of the Irish Republican Army, the ARA robbed 22 banks in seven states before they were captured. Their goal had been to finance racial supremacist causes and to hasten the overthrow of what they called the Zionist Occupation Government. Some members also considered themselves Christian Identity fundamentalist Phineas Priests.

Asahara, Shoko The spiritual leader of the Aum Shinrikyō cult.

Ásatrú A mystical belief in the ancient Norse gods' pantheon. Some Ásatrú believers are racial supremacists.

Askaris Government-supported death squads in South Africa that assassinated members of the African National Congress and their supporters prior to the end of apartheid.

Assassination The act of killing a symbolic victim in a sudden and premeditated attack. Many assassinations are politically motivated.

Assault rifles Automatic military weapons that use rifle ammunition.

Asymmetrical warfare A term used to describe tactics, organizational configurations, and methods of conflict that do not use previously accepted or predictable rules of engagement.

Augustine, Saint A Christian philosopher who developed the concept of the just war.

Aum Shinrikyō A cult based in Japan and led by Shoko Asahara. Responsible for releasing nerve gas into the Tokyo subway system, injuring 5,000 people.

Authoritarian regimes Governments that practice strict control over public and political institutions and emphasize public order. The media and other public information outlets are regulated and censored by the government. Some authoritarian regimes have democratic institutions.

Auto-genocide Self-genocide. When members of the same ethnic or religious group commit genocide against fellow members.

Axis of evil In January 2002, U.S. President Bush identified Iraq, Iran, and North Korea as the axis of evil. In that speech, he promised that the United States "will not permit the world's most dangerous regimes to threaten us with the world's most destructive weapons."

Ayyash, Yehiya ("The Engineer") A Palestinian terrorist bomb maker affiliated with HAMAS. He was responsible for scores of Israeli casualties and was eventually assassinated by a remotely controlled explosive device hidden in his cell phone.

Ba'ath Party A pan-Arab nationalist party.

Bakunin, Mikhail An early philosophical proponent of anarchism in Russia.

Basque Fatherland and Liberty (Euskadi Ta Azkatasuna, or ETA) Founded in 1959 to promote the independence of the Basque region in northern Spain. Although ETA adopted terrorism as a tactic in reply to the Franco government's violent repression of Basque nationalism, its campaign of violence escalated in the post-Franco era. At least six ETA factions and subfactions have been formed.

Beka'a Valley A valley in eastern Lebanon that became a center for political extremism and a safe haven for terrorists.

Berri, Nabih A leader of the Shi'a Amal paramilitary, prominent during the Lebanese Civil War during the 1970s and 1980s, as well as during the TWA Flight 847 incident.

Bhagwan Shree Rajneesh The leader of a Hindu-oriented cult based in the Pacific Northwest of the United States. The group was responsible for poisoning the salad bars of 10 Oregon restaurants with *Salmonella* bacteria in 1984. More than 700 people fell ill.

bin Laden, Osama Founder and leader of the Islamic terrorist Al Qaeda network.

Biological agents A term used to refer to potential ingredients in biological weapons.

Biometric technologies Digital technologies that allow digital photographs of faces to be matched against wanted suspects. Biometrics was used at American football's 2001 Super Bowl championship, when cameras scanned the faces of sports fans as they entered the stadium and matched their digital images against those of criminal fugitives and terrorists. The game became derisively known as the "Snooperbowl."

Birmingham Six Six men who were wrongfully convicted of a 1974 bombing of two pubs in Birmingham, England. They were released in 1991 after an appellate court ruled that the police had used fabricated evidence.

Black Hebrew Israelites An American racial supremacist cult that promotes African racial supremacy. Branches are also known as the Tribe of Judah, Nation of Israel, and Temple of Love. One branch based in Miami, Florida, and led by Hulon Mitchell (also known as Yahweh Ben Yahweh) was responsible for at least 14 murders during the 1980s.

Black Liberation Army (BLA) An African American terrorist group active during the 1970s. The BLA tended to target police officers and banks.

Black Panther Party for Self-Defense An African American nationalist organization founded in 1966 in Oakland, California. The Black Panthers eventually became a national movement. It was not a terrorist movement, but some members eventually engaged in terrorist violence.

Black Power An African American nationalist ideology developed during the 1960s that stressed self-help, political empowerment, cultural chauvinism, and self-defense.

Black Pride A movement in the United States that emphasized Afrocentric political agendas, experiments in economic development of African American communities, and cultural chauvinism that was expressed in music, art, and dress.

Black September A campaign waged by the Jordanian army in September 1970 to suppress what was perceived as a threat to Jordanian sovereignty from Palestinian fighters and leaders based in Jordan.

Black Widows The term given by the Russian media and authorities to Chechen women who participate in terrorist attacks against Russian interests. Many Black Widows engage in suicide operations, and such women volunteer, are manipulated, or are coerced to enlist. They are allegedly the relatives of Chechen men who have been killed in the conflict.

Blacklisted A policy of prohibiting political activists from obtaining employment in certain industries.

Bloody Sunday An incident on January 30, 1972, in Londonderry, Northern Ireland, when British paratroopers fired on demonstrators, killing 13 people.

Boko Haram An Islamist insurgency active in northeast Nigeria and bordering nations. Founded in 2002, its name is roughly translated as "Western education is forbidden."

Boland Amendment A bill passed by Congress in December 1982 that forbade the expenditure of U.S. funds to overthrow the Sandinista government.

Booth, John Wilkes A Confederate sympathizer who assassinated President Abraham Lincoln after the conclusion of the American Civil War.

Botulinum toxins (botulism) A rather common form of food poisoning. It is a bacterium rather than a virus or fungus and can be deadly if inhaled or ingested even in small quantities.

Brothers, Richard The English founder of Anglo-Israelism during the 18th century.

Bubonic plague Known as the Black Death in medieval Europe, this disease is spread by bacteria-infected fleas that infect hosts when bitten. The disease is highly infectious and often fatal.

Bureau for the Protection of the Constitution A government agency in Germany responsible for domestic security and intelligence.

Bureaucracy Operational arrangements of government. Max Weber used the term to describe and explain rationality and efficiency in managing governments—a field of public administration known as organizational theory.

Burke, Edmund The British father of conservatism. An 18th-century intellectual who denounced the excesses of the French Revolution and other challenges to the traditional European order.

Butler, Richard The founder and leader of the Aryan Nations organization. Also a promulgator of Christian Identity mysticism.

Cadres Politically indoctrinated and motivated activists. Frequently the core of a revolutionary movement.

Carlos the Jackal The nom de guerre for Ilich Ramirez Sanchez, a Venezuelan revolutionary who became an international terrorist. He acted primarily on behalf of the Popular Front for the Liberation of Palestine.

Carmichael, Stokely A leader of the Student Nonviolent Coordinating Committee in the American South during the 1960s. One of the first advocates of Black Power.

Carnivore A surveillance technology developed for use by the FBI that could reportedly monitor Internet communications. Under law, the FBI could not use Carnivore without a specific court order under specific guidelines, much like other criminal surveillance orders. The FBI eventually redesignated the system DCS-1000.

Castro, Fidel The leader of the Cuban Revolution.

Cell-based terrorist environment A terrorist environment in which terrorists have organized themselves into small semiautonomous units rather than in traditionally hierarchical configurations. Difficult to combat because there is no central organization.

Cells Autonomous groups of terrorists who may be loosely affiliated with a larger movement but who are largely independent of hierarchical control.

Central Intelligence Agency (CIA) The principal intelligence agency in the United States. The theoretical coordinator of American foreign intelligence collection.

Chemical agents Chemicals that can potentially be converted into weapons. Some chemical agents, such as pesticides, are commercially available. Other chemical agents can be manufactured by terrorists using commonly available instruction guides.

Child soldiers Children who have been pressed into military service.

Chlorine gas A chemical agent that destroys the cells that line the respiratory tract.

Christian Identity The American adaptation of Anglo-Israelism. A racial supremacist mystical belief that holds that Aryans are the chosen people of God, the United States is the Aryan Promised Land, nonwhites are soulless beasts, and Jews are biologically descended from the devil.

Christian Right A mostly Protestant fundamentalist movement in the United States that links strict evangelical Christian values to political agendas.

Cinque *See* DeFreeze, Donald.

Classical ideological continuum Symbolic political designations derived from the French Revolution. The concepts of left, center, and right have become part of modern political culture.

Codes of self-sacrifice Philosophical, ideological, or religious doctrines that create a warrior ethic in followers of the doctrine. Codes of self-sacrifice instill a sense of a higher calling that allows for the adoption of a superior morality. Followers consider acts of violence carried out in the name of the code completely justifiable.

Coercive covert operations Covert counterterrorist measures that seek to resolve terrorist crises by disrupting and destroying terrorist groups.

Collateral damage A term used to describe unintended casualties. Usually applied to civilians who have been mistakenly killed.

Collective nonviolence An activist philosophy of the civil rights movement in the American South that advocated peaceful civil disobedience.

Communal terrorism Group-against-group terrorism, in which rival demographic groups engage in political violence against each other.

Composite-4 (C-4) A powerful military-grade plastic explosive.

Concessionary options Conciliatory counterterrorist measures that seek to resolve terrorist crises by acceding to the terrorists' demands.

Conciliatory responses Counterterrorist measures that seek to resolve terrorist crises by addressing the underlying conditions that cause extremist violence.

Conservatism A political ideology that seeks to preserve traditional values.

Contagion effect Copycat terrorism in which terrorists imitate each other's behavior and tactics. This theory is still debated.

Contras Rightist Nicaraguan counterrevolutionaries trained and supported by the United States during the 1980s.

Convention to Prevent and Punish Acts of Terrorism Taking the Form of Crimes Against Persons and Related Extortion That Are of International Significance A treaty among members of the Organization of American States that defined attacks against internationally protected persons as common crimes. Its goal was to establish common ground for recognizing the absolute inviolability of diplomatic missions.

Counterculture A youth-centered movement in the United States and other Western countries during the 1960s and 1970s. It questioned status quo social and political values.

Counterterrorism Proactive policies that specifically seek to eliminate terrorist environments and groups. There are a number of possible categories of counterterrorist response, including counterterrorist laws, which specifically criminalize terrorist behavior and supportive operations.

Crazy states States where behavior is not rational, in which the people live at the whim of the regime or a dominant group. Some crazy states have little or no central authority and are ravaged by warlords or militias. Other crazy states have capricious, impulsive, and violent regimes in power that act out with impunity.

Creativity A mystical belief practiced by the racial supremacist World Church of the Creator in the United States. Creativity is premised on a rejection of the white race's reliance on Christianity, which is held to have been created by the Jews as a conspiracy to enslave whites. According to Creativity, the white race itself should be worshipped.

Criminal profiles Descriptive profiles of criminal suspects developed by law enforcement agencies to assist in the apprehension of the suspects.

Crucifixion A form of public execution during the time of the Roman Empire. It involved affixing condemned persons to a cross or other wooden platform. The condemned were either nailed through the wrist or hand or tied on the platform; they died by suffocation as their bodies sagged.

Crusades A series of Christian military campaigns during the Middle Ages instigated by the Pope and Western Christian rulers. Most of these campaigns were invasions of Muslim territories, although the Crusaders also attacked Orthodox Christians, conducted pogroms against Jews, and suppressed "heresies."

Cult of personality The glorification of a single strong national leader and political regime.

Customer anonymity A policy adopted in some countries that allows national banks to guarantee customer privacy.

Cyberterrorism The use of technology by terrorists to disrupt information systems.

Cyberwar The targeting of terrorists' electronic activities by counterterrorist agencies. Bank accounts, personal records, and other data stored in digital databases can theoretically be intercepted and compromised.

Days of Rage Four days of rioting and vandalism committed by the Weathermen in Chicago, Illinois, in October 1969.

DCS-1000 The redesignated name given to Carnivore, the FBI's Internet surveillance technology.

Death squads Rightist paramilitaries and groups of people who have committed numerous human rights violations. Many death squads in Latin America and elsewhere have been supported by the government and the upper classes.

Decommissioning The process of disarmament by the Irish Republican Army that was set as a condition for the Good Friday Agreement peace accords.

Defense Intelligence Agency (DIA) The central agency for military intelligence of the U.S. armed forces.

DeFreeze, Donald The leader of the Symbionese Liberation Army, a California-based American terrorist group active during the 1970s. DeFreeze adopted the nom de guerre Cinque.

Delta Force (1st Special Forces Operational Detachment-Delta) A secretive American special operations unit that operates in small covert teams. Its mission is similar to those of the British Special Air Service and French 1st Navy Parachute Infantry Regiment. Delta Force operations probably include abductions, reconnaissance, and punitive operations.

Democratic Front for the Liberation of Palestine (DFLP) A faction of the Palestine Liberation Organization, which split from the Popular Front for the Liberation of Palestine in 1969 and further split into two factions in 1991. It is a Marxist organization that believes in ultimate victory through mass revolution, and it has committed small bombings and assaults against Israel, including border raids.

Department of Homeland Security A new department of the U.S. government created to coordinate homeland security in the aftermath of the September 11, 2001, homeland attacks.

Department of Homeland Security Act of 2002 Statutory authorization for the creation of the Department of Homeland Security in the United States.

Dictatorship of the proletariat The Marxist belief that the communist revolution will result in the establishment of a working class–centered government.

Diplock Courts Special courts created in Northern Ireland in response to repeated intimidation of jurors by paramilitaries. Named after Lord Diplock, who reported to Parliament on the problem, they held trials before a single judge without recourse to jury trial.

Diplomacy Conciliatory counterterrorist measures that seek to resolve terrorist crises by negotiating with terrorists or their supporters.

Diplomatic Security Service A security bureau within the U.S. Department of State that protects diplomats and other officials.

Direct action A philosophy of direct confrontation adopted by the Students for a Democratic Society and other members of the American New Left movement.

Direct Action (Action Directe) An anti-American and anti-NATO terrorist group in France that was founded in 1979. Direct Action operated mainly in Paris and committed approximately 50 terrorist attacks. It acted in solidarity with Germany's Red Army Faction, Italy's Red Brigades, Belgium's Combatant Communist Cells, and Palestinian extremists.

Directorate for Inter-Services Intelligence (ISI) The chief Pakistani security service.

Dirty bomb A highly toxic bomb that contains conventional bomb components and toxic substances such as radioactive materials or toxic chemicals. The conventional bomb sends out a cloud of radioactive or chemical toxins.

Dirty War A term given to a campaign of state-sponsored terror waged in Argentina during the 1970s. Tens of thousands of people were tortured, disappeared, or killed.

Disinformation Counterterrorist measures that seek to resolve terrorist crises by disseminating damaging information, thus perhaps causing internal dissension and distrust among the terrorists and their supporters.

Dissident terrorism Bottom-up terrorism perpetrated by individuals, groups, or movements in opposition to an existing political or social order.

Duvdevan An elite unit in the Israel Defense Forces that specializes in urban covert operations disguised as Arabs.

Dynamite A commercially available high explosive that has nitroglycerin as its principal chemical ingredient.

Earth Liberation Front (ELF) A single-issue movement that protests environmental degradation and pollution. A splinter group from the environmentalist group Earthfirst!, the ELF is potentially more radical than the Animal Liberation Front.

Echelon A satellite surveillance network maintained by the U.S. National Security Agency. It is a kind of global wiretap that filters through communications using antennae, satellite, and other technologies. Internet transfers, telephone conversations, and data transmissions are the types of communications that can reportedly be intercepted.

Economic sanctions Counterterrorist measures that seek to influence the behavior of terrorist states by pressuring their national economies.

Electromagnetic pulse (EMP) technologies Technologies using an electromagnetic burst from a generator that can disable electronic components such as microchips. If used on a sizable scale, EMP could destroy large quantities of military or financial information.

Electronic trigger Remotely controlled bombs are commonly employed by terrorists. The trigger is activated by a remote electronic or radio signal.

Emergency Search Team A paramilitary unit within the U.S. Department of Energy that has counterterrorist capabilities.

End justifies the means, The A concept wherein the desired goal is so just that the methods used to obtain the goal are acceptable regardless of their immediate consequences.

Engels, Friedrich Karl Marx's colleague and compatriot during the genesis of what was to become communist ideology.

Engineer, the The designation given to the HAMAS bomb maker Yehiya Ayyash.

Enhanced security Counterterrorist measures that harden targets to deter or otherwise reduce the severity of terrorist attacks.

Ensslin, Gudrun A founder and leader of the Red Army Faction/Baader-Meinhof Gang in West Germany. She committed suicide in prison in October 1977 along with Andreas Baader and Jan-Carl Raspe. The incident became known as Death Night.

Episode-specific Sponsorship State-sponsored terrorism limited to a single episode or campaign.

Establishment, the A designation coined by the New Left in the United States during the 1960s. It referred to mainstream American political and social institutions.

ETA (Euskadi Ta Azkatasuna) *See* Basque Fatherland and Liberty.

Ethnic cleansing A term created by Serb nationalists during the wars following the breakup of Yugoslavia. It described the suppression and removal of non-Serbs from regions claimed for Serb settlement. A euphemism for genocide.

Ethno-nationalist communal terrorism Violence involving conflict between populations that have distinct histories, customs, ethnic traits, religious traditions, or other cultural idiosyncrasies.

Euphemistic language Code words used by all participants in a terrorist environment to describe other participants and their behavior.

European Police Office (EUROPOL) A cooperative investigative consortium of members of the European Union. It has a mission similar to INTERPOL.

Extradition treaties International agreements to turn over criminal fugitives to the law enforcement agencies of fellow signatories.

Extraordinary renditions A practice initially sanctioned during the Reagan administration in about 1987 as a measure to capture drug traffickers, terrorists, and other wanted persons. It involves an uncomplicated procedure: Find the suspects anywhere in the world, seize them, transport them to the United States, and force their appearance before a federal court. Following the September 11, 2001, terrorist attacks, suspects were not brought before federal courts and were instead confined in classified "black site" facilities and the Guantánamo Bay military base in Cuba. The black sites were eventually closed, but the Guantánamo Bay facility remained in operation.

Extremism Political opinions that are intolerant toward opposing interests and divergent opinions. Extremism forms the ideological foundation for political violence. Radical and reactionary extremists often rationalize and justify acts of violence committed on behalf of their cause.

"Extremism in defense of liberty is no vice" An uncompromising belief in the absolute righteousness of a cause. A moralistic concept that clearly defines good and evil. The statement was made by Senator Barry Goldwater during the 1964 presidential election in the United States.

Fallout Dangerous radioactive debris emitted into the atmosphere by a nuclear explosion that falls to earth as toxic material.

FALN *See* Armed Forces for National Liberation (Fuerzas Armadas de Liberación Nacional)

Far left The extremist, but not necessarily violent, left wing. Usually strongly influenced by Marxist ideology. Radical in political orientation.

Far right The extremist, but not necessarily violent, right wing. Reactionary in political orientation.

Fascism An ideology developed during the mid-20th century that emphasized strong state-centered authority, extreme law and order, militarism, and nationalism. Variants of fascism were applied during the 1930s in Italy, Germany, and Spain, as well as in Latin America during the postwar era.

Federal Bureau of Investigation (FBI) An investigative bureau within the U.S. Department of Justice, it is the largest federal law enforcement agency. Among its duties are domestic counterterrorism and intelligence collection.

Fhima, Lamen Khalifa An alleged agent of Libya's security service who was acquitted by a Scottish court sitting near the Hague, Netherlands, of charges that he participated in the bombing of Pan Am Flight 103 over Lockerbie, Scotland.

Force 17 An elite security unit within Al Fatah, founded in 1970. It has engaged in paramilitary and terrorist attacks and has served as Yasir Arafat's guard force.

Force 777 An elite Egyptian counterterrorist unit that has had mixed success in resolving terrorist crises.

Force multiplier Also known as force multiplication. An attribute or combination of attributes that contribute to increasing the effectiveness of a movement or fighting group.

Four Olds During the Great Proletarian Cultural Revolution in China, Maoists waged an ideological struggle to eliminate what they termed the *Four Olds:* old ideas, old culture, old customs, and old habits.

Fourteen Words A rallying slogan for the racial supremacist right wing in the United States. Originally coined by a convicted member of the terrorist group the Order, the Fourteen Words are "We must secure the existence of our people and a future for White children."

Franco, Francisco The leader of the right-wing rebellion in Spain against the leftist republic during the Civil War of the 1930s. He became the dictator of postwar Spain.

Free press A media environment in which few official restrictions are placed on reporting the news. The free press relies on ethical and professional standards of behavior to regulate reporting practices.

Freedom Birds A term given to female combatants in the Liberation Tigers of Tamil Eelam.

Freedom fighter One who fights on behalf of an oppressed group. A very contextual term.

French Navy Special Assault Units Elite units of the French Navy that are trained for operations against seaborne targets, coastlines, and harbors. Their mission is similar to those of the British Special Boat Service and the U.S. Navy SEALs.

Fringe left The revolutionary left. Often violent.

Fringe right The revolutionary right. Often violent.

Fund for the Martyrs An Iranian fund established for the benefit of Palestinian victims of the intifada against Israel.

Furrow, Buford Oneal A former member of Aryan Nations who went on a shooting spree in Los Angeles, California, in August 1999. His spree included an attack at a Jewish community center, in which five people were wounded, and the murder of an Asian mail carrier.

Gasoline bomb A simple explosive consisting of a gasoline-filled container with a detonator. Perhaps the most common gasoline bomb is the Molotov cocktail.

Genocidal domestic state terrorism State-initiated genocide. The state either involves itself directly in the genocidal campaign or deploys proxies to carry out the genocide.

Genocide The suppression of a targeted demographic group with the goal of repressing or eliminating its cultural or physical distinctiveness. The group is usually an ethno-nationalist, religious, or ideological group.

GIGN (Groupe d'Intervention Gendarmerie Nationale) An elite paramilitary unit recruited from the French gendarmerie, or military police. GIGN is a counterterrorist unit with international operational duties.

Golani Brigade An elite unit within the Israel Defense Force that normally operates in conventionally organized military units. It has been deployed frequently for suppression campaigns against Hezbollah in southern Lebanon.

Goldstein, Baruch A lone-wolf terrorist who fired on worshippers inside the Ibrahim Mosque at the Cave of the Patriarchs holy site in the city of Hebron, Israel. According to official government estimates, he killed 29 people and wounded another 125. In reprisal for the Hebron massacre, the Palestinian Islamic fundamentalist movement HAMAS launched a bombing campaign that included the first wave of human suicide bombers.

Good Friday Agreement A significant outcome of the Northern Ireland peace process. The agreement was overwhelmingly approved by voters on April 10, 1998, in both the Republic of Ireland and Northern Ireland. It signaled the mutual acceptance of a Northern Ireland assembly and the disarmament, or decommissioning, of all paramilitaries. Also known as the Belfast Agreement.

Grail A designation for the Soviet-made SA-7 surface-to-air missile.

Great Proletarian Cultural Revolution A period from 1965 to 1969 in China during which the Communist Party instigated a mass movement to mobilize the young postrevolution generation. Its purpose was to eliminate so-called revisionist tendencies in society and to create a newly indoctrinated revolutionary generation.

Greater jihad In Muslim belief, an individual struggle to do what is right in accordance with God's wishes. All people of faith are required to do what is right and good.

Green Berets (Special Forces Group) A special operations unit of the U.S. Army. Green Berets usually operate in units called A Teams, comprising specialists whose skills include languages, intelligence, medicine, and demolitions. The traditional mission of the A Team is force multiplication.

Green Police The popular name for Israel's Police Border Guards.

GSG-9 (Grenzschutzgruppe 9) An elite German paramilitary unit that was organized after the disastrous failed attempt to rescue Israeli hostages taken by Black September at the 1972 Munich Olympics. It is a paramilitary force that has been used domestically and internationally as a counterterrorist and hostage rescue unit.

Guerrilla A term first used during Spanish resistance against French occupation troops during the Napoleonic Wars. It refers to irregular hit-and-run tactics.

Guevara, Ernesto "Che" An Argentine revolutionary and intellectual who was instrumental in the success of the Cuban Revolution. Eventually killed in Bolivia, he developed his own philosophy of a continent-wide revolution in Latin America.

Guildford Four Four people who were wrongfully convicted of an October 1974 bombing in Guildford, England. They served 15 years in prison before being released in 1989 when their convictions were overturned on appeal.

Hague Convention of 1970 A treaty requiring the extradition or prosecution of hijackers.

Hague Convention A series of international agreements that tried to establish rules for conflict.

HAMAS (Islamic Resistance Movement) A Palestinian Islamic movement that waged a protracted terrorist campaign against Israel.

Hate crimes Crimes motivated by hatred against protected groups of people. They are prosecuted as aggravated offenses rather than as acts of terrorism.

Hawala An ancient transnational trust-based system used to transfer money via brokers.

Heinzen, Karl A 19th-century revolutionary theorist in Germany who advocated revolutionary terrorism and the use of explosives. Heinzen supported the acquisition of new weapons technologies to utterly destroy the enemies of the people. According to Heinzen, these weapons should include poison gas and new high-yield explosives.

Hezbollah A Lebanese Shi'a movement that promotes Islamic revolution. It was prominent in the resistance against the Israeli presence in South Lebanon and frequently engaged in terrorism.

Hitler, Adolf The leader of the National Socialist German Workers, or Nazi, Party in Germany during the 1930s and 1940s.

Holy Spirit Mobile Force A cultic insurgency in Uganda inspired and led by Alice Lakwena. In late 1987, she led thousands of her followers against the Ugandan army. To protect themselves from death, the fighters anointed themselves with holy oil, which they believed would ward off bullets. Thousands of Lakwena's followers were slaughtered in the face of automatic weapons and artillery fire.

Hostage Rescue Team A paramilitary group organized under the authority of the U.S. Federal Bureau of Investigation. The hostage rescue team is typical of American paramilitary units in that it operates under the administrative supervision of federal agencies that perform traditional law enforcement work.

House Un-American Activities Committee A congressional committee created in the aftermath of a Red Scare during the 1930s to investigate threats to American security.

Human intelligence Intelligence that has been collected by human operatives rather than through technological resources. Also referred to as HUMINT.

Hussein, Saddam The ruler of Iraq who became a prominent figure in state sponsorship of international terrorism and the development of weapons of mass destruction during the 1980s and 1990s. He also attempted to annex Kuwait during the early 1990s, causing the Gulf War.

Ideological communal terrorism Communal violence in the postwar era that usually reflected the global ideological rivalry between the United States and the Soviet Union.

Ideologies Systems of political belief.

Imperialism A term used to describe the doctrine of national expansion and exploitation.

Improvised explosive devices (IEDs) So-called roadside bombs that were constructed and deployed by Iraqi insurgents during the U.S.-led occupation.

Information is power A political and popular concept that the control of the dissemination of information, especially through media outlets, enhances the power of the controlling interest.

Inkatha Freedom Party A Zulu-based movement in South Africa.

Intelligence The collection of data for the purpose of creating an informational database about terrorist movements and predicting their behavior.

Intelligence community The greater network of intelligence agencies. In the United States, the Central Intelligence Agency is the theoretical coordinator of intelligence collection.

International Court of Justice The principal judicial arm of the United Nations. Its 15 judges are elected from among member states, and each sits for a nine-year term. The court hears disputes between nations and gives advisory opinions to recognized international organizations.

International Criminal Court (ICC) A court established to prosecute crimes against humanity, such as genocide. Its motivating principle is to promote human rights and justice. In practice, this has meant that the ICC has issued arrest warrants for the prosecution of war criminals.

International Criminal Police Organization (INTERPOL) An international network of law enforcement that cooperates in the investigation of crimes. It is based in Ste. Cloud, France.

International Criminal Tribunal for Rwanda (ICTR) A tribunal that has investigated allegations of war crimes and genocide resulting from the breakdown of order in Rwanda during the 1990s. The indictments against suspected war criminals detail what can only be described as genocide on a massive scale.

International Criminal Tribunal for the Former Yugoslavia (ICTY) A tribunal that has investigated allegations of war crimes and genocide arising out of the wars that broke out after the fragmentation of Yugoslavia during the 1990s. Several alleged war criminals, including former Yugoslavian president Slobodan Milosevic, have been brought before the court. Others remain at large but under indictment.

International mujahideen Islamic revolutionaries who have adopted a pan-Islamic ideology.

International terrorism Terrorism that is directed against targets symbolizing international interests. These attacks can occur against domestic targets that have international symbolism or against targets in the international arena.

Internment Camps After the December 7, 1941, Japanese air attack on Pearl Harbor, the administration of U.S. president Franklin Delano Roosevelt established the War Relocation Authority. The U.S. Army was tasked with moving ethnic Japanese to internment facilities on the West Coast and elsewhere. More than 100,000 ethnic Japanese were forced to relocate to these facilities. The internment facilities were operational until 1945.

Intifada The protracted Palestinian uprising against Israel. Literally, "shaking off."

Iran-Contra scandal Lieutenant Colonel Oliver North's efforts to circumvent the Boland Amendment were revealed by the press when a covert American cargo plane was shot down inside Nicaragua and an American mercenary was captured.

Irish National Liberation Army (INLA) The INLA grew out of the split in the IRA during the 1970s. The group adopted Marxist theory as its guiding ideology and fought to reunite Northern Ireland with Ireland. The INLA considered itself to be fighting in unity with other terrorist groups that championed oppressed groups around the world. Its heyday was during the 1970s and mid-1980s.

Islamic jihad A label adopted by some Islamic terrorists seeking to establish an Islamic state. Groups known as Islamic Jihad exist in Lebanon, Palestine, and Egypt.

Islamic State of Iraq and the Levant Also known as the self-proclaimed Islamic State and the Islamic State of Iraq and al-Sham (ISIS). An Islamist insurgency originating in Iraq and Syria in 2013. Other Islamist insurgencies later declared allegiance to the ISIS "brand."

"It became necessary to destroy the town to save it" An extremist goal to destroy an existing order without developing a clear vision for the aftermath. A moralistic concept to justify terrorist behavior. The statement was allegedly made by an American officer during the war in Vietnam.

Izzedine al-Qassam Brigade A militant movement within the overarching HAMAS movement of Palestinian Islamic revolutionaries.

Jamahiriya Security Organization (JSO) The Libyan state security agency during the reign of Muammar el-Qaddafi. Apparently responsible for promoting Libya's policy of state-sponsored terrorism.

Janjaweed An alliance of Arab militias in Darfur, Sudan. When a rebellion broke out among African residents of Darfur in early 2003, the Sudanese government armed and provided air support for a Janjaweed campaign of ethnic cleansing. About 2 million Africans became refugees when they were forced from the land, and about 50,000 were killed. The Janjaweed systematically sexually assaulted African women and girls.

Japanese Red Army A nihilistic terrorist group active during the 1970s and 1980s. Responsible for many attacks, including the May 1972 attack in Lod Airport in Israel on behalf of the Popular Front for the Liberation of Palestine.

Jewish Defense League (JDL) A militant Jewish organization founded in the United States by Rabbi Meir Kahane.

Jihad A central tenet in Islam that literally means a sacred "struggle" or "effort." Although Islamic extremists have interpreted jihad to mean waging holy war, it is not synonymous with the Christian concept of a crusade.

Jihadi One who wages jihad.

Joint operations supportive sponsorship State-sponsored terrorism in which state personnel participate in the terrorist enterprise.

Jones, Jim Founder and leader of the American apocalyptic cult People's Temple of the Disciples of Christ. Founded in California, the group relocated to Guyana in the late 1970s. More than 900 followers committed suicide in November 1978 by drinking flavored sugar water laced with poison.

Journalistic self-regulation The theoretical practice of ethical reporting among members of the press.

Jus ad bellum Correct conditions for waging war. An element of the just war doctrine.

Jus in bello One's correct behavior while waging war. An element of the just war doctrine.

Just war doctrine A moral and ethical doctrine that raises the questions of whether one can ethically attack an opponent, how one can justifiably defend oneself, and what types of force are morally acceptable in either context. The doctrine also addresses who can morally be defined as an enemy and what kinds of targets may be morally attacked.

Justice Commandos of the Armenian Genocide One of several Armenian terrorist groups active in the postwar era that targeted Turkish interests to avenge the Turkish genocide of Armenians.

Kach (Kahane Chai) Militant movements in Israel that carried on after Rabbi Meir Kahane was assassinated. They advocate the expulsion of Arabs from territories claimed as historically Jewish land. *Kach* means "only thus." *Kahane Chai* means "Kahane lives."

Kaczynski, Theodore "Ted" The Unabomber in the United States who sent bombs hidden in letters and packages to protest technological society. A case study in politically motivated lone-wolf attacks. Also a case study of a medium degree of criminal skill.

Kahane, Rabbi Meir Founder and leader of the Jewish Defense League.

Kalashnikov, Mikhail The inventor of the famous AK-47 assault rifle.

Kansi, Mir Aimal A terrorist who used an AK-47 assault rifle against employees of the Central Intelligence Agency who were waiting in their cars to enter the CIA's headquarters in Langley, Virginia. Two people were killed, and three were wounded. He was later captured in Pakistan, sent to the United States for prosecution, and convicted of murder.

Kerner Commission A term given to the presidentially appointed National Advisory Commission on Civil Disorders, which released a report in 1968 on civil disturbances in the United States.

Khaled, Leila A Palestinian nationalist who successfully hijacked one airliner and failed in an attempt to hijack another. She acted on behalf of the Popular Front for the Liberation of Palestine.

Khmer Rouge A Cambodian Marxist insurgency that seized power in 1975. During its reign, between 1 and 2 million Cambodians died, many of them in the infamous Killing Fields.

"Kill one man, terrorize a thousand" A paraphrasing of a quotation by the Chinese military philosopher Wu Ch'i. Variously ascribed to the Chinese military philosopher Sun Tzu and Chinese communist leader Mao Zedong.

Komitehs Revolutionary tribunals established after the Islamic revolution in Iran.

Kony, Josef Founder and leader of Uganda's cultic Lord's Resistance Army.

Kosovo A region in southern Yugoslavia that many Serbs consider their spiritual homeland. It became an international flash point when ethnic Albanian Kosovars sought to secede from Yugoslavia.

Kosovo Liberation Army (KLA) An ethnic Albanian dissident movement seeking independence for the Kosovo region of the former Yugoslavia. The group has used terrorism against Serb civilians and security forces.

Kropotkin, Petr An early philosophical proponent of anarchism in Russia.

Ku Klux Klan (KKK) A racial supremacist organization founded in 1866 in Pulaski, Tennessee. During its five eras, the KKK was responsible for thousands of acts of terrorism.

Kuclos A symbol adopted by the Ku Klux Klan consisting of a cross and a teardrop-like symbol enclosed by a circle. Literally, Greek for "circle."

Kurdistan The regional homeland of the Kurdish people. It is divided between Iran, Iraq, Syria, and Turkey.

Kurds An ethno-nationalist group in the Middle East. Several nationalist movements fought protracted wars on behalf of Kurdish independence.

Labeling Attaching euphemistic terms to the participants in a terrorist environment.

Lakwena, Alice Auma Leader of the cultic Holy Spirit Mobile Force in Uganda. She claimed to be inspired by the Christian Holy Spirit and preached that her movement would defeat government forces and purge Uganda of witchcraft and superstition. Her followers were annihilated, and she fled the country.

Laskar Jihad (Militia of the Holy War) An armed Islamic group organized in April 2000 in Indonesia. Under the leadership of Ja'afar Umar Thalib, the group waged a communal holy war in Indonesia, primarily against Christians on Indonesia's Molucca Islands.

Law enforcement The use of law enforcement agencies and criminal investigative techniques in the prosecution of suspected terrorists.

Leaderless resistance A cell-based strategy of the Patriot and neo-Nazi movements in the United States requiring the formation of "phantom cells" to wage war against the government and enemy interests. Dedicated Patriots and neo-Nazis believe that this strategy will prevent infiltration from federal agencies.

Left, center, right Designations on the classical ideological continuum. The left tends to promote social change. The center tends to favor incremental change and the status quo. The right tends to favor traditional values.

Legalistic responses Counterterrorist measures that use the law to criminalize specific acts as terrorist behaviors and that use law enforcement agencies to investigate, arrest, and prosecute suspected terrorists.

Lemkin, Raphael The creator of the word *genocide*, which first appeared in print in his influential book *Axis Rule in Occupied Europe*, published in 1944.

Lenin, Vladimir Ilyich The Russian revolutionary leader and theorist who was the principal leader of the Russian Revolution of 1917. He became the first leader of the Soviet Union and was also the author of several books that were very influential in the international communist movement throughout the 20th century.

Lesser jihad The defense of Islam against threats to the faith. This includes military defense and is undertaken when the Muslim community is under attack.

Liberation Tigers of Tamil Eelam (LTTE) A nationalist group in Sri Lanka that champions the independence of the Tamil people. Responsible for many acts of terrorism.

Liquid metal embrittlement The process of using chemicals to weaken metals. Such chemicals can embrittle, or make rigid, various metals.

Logistically supportive sponsorship State-sponsored terrorism in which the state provides a great deal of logistical support to the terrorists but stops short of directly participating in the terrorist incident or campaign.

Lone wolf model A designation describing political violence committed by individuals who are motivated by an ideology but who have no membership in a terrorist organization.

Long hot summers A term used during the 1960s to describe urban racial tensions that sometimes led to rioting.

Lord's Resistance Army Josef Kony reorganized Uganda's cultic Holy Spirit Mobile Force into the Lord's Resistance Army. He blended together Christianity, Islam, and witchcraft into a bizarre mystical foundation for his movement. The group was exceptionally brutal and waged near-genocidal terrorist campaigns—largely against the Acholi people that it claimed to champion.

Luddites A movement of English workers during the early 1800s. The Luddites objected to the social and economic transformations of the Industrial Revolution. They targeted the machinery of the new textile factories, and textile mills and weaving machinery were disrupted and sabotaged. After 17 Luddites were executed in 1813, the movement gradually died out.

M-16 The standard assault rifle for the U.S. military; first introduced in the mid-1960s.

MacDonald, Andrew *See* William Pierce.

Mala in se An act designated as a crime that is fundamentally evil, such as murder and rape.

Mala prohibita An act designated as a crime that is not fundamentally evil, such as prostitution and gambling.

Manifesto of the Communist Party The seminal document of communism, written by Karl Marx and Friedrich Engels.

Manipulation of the media The attempt by state and substate participants in a terrorist environment to control or otherwise affect the reporting of news by the media.

Mao Zedong The leader of the Chinese Revolution. His tactical and strategic doctrine of People's War was practiced by a number of insurgencies in the developing world. Mao's interpretation of Marxism was also very influential among communist revolutionaries.

Marighella, Carlos A Brazilian Marxist revolutionary and theorist who developed an influential theory for waging dissident terrorist warfare in urban environments.

Martyrdom Martyrdom is achieved by dying on behalf of a religious faith or for some other greater cause. A common concept among religious movements.

Marx, Karl A mid-19th-century philosopher who, along with Friedrich Engels, developed the ideology of class struggle.

Marxism An ideology that believes in the historical inevitability of class conflict, culminating in the final conflict that will establish the dictatorship of the proletariat.

Mass communications The technological ability to convey information to a large number of people. It includes technologies that allow considerable amounts of information to be communicated through printed material, audio broadcasts, video broadcasts, and expanding technologies such as the Internet.

Mathews, Robert Jay The founder and leader of the American neo-Nazi terrorist group the Order, founded in 1983.

May 19 Communist Organization (M19CO) An American Marxist terrorist group that was active in the late 1970s and early 1980s. It was composed of remnants of the Republic of New Africa, the Black Liberation Army, the Weather Underground, and the Black Panthers. M19CO derived its name from the birthday of Malcolm X and Vietnamese leader Ho Chi Minh.

McCarthy, Senator Joseph A Wisconsin senator who initiated a purge of suspected communists in the United States during the early 1950s.

McCarthyism The term used to describe procedures and the underlying policy applied by Senator Joseph McCarthy in the United States during the purge of suspected communists in the early 1950s.

McVeigh, Timothy A member of the Patriot movement in the United States and probably a racial supremacist. Responsible for constructing and detonating an ANFO bomb that destroyed the Alfred P. Murrah Federal Building in Oklahoma City, Oklahoma, on April 19, 1995. One hundred sixty-eight people were killed.

Means of production A Marxist concept describing the primary source of economic production and activity during the stages of human social evolution.

Media as a weapon For terrorists and other extremists, information can be wielded as a weapon of war. Because symbolism is at the center of most terrorist incidents, the media are explicitly identified by terrorists as potential supplements to their arsenal.

Media gatekeeping Similar to journalistic self-regulation. The theoretical practice of ethical self-regulation by members of the free press.

Media spin The media's inclusion of subjective and opinionated interpretations when reporting the facts.

Media-oriented terrorism Acts of terrorism carried out to attract and manipulate media coverage.

Meinhof, Ulrike A founder and leader of the Red Army Faction/Baader-Meinhof Gang in West Germany. Meinhof hanged herself in prison on May 9, 1976.

Meredith, James An American civil rights activist who was ambushed, shot, and wounded in June 1966 as he walked through Mississippi to demonstrate that African Americans could safely go to polling places to register to vote.

MI-5 An intelligence agency in Great Britain responsible for domestic intelligence collection.

MI-6 An intelligence agency in Great Britain responsible for international intelligence collection.

Military Intelligence Service A government agency in Germany responsible for international intelligence collection.

Militias Organized groups of armed citizens who commonly exhibit antigovernment tendencies and subscribe to conspiracy theories. The armed manifestation of the Patriot movement.

Mines Military-grade explosives that are buried in the soil or rigged to be detonated as booby traps. Antipersonnel mines are designed to kill people, and antitank mines are designed to destroy vehicles. Many millions of mines have been manufactured and are available on the international market.

Mini-Manual of the Urban Guerrilla An influential essay written by Carlos Marighella that outlined his theory of urban dissident terrorist warfare.

Mitchell, Hulon, Jr. Also known as Yahweh Ben Yahweh (God, Son of God). Founder and leader of a Miami branch of the Black Hebrew Israelites. He taught that whites are descendants of the devil and worthy of death. Followers who did not practice complete obedience were dealt with harshly, and some were beaten or beheaded. Mitchell and some of his followers were imprisoned. Mitchell's group was implicated in 14 murders during the 1980s.

Molotov cocktail A simple gasoline bomb consisting of a gasoline-filled bottle with a rag inserted as a wick.

Molotov, Vyacheslav The Soviet foreign minister during World War II, for whom the Molotov cocktail is named.

Monolithic terrorist environment A terrorist environment in which a single national sponsor supports and directs international terrorism. Combating this environment is relatively uncomplicated because attention can theoretically be directed against a single adversary.

Montreal Convention of 1971 A treaty that extended international law to terrorist attacks on airports and grounded aircraft.

Moussaoui, Zacarias A suspected member of the cell that carried out the attacks of September 11, 2001. He was being held in custody on other charges at the time of the attacks and was later prosecuted in federal court.

Mud People A derogatory term given to non-Aryans by followers of the Christian Identity movement. Mud People are considered nonhuman, soulless beasts who dwelt outside the Garden of Eden.

Mujahideen Individuals who wage war in defense of Islam. Literally, "holy warriors."

Multinational corporations Large corporations that conduct business on a global scale. They are usually centered in several countries.

Muslim Brotherhood A transnational Sunni Islamic fundamentalist movement that is very active in several North African and Middle Eastern countries. It has been implicated in terrorist violence committed in Egypt, Syria, and elsewhere.

Mussolini, Benito The Italian dictator who led the first successful fascist seizure of power during the 1920s.

Mustard gas A chemical agent that is a mist rather than a gas. It is a blistering agent that blisters the skin, eyes, and nose, and it can severely damage the lungs if inhaled.

Narco-terrorism Political violence committed by dissident drug traffickers who are primarily concerned with protecting their criminal enterprise. This is in contradistinction to drug-related violence.

Narcotraficantes Latin American drug traffickers.

Narodnaya Volya (People's Will) A 19th-century terrorist group in Russia.

National Alliance An overtly Nazi organization based in West Virginia that was founded in 1970 by William Pierce, a former member of the American Nazi Party.

National Counterterrorism Center (NCTC) An agency established in the United States to integrate the counterterrorism efforts of the intelligence community.

National Security Agency (NSA) An American intelligence agency charged with signal intelligence collection, code making, and code breaking.

Nationalist dissident terrorism Political violence committed by members of ethno-nationalist groups who seek greater political rights or autonomy.

Nativism American cultural nationalism. A cornerstone of Ku Klux Klan ideology.

Nazi Holocaust The genocide waged against European Jews by Germany before and during World War II. The first significant anti-Semitic racial decree promulgated by the Nazis was the Law for the Protection of German Blood and German Honor, passed in September 1935. In the end, approximately six million Jews were murdered.

Nechayev, Sergei An early philosophical proponent of anarchism in Russia. Author of *Revolutionary Catechism*.

Neocolonialism A postwar Marxist concept describing Western economic exploitation of the developing world.

Nerve gas A chemical agent, such as sarin, tabun, and VX, that blocks (or short-circuits) nerve messages in the body. A single drop of a nerve agent, whether inhaled or absorbed through the skin, can shut down the body's neurotransmitters.

Netwar An emerging method of conflict that uses network forms of organization and information-age strategies, doctrines, and technologies. Participants in these networks are dispersed small groups who operate as a "flat" organizational network rather than under chains of command.

New African Freedom Fighters The self-defined military wing of an African American nationalist organization called the Republic of New Africa. Composed of former members of the Black Liberation Army and Black Panthers, the group operated in collaboration with other members of the revolutionary underground. It was eventually broken up in 1985 after members were arrested for conspiring to free an imprisoned comrade, bomb the courthouse, and commit other acts of political violence.

New Left A movement of young leftists during the 1960s who rejected orthodox Marxism and took on the revolutionary theories of Frantz Fanon, Herbert Marcuse, Carlos Marighella, and other new theorists.

New Media The use of existing technologies and alternative broadcasting formats to analyze and disseminate information. These formats include talk-show models, tabloid styles, celebrity status for hosts, and blatant entertainment spins. Strong and opinionated political or social commentary also makes up a significant portion of New Media content.

New Terrorism A typology of terrorism characterized by a loose cell-based organizational structure, asymmetrical tactics, the threatened use of weapons of mass destruction, potentially high casualty rates, and usually a religious or mystical motivation.

New World Liberation Front The name of an American terrorist group active during the mid-1970s. Organized as a "reborn" manifestation of the Symbionese Liberation Army by former SLA members and new recruits.

New World Order A conspiracy theory common among American neo-Nazis and members of the Patriot movement. It holds that non-American interests are threatening to take over—or have already taken over—key governmental centers of authority. This takeover is part of an international plot to create a one-world government.

News scoop Media competition to preempt competitors' stories by being the first to report breaking news.

News triage The decision-making process within the media that determines what news to report and how to report it.

Nidal, Abu A Palestinian nationalist responsible for numerous acts of terrorism. Frequently an agent of state-sponsored terrorism.

Nihilism A 19th-century Russian philosophical movement of young dissenters who believed that only scientific truth could end ignorance. Nihilists had no vision for a future society; they asserted only that the existing society was intolerable. Modern nihilist dissidents exhibit a similar disdain for the existing social order but offer no clear alternative for after its destruction.

Nihilist dissident terrorism The practice of political violence with the goal of destroying an existing order, committed with little or no regard for the aftermath of the revolution.

Nihilist dissidents Antistate dissidents whose goal is to destroy the existing social order with little consideration given for the aftermath of the revolution. They practice "revolution for revolution's sake."

Nonviolent covert operations Counterterrorist options that include infiltration, disinformation, cyberwar, intelligence, economic sanctions, and target hardening.

Northern Ireland Act A law passed in Northern Ireland in 1993 that created conditions of quasi-martial law. The act suspended several civil liberties and empowered the British military to engage in warrantless searches of civilian homes, temporarily detain people without charge, and question suspects. The military could also intern suspected terrorists and turn over for prosecution those for whom enough evidence had been seized.

Nuclear weapons High-explosive military weapons using weapons-grade plutonium and uranium. Nuclear explosions devastate the area within their blast zone, irradiate an area outside the blast zone, and are capable of sending dangerous radioactive debris into the atmosphere that descends to earth as toxic fallout.

Off the grid A tactic used by hard-core members of the Patriot movement who believe in the New World Order conspiracy theory. Believers typically refuse to use credit cards, driver's licenses, and Social Security numbers as a way to lower their visibility from the government, banks, and other potential agents of the New World Order.

Office of Homeland Security An American agency established immediately after the September 11, 2001, attacks. Its ostensible purpose was to coordinate domestic security. Because it lacked the authority to set policy for other federal agencies, it was replaced by the Department of Homeland Security.

Official domestic state terrorism Terrorism undertaken as a matter of official government policy.

Official Secrets Act An act in Great Britain that permitted the prosecution of individuals for the reporting of information that was deemed to endanger the security of the British government.

Okhrana The secret police of czarist Russia. Responsible for writing the anti-Semitic *Protocols of the Learned Elders of Zion.*

"One man willing to throw away his life is enough to terrorize a thousand" The symbolic power of a precise application of force by an individual who is willing to sacrifice himself or herself can terrorize many other people. A moralistic concept that illustrates how a weak adversary can influence a strong adversary. The statement was made by the Chinese military philosopher Wu Ch'i.

"One person's terrorist is another person's freedom fighter" The importance of perspective in the use of violence to achieve political goals. Championed groups view violent rebels as freedom fighters, whereas their adversaries consider them terrorists.

One-Seedline Christian Identity A Christian Identity mystical belief that argues that all humans, regardless of race, are descended from Adam. However, only Aryans (defined as northern Europeans) are the true elect of God. They are the Chosen People whom God has favored and who are destined to rule over the rest of humanity. In the modern era, those who call themselves the Jews are actually descended from a minor Black Sea ethnic group and therefore have no claim to Israel.

Operation Death Trains The synchronized detonation of 10 bombs aboard commuter trains in Madrid, Spain, on March 11, 2004. The operation, carried out by the Abu Hafs al-Masri Brigades, killed 191 people and wounded more than 1,500. The attack led to the ouster of Spanish prime minister Jose Maria Aznar's government and the withdrawal of 1,300 Spanish troops from Iraq.

Operation Eagle Claw An operation in April 1980 launched by the United States to rescue Americans held hostage by Iran at the U.S. embassy in Tehran. The operation failed on the ground in Iran when a helicopter flew into an airplane and both exploded. Eight soldiers were killed, and the mission was aborted.

Operation El Dorado Canyon On April 14, 1986, the United States bombed targets in Libya using Air Force bombers based in Great Britain and Navy carrier-borne aircraft based in the Mediterranean. The strike was in retaliation for terrorist attacks against American personnel in Europe.

Operation Enduring Freedom The designation given to the counterterrorist war waged in the aftermath of the September 11, 2001, homeland attacks.

Operation Infinite Justice The original designation given to the counterterrorist war waged in the aftermath of the attacks of September 11, 2001.

Operation Iraqi Freedom The designation given to the U.S.-led invasion of Iraq in March 2003.

Order, the An American neo-Nazi terrorist group founded by Robert Jay Mathews in 1983. Centered in the Pacific Northwest, the Order's methods for fighting its war against what it termed the Zionist Occupation Government were counterfeiting, bank robberies, armored car robberies, and murder. The Order had been suppressed by December 1985.

Order of Assassins A religious movement established in the Middle East during the 11th century. It sought to purge the Islamic faith and resist the Crusader invasions. The Assassins were noted for using stealth to kill their opponents.

Organizational theory A term used in the field of public administration to describe the study of bureaucracy.

Osawatomie An underground periodical published by the Weather Underground Organization during the 1970s.

Pahlavi, Shah Mohammad Reza The last Shah of Iran, who was ousted in an Islamic revolution led by the Ayatollah Ruhollah Khomeini.

Palestine Islamic Jihad (PIJ) The PIJ is not a single organization but a loose affiliation of factions. It is an Islamic fundamentalist revolutionary movement that seeks to promote jihad, or holy war, and to form a Palestinian state; it is responsible for assassinations and suicide bombings.

Palestine Liberation Front (PLF) The PLF split from the Popular Front for the Liberation of Palestine—General Command in the mid-1970s and further split into pro-PLO, pro-Syrian, and pro-Libyan factions. The pro-PLO faction was led by Abu Abbas, who committed a number of attacks against Israel.

Palestine Liberation Organization (PLO) An umbrella Palestinian nationalist organization. It comprises numerous activist factions, many of which engage in political violence.

Palmer, A. Mitchell The attorney general who served during the administration of American President Woodrow Wilson.

Palmer Raids A series of raids in the United States during the administration of President Woodrow Wilson targeting communist and other leftist radical groups.

Pan Am Flight 103 An airliner that exploded over Lockerbie, Scotland, on December 21, 1988. In the explosion, 270 people were killed, including all 259 passengers and crew and 11 persons on the ground. Libya was implicated in the incident.

Pan-Arabism An international Arab nationalist movement that held momentum after World War II.

Parachute Sayaret An elite reconnaissance unit within the Israel Defense Force. It has been deployed in small and large units, relying on high mobility to penetrate deep into hostile territory. It participated in the Entebbe rescue in Uganda and was used against Hezbollah in southern Lebanon.

Paramilitaries A term used to describe rightist irregular units and groups that are frequently supported by governments or progovernment interests. Many paramilitaries have been responsible for human rights violations.

Paramilitary repressive options Counterterrorist measures that seek to resolve terrorist crises by deploying armed nonmilitary personnel. These personnel can include covert operatives, localized militia units, or large armed units.

Party of God Lebanon's Hezbollah.

Peace process An ongoing process of negotiations between warring parties with the goal of addressing their underlying grievances and ending armed conflict.

People's Liberation Army The Chinese communist national army, founded by Mao Zedong.

People's Temple of the Disciples of Christ A cult founded and led by Jim Jones. After relocating to Guyana, hundreds of members of the group committed ritual suicide when followers shot and killed Congressman Leo Ryan and several others; 914 people died, including 200 children.

People's war A concept in irregular warfare in which the guerrilla fighters and the populace are theoretically indistinguishable.

People's Will *See* Narodnaya Volya.

Phansi A rope used by the Thuggees of India to ritualistically strangle their victims.

Phantom cells An organizational concept articulated by former Klansman Louis Beam in the early 1990s. Rightist dissidents were encouraged to organize themselves into autonomous subversive cells that would be undetectable by the enemy U.S. government or agents of the New World Order.

Phineas Priesthood A shadowy movement of Christian Identity fundamentalists in the United States who believe that they are called by God to purify their race and Christianity. They are opposed to abortion, homosexuality, interracial mixing, and whites who "degrade" white racial supremacy. It is a calling for men only, so no women can become Phineas Priests. The name is taken from the Bible at Chapter 25, Verse 6 of the Book of Numbers, which tells the story of a Hebrew man named Phineas who killed an Israelite man and his Midianite wife in the temple.

Phoenix Program A three-year campaign conducted during the Vietnam War to disrupt and eliminate the administrative effectiveness of the communist Viet Cong.

Phosgene gas A chemical agent that causes the lungs to fill with water, choking the victim.

Pierce, William The founder and leader of the neo-Nazi National Alliance in the United States. Also author of *The Turner Diaries*, under the nom de plume of Andrew MacDonald.

Pipe bombs Devices constructed from common pipes that are filled with explosives (usually gunpowder) and then capped on both ends. Nuts, bolts, screws, nails, and other shrapnel are usually taped or otherwise attached to these devices.

Plastic explosives A malleable explosive compound commonly used by terrorists.

Pogroms Anti-Semitic massacres in Europe that occurred periodically from the time of the First Crusade through the Nazi Holocaust. Usually centered in Central and Eastern Europe.

Pol Pot The principal leader of Cambodia's Khmer Rouge during its insurgency and consolidation of power.

Police Border Guards An elite Israeli paramilitary force that is frequently deployed as a counterterrorist force. Known as the Green Police, it operates in two subgroups: YAMAS is a covert group that has been used extensively during the Palestinian intifada, and YAMAM was specifically created to engage in counterterrorist and hostage rescue operations.

Politically sympathetic sponsorship State-sponsored terrorism that does not progress beyond ideological and moral support.

Pope Urban II The Roman Catholic pope from 1088 to 1099 who commissioned the first Christian Crusade with the goal of seizing Jerusalem and other territories from Muslim control. He promised forgiveness for sins to all who fought for the Crusade.

Popular Front for the Liberation of Palestine (PFLP) Founded in 1967 by George Habash, it is a Marxist organization that advocates a multinational Arab revolution, and it has been responsible for dramatic international terrorist attacks. Its hijacking campaign in 1969 and 1970, its collaboration with Western European terrorists, and its mentorship of Carlos the Jackal arguably established the model for modern international terrorism.

Popular Front for the Liberation of Palestine— General Command (PFLP-GC) Ahmid Jibril formed the PFLP-GC in 1968 when he split from the Popular Front for the Liberation of Palestine (PFLP) because he considered the PFLP too involved in politics and not sufficiently committed to the armed struggle against Israel. The PFLP-GC was probably directed by Syria and has been responsible for many cross-border attacks against Israel.

Port Huron Statement A document crafted in the United States in 1962 by members of Students for a Democratic Society. It harshly criticized mainstream American values and called for the establishment of a New Left movement in the United States.

Prairie Fire An underground manifesto published by the Weather Underground Organization during the 1970s.

Precision-guided munitions (PGMs) Technologically advanced weapons that can be remotely guided to targets. Some PGMs are referred to as smart bombs.

Preemptive strikes Counterterrorist measures that proactively seek out and attack terrorist centers prior to a terrorist incident.

Pressure trigger Weapons such as mines are detonated when physical pressure is applied to a trigger. A variation on physical pressure triggers is trip-wire booby traps. More sophisticated pressure triggers react to atmospheric (barometric) pressure, such as changes in pressure when an airliner ascends or descends.

Prevention and Punishment of Crimes Against Internationally Protected Persons, Including Diplomatic Agents. A treaty that sought to establish a common international framework for suppressing extremist attacks against those who are protected by internationally recognized status.

Progressive Labor Party A Maoist faction of the Students for a Democratic Society in the United States. Active during the late 1960s and 1970s.

Proletariat A Marxist term for the working class.

Propaganda by the deed The notion that revolutionaries must violently act on their beliefs to promote the ideals of the revolution. Originally promoted by the anarchists.

"Property is theft!" The anarchist philosopher Pierre-Joseph Proudhon's belief that systems based on the acquisition of private property are inherently exploitative.

Protocols of the Learned Elders of Zion A forgery written under the direction of the czarist secret police in the late 19th century. It purports to be the proceedings of a secret international society of Jewish elders who are plotting to rule the world.

Proudhon, Pierre-Joseph Nineteenth-century philosopher and father of anarchism.

Provisional Irish Republican Army (Provos) A terrorist organization in Northern Ireland that champions the rights of Northern Irish Catholics. The PIRA was formed with the goal of uniting Northern Ireland with the Irish Republic. Also known as the Provos.

Provos The popular name given to the Provisional Irish Republican Army.

Publicize the cause The practice by terrorists of disseminating information about their grievances and championed groups. This can be done through symbolic violence and the manipulation of the media.

Punitive strikes Counterterrorist measures that seek out and attack terrorist centers to damage the terrorist organization. Frequently conducted as retribution for a terrorist incident.

Qaddafi, Muammar el- The ruler of Libya who became a prominent figure in state sponsorship of international terrorism during the 1980s.

Qassam A relatively unsophisticated surface-to-surface missile developed by the military arm of HAMAS in Gaza. Thousands of Qassams have been fired into Israel. Newer designs of the rocket are more sophisticated.

Qods (Jerusalem) Force A unit of Iran's Revolutionary Guards Corps that promotes the "liberation" of Jerusalem from non-Muslims.

Racial holy war (Rahowa) A term given by racial supremacists to a future race war that they believe will inevitably occur in the United States.

Racial profiling Similar to criminal profiling, but it uses race or ethnicity as the overriding descriptor to assist in the apprehension of suspects. Race is a legitimate element for criminal profiling, but it cannot be the principal element. Unfortunately, incidents of racial profiling have been documented for some time in the United States.

Radiological agents Materials that emit radiation that can harm living organisms when inhaled or otherwise ingested. Non-weapons-grade radiological agents could theoretically be used to construct a toxic dirty bomb.

Rajneeshees Followers of the cult leader Bhagwan Shree Rajneesh. In September 1984, the group poisoned the salad bars of 10 Oregon restaurants with *Salmonella* bacteria. More than 700 people fell ill.

RDX The central component of most plastic explosives.

Reactionary A term given to far-right and fringe-right political tendencies.

Red Army Faction (RAF) A leftist terrorist movement active in West Germany during the 1970s and 1980s. Also referred to as the Baader-Meinhof Gang.

Red Brigade A leftist terrorist movement active in Italy during the 1970s and 1980s.

Red Guards Groups of young Communist radicals who sought to purge Chinese society during the Great Proletarian Cultural Revolution.

Red Scares Periodic anticommunist security crises in the United States, when national leaders reacted to the perceived threat of communist subversion.

Regicide The killing of kings.

Reign of Terror (régime de la terreur) A period during the French Revolution when the new republic violently purged those who were thought a threat to the prevailing ideals of the revolution. Terrorism was considered a necessary and progressive revolutionary tactic.

Relative deprivation theory A sociological term that indicates the lack of human needs vis-à-vis other members of a particular society.

Religious communal terrorism Conflict between religious groups involving terrorist violence.

Repentance laws An offer of qualified amnesty by the Italian government to Red Brigades members, requiring them to demonstrate repentance for their crimes. Repentance was established

by cooperating within a sliding scale of collaboration. A significant number of imprisoned Red Brigades terrorists accepted repentance reductions in their sentences.

Repressive responses Counterterrorist measures that seek to resolve terrorist crises by disrupting or destroying terrorist groups and movements. These responses include military and nonmilitary options.

Republic of New Africa (RNA) An African American nationalist organization. Its goal was to form a separate African American nation from portions of several southern states. Some members opted to engage in political violence under the name of the New African Freedom Fighters.

Resistance A cover name used by the leftist May 19 Communist Organization in the United States.

Revolutionary Armed Forces of Colombia (Fuerzas Armados Revolucionarios de Colombia, or FARC) An enduring Marxist insurgent movement in Colombia that has engaged in guerrilla warfare and terrorism since its inception during the 1960s.

Revolutionary Catechism A revolutionary manifesto written by the Russian anarchist Sergei Nechayev.

Revolutionary dissident terrorism The practice of political violence with the goal of destroying an existing order, committed with a plan for the aftermath of the revolution.

Revolutionary Fighting Group *See* May 19 Communist Organization.

Revolutionary Guards Corps Iranian Islamic revolutionaries who have been deployed abroad, mainly to Lebanon, to promote Islamic revolution.

Revolutionary Justice Organization An adopted alias of Lebanon's Hezbollah.

Revolutionary Tribunal The revolutionary court established during the French Revolution.

Revolutionary United Front (RUF) A rebel movement that arose in Sierra Leone in 1991. Led by Foday Sankoh, RUF forces were responsible for widespread human rights abuses and atrocities.

Revolutionary Youth Movement II A faction of Students for a Democratic Society in the United States. The group adapted its ideological motivations to the political and social context of the 1960s by tailoring the ideologies of orthodox Marxism to the political environment of the 1960s.

Rewards for Justice Program An international bounty program managed by the U.S. Diplomatic Security Service. The program offered cash rewards for information leading to the arrest of wanted terrorists.

Roadside bomb An improvised explosive device (IED) constructed and deployed by Iraqi insurgents against U.S.-led occupation forces.

Rocket-propelled grenades (RPGs) Handheld military weapons that use a propellant to fire a rocket-like explosive.

Royal Marine Commandos British rapid-reaction troops that deploy in larger numbers than the Special Air Service and Special Boat Service. They are organized around units called commandos that are roughly equivalent to a conventional battalion.

RPG-7 A rocket-propelled grenade weapon manufactured in large quantities by the Soviet Bloc.

Ruby Ridge An August 1992 incident in Idaho when racial supremacist Randy Weaver and his family were besieged by federal agents for failure to reply to an illegal weapons charge. Weaver's wife and son were killed during the incident, as was a U.S. Marshal. Members of the Patriot movement and other right-wing extremists cite Ruby Ridge as evidence of a broader government conspiracy to deprive freedom-loving "true" Americans of their right to bear arms and other liberties.

SA-7 An infrared-targeted Soviet-made surface-to-air missile, also known as the Grail.

Sam Melville–Jonathan Jackson Unit A group that took credit for bombing the Boston State House in Boston, Massachusetts, in 1975. It was a term used by the leftist United Freedom Front.

Sanchez, Ilich Ramirez *See* Carlos the Jackal.

Sandinistas A Marxist movement in Nicaragua that seized power after a successful insurgency against the regime of Anastasio Somoza Debayle. The Sandinista regime became the object of an American-supported insurgency.

Sarin A potent nerve gas. The Aum Supreme Truth cult released sarin gas into the Tokyo, Japan, subway system in March 1995, killing 12 and injuring thousands.

Sayaret Elite Israeli reconnaissance units that engage in counterterrorist operations. Sayaret have been attached to General Headquarters (Sayaret Matkal) and the Golani Brigade. There is also a Parachute Sayaret.

Sayaret Matkal An elite reconnaissance unit within the Israel Defense Force, attached to the IDF General Headquarters. It is a highly secretive formation that operates in small units and is regularly used for counterterrorist operations.

Sea Air Land Forces (SEALs) Similar to the British Special Boat Service and French Navy special assault units, the primary mission of the U.S. Navy SEALs is to conduct seaborne, riverine, and harbor operations. They have also been used extensively on land.

Sectarian violence Religious communal violence.

Semtex A high-grade and high-yield plastic explosive originally manufactured in Czechoslovakia when it was a member of the Soviet Bloc.

Shadow wars Covert campaigns to suppress terrorism.

Shining Path (Sendero Luminoso) A Marxist insurgent movement in Peru. Founded and led by former philosophy professor Abimael Guzmán, the group regularly engaged in terrorism.

Sicarii The Zealot rebels who opposed Roman rule. Named for the curved dagger, or *sica*, that was a preferred weapon.

Signal intelligence Intelligence that has been collected by technological resources. Also referred to as SIGINT.

Signature method Methods that become closely affiliated with the operational activities of specific extremist groups.

Sinn Féin An aboveground political party in Northern Ireland that champions Catholic rights and union with the Irish Republic.

Skinheads A countercultural youth movement that began in England in the late 1960s. An international racist skinhead movement eventually developed in Europe and the United States. The term *skinhead* refers to the members' practice of shaving their heads.

Sleeper cells A tactic used by international terrorist movements in which operatives theoretically establish residence in another country to await a time when they will be activated by orders to carry out a terrorist attack.

Smallpox A formerly epidemic disease that has been eradicated in nature but that has been preserved in research laboratories. A possible ingredient for biological weapons.

Social cleansing The practice of eliminating defined undesirables from society. These undesirables can include those who practice defined morals crimes or who engage in denounced political and social behaviors.

Social reform Conciliatory counterterrorist measures that seek to resolve terrorist crises by resolving political and social problems that are the focus of the terrorists' grievances.

Social Revolutionary Party A Russian revolutionary movement during the late 19th and early 20th centuries. The group adopted terrorism as a revolutionary method.

Soft targets Civilian and other undefended targets that are easily victimized by terrorists.

Somoza Debayle, Anastasio The U.S.-supported Nicaraguan dictator overthrown by the Sandinista-led insurgency.

Special Air Service (SAS) A secretive organization in the British Army that has been used repeatedly in counterterrorist operations. Organized at a regimental level, but operating in very small teams, the SAS is similar to the French 1st Navy Parachute Infantry Regiment and the American Delta Force.

Special Boat Service (SBS) A special unit under the command of the British Royal Navy. The SBS specializes in operations against seaborne targets and along coastlines and harbors.

They are similar to the French Navy's special assault units and the American SEALs.

Special Operations Command The general headquarters for U.S. Special Operations Forces.

Special operations forces Elite military and paramilitary units deployed by many armed forces. They are highly trained and are capable of operating in large or small formations, both overtly and covertly.

Spillover effect Terrorist violence that occurs beyond the borders of the countries that are the target of such violence.

State assistance Tacit state participation in and encouragement of extremist behavior. Its basic characteristic is that the state, through sympathetic proxies and agents, implicitly takes part in repression, violence, and terrorism.

State patronage Active state participation in and encouragement of extremist behavior. Its basic characteristic is that the state, through its agencies and personnel, actively takes part in repression, violence, and terrorism.

Stateless revolutionaries International terrorists who are not sponsored by, or based in, a particular country.

State-regulated press State-regulated media exist in environments where the state routinely intervenes in the reporting of information by the press. This can occur in societies that otherwise have a measure of democratic freedoms as well as in totalitarian societies.

Stinger A technologically advanced handheld anti-aircraft missile manufactured by the United States.

Stockholm syndrome A psychological condition in which hostages begin to identify and sympathize with their captors.

Strong multipolar terrorist environment A terrorist environment that presumes that state sponsorship guides terrorist behavior but that several governments support their favored groups. It also presumes that there are few truly autonomous international terrorist movements; they all have a link to a state sponsor.

Structural theory A theory used in many disciplines to identify social conditions (structures) that affect group access to services, equal rights, civil protections, freedom, or other quality-of-life measures.

Struggle meetings Revolutionary rallies held during the Chinese Revolution. Denunciations were often made against those thought to be a threat to the revolution.

Students for a Democratic Society (SDS) A leftist student movement founded in 1962 in the United States. It rose to become the preeminent activist organization on American campuses throughout the 1960s. Its factions—the Progressive Labor Party, Revolutionary Youth Movement II, and the Weathermen—were highly active during the 1960s and early 1970s.

Submachine guns Light automatic weapons that fire pistol ammunition.

Suicide bombers Terrorists trained to detonate explosives that have been strapped to their bodies.

Sun Tzu Chinese military philosopher whose book *The Art of War* has been a significant influence on military theory.

Supergrass A policy in Northern Ireland during the 1980s of convincing Provos and members of the Irish National Liberation Army to defect from their movements and inform on their former comrades.

Suppression campaigns Counterterrorist measures that seek to resolve terrorist crises by waging an ongoing campaign to destroy the terrorists' capacity to strike.

Survivalism A philosophy of complete self-sufficiency. Sometimes adopted by those who practice the tactic of going "off the grid."

Tamil Tigers *See* Liberation Tigers of Tamil Eelam.

Terminal institutions Institutions under the jurisdiction of criminal justice and military justice systems that provide final resolution to individual terrorists' careers after they have been captured, prosecuted, convicted, and imprisoned.

Terrorism Elements from the American definitional model define terrorism as a premeditated and unlawful act in which groups or agents of some principal engage in a threatened or actual use of force or violence against human or property targets. These groups or agents engage in this behavior intending the purposeful intimidation of governments or people to affect policy or behavior with an underlying political objective. There are more than 100 definitions of terrorism.

Terrorist One who practices terrorism. Often a highly contextual term.

Terrorist profiles Descriptive profiles of terrorist suspects developed by law enforcement agencies to assist in the apprehension of terrorist suspects. Similar to criminal profiling.

Third World A postwar term created to describe the developing world.

Thuggee A mystical cult that existed for centuries in India. Members ritualistically murdered travelers to honor the goddess Kali.

TNT A commercially available explosive.

Tokyo Convention on Offences and Certain Other Acts Committed on Board Aircraft A treaty enacted in 1963 as the first airline crimes treaty.

Torture Physical and psychological pressure and degradation.

Total war The unrestrained use of force against a broad selection of targets to utterly defeat an enemy.

Totalitarian regimes Governments that practice total control over public and political institutions. The media and other public information outlets are completely controlled.

Troubles, the The term given to sectarian violence between Catholics and Protestants in Northern Ireland.

Turner Diaries, The A short novel written by National Alliance founder William Pierce under the pseudonym Andrew MacDonald. It depicts an Aryan revolution in the United States and is considered by many neo-Nazis to be a blueprint for the eventual racial holy war.

TWA Flight 847 In June 1985, hijackers belonging to Lebanon's Hezbollah hijacked a TWA airliner, taking it on a high-profile and media-intensive odyssey around the Mediterranean.

Two-Seedline Christian Identity A Christian Identity mystical belief that rejects the notion that all humans are descended from Adam (see One-Seedline Christian Identity). According to this belief, Eve bore Abel as Adam's son but bore Cain as the son of the Serpent. Outside of the Garden of Eden lived nonwhite, soulless beasts who were a separate species from humans. When Cain slew Abel, he was cast out of the Garden to live among the soulless beasts. Those who became the descendants of Cain are the modern Jews. They are biologically descended from the devil and are a demonic people worthy of extermination.

Tyrannicide The assassination of tyrants for the greater good of society.

Unabomber The popular nickname applied to Theodore Kaczynski.

United Freedom Front (UFF) A leftist terrorist group in the United States that was active from the mid-1970s through the mid-1980s.

USA PATRIOT Act The Uniting and Strengthening America by Providing Appropriate Tools Required to Intercept and Obstruct Terrorism Act of 2001. Passed by the U.S. Congress on October 26, 2001. Its provisions are designed to authorize homeland security–related measures to combat terrorist threats to the U.S. homeland.

USA PATRIOT Improvement and Reauthorization Act of 2005 Legislation mandating the periodic review and reauthorization of the provisions of the USA PATRIOT Act.

USS Cole An American destroyer that was severely damaged on October 12, 2000, while berthed in the port of Aden, Yemen. Two suicide bombers detonated a boat bomb next to the Cole, killing themselves and 17 crew members and wounding 39 other Navy personnel.

Utopia An ideal society.

Vanguard strategy In Marxist and non-Marxist theory, the strategy of using a well-indoctrinated and motivated elite to lead the working-class revolution. In practice, this strategy was adopted in the postwar era by terrorist organizations and extremist movements.

Vehicular bombs Include car bombs and truck bombs; they are mobile, covert in the sense that they are not readily identifiable, capable of transporting large amounts of explosives, and rather easily constructed. They have been used on scores of occasions throughout the world.

Viet Cong The name given by the United States and its noncommunist South Vietnamese allies to South Vietnamese communist insurgents.

Vigilante state terrorism Unofficial state terrorism in which state personnel engage in nonsanctioned political violence. It can include the use of death squads.

Waco The location in Texas of an April 1993 incident in which federal agents besieged the Branch Davidian cult's compound after a failed attempt in February to serve a search warrant for illegal firearms had ended in the deaths of four federal agents and several cult members. During an assault on April 19, led by the FBI, about 80 Branch Davidians—including more than 20 children—died in a blaze that leveled the compound. Patriots and other rightists consider this tragedy to be evidence of government power run amok.

Warfare Making war against an enemy. In the modern era, it usually refers to conventional and guerrilla conflicts.

Wars of national liberation A series of wars fought in the developing world in the postwar era. These conflicts frequently pitted indigenous guerrilla fighters against European colonial powers or governments perceived as pro-Western. Insurgents were frequently supported by the Soviet Bloc or China.

Weak multipolar terrorist environment A terrorist environment that presupposes that state sponsorship exists but that the terrorist groups are more autonomous. Under this scenario, several governments support their favored groups, but many of these groups are relatively independent international terrorist movements.

Weapons of mass destruction High-yield weapons that can potentially cause a large number of casualties when used by terrorists. Examples of these weapons include chemical, biological, radiological, and nuclear weapons. They can also be constructed from less exotic compounds, such as ANFO.

Weather Bureau The designation adopted by the leaders of the Weatherman faction of Students for a Democratic Society.

Weather Underground Organization (WUO) The adopted name of the Weathermen after they moved underground.

Weathermen A militant faction of Students for a Democratic Society that advocated, and engaged in, violent confrontation with the authorities. Some engaged in terrorist violence.

Weinrich, Johannes A former West German terrorist "purchased" by the German government from the government of Yemen. He stood trial in Germany for the 1983 bombing of a French cultural center in Berlin, in which one person was killed and 23 others were wounded. He had also been a very close associate of Carlos the Jackal.

White Aryan Resistance A California-based racial supremacist hate group founded by former Klansman Tom Metzger in the early 1980s.

Wrath of God A counterterrorist unit created by the Israelis to eliminate Palestinian operatives who had participated in the massacre of Israeli athletes at the 1972 Munich Olympics. Also called Mivtzan Elohim.

Wu Ch'i Chinese military philosopher who is usually associated with Sun Tzu.

YAMAM One of two operational subgroups deployed by Israel's Police Border Guards (the other subgroup is YAMAS). It engages in counterterrorist and hostage rescue operations.

YAMAS One of two operational subgroups deployed by Israel's Police Border Guards (the other subgroup is YAMAM). It is a covert unit that has been used to neutralize terrorist cells in conjunction with covert Israel Defense Force operatives.

Year Zero The ideological designation given by the Khmer Rouge to the beginning of their genocidal consolidation of power.

Zapatista National Liberation Front Leftist rebels originally centered in Chiapas, Mexico. During the late 1990s, they engaged in guerrilla fighting that ended when they were integrated into the Mexican political process.

Zealots Hebrew rebels who uncompromisingly opposed Roman rule in ancient Palestine.

Zionism An intellectual movement within the Jewish community describing the conditions for the settlement of Jews in Israel.

NOTES

Chapter One

1. *Webster's New Twentieth-Century Dictionary of the English Language,* unabridged, 2nd ed. (New York, NY: Publishers Guild, 1966).

2. Laird Wilcox, "What Is Extremism? Style and Tactics Matter More Than Goals," in *American Extremists: Militias, Supremacists, Klansmen, Communists, & Others,* eds. John George and Laird Wilcox (Amherst, NY: Prometheus, 1996), 54.

3. Jeffrey Goldberg, "Inside Jihad U.: The Education of a Holy Warrior," *New York Times Magazine,* June 25, 2000, 35.

4. For an excellent list of traits of extremists, see Laird Wilcox, "What Is Extremism?" 54.

5. For references to the Cuban perspective, see Martin Kenner and James Petras, *Fidel Castro Speaks* (New York, NY: Grove, 1969).

6. Walter Laqueur, *The New Terrorism: Fanaticism and the Arms of Mass Destruction* (New York, NY: Oxford University Press, 1999), 5.

7. See Alex P. Schmid and Albert J. Jongman, *Political Terrorism* (Amsterdam: North Holland, 1988). The book reports the results of a survey of 100 experts asked for their definitions of terrorism.

8. David J. Whittaker, ed., *The Terrorism Reader* (New York, NY: Routledge, 2001), 8.

9. Ibid., 1.

10. Office for the Protection of the Constitution, 1. See Whittaker, *The Terrorism Reader.*

11. Ibid.

12. Ted Robert Gurr, "Political Terrorism: Historical Antecedents and Contemporary Trends," in *Violence in America: Protest, Rebellion, Reform,* vol. 2 (Newbury Park, CA: Sage, 1989).

13. J. P. Gibbs, "Conceptualization of Terrorism," *American Sociological Review* 54 (1989): 329, quoted in Mark S. Hamm, ed. *Hate Crime: International Perspectives on Causes and Control* (Highland Heights: Northern Kentucky University, Academy of Criminal Justice Sciences, 1994), 111.

14. Bruce Hoffman, *Inside Terrorism* (New York, NY: Columbia University Press, 1998), 43.

15. Whittaker, *The Terrorism Reader,* 8.

16. U.S. Departments of the Army and the Air Force, *Military Operations in Low Intensity Conflict,* Field Manual 100-20/Air Force Pamphlet 3-20 (Washington, DC: Government Printing Office, 1990), 3–1.

17. 18 U.S.C. 3077.

18. Terrorist Research and Analytical Center, National Security Division, Federal Bureau of Investigation, *Terrorism in the United States 1995* (Washington, DC: U.S. Department of Justice, 1996), ii.

19. Office of the Coordinator for Counterterrorism, *Patterns of Global Terrorism 1996,* U.S. Department of State Publication 10433 (Washington, DC: U.S. Department of State, 1997), vi.

20. Steven E. Barkan and Lynne L. Snowden, *Collective Violence* (Boston, MA: Allyn & Bacon, 2001).

21. Hoffman, *Inside Terrorism.*

22. Laqueur, *The New Terrorism.*

23. Rachel Ehrenfeld, *Narco Terrorism* (New York, NY: Basic Books, 1990); Jonathan B. Tucker, ed., *Toxic Terror: Assessing Terrorist Use of Chemical and Biological Weapons* (Cambridge, MA: MIT Press, 2000).

24. Paul R. Pillar, *Terrorism and U.S. Foreign Policy* (Washington, DC: Brookings Institution Press, 2001), 178.

25. Ibid., 86.

26. Kevin Jack Riley and Bruce Hoffman, *Domestic Terrorism: A National Assessment of State and Local Preparedness* (Santa Monica, CA: RAND, 1995), 2.

27. The quote has been more widely reported since the Vietnam War as "we had to destroy the village to save it." See Don Oberdorfer, *Tet!* (Garden City, NY: Doubleday, 1971), 184–85, 332. See also Neil Sheehan, *A Bright Shining Lie: John Paul Vann and America in Vietnam* (New York, NY: Random House, 1988), 719.

28. In Chinese literature and propaganda, *bandit* is often a synonym for *rebel.* Sun Tzu, *The Art of War* (New York, NY: Oxford University Press, 1963), 168.

29. Within the context of the campaign, Lyndon Johnson's anti-Communist credentials were decisively validated during the Gulf of Tonkin crisis in August 1964. The destroyer USS *Maddox* was reported to have been attacked by North Vietnamese torpedo boats off the coast of North Vietnam. American air strikes were launched in reprisal, and Congress unanimously passed the Gulf of Tonkin Resolution, which supported President Johnson's use of measures to protect U.S. interests in Vietnam and elsewhere. For a discussion of the incident within the context of the politics at the time, see Doris Kearns, *Lyndon Johnson and the American Dream* (New York, NY: Harper & Row, 1976), 195. For an insider's discussion, see Merle Miller, *Lyndon: An Oral Biography* (New York, NY: Ballantine, 1980), 465–77.

30. For a discussion of this subject from the cultural perspectives of Bosnian Muslims and Serbs, see

Steven M. Weine, *When History Is a Nightmare: Lives and Memories of Ethnic Cleansing in Bosnia-Herzegovina* (New Brunswick, NJ: Rutgers University Press, 1999).

31. Associated Press reporter Peter Arnett attributed the source of the quotation to a U.S. soldier at the city of Ben Tre in South Vietnam during the Tet offensive in 1968. As reported, it was the statement of an officer higher up in the chain of command—a U.S. army major. Although widely repeated at the time and since the war, only Arnett said he heard the statement at the site, and only Arnett filed the quotation from the Ben Tre visit. The U.S. officer was not identified and has not been identified since the war (see Oberdorfer, *Tet!*, and Sheehan, *A Bright Shining Lie*). The U.S. Department of Defense launched an investigation to find the source of the quote. No officer or enlisted man was identified (see Oberdorfer, *Tet!*).

32. Gabriel Weimann and Conrad Winn, *The Theater of Terror: Mass Media and International Terrorism* (New York, NY: Longman, 1994), 104. The authors mention the following societal participants in media events: the direct victims, the terrorists, the broadcasting audience, journalists, and governments.

33. David L. Paletz and Alex P. Schmid, *Terrorism and the Media* (Newbury Park, CA: Sage, 1992), 179.

34. For a discussion of the ambiguities about defining combatants and noncombatants, see Peter C. Sederberg, *Terrorist Myths: Illusion, Rhetoric, and Reality* (Englewood Cliffs, NJ: Prentice Hall, 1989), 37–39.

35. For a discussion of the ambiguities about defining indiscriminate force, see ibid., 39–40.

Chapter Two

1. See Walter Laqueur, *The New Terrorism: Fanaticism and the Arms of Mass Destruction* (New York, NY: Oxford University Press, 1999), 90.

2. An extraordinary and classic history of the Roman Empire is found in Edward Gibbon's great work of literature, *The History of the Decline and Fall of the Roman Empire* (New York, NY: AMS Press, 1974, reprinted from J. B. Bury, ed., London, UK: Methuen, 1909).

3. For a discussion of the Roman occupation of Judea and the First Jewish Revolt in the broader context of Roman politics, see Michael Grant, *The Twelve Caesars* (New York, NY: Scribner, 1975).

4. Burke, a Whig member of Parliament, was a progressive in his time. He opposed absolutism, poor treatment of the American colonists, and the slave trade. He expressed his opposition to Jacobin extremism in a series of writings, including *Reflections on the French Revolution* and *Letters on a Regicide Peace*.

5. For a classic account of the Terror, see Stanley Loomis, *Paris in the Terror: June 1793–July 1794* (Philadelphia, PA: J. B. Lippincott, 1964).

6. A French physician, Joseph Ignace Guillotin, invented the guillotine. He was loyal to the revolution and a deputy to the States-General. Guillotin encouraged the use of the beheading machine as a painless, humane, and symbolically revolutionary method of execution.

7. Pamala L. Griset and Sue Mahan, *Terrorism in Perspective* (Thousand Oaks, CA: Sage, 2002), 4.

8. Ibid.

9. For a good discussion about the consolidation of the Chinese revolution and the Great Proletarian Cultural Revolution that occurred later, see John King Fairbank, *The Great Chinese Revolution: 1800–1985* (New York, NY: Harper & Row, 1987). For an analysis of the ideology of the Ayatollah Khomeini and the Iranian revolution, see Vanessa Martin, *Creating an Islamic State: Khomeini and the Making of a New Iran* (London, UK: I. B. Tauris, 2000).

10. Karl Marx and Friedrich Engels, "Manifesto of the Communist Party," in *The Marx-Engels Reader*, ed. Robert C. Tucker (New York, NY: Norton, 1972), 335.

11. Laqueur, *The New Terrorism*, 13.

12. Ibid., 81.

13. Ibid., 82.

14. The politics of the French Revolution are evaluated in Theda Skocpol, *States and Social Revolutions: A Comparative Analysis of France, Russia, and China* (Cambridge, UK: Cambridge University Press, 1990), 174–205.

15. For a comparative discussion of ideological conflict in revolutionary environments, see Skocpol, *States and Social Revolutions*. For seminal discussions that formed the ideological foundation for the U.S. Constitution and Bill of Rights, see Alexander Hamilton, John Jay, and James Madison, *The Federalist: A Commentary on the Constitution of the United States, Being a Collection of Essays Written in Support of the Constitution Agreed Upon September 17, 1787* (New York, NY: Modern Library, 2000).

16. Laqueur, *The New Terrorism*, 230.

17. Konrad Kellen, "Ideology and Rebellion: Terrorism in West Germany," in *Origins of Terrorism: Psychologies, Ideologies, Theologies, States of Mind*, ed. Walter Reich (Washington, DC: Woodrow Wilson Center Press, 1998), 57.

18. See Harry B. Ellis, *Ideals and Ideologies: Communism, Socialism, and Capitalism* (New York, NY: World, 1972).

19. Leonard Weinberg, "An Overview of Right-Wing Extremism in the Western World: A Study of Convergence, Linkage, and Identity," in *Nation and Race: The Developing Euro-American Racist Subculture*, eds. Jeffrey Kaplan and Tore Bjørgo (Boston, MA: Northeastern University Press, 1998), 8.

20. Ibid., 10.

21. See Anthony Faiola and Stephany Kirchner, "Merkel Condemns Rash of Neo-Nazi Attacks in Germany," *Los Angeles Times*, August 26, 2015.

22. For a good journalistic chronology of the Spanish Civil War, see R. H. Haigh, D. S. Morris, and A. R. Peters, *The*

Guardian Book of the Spanish Civil War (Aldershot, UK: Wildwood House, 1987).

23. Mark W. Janis, An Introduction to International Law, 3d ed. (New York, NY: Aspen Law & Business, 1999), 171.

24. Jessica Stern, The Ultimate Terrorists (Cambridge, MA: Harvard University Press, 1999), 18.

25. See Bernhardt J. Hurwood, Society and the Assassin: A Background Book on Political Murder (New York, NY: Parents' Magazine Press, 1970), 17.

26. David E. Sanger, "In Speech, Bush Focuses on Conflicts Beyond Iraq," New York Times, May 1, 2003.

27. National Commission on Terrorist Attacks Upon the United States, The 9/11 Commission Report (New York, NY: W. W. Norton, 2004), 32–33, 305, 311.

28. Carol J. Williams, "Suicide Attacks Rising Rapidly," Los Angeles Times, June 2, 2005.

Chapter Three

1. See Clifford E. Simonsen and Jeremy R. Spindlove, Terrorism Today: The Past, the Players, the Future (Upper Saddle River, NJ: Prentice Hall, 2000), 22–24.

2. Steven E. Barkan and Lynne L. Snowden, Collective Violence (Boston, MA: Allyn & Bacon, 2001), 6.

3. Ibid., 7.

4. Relative deprivation theory was pioneered by James Chowning Davies. See James Chowning Davies, "Toward a Theory of Revolution," American Sociological Review 25 (1962): 5–19.

5. Jack A. Goldstone, "Introduction: The Comparative and Historical Study of Revolutions," in Revolutions: Theoretical, Comparative, and Historical Studies (San Diego, CA: Harcourt Brace Jovanovich, 1986), 1–17, cited in Barkan and Snowden, Collective Violence, 53.

6. See Barkan and Snowden, Collective Violence, 55.

7. Ibid., 17.

8. See Ted Robert Gurr, Why Men Rebel (Princeton, NJ: Princeton University Press, 1970).

9. Ibid., p. 52.

10. See Alan Krueger and Jitka Malečková "Education, Poverty, and Terrorism: Is There a Causal Connection?," Journal of Economic Perspectives 17, no. 4 (2003): 119–44. See also Joshua Angrist, "The Economic Returns to Schooling in the West Bank and Gaza Strip," American Economic Review 85, no. 5 (1995): 1065–87.

11. Discussed in Barkan and Snowden, Collective Violence, 18.

12. Jerrold M. Post, "Terrorist Psycho-logic: Terrorist Behavior as a Product of Psychological Forces," in Origins of Terrorism: Psychologies, Ideologies, Theologies, States of Mind, ed. Walter Reich (Washington, DC: Woodrow Wilson Center Press, 1998), 9.

13. Ibid., 28, reporting findings of the Ministry of the Interior, Federal Republic of Germany, Analysen zum Terrorismus 1–4 (Darmstadt, Germany: Deutscher Verlag, 1981, 1982, 1983,

1984); Herbert Jäger, Gerhard Schmidtchen, and Lieselotte Süllwold, eds., Analysen zum Terrorismus 2: Lebenslaufanalysen (Darmstadt, Germany: Deutscher Verlag, 1981); Wanda von Baeyer-Kaette, Dieter Classens, Hubert Feger, and Friedhelm Neidhardt, eds., Analysen zum Terrorismus 3: Gruppenprozesse (Darmstadt, Germany: Deutscher Verlag, 1982).

14. Ibid., 28.

15. Ibid., 20.

16. Ibid.

17. Ibid., 25–42.

18. Ibid., 31.

19. See Émile Durkheim, Suicide, J. A. Spaulding and G. Simpson, Trans. (New York, NY: Free Press, 1951); see also Émile Durkheim, The Division of Labor in Society, W. D. Halls, Trans. (New York: Free Press, 1994).

20. See Robert K. Merton, "Social Structure and Anomie," American Sociological Review 3 (1938); see also Robert K. Merton, Social Theory and Social Structure, Enlarged ed. (New York, NY: Free Press, 1968).

21. Lawrence Cohen and Marcus Felson, "Social Change and Crime Rate Trends: A Routine Activity Approach," American Sociological Review 44, no. 4 (1979): 588–608.

22. See B. Krisberg, Crime and Privilege: Toward a New Criminology (Englewood Cliffs, NJ: Prentice Hall, 1975).

23. See William J. Chambliss and Robert B. Seidman. Law, Order and Power (Reading, MA: Addison-Wesley, 1982).

24. Ibid.; see also Richard Quinney, The Social Reality of Crime (Boston, MA: Little, Brown, 1970).

25. For a good summary of Mao's political ideology, see Stuart R. Schram, The Political Thought of Mao Tse-tung (New York, NY: Praeger, 1974).

26. Quotation in Peter Ford, "Why Do They Hate Us?" Christian Science Monitor, September 27, 2001.

27. Michael Scheuer (as Anonymous), Imperial Hubris: Why the West Is Losing the War on Terror (Dulles, VA: Brassey's, 2004), 1.

28. Office of the Director of National Intelligence, National Intelligence Estimate: The Terrorist Threat to the US Homeland (Washington, DC: National Intelligence Council, 2007).

29. Dana Priest, "Report Says Iraq Is New Terrorist Training Ground," Washington Post, January 14, 2005.

30. For a profile of one foreign volunteer's experience in Iraq, see Megan K. Stack, "Getting an Education in Jihad," Los Angeles Times, December 29, 2004.

31. For an analysis of American intervention in Central America and the Caribbean, see Lester D. Langley, The Banana Wars: United States Intervention in the Caribbean, 1898–1934 (Chicago, IL: Dorsey, 1985).

32. See Jay Mallin, Terror and Urban Guerrillas: A Study of Tactics and Documents (Coral Gables, FL: University of Miami Press, 1971).

33. Marighella's name has been alternatively spelled with one l and two ls. Marighella himself alternated between spellings.

34. Carlos Marighella, *Mini-Manual of the Urban Guerrilla*, cited in Mallin, *Terror and Urban Guerrillas*, 70–71.

35. For an interesting attack against Marxist ideology, see Milovan Djilas, *The Unperfect Society: Beyond the New Class* (New York, NY: Harcourt, Brace & World, 1969).

36. Barkan and Snowden, *Collective Violence*, 27.

37. Ibid., 27–28.

38. Ibid.

Chapter Four

1. Brian Jenkins, quoted in Bruce Hoffman, *Inside Terrorism* (New York, NY: Columbia University Press, 1998), 132.

2. Michael Moss, "An Internet Jihad Aims at U.S. Viewers," *New York Times*, October 15, 2007. See also Mary Beth Sheridan, "Terrorism Probe Points to Reach of Web Networks," *Washington Post*, January 24, 2008.

3. See Geisal G. Mohamed, "The Globe of Villages: Digital Media and the Rise of Homegrown Terrorism," *Dissent* (Winter 2007): 61–64. See also John Gray, "A Violent Episode in the Virtual World," *New Statesman*, July 18, 2005.

4. Ariana Eunjung Cha, "From a Virtual Shadow, Messages of Terror," *Washington Post*, October 2, 2004.

5. Richard Davis and Diana Owen, *New Media and American Politics* (New York, NY: Oxford University Press, 1998), 7.

6. Ibid., 9–15.

7. Ibid.

8. For a discussion of selective reporting, see James Rainey, "Unseen Pictures, Untold Stories," *Los Angeles Times*, May 21, 2005.

9. Hoffman, *Inside Terrorism*, 36–37.

10. See Albert Bandura, "Mechanisms of Moral Disengagement," in *Origins of Terrorism: Psychologies, Ideologies, Theologies, States of Mind*, ed. Walter Reich (Washington, DC: Woodrow Wilson Center, 1998), 169.

11. Hoffman, *Inside Terrorism*, 142.

12. Ibid.

13. See ibid.

14. Steven E. Barkan and Lynne L. Snowden, *Collective Violence* (Boston, MA: Allyn & Bacon, 2000), 84.

15. Peter Taylor, *States of Terror: Democracy and Political Violence* (London, UK: Penguin, 1993), 8, cited in Hoffman, *Inside Terrorism*, 74.

16. Abu Iyad with Eric Rouleau, *My Home, My Land: A Narrative of the Palestinian Struggle* (New York, NY: Time Books, 1981), 111–12, quoted in Hoffman, *Inside Terrorism*, 73.

17. Hoffman, *Inside Terrorism*, 132.

18. Gabriel Weimann and Conrad Winn, *The Theater of Terror: Mass Media and International Terrorism* (New York, NY: Longman, 1994), 1.

19. Barkan and Snowden, *Collective Violence*.

20. Lawrence Howard, ed., *Terrorism: Roots, Impact, Responses* (New York, NY: Praeger, 1992), 102.

21. For a discussion of the contagion effect and additional discussions, see Weimann and Winn, *The Theater of Terror*, 157–60, 211.

22. Ibid., 158. See also C. S. Spilerman, "The Causes of Racial Disturbances," *American Psychological Review 35* (1970): 627–49, and Leonard Berkowitz and Jacqueline Macaulay, "The Contagion of Criminal Violence," *Psychometry 34* (1971): 238–60.

23. For a discussion of the contagion effect and additional discussions, see Weimann and Winn, *The Theater of Terror*, 157–60, 211.

24. See David L. Paletz and Laura L. Tawney, "Broadcasting Organizations' Perspectives," in *Terrorism and the Media*, eds. David Paletz and Alex P. Schmid (Newbury Park, CA: Sage, 1992), 105.

25. Ibid., 107, 109.

Chapter Five

1. The one noncommunal dissident terrorist incident that approximated state terrorism in sheer scale was the September 11, 2001, Al Qaeda attack on the United States.

2. Paul R. Pillar, *Terrorism and U.S. Foreign Policy* (Washington, DC: Brookings Institution Press, 2001), 157–98.

3. Ibid., 157.

4. Ibid., 178.

5. Ibid., 86.

6. Article 1.1 of the United Nations Convention against Torture and Other Cruel, Inhuman or Degrading Treatment or Punishment provides the following definition of torture: "For the purpose of this Convention, the term 'torture' means any act by which severe pain or suffering, whether physical or mental, is intentionally inflicted on a person for such purposes as obtaining from him, or a third person, information or a confession, punishing him for an act he or a third person has committed or is suspected of having committed, or intimidating or coercing him or a third person, or for any reason based on discrimination of any kind, when such pain or suffering is inflicted by or at the instigation of or with the consent or acquiescence of a public official or other person acting in an official capacity. It does not include pain or suffering arising only from, inherent in, or incidental to, lawful sanctions."

7. See Peter Iadicola and Anson Shupe, *Violence, Inequality, and Human Freedom* (Dix Hills, NY: General Hall, 1998), 276–89.

8. For a good discussion of U.S. policy in Nicaragua, see Thomas W. Walker, ed., *Revolution and Counterrevolution in Nicaragua* (Boulder, CO: Westview, 1991).

9. In Syria and other countries during the Arab Spring protests (particularly Egypt), the Muslim Brotherhood proved to

be a participatory faction of the protests rather than at the vanguard of insurgency.

10. See John King Fairbank, *The Great Chinese Revolution: 1800–1985* (New York, NY: Harper & Row, 1987), 316–41.

11. Ibid., 317.

12. Yehezkel Dror, *Crazy States: A Counterconventional Strategic Problem* (New York, NY: Kraus, Milwood, 1980).

13. Peter C. Sederberg, *Terrorist Myths: Illusion, Rhetoric, and Reality* (Englewood Cliffs, NJ: Prentice Hall, 1989).

14. Raphael Lemkin, *Axis Rule in Occupied Europe: Laws of Occupation, Analysis of Government, Proposals for Redress* (Washington, DC: Carnegie Endowment for International Peace, 1944). Chapter 9 discusses genocide in detail.

15. Quoted from Gerhard von Glahn, *Law Among Nations: An Introduction to Public International Law*, 5th ed. (New York, NY: Macmillan, 1986), 303–304.

16. Bruce Hoffman, *Inside Terrorism* (New York, NY: Columbia University Press, 1998), 195.

17. Frances FitzGerald, *Fire in the Lake: The Vietnamese and the Americans in Vietnam* (New York, NY: Vintage, 1972), 549.

Chapter Six

1. David J. Whittaker, ed., *The Terrorism Reader* (New York, NY: Routledge, 2001), 33.

2. Richard Schultz, "Conceptualizing Political Terrorism," *Journal of International Affairs 32* (1978): 1, 7–15, quoted in Whittaker, *The Terrorism Reader*.

3. Steven E. Barkan and Lynne L. Snowden, *Collective Violence* (Boston, MA: Allyn & Bacon, 2001), 70.

4. Ted Robert Gurr, "Political Terrorism: Historical Antecedents and Contemporary Trends," in *Violence in America: Protest, Rebellion, Reform*, vol. 2., ed. Ted Robert Gurr (Newbury Park, CA: Sage, 1989), 204.

5. Peter C. Sederberg, *Terrorist Myths: Illusion, Rhetoric, and Reality* (Englewood Cliffs, NJ: Prentice Hall, 1989).

6. The *Mini-Manual* is reprinted in Jay Mallin, ed., *Terror and Urban Guerrillas: A Study of Tactics and Documents* (Coral Gables, FL: University of Miami Press, 1971), 70–115.

7. Christopher Hewitt, "Public's Perspectives," in *Terrorism and the Media*, eds. David L. Paletz and Alex P. Schmid (Newbury Park, CA: Sage, 1992), 182.

8. Karen DeYoung and Douglas Farah, "Al Qaeda Shifts Assets to Gold," *Washington Post*, June 18, 2002.

9. For an excellent discussion of this progression, see Brent L. Smith, *Terrorism in America: Pipe Bombs and Pipe Dreams* (Albany: State University of New York Press, 1994).

10. The Provisional IRA was formed in 1969 when radicals broke from the official IRA, which was more political than military.

11. For an excellent analysis of the IRA and the Troubles in Northern Ireland, see J. Boywer Bell, *The IRA 1968–2000: Analysis of a Secret Army* (London, UK: Frank Cass, 2000).

12. Whittaker, *The Terrorism Reader*, 126.

13. Don Podesta, "The Terrible Toll of Human Hatred," *Washington Post National Weekly Edition*, June 8, 1987, quoted in *Violence and Terrorism*, 3rd ed., eds. Bernard Schechterman and Martin Slann (Guilford, CT: Dushkin, 1993), 33.

14. Ibid.

15. Trent N. Thomas, "Global Assessment of Current and Future Trends in Ethnic and Religious Conflict," in *Ethnic Conflict and Regional Instability*, eds. Robert L. Pfaltzgraff Jr. and Richard A. Schultz (Carlisle, PA: Strategic Studies Institute, 1994), 33–41, quoted in *Violence and Terrorism*, 5th ed., eds. Bernard Schechterman and Martin Slann (Guilford, CT: Dushkin, 1999), 24.

16. Richard Clutterbuck, *Terrorism, Drugs and Crime in Europe After 1992* (New York, NY: Routledge, 1990), 73.

17. *Irish News*, November 30, 1993. Reporting on a joint study by the Northern Ireland Economic Research Centre in Belfast and the Economic and Social Research Institute in Dublin.

18. Some northerners are ethnic Arabs, but many are not. Nevertheless, non-Arab Muslims have been heavily influenced by their Arab neighbors and fellow Muslims and hence have developed an Arabized culture.

19. The Axis powers were an alliance of Germany, Japan, Italy, and their allies.

20. Podesta, "The Terrible Toll."

21. See Bruce Hoffman, "Terrorism Trends and Prospects," in *Countering the New Terrorism*, eds. Ian O. Lesser, Bruce Hoffman, John Arquilla, David Ronfeldt, and Michele Zanini (Santa Monica, CA: RAND, 1999), 28ff.

22. See Joby Warrick, "An Easier, but Less Deadly, Recipe for Terror," *Washington Post*, December 31, 2004.

Chapter Seven

1. Joshua 11, in *The Holy Bible, New Revised Standard Version* (Nashville, TN: Thomas Nelson, 1990).

2. Ralph A. Scott, *A New Look at Biblical Crime* (Chicago, IL: Nelson-Hall, 1979), 66, cited in Peter Iadicola and Anson Shupe, *Violence, Inequality, and Human Freedom* (New York, NY: General Hall, 1998), 175.

3. Norman Cohn, *The Pursuit of the Millennium* (New York, NY: Oxford University Press, 1971), 61, quoted in Iadicola and Shupe, *Violence, Inequality, and Human Freedom*, 177.

4. For a history of the Assassin movement, see Bernard Lewis, *The Assassins: A Radical Sect in Islam* (New York, NY: Oxford University Press, 1987).

5. In *The Assassins*, Bernard Lewis discounts the assertion that the Assassins drugged themselves and argues, "In all probability it was the name that gave rise to the story, rather than the reverse," 12.

6. James A. Haught, *Holy Horrors* (Buffalo, NY: Prometheus, 1990), 34, cited in Iadicola and Shupe, *Violence, Inequality, and Human Freedom*, 181.

7. Much of the discussion has been adapted from Human Rights Watch, *The Scars of Death: Children Abducted by the Lord's Resistance Army in Uganda* (New York, NY: Human Rights Watch, 1997).

8. The *Protocols of the Learned Elders of Zion* has been extensively published on the Internet. It is readily available from websites promoting civil liberties, neo-Nazi propaganda, anti-Semitism, and Islamist extremism.

9. See Michael A. Hiltzik, "Russian Court Rules 'Protocols' an Anti-Semitic Forgery," *Los Angeles Times*, November 28, 1993.

10. Walter Laqueur, *The New Terrorism: Fanaticism and the Arms of Mass Destruction* (New York, NY: Oxford University Press, 1999), 129.

11. Robin Wright, "Iranian Unit to Be Labeled 'Terrorist,'" *Washington Post*, August 15, 2007.

12. Ali Alfoneh, "Iran's Suicide Brigades," *Middle Eastern Quarterly 14*, no. 1 (2007).

13. Robert J. Kelly and Jess Maghan, eds., *Hate Crime: The Global Politics of Polarization* (Carbondale: Southern Illinois University Press, 1998), 105.

14. See Samuel M. Katz, *The Hunt for the Engineer: How Israeli Agents Tracked the Hamas Master Bomber* (New York, NY: Fromm International, 2001), 97–99.

15. Ibid., 225.

16. "Rabin's Alleged Killer Appears in Court," *CNN World News*, November 7, 1995.

17. Data derived from Central Intelligence Agency, *World Fact Book* (Washington, DC: U.S. Central Intelligence Agency), https://www.cia.gov/library/publications/resources/the-world-factbook/index.html.

18. See Monte Morin, "In Iraq, to Be a Hairstylist Is to Risk Death," *Los Angeles Times*, February 22, 2005.

19. A jihadist is one who wages jihad, regardless of whether it is an armed jihad. Mujahideen are jihadists who have taken up arms.

20. David Rohde and C. J. Chivers, "Al Qaeda's Grocery Lists and Manuals of Killing," *New York Times*, March 17, 2002.

21. Robert D. McFadden, "Bin Laden's Journey From Rich Pious Lad to the Mask of Evil," *New York Times*, September 30, 2001.

22. Simon Reeve, *The New Jackals: Ramzi Yousef, Osama bin Laden and the Future of Terrorism* (Boston, MA: Northeastern University Press, 1999), 181.

23. The Levant refers to the Eastern Mediterranean region, traditionally encompassing Syria, Lebanon, Israel, Jordan, and Cyprus.

24. U.S. Department of State, "Aum Supreme Truth (Aum)," in *Patterns of Global Terrorism, 2000* (Washington, DC: U.S. Department of State, April 2001).

25. Andrew Marshall, "It Gassed the Tokyo Subway, Microwaved Its Enemies and Tortured Its Members. So Why Is the Aum Cult Thriving?" *The Guardian*, July 15, 1999.

26. U.S. Department of State, "Aum Supreme Truth."

27. Marshall, "It Gassed the Tokyo Subway."

28. Ibid.; Laqueur, *The New Terrorism*, 54.

29. Initial reports cited this figure. Later studies suggest that physical injuries numbered 1,300 and that the rest were psychological injuries. U.S. Department of State, "Aum Supreme Truth."

30. For interesting insight about Al Qaeda's use of computers, see Alan Cullison, "Inside Al-Qaeda's Hard Drive," *The Atlantic*, September 2004.

31. Dana Priest, "Report Says Iraq Is New Terrorist Training Ground," *Washington Post*, January 14, 2005.

32. Josh Meyer, "Bin Laden, in Tape, May Have Sights on New Role," *Los Angeles Times*, October 31, 2004.

33. See Alan Cowell, "British Muslims Are Seen Moving Into Mideast Terrorism," *New York Times*, May 1, 2003; Alan Cowell, "Zeal for Suicide Bombing Reaches British Midlands," *New York Times*, May 2, 2003; Craig Whitlock, "Moroccans Gain Prominence in Terror Groups," *Washington Post*, October 14, 2004; Tony Czuczka, "Germans Suspect Terror Pipeline," *Dallas Morning News*, January 9, 2005; Sebastian Rotella, "Europe's Boys of Jihad," *Los Angeles Times*, April 2, 2005.

34. For a discussion of Christian evangelizing in Iraq, see Jane Lampman, "A Crusade After All?" *Christian Science Monitor*, April 17, 2003.

Chapter Eight

1. Charles W. Kegley Jr., "An Introduction," in *International Terrorism: Characteristics, Causes, Controls* (New York, NY: St. Martin's, 1990), 3.

2. Reuters, "Chronology: Previous Attacks on American Embassies," *New York Times*, January 12, 2007.

3. Kegley, "An Introduction," 21.

4. See Peter C. Sederberg, *Terrorist Myths: Illusion, Rhetoric, and Reality* (Englewood Cliffs, NJ: Prentice Hall, 1989), 117.

5. Simon Reeve, *The New Jackals: Ramzi Yousef, Osama bin Laden and the Future of Terrorism* (Boston, MA: Northeastern University Press, 1999), 3.

6. James Bruce, "Arab Veterans of the Afghan War," *Jane's Intelligence Review*, April 1, 1995, 175.

7. Donald G. McNeil, "What Will Rise if bin Laden Falls?" *New York Times*, December 2, 2001.

8. From Richard C. Paddock and Bob Drogin, "A Terror Network Unraveled in Singapore," *Los Angeles Times*, January 20, 2002; quoted with permission.

9. Ibid.

Chapter Nine

1. See Brent L. Smith, *Terrorism in America: Pipe Bombs and Pipe Dreams* (Albany: State University of New York Press, 1994), 35.

2. For good histories of the civil rights movement, see Taylor Branch, *Parting the Waters: America in the King Years, 1954–63* (New York, NY: Simon & Schuster, 1988). See also Henry Hampton and Steve Fayer, *Voices of Freedom: An Oral History of the Civil Rights Movement From the 1950s Through the 1980s* (New York, NY: Bantam Books, 1990).

3. Ted Robert Gurr, "Terrorism in Democracies: Its Social and Political Bases," in *Origins of Terrorism: Psychologies, Ideologies, Theologies, and States of Mind*, ed. Walter Reich (Washington, DC: Woodrow Wilson Center, 1998), 89.

4. Data are derived from *Riots, Civil and Criminal Disorders— Hearings Before the Permanent Subcommittee on Investigations of the Committee on Government Operations*, United States Senate, Part 25 (Washington, DC: Government Printing Office, 1970), cited in George Prosser, "Terror in the United States: 'An Introduction to Elementary Tactics' and 'Some Questions on Tactics,'" in *Terror and Urban Guerrillas: A Study of Tactics and Documents*, ed. Jay Mallin (Coral Gables, FL: University of Miami Press, 1971), 52.

5. A former professor, Leary was best known for his recreational and spiritual experimentation with the hallucinogenic drug LSD, which he advocated as a consciousness-raising drug.

6. Possibly 26 police officers died in BLA ambushes. Ted Robert Gurr, "Political Terrorism: Historical Antecedents and Contemporary Trends," in *Violence in America: Protest, Rebellion, Reform*, vol. 2, ed. Ted R. Gurr (Newbury Park, CA: Sage, 1989).

7. For sources and further discussion of the FALN, see Brent L. Smith, *Terrorism in America: Pipe Bombs and Pipe Dreams* (Albany: State University of New York Press, 1994).

8. See Smith, *Terrorism in America*, for sources and further discussion of left-wing hard cores.

9. See Smith, *Terrorism in America*, for sources and further discussion of the United Freedom Front.

10. A copy of *The Turner Diaries* was found with Timothy McVeigh when he was arrested after the Oklahoma City bombing in 1995. See Andrew MacDonald, *The Turner Diaries* (New York, NY: Barricade, 1980).

11. For a discussion of the Aryan Republican Army, see Mark Hamm, *In Bad Company: America's Terrorist Underground* (Boston, MA: Northeastern University Press, 2002).

12. The chronology of the Order's terrorist spree is adapted from the Anti-Defamation League, *Danger: Extremism, The Major Vehicles and Voices on America's Far-Right Fringe* (New York, NY: Anti-Defamation League, 1996), 270–71.

13. Southern Poverty Law Center, *Intelligence Report*, Summer 2001.

14. Ibid.

15. See Southern Poverty Law Center, "Patriot Free Fall," *Intelligence Report*, Summer 2002.

16. See Southern Poverty Law Center, "The Second Wave: Return of the Militias" (Montgomery, AL: Southern Poverty Law Center, August 2009).

17. For a discussion of Timothy McVeigh's immersion in the fringe right—from the perspective of McVeigh himself—see Lou Michel and Dan Herbeck, *American Terrorist: Timothy McVeigh and the Oklahoma City Bombing* (New York, NY: HarperCollins, 2001).

18. Ibid., 164.

19. Ibid., 224.

20. Ibid., 234.

Chapter Ten

1. Only the United States, Great Britain, Russia, and France have the capability to deploy large numbers of seaborne troops.

2. Muslim commentators criticized the term *infinite justice*, arguing that only God is capable of infinite justice.

3. David J. Whittaker, ed., *The Terrorism Reader* (New York, NY: Routledge, 2001), 144–45.

4. Jack Serle, "More than 2400 Dead as Obama's Drone Campaign Marks Five Years," *Bureau of Investigative Journalism*, January 23, 2014.

5. Bill Roggio, "Charting the Data for U.S. Airstrikes in Pakistan," https://www.longwarjournal.org/.

6. For a history of the Foreign Legion, see Tony Geraghty, *March or Die: A New History of the French Foreign Legion* (New York, NY: Facts on File, 1986).

7. Craig Whitlock, "After a Decade at War With the West, Al-Qaeda Still Impervious to Spies," *Washington Post*, March 20, 2008.

8. Robert M. Clark, *Intelligence Collection* (Thousand Oaks, CA: CQ Press, 2014), 490.

9. Ibid., p. 492.

10. Ibid., p. 489.

11. See Nick Anderson, "More Ports of Entry to Use Digital Screening," *Los Angeles Times*, January 4, 2005; see also Philip Shenon, "New Devices to Recognize Bodily Features on Entry Into the U.S.," *New York Times*, April 30, 2003.

12. See T. R. Reid, "IRA Issues Apology for All Deaths It Caused," *Washington Post*, July 17, 2002.

13. Jim Dwyer and Brian Lavery, "I.R.A. to Renounce Violence in Favor of Political Struggle," *New York Times*, July 27, 2005.

14. Glenn Franke and William Branigin, "IRA Announces End to Armed Campaign," *Washington Post*, July 28, 2005.

15. For the complete text of the findings of Senate investigations into the scandal, see *New York Times*, the *Tower Commission Report* (New York, NY: Bantam Books and Times Books, 1987).

16. Paul Wilkinson, "Fighting the Hydra: Terrorism and the Rule of Law," in *International Terrorism: Characteristics, Causes, Controls*, ed. Charles W. Kegley (New York, NY: St. Martin's, 1990), 255.

17. Ibid.

18. Ibid.

19. Ibid.
20. Ibid.

Chapter Eleven

1. Executive Order 13228. This executive order was amended by Executive Order 12656, which clarified that policies enacted in reply to terrorist events outside of the United States would remain within the authority of the National Security Council.
2. U.S. Department of Homeland Security, "Preventing Terrorism Overview" (July 16, 2015), http://www.dhs.gov/preventing-terrorism-overview.
3. Keith B. Richburg and Fred Barbash, "Madrid Bombings Kill at Least 190," *Washington Post*, March 11, 2004.
4. Doreen Carvajal, "Spaniards Turn Out in Huge Numbers to Mourn Blast Victims," *New York Times*, March 12, 2004.
5. Victoria Burnett, "7 Are Acquitted in Madrid Bombings," *New York Times*, November 1, 2007.
6. Glenn Frankel, "London Subway Blasts Almost Simultaneous, Investigators Conclude," *Washington Post*, July 10, 2005.
7. Sarah Lyall, "3 Main British Parties to Back Tougher Antiterrorism Laws," *New York Times*, July 27, 2005.
8. The Department of Homeland Security absorbed the Immigration and Naturalization Service, the Coast Guard, the Customs Service, the Federal Emergency Management Agency, and many other smaller bureaus.
9. National Commission on Terrorist Attacks on the United States, *The 9/11 Commission Report: Final Report of the National Commission on Terrorist Attacks Upon the United States* (New York, NY: Norton, 2004).
10. Department of Homeland Security, "About DHS." http://www.dhs.gov/about-dhs.
11. Department of Agriculture, "What We Do," https://www.usda.gov/our-agency/about-usda.
12. Department of Defense, "Mission Statement," http://govinfo.library.unt.edu/npr/library/status/mission/mdod.htm.
13. Department of Energy, "About Us," http://energy.gov/about-us.
14. Department of Health and Human Services, "About HHS," http://www.hhs.gov/about/.
15. Department of the Interior, "Mission Statement," http://www.doi.gov/whoweare/Mission-Statement.cfm.
16. Department of the Treasury, "About," http://www.treasury.gov/about/role-of-treasury/Pages/default.aspx.
17. Environmental Protection Agency, "About EPA," http://www.epa.gov/aboutepa/whatwedo.html.
18. Peter Finn, "Arrests Reveal Al Qaeda Plans," *Washington Post*, June 16, 2002.
19. Paul R. Pillar, *Terrorism and U.S. Foreign Policy* (Washington, DC: Brookings Institution Press, 2001), 115.
20. United States Select Committee on Intelligence, *Report on the U.S. Intelligence Community's Prewar Intelligence Assessments on Iraq* (Washington, DC: United States Senate, July 7, 2004).
21. Ibid., 14.
22. See Shane Schot and David E. Sanger, "Bush Panel Finds Big Flaws Remain in U.S. Spy Efforts," *New York Times*, April 1, 2005.
23. See *Frisbie v. Collins* 342 U.S. 519, 522 (1954); see also *Ker v. Illinois* 119 U.S. 436, 444 (1886).
24. See Craig Whitlock, "From CIA Jails, Inmates Fade Into Obscurity," *Washington Post*, October 27, 2007.
25. See Tracy Wilkinson, "Italy Orders Arrest of 13 CIA Operatives," *Los Angeles Times*, June 25, 2005.

Chapter Twelve

1. See Mark Ehrman, "Terrorism From a Scholarly Perspective," *Los Angeles Times Magazine*, May 4, 2003.
2. Samuel P. Huntington, *The Clash of Civilizations and the Remaking of World Order* (New York, NY: Touchstone, 1996).
3. Andrew MacDonald [William Pierce], *The Turner Diaries* (New York, NY: Barricade Books, 1996).
4. E. L. Anderson [David L. Hoggan], *The Myth of the Six Million* (Newport Beach, CA: Noontide, 1969).
5. Audrey Kurth Cronin, *How Terrorism Ends: Understanding the Decline and Demise of Terrorist Campaigns* (Princeton, NJ: Princeton University Press, 2009).
6. Adam Cohen, "Following the Money," *Time*, October 8, 2001.
7. One HAMAS leader bragged that suicide bombings were cheap—costing approximately $1,500 each in 2001 U.S. dollars.
8. For a report on charities, see David B. Ottaway, "U.S. Eyes Money Trails of Saudi-Backed Charities," *Washington Post*, August 19, 2004.
9. Karen DeYoung and Douglas Farah, "Al Qaeda Shifts Assets to Gold," *Washington Post*, June 18, 2002.
10. For online access to EPIC's DCS-1000 FOIA documents, see http://epic.org/.

INDEX

Page numbers in *italics* indicate photos. Page numbers followed by "*t*" and "*f*" indicate tables and figures respectively.